The Songs of Psalms

Text, Translation and Interpretation

by

Heinrich W. Guggenheimer

KTAV PUBLISHING HOUSE

2020

Published by
KTAV PUBLISHING HOUSE
527 Empire Blvd
Brooklyn NY 11225
www.ktav.com
orders@ktav.com

Ph: (718)972-5445/Fax: (718)972-6307

ISBN 978-1-60280-4012

Table of Contents

TABLE OF CONTENT

Introduction

The big question is, what makes the Psalms poetry? They do not exhibit the fixed sequence of stresses as in Greek, Roman, and Arabic poetry, nor have a fixed count of syllables or rhyme. What is clear is that the diction shows the signs of poetry, characterized by an almost complete absence of the definite article, the accusative particle, אשר, של, שֶׁ, and *vaw conversive*. It has been asserted that the basic pattern of Psalms is a verse of four stresses. Since we cannot reconstruct the actual presentation of Psalms in biblical times all we can do is to try to understand how the Masoretes understood the situation. Now there are two Psalms which have parallels in prose books (*2Sam.* 22, *1Chr.* 16:8-36), which really are built on reading this pattern, in contrast to the same verses in Psalms which are scanned as exhibiting varying speeds even in one verse. A reasonable explanation would be that the prose texts are punctuated for declamation whereas Psalms are treated as songs. For example, taking each verse as one strophe, the division into lines as indicated by the dividing accents is as follows:

2Sam22	Psalm18
כא יִגְמְלֵנִי יְיָ כְּצִדְקָתִי כְּבֹר יָדַי יָשִׁיב לִי׃	כא יִגְמְלֵנִי יְיָ כְּצִדְקִי כְּבֹר יָדַי יָשִׁיב לִי׃
כב כִּי שָׁמַרְתִּי דַּרְכֵי יְיָ וְלֹא רָשַׁעְתִּי מֵאֱלֹהָי׃	כב כִּֽי־שָׁמַרְתִּי דַּרְכֵי יְיָ לֹא־רָשַׁעְתִּי מֵאֱלֹהָי
כג כִּי כָל־מִשְׁפָּטָו לְנֶגְדִּי וְחֻקֹּתָיו לֹא־אָסוּר מִמֶּנָּה׃	כג כִּי כָל־מִשְׁפָּטָיו לְנֶגְדִּי וְחֻקֹּתָיו לֹא־אָסִיר מֶנִּי׃
כד וָאֶהְיֶה תָמִים לוֹ וָאֶשְׁתַּמְּרָה מֵעֲוֹנִי׃	כד וָאֱהִי תָמִים עִמּוֹ וָאֶשְׁתַּמֵּר מֵעֲוֹנִי׃
כה וַיָּשֶׁב יְיָ לִי כְּצִדְקָתִי כְּ בֹ רִי לְ נֶגֶד עֵינָיו׃	כה וַיָּֽשֶׁב־יְיָ לִי כְצִדְקִי כְּבֹר יָדַי לְנֶגֶד עֵינָיו׃

It can be seen that the prose text has each verse split into four parts of approximately even weights, whereas the Psalm text implies that frequently there are only three parts of which one has to be produced at a different speed. A similar situation holds for the other text, as can be seen at Ps. 105. Unfortunately, the musical tradition underlying the text has been lost. Together with this tradition we lost also a safe basis for syllable count, since for some masoretic rules semivowels are considered syllable forming but for others they are disregarded. One may assume that a poet has considerable leeway in treating semivowels one way or the other; that leeway is found both in Spanish (quantitative) and German (syllable counting) Hebrew medieval poetry, cf. Ps. 14:1. We know that syllables were counted since sometimes in poetry words are lengthened to yield an otherwise unnecessary additional syllable (e.g., ישועתה *Jon.* 3:10, *Ps.* 3:3, 80:3, used by three different authors). In any case, the long periods of modern translations of Psalms are certainly giving an incorrect picture. Most of the verses of Psalms are stanzas composed of short lines, many being just outcries. In the interpretation of the text as songs composed of strophes I have followed the masoretic divisions strictly. These divisions will hopefully give the reader a sense of the dynamics of the text and encourage him to discover the everchanging patterns in the poems. Most textual difficulties of Psalms disappear if verses are not considered as sentences (with subject, predicate, and objects) but stanzas to be split into different sentences more or less connected with one another. The masoretic division into minor (continuing text) and major (allowing jumps in thought and style) division has been completely followed. After a major divider, the next line starts on the margin; after a minor divider the next line is indented. This graphic representation permits the study of the rhythmic structure of different kinds of Psalms. This might in some instances give a few lines too many but it is our best indication of the masoretic reading of the poet's intention, and decreasing the number of lines in a stanza often will obscure the meaning. The masoretic accents recognize different levels of caesuras. The separate set of poetic accents for the poetic books was necessary, because poetic lines are so very short! The full set of these accents is explained at the end of this Introduction.

In my translation, I have in general followed the classical interpretations of R. Saadya Gaon, Rashi, and Abraham Ibn Ezra. These authors (to whom one has to add, as a source of principles of poetic grammar, Nachmanides in his commentary to the Pentateuch) have a great advantage over modern scholars. In addition to being very learned, all of them were practicing poets. Also I am following the principle that the same root used repeatedly but not repetitively in the same Psalm should be traced to different roots, possibly representing different Semitic languages (in order of importance, Arabic, Aramaic, Ugaritic-Phenician, Accadic), or different Semitic consonants fused in Hebrew. This principle has already been stated as a major poetic technique by Ibn Ezra to *Ex.* 22:4. Its action is obvious in all poetic parts of the Pentateuch but is more hidden in Psalms. A note has been appended to the translation when the principle is applied.

The poetic devices discovered in Psalms by modern authors have been recognized in the present translation since most of them appear in the works of the classical commentators. So the contracted כ meaning "as if" is given by Nachmanides (*Gen.* 25: 31), the emphatic כ (*Gen.* 39:19) and double duty prefix ל (*Ex.* 21:8) by the same author, other double duty words by Ibn Ezra (*Ps.* 140:9, 147:2), the enclitic מ (or absolute instead of construct) by Ibn Janah (*Riqmah*, Chap. 31, on *Deut.* 33:11), and the identification of כָּבֵד and כָּבוֹד by Rashi (*Baba Mezia`* 112a). Note that Rashi sees no need for either emendation or revocalization!

For a readable modern translation, I have dispensed with Thee and Thou but have capitalized all words addressed to Divinity. The tetragrammaton YHWH is translated as Eternal, following the German tradition. It is the fashion in scholarly texts to vocalize this Name as a kind of *hiph`il* but that vocalization is an antihistoric reconstruction. In fact, it is reported (*Yoma* 39b) that after the death of the high priest, Simeon the Just, the priests in the Temple of Jerusalem refrained from pronouncing the priestly blessing with the Name in its proper vocalization and from that point on the knowledge of the proper vocalization was lost within one generation. If the proper vocalization of the Name as it was used in Israel were not a magic act but a simple exercise in grammar, it could not have been lost. (Compare also Ben Yehuda's discussion of the Name YHWH in his Thesaurus). In addition, in order to make the sense clear without having to introduce any notes, I am writing earth and heaven for the visible earth and heaven, but Earth and Heaven for the world of the damned and that of the rewarded souls, similarly Life and Death express life and death everlasting. In my understanding of the theology of the psalmist, the just can expect their souls to participate in life everlasting in the presence of God but the souls of the wicked are permanently destroyed in a place called the Pit.

Since a line after a major stop together with the indented line following form a syntactic unit, many times English grammar requires that the second part be put in front of the first part. This rather frequent occurrence has to be understood and is not noted in the commentary. The switch is restricted to the couple formed by a line started at the margin followed by an indented one.

Reading Psalms

As already noted, Psalms were written to be sung, not read. Since we have lost the melodies, the second best way is to read the Hebrew text aloud. In this edition, each verse is treated as a stanza in a poem. To help the declamation, an indented line is more or less read on with the preceding one but a not indented line requires a stop before reading. In the Hebrew text, the caesuras and minor stops are indicated by musical signs.

1. If a verse has one caesura, it almost always is indicated by Atnah: -.
2. If a verse has two caesuras, the first usually is Oleh Weyored -, the second is Atnah. Oleh Weyored is stronger that Atnah and requires a longer stop. It is notable that in the prose version (*1 Chr.* 16) of the first part of *Ps.* 105, the translation of Psalm - is Zaqef -, a secondary divider.
3. If there are three caesuras, the first usually is the Major Revia -, followed by Oleh Weyored

and Atnah. The Minor Revia has exactly the same form as the Major but is a connecting accent. A Revia is minor if and only if it is immediately followed by a dividing accent.

Minor dividing accents are the following:
4. Revia Mugrash --, usually the last dividing accent in a verse, preceding the final stop -.
5. Zinnor -. This always is written over the last letter in the word, irrespective of the position of the stress. If immediately followed by a strong divider, its status as dividing accent is questionable.
6. Dehi -. This always is written in front of the first letter of the word; at any other position it denotes the connecting accent Tirha. In a sequence of unaccented words joined to the accented one by *maqqef*, the Dehi is written at the accented word.
7. Pazer -.
8. Legarmeh I-, I-, or I-. I- is a dividing accent only if not followed immediately by a dividing accent, in which case it is the connecting accent Mahpah (cf. Revia).
9. Major Shalshelet I-.

The musical and grammatical meanings of the connecting accents have been lost. One only can list them for orientation:
10-18: Merkha -. Munah -. Illuy -. Tirha - (see Dehi). Galgal -. Mahpah - (see Legarmeh). Azla - (see Legarmeh). Minor Shalshelet -. Zinnorit -- --, mostly following Revia Mugrash.

Psalm 1

1 Hail to the man
Who did not go
By the wicked ones' counsel,
Who did not stay
At sinners' rank,
Nor did sit down
At scoffers' seat.

א אַ֥שְֽׁרֵי־הָאִ֗ישׁ
אֲשֶׁ֤ר לֹ֥א הָלַךְ֮
בַּעֲצַ֪ת רְשָׁ֫עִ֥ים
וּבְדֶ֣רֶךְ חַ֭טָּאִים
לֹ֣א עָמָ֑ד
וּבְמוֹשַׁ֥ב לֵ֝צִ֗ים
לֹ֣א יָשָֽׁב׃

2 Rather in the Eternal's Law is his pleasure
And he meditates His teachings
Day and night.

ב כִּ֤י אִ֥ם־בְּתוֹרַ֥ת יהוה חֶ֫פְצ֥וֹ
וּֽבְתוֹרָת֥וֹ יֶהְגֶּ֗ה
יוֹמָ֥ם וָלָֽיְלָה׃

3 He will be like a tree
Planted at water rivulets
Whose fruit
Will be given at the right time
And whose leaf will not wither
And all that he produces succeeds.

ג וְֽהָיָ֗ה כְּעֵץ֮
שָׁת֪וּל עַֽל־פַּלְגֵ֫י מָ֥יִם
אֲשֶׁ֤ר פִּרְי֨וֹ ׀
יִתֵּ֬ן בְּעִתּ֗וֹ
וְעָלֵ֥הוּ לֹֽא יִבּ֑וֹל
וְכֹ֖ל אֲשֶׁר־יַעֲשֶׂ֣ה יַצְלִֽיחַ׃

4 Not so the wicked:
Rather like chaff
That the wind disperses.

ד לא־כֵ֥ן הָרְשָׁעִ֑ים
כִּ֥י אִם־כַּ֝מֹּ֗ץ
אֲֽשֶׁר־תִּדְּפֶ֥נּוּ רֽוּחַ׃

5 Therefore
The wicked will not rise
In judgment
Nor will the sinners
In the assembly of the just.

ה עַל־כֵּ֤ן ׀
לֹא־יָקֻ֣מוּ רְ֭שָׁעִים
בַּמִּשְׁפָּ֑ט
וְ֝חַטָּאִ֗ים
בַּעֲדַ֥ת צַדִּיקִֽים׃

6 Truly, the Eternal understands
The action of the just
But the action of the wicked will vanish.

ו כִּֽי־יוֹדֵ֣עַ יהוה
דֶּ֣רֶךְ צַדִּיקִ֑ים
וְדֶ֖רֶךְ רְשָׁעִ֣ים תֹּאבֵֽד׃

A didactic poem (characterized as such by the repeated use of the prosaic word אשר) which sets the tone for the entire book of Psalms.

1. אשרי is a nominal form related to the verb אשר "to be rich, happy". The corresponding noun could possibly be אשר but it is not documented anywhere in Hebrew or related texts. אשרי has to be taken as an acclamation. The version "hail" chosen here underlines the word as an acclamation; "Happy!" might be less idiomatic but more correct.

In Mishnaic and Rabbinic Hebrew, עדה means both "counsel" and "council". The second meaning is found in some Psalms by some authors, but this is conjectural. In the third part of the stanza, "seat" is certainly a static object and by parallelism דרך in the second part also must be something static. But the first part is different from the other two both metrically, 3 parts instead of 2, and syntactically, verb before subject instead of subject before verb. Therefore, there is no need to extend the parallelism to the first part. Since the last two parts are parallel, one cannot treat the arrangement as chiastic. In addition, a translation as "council" would mean a translation "Who did not perambulate in the council of the wicked" which would weaken the impact of the statement. An interpretation "Who did not go to the council" would need לעצת .

The word דרך in Hebrew can be both feminine and masculine. There seem to be no fixed gender rules. (The Babylonian Talmud, *Qiddushin* 2a, declares the gender to be dependent on the context). Now it is a principle that I hope to illustrate many times in this translation of Psalms that the same word used repeatedly in one poem carries different meanings each time it is used in the same poem . This is particularly true for the repeated use of the same word in one and the same stanza, as here in verses 3 and 6; such a repetition is not even good prose unless a multiple repetition indicates emphasis. Accadic distinguishes strictly between masculine *durku* "way" and feminine *derkatu* "status, rank; dominion" that appears also as *drkt* in Ugaritic. The second meaning seems to be most appropriate here, the simple prose meaning "way" is used in v. 6, together with another of the many meanings of דרך, either "way of acting, modus operandi" (parallel its synonym ארח) or possibly "worship", usually associated with דֶּ֫רֶךְ בְּאֵֽר־שָׁ֑בַע in *Amos* 8:14.

2. In both cases in this Psalm, כי אם means "on the contrary, rather". There are quite a number of possible meanings of this combination.

It would seem quite unpoetic to use the same word Torah twice in the same verse unless used in identical clauses for emphasis. The word is usually connected to the root הורה "to teach, instruct". But this meaning is impossible, e.g., in *Deut*. 33:4: תּוֹרָ֥ה צִוָּה־לָ֖נוּ מֹשֶׁ֑ה "Moses commanded us Torah". It is possible to command the obligation to study, but the result of study, *Torah*, must be personally acquired by study. The verse does not say "Moses commanded us to study Torah". The meaning is rather connected with Accadic *tertu* "(Divine) command", removed from its original meaning "omen". This was already recognized by the Aramaic paraphrase of Psalms which has אלהן בנימוסא דיי רעותיה ובאורייתיה מרנן ימם ולילי "but his pleasure is in the laws of the Lord and its His teachings he sounds by day and by night". The second half of the verse is a clear allusion to *Jos*. 1:8. The subjunctive in the last clause implies that while certainly the just do not always utter the Lord's teachings, they are always prepared to do so.

3. It is clear from *Prov*. 21:1 that פלגי מים is a water canal, diverted from a river and controlled by a sluice. In Torczyner's opinion, the primary meaning of the root פלג is "making a diversion, a branch" as in Accadic; in other derivations its primary meaning is "making a cleavage". In classical Arabic, فلج is a brook. The usefulness of Arabic for old Judean Hebrew should not be underestimated; for example, Abigail's first husband, Nabal the Calebite (*1S*. 25:3), has an Arabic name, "nobleman", not a Hebrew one "scoundrel". Therefore, another possible interpretation of the verse would be "transplanted to a water cleft". Note that the first verse is in the past tense, the second starts with a present clause, and the third is in the future, referring to the future Life of the Just.

At the start of the verse, ֗ is a minor *revia`* since it is followed directly by a strong dividing accent, but, as noted by *Minḥat Shay*, the preceding *g`aya*, essentially unnecessary under initial *sheva*, makes it close to a dividing accent (*deḥiq*), inducing *dagesh lene* in the following בגד כפת, without requiring a stop in the recitation.

4. The main clause of the verse has no verb; the implied "will be" is supplied by v. 3, notwithstanding the change in number which is never a hindrance in Hebrew poetry.

5. It is not clear whether the wicked will not be judged at all, their souls having been blown away like like chaff even before they could appear before the Divine court, or that they appear in court but cannot stand up against the evidence of their guilt.

6. In most of Hebrew poetry כי means emphatic “certainly”, not logical “therefore” or “because”. For example, *Gen*. 18:20: זַעֲקַ֛ת סְדֹ֥ם וַעֲמֹרָ֖ה כִּי־רָ֑בָּה "the outcry about Sodom and Gomorra is certainly great". Nachmanides also points to *Gen*. 39:19, כַּדְּבָרִ֣ים הָאֵ֔לֶּה עָ֥שָׂה לִ֖י עַבְדֶּ֑ךָ "truly in this way did your slave behave towards me".
The meanings of דרך, and a possible translation of "worship" instead "actions", have been discussed in v.1. Probably the ambiguity in meaning is intended by the poet and is untranslatable.

Psalm 2

Why
Are peoples excited,
And nations
Think about armaments?

א לָ֭מָּה
רָגְשׁ֣וּ גוֹיִ֑ם
וּ֝לְאֻמִּ֗ים
יֶהְגּוּ־רִֽיק׃

2 Kings of the earth
Station themselves
And princes consult together,
Against the Eternal
And against His anointed.

ב יִ֥תְיַצְּב֨וּ ׀
מַלְכֵי־אֶ֗רֶץ
וְרוֹזְנִ֥ים נֽוֹסְדוּ־יָ֑חַד
עַל־ יהוה
וְעַל־מְשִׁיחֽוֹ׃

3 “Let us break
Their chains,
And throw from us their ropes!”

ג נְֽ֭נַתְּקָה
אֶת־מֽוֹסְרוֹתֵ֑ימוֹ
וְנַשְׁלִ֖יכָה מִמֶּ֣נּוּ עֲבֹתֵֽימוֹ׃

4 He Who is throning in Heaven is laughing,
The Lord
Will scoff at them!

ד יוֹשֵׁ֣ב בַּשָּׁמַ֣יִם יִשְׂחָ֑ק
אֲ֝דֹנָ֗י
יִלְעַג־לָֽמוֹ׃

5 Then He will talk to them in His rage
And in His fury will confound them.

ה אָ֤ז יְדַבֵּ֣ר אֵלֵ֣ימוֹ בְאַפּ֑וֹ
וּֽבַחֲרוֹנ֥וֹ יְבַהֲלֵֽמוֹ׃

6 But I
Was dedicated as His king,
On Zion,
His holy mountain.

ו וַ֭אֲנִי
נָסַ֣כְתִּי מַלְכִּ֑י
עַל־צִ֝יּ֗וֹן
הַר־קָדְשִֽׁי׃

7 I shall tell the decree:
The Eternal
Said to me: you are My son,
I
Today I made you my creature.

ז אֲסַפְּרָ֗ה אֶֽ֫ל חֹ֥ק
יהוה
אָמַ֘ר אֵלַ֣י בְּנִ֣י אַ֑תָּה
אֲ֝נִ֗י
הַיּ֥וֹם יְלִדְתִּֽיךָ׃

8 Ask of Me,
And I shall give peoples
As your holdings,
And your heirloom
The ends of the earth.

ח שְׁאַ֤ל מִמֶּ֗נִּי
וְאֶתְּנָ֣ה ג֭וֹיִם
נַחֲלָתֶ֑ךָ
וַ֝אֲחֻזָּתְךָ֗
אַפְסֵי־אָֽרֶץ׃

9 Smash them
With an iron rod,
Shatter them like a potter’s vessel!

ט תְּ֭רֹעֵם
בְּשֵׁ֣בֶט בַּרְזֶ֑ל
כִּכְלִ֖י יוֹצֵ֣ר תְּנַפְּצֵֽם׃

10 But now,
Kings be wise,
Take heed
Rulers of the earth.

י וְ֭עַתָּה
מְלָכִ֣ים הַשְׂכִּ֑ילוּ
הִ֝וָּסְר֗וּ
שֹׁ֣פְטֵי אָֽרֶץ׃

11 Worship the Eternal in fear
And shake
In trembling.

יא עִבְדוּ אֶת־ יהוָה בְּיִרְאָה
וְגִילוּ
בִּרְעָדָה׃

12 Arm yourselves in purity
Lest He rebuke you
And you lose dominion;
Certainly His rage will soon burn.
Fortunate are
All who trust in Him.

יב נַשְּׁקוּ־בַ֗ר
פֶּן־יֶאֱנַף |
וְתֹאבְדוּ דֶרֶךְ
כִּי־יִבְעַר כִּמְעַט אַפּוֹ
אַשְׁרֵי
כָּל־חוֹסֵי בוֹ׃

A kingly poem. It is not clear whether the king is David, another king of the Davidic dynasty, or the Messiah.

1. The verb stem רגש appears only in Psalms (nouns, 55:15, 64:3). The corresponding verb in Rabbinic Hebrew appears only in the causative where it means "to feel, to notice"; the derived Aramaic noun רגשא means noise, noisy upheaval. This fits in with Arabic רגש describing either the roaring of a camel or the echo of thunder. In any case, the meaning is an irregular noise or roar.

The root ריק as "arming somebody" appears in *Gen*. 14:14, וַיָּרֶק אֶת־חֲנִיכָיו "he armed those whom he had raised".

The structure of the verse is chiastic, verb (V) noun (N), noun (N) verb (V).

2. The first clause could be translated: "Kings of the earth mobilize" but the root יצב is static, "to stand up, to stay put", and does not denote mobility. The meaning is that the kings put their armies on stand-by alert. The chiasmus again is VNNV.

3. "They" here are God's anointed and his people or army. This verse is parallel, VNVN. Verse 4 is parallel, NVNV.

5. Chiastic, VNNV. The possibility that the first clause means "Then He will subdue (יַדְבֵּר) their strongmen (אֵלִים) in His rage" would make v. 9 superfluous and is disregarded as unfitting at this position

6. It is difficult to determine who is talking in this verse. It cannot be God who is the speaker since, in the following verses, clearly God's anointed king is the speaker,. The suffixes in קָדְשִׁי מַלְכִּי are third person (Phoenician) singular possessive pronouns "his", cf. the *qere* נפשי "his soul" in Ps. 24:4. The verbal stem נסך in its other occurrences in the Bible means "to pour", either water, wine, or molten metal. It may be that the title נסיך " prince", really means "the person with the right to pour out libations as sacrifices"; this seems to be the meaning of *nisakku* in Accadic. The expression נָסַכְתִּי cannot mean "I was appointed נסיך" since it is an active form and the initial *nun* is part of the root. The best guess is to appeal to the Arabic where נסכ means "to dedicate (oneself, somebody, or something) to God's service". If God is the speaker, the translation would be "I dedicated My king on Zion, My holy mountain." This is one straight sentence.

7. The decree, חק, is a decree imposed from above. יְלִדְתִּיךָ means "I made you a creature", or maybe even "My creature". It cannot be "I gave birth to You" , יְלַדְתִּיךָ .

8. Here the chiliastic arrangement is nominal: direct object - indirect object; indirect object - direct object.

9. The imprecation is chiliastic, VNNV. The exhortation in v. 10 is inverted chiliastic, NVVN. The first verb, השכילו, can also be translated "be intelligent", and the second one, הוסרו, "be forewarned".
10. שופט is not a "judge" in the modern sense, but "ruler" (one of his main obligations being dispensing justice), like *suffetes*, rulers of Karthage in Roman sources.

11. Usually, גיל means either "joy" (*Hos*. 9:1, *Jer*. 48:33), "age, generation" (*Dan*. 1:10). The verbal stem גיל usually means "rejoice" (as in Accadic) but here and in *Hos*. 10:5 it seems to be Arabic גאל "to hobble, to go lame".
The parallelism is VNVN.

12. The first clause means neither "kiss the son" (Septuagint), nor "adore in purity" (Vulgate). Since this is a Psalm about a king, the reasonable comparison is with the only other occurrence of the verbal root נשק in a royal setting, in the story of Joseph where Pharao appoints him (*Gen*. 41:10) "You shall be over my house, by your orders shall my people be equipped (to withstand the seven years of famine)" (translation of S.R. Hirsch). This gives a fitting bracket for the entire poem: in v. 1-2, peoples and kings attempt to arm themselves against the Eternal and His anointed, whereas here they are admonished to pursue only good-faith military equipment. Instead of “purity” one might choose the nuance "good faith" for בר "purity, innocence" noted in classical Arabic. "Innocently" would also be an acceptable translation.

For דרך, אשרי see *Ps*. 1. The last clause seems to be independent of the preceding text; in the opinion of the Talmudim (b/ *Berakhot* 10a, y. *Berakhot* 4:3 (8a), *Taaniot* 2:2 (65c)) its role is to bracket *Ps*. 1,2 as one unit.

Psalm 3

1 A Psalm of David
When he was fleeing
From before
His son Absalom.

א מִזְמ֥וֹר לְדָוִ֑ד
בְּ֝בָרְח֗וֹ
מִפְּנֵ֤י ׀
אַבְשָׁל֬וֹם בְּנֽוֹ׃

2 Eternal,
How many are my enemies!
The mighty
Are rebelling against me.

ב יהוה
מָֽה־רַבּ֥וּ צָרָ֑י
רַ֝בִּ֗ים
קָמִ֥ים עָלָֽי׃

3 The mighty
Say about my person:
There is no help for him in God, Sela.

ג רַבִּים֮
אֹמְרִ֪ים לְנַ֫פְשִׁ֥י
אֵ֤ין יְֽשׁוּעָ֓תָה לּ֬וֹ בֵֽאלֹהִ֬ים סֶֽלָה׃

4 But You, Eternal,
Are a shield around me.
My glory,
Who gives me success.

ד וְאַתָּ֣ה יהוה
מָגֵ֣ן בַּעֲדִ֑י
כְּ֝בוֹדִ֗י
וּמֵרִ֥ים רֹאשִֽׁי׃

5 Attentively
I call to the Eternal,
He answers me from His holy mountain, Sela.

ה ק֭וֹלִי
אֶל־יהוָ֣ה אֶקְרָ֑א
וַיַּעֲנֵ֨נִי מֵהַ֖ר קָדְשׁ֣וֹ סֶֽלָה׃

6 I was laying down and went to sleep;
I awoke,
Truly the Eternal will support me.

ו אֲנִ֥י שָׁכַ֗בְתִּי וָֽאִ֫ישָׁ֥נָה
הֱקִיצ֑וֹתִי
כִּ֖י יהוָ֣ה יִסְמְכֵֽנִי׃

7 I am not afraid
Before the myriads of people,
Who all around
Are arraigned against me.

ז לֹֽא־אִ֭ירָא
מֵרִבְב֣וֹת עָ֑ם
אֲשֶׁ֥ר סָ֝בִ֗יב
שָׁ֣תוּ עָלָֽי׃

8 Please arise, Eternal,
Save me, my God,
Truly You will slap all my enemies on the jaw,
You will have broken the wicked's teeth.

ח ק֘וּמָ֤ה יהוה ׀
הוֹשִׁ֘יעֵ֤נִי אֱלֹהַ֗י
כִּֽי־הִכִּ֣יתָ אֶת־כָּל־אֹיְבַ֣י לֶ֑חִי
שִׁנֵּ֖י רְשָׁעִ֣ים שִׁבַּֽרְתָּ׃

9 The salvation is the Eternal's,
Your blessing is on Your people, Sela.

ט לַיהוָ֥ה הַיְשׁוּעָ֑ה
עַל־עַמְּךָ֖ בִרְכָתֶ֣ךָ סֶּֽלָה׃

1. From the count of full syllables in this verse, 4 - 4 - 4, it is seen that the header itself is poetry, not prose. The normal structure of a Psalm is a complaint followed by a victory song. While שִׁיר is a song, the Arabic shows that מִזְמוֹר is performed accompanied by flutes or other wind instrument. This is appropriate both for a dirge and a victory song.

2. The root רבב, רוב means mainly "to be many, to be great." The connected noun רב can mean "head, noble" both in Biblical Hebrew (where it is mostly used for non-Jewish office holders) and in Accadic where *rubū* means "noble, prince, magnate". Since the root appears twice in the same verse, I am translating the verb in its standard sense and take the noun to mean "nobles, important people".

2. The pronunciation of the Divine name cannot be determined. All we can say from this verse, as also from previous Psalms, that the Name must have two full syllables. The rhyme of the two parts is -ay. Comparing verse 2 to verse 4 which has 3 part rhyming in -y one is tempted to assume that the poet circumscribed the Divine name by the traditional Adonay, to obtain three rhyming clauses

3. This verse shows that we know nothing about the prosody of the Psalms. At a first glance, verses 3 and 5 seem badly out of balance, with short outcries at the start of the verse and a very long uninterrupted second part. Since the poet replaces the standard word ישועה by the poetic ישועתה with a double feminine ending, obviously to add another syllable required by melody or meter, it is clear that these lengths are intended poetic devices. One might fault the Masoretic accents as untrue to the poets intentions and break up this long clause of 10 full syllables into two or more shorter units; this will not do since the poem has another two clauses of 10 syllables and one of 9. Verse 3 is singular in that it has *`oleh weyored* not followed by *athnaḥ*. Also *Ps.* 1 has a long intrusive clause in v. 2; one has to recognize these pattern-breaking lengths as part of poetic technique.

It is not clear what the word *Sela* means. In the Bible the word appears only in poetry, in Psalms and the Psalm of Habakkuk, and only at the end of a sentence after a connecting accent. According to some, it is a musical note. The translation of the Aramaic Targum is "forever". Ibn Ezra declares it to be an affirmation and this is accepted by Qimḥi. The root סלה appears both as a derogatory (*Lam.*1:15, *Ps.* 119:118) and a positive (*Job* 28:16,19) verbal stem; the positive may be just a form of סלא (*Lam.* 4:2) whose meaning also is not completely clear but which may be described by the identical Sabean root "to dedicate, to present as an offering". It seem that *Sela* indicates the end of a unit in the poem.

4. The exclamation קוֹל "attention!" is found several times in Psalms and is retained in the old version of the prayer formula על הקוֹל " pay attention!", replaced in our *maḥzorim* by the rather unintelligible על הכול in the recitation of the reader before the Torah reading on Sabbath and Holidays.

8. The jussives in the first part of the verse show that the past tenses of the second half must be translated as future perfects.

9. The *dagesh* in סֶּלָה is an example of דחיק after unstressed final *qamaz* as is לּוֹ in v. 3 .

Psalm 4

1 For the conductor of an orchestra, A psalm of David.	א לַֽמְנַצֵּ֥חַ בִּנְגִינ֗וֹת מִזְמ֥וֹר לְדָוִֽד׃
2 When I am calling answer me, God Who justifies me. In straits, You expanded me; Be gracious to me And hear my prayer.	ב בְּקָרְאִ֡י עֲנֵ֤נִי ׀ אֱלֹ֘הֵ֤י צִדְקִ֗י בַּ֭צָּר הִרְחַ֣בְתָּ לִּ֑י חָ֝נֵּ֗נִי וּשְׁמַ֥ע תְּפִלָּתִֽי׃
3 Important people? Until when shall my honor be put to shame Do you love emptiness, Do you desire lies? Sela.	ג בְּנֵי־אִ֡ישׁ עַד־מֶ֬ה כְבוֹדִ֣י לִ֭כְלִמָּה תֶּאֱהָב֣וּן רִ֑יק תְּבַקְשׁ֖וּ כָזָ֣ב סֶֽלָה׃
4 So know: The Eternal truly has distinguished His pious, The Eternal will hear When I am calling to Him.	ד וּדְע֗וּ כִּֽי־הִפְלָ֣ה יְ֭הוָה חָסִ֣יד ל֑וֹ יְיָ֥ יִ֝שְׁמַ֗ע בְּקָרְאִ֥י אֵלָֽיו
5 Be excited but do not sin; Talk in your hearts On your couches, But be silent, Sela.	ה רִגְז֗וּ וְֽאַל־תֶּ֫חֱטָ֥אוּ אִמְר֣וּ בִ֭לְבַבְכֶם עַל־מִשְׁכַּבְכֶ֗ם וְדֹ֣מּוּ סֶֽלָה׃
6 Bring honest sacrifices And trust In the Eternal.	ו זִבְח֥וּ זִבְחֵי־צֶ֑דֶק וּ֝בִטְח֗וּ אֶל־יְהוָֽה׃
7 Grandees are saying: "Who will show us the good?" Turn to us The light of Your presence, Eternal.	ז רַבִּ֥ים אֹמְרִים֮ מִֽי־יַרְאֵ֪נ֫וּ ט֥וֹב נְֽסָה־עָ֭לֵינוּ א֨וֹר פָּנֶ֬יךָ יְהוָֽה׃
8 You put joy into my heart The moment their grain and cider increased.	ח נָתַ֣תָּה שִׂמְחָ֣ה בְלִבִּ֑י מֵעֵ֬ת דְּגָנָ֖ם וְתִירוֹשָׁ֣ם רָֽבּוּ׃
9 In isolated peace I shall lie down and sleep Truly, You alone, Eternal, Safely Will make me dwell!	ט בְּשָׁל֣וֹם יַחְדָּו֮ אֶשְׁכְּבָ֪ה וְאִ֫ישָׁ֥ן כִּֽי־אַתָּ֣ה יְהוָ֣ה לְבָדָ֑ד לָ֝בֶ֗טַח תּוֹשִׁיבֵֽנִי׃

1. This royal psalm should be sung accompanied by an orchestra, led by a conductor.

2. The expression אלהי צדקי cannot be translated "God of my righteousness", since the צדק here is God's gift, a not-guilty verdict in the heavenly court. Similarly in v. 6, the sacrifices are not "of righteousness" but are justified or justifiable. An unjustified sacrifice is sinful, it is profane matter known in Talmudic theory as חולין

לעזרה.

3. איש and בני איש very often means the upper classes of society, in contrast to בני אדם "everbody" or "the lower classes".

For עד מה we follow the Aramaic Targum, מטול מה "because of what", which conforms with the usage of Rabbinic and modern Hebrew, but not the Septuagint , whose "how long, until which time" is followed by almost all translators. One could translate here ריק with "nothings, vain things" with practically all other translators. However, since רגזו in v.5 is clearly an echo of רגשו in Ps.2, it is best to follow the language of that Psalm.

7. M. Dahood has correctly identified טוב as beneficial rain, the lifeblood of an agricultural society.

נסה stands for נשׂה, the root used in the third part of the Priestly Blessing *Num.* 6:26, יִשָּׂא יְיָ | פָּנָיו אֵלֶיךָ, on which the second half of the verse is modelled.

v.8,9 These verses show that the entire psalm is a supplication by the king for his people. He is justified if his rule produces ample supplies for his people; then he, in his royal isolation, can sleep well.

כי as usual in Psalms is not a logical connective but an emphatic exclamation.

Psalm 5

1 For the director, on flutes,
A Psalm of David.

א לַמְנַצֵּ֥חַ אֶֽל־הַנְּחִיל֗וֹת
מִזְמ֥וֹר לְדָוִֽד׃

2 Eternal,
Bend Your ear to my sayings,
Please understand my thoughts.

ב אֲמָרַ֣י הַאֲזִ֘ינָ֤ה ׀
יְהוָ֗ה
בִּ֣ינָה הֲגִֽיגִי׃

3 Pay attention to the sound of my outcry,
My King, and my God,
Truly, to You
I am praying.

ג הַקְשִׁ֤יבָה ׀ לְק֬וֹל שַׁוְעִ֗י
מַלְכִּ֥י וֵאלֹהָ֑י
כִּֽי־אֵ֝לֶ֗יךָ
אֶתְפַּלָּֽל׃

4 Eternal, at dawn
Hear my voice,
At dawn I shall present my case to You,
And I shall await.

ד יְֽהוָ֗ה בֹּ֭קֶר
תִּשְׁמַ֣ע קוֹלִ֑י
בֹּ֥קֶר אֶֽעֱרָךְ־לְ֝ךָ֗
וַאֲצַפֶּֽה׃

5 Certainly,
You
Are not a god who desires crime,
No evil may dwell with You.

ה כִּ֤י ׀
לֹ֤א אֵֽל־חָפֵ֘ץ רֶ֥שַׁע ׀
אָ֑תָּה
לֹ֖א יְגֻרְךָ֣ רָֽע׃

6 Hooligans cannot stand up
Before Your eyes;
You hate
All evil doers.

ו לֹֽא־יִתְיַצְּב֣וּ ה֭וֹלְלִים
לְנֶ֣גֶד עֵינֶ֑יךָ
שָׂ֝נֵ֗אתָ
כָּל־פֹּ֥עֲלֵי אָֽוֶן׃

7 Destroy
The speakers of lies!
A man of invention and lies
The Eternal will despise.

ז תְּאַבֵּד֮
דֹּבְרֵ֪י כָ֫זָ֥ב
אִישׁ־דָּמִ֥ים וּמִרְמָ֗ה
יְתָ֘עֵ֥ב ׀
יְהוָֽה׃

8 But I,
In the immensity of Your grace
Shall come to Your House,
I shall prostrate myself at Your holy Hall
In fear of You.

ח וַאֲנִ֗י
בְּרֹ֣ב חַ֭סְדְּךָ
אָב֣וֹא בֵיתֶ֑ךָ
אֶשְׁתַּחֲוֶ֥ה אֶל־הֵֽיכַל־קָ֝דְשְׁךָ֗
בְּיִרְאָתֶֽךָ׃

9 Eternal,
Lead me to Your justification
Because of those who ambush me,
Make my way straight before You.

ט יְהוָ֤ה ׀
נְחֵ֬נִי בְצִדְקָתֶ֗ךָ
לְמַ֥עַן שׁוֹרְרָ֑י
הַוְשַׁ֖ר [הַיְשַׁ֖ר] לְפָנַ֣י דַּרְכֶּֽךָ׃

10 Truly, Nothing in his mouth is correct,
Their innards are ardent desires;
An open grave are their throats;
Their tongues
They make slick!

י כִּ֤י אֵ֪ין בְּפִ֡יהוּ נְכוֹנָה֮
קִרְבָּ֪ם הַ֫וּ֥וֹת
קֶֽבֶר־פָּת֥וּחַ גְּרוֹנָ֑ם
לְ֝שׁוֹנָ֗ם
יַחֲלִֽיקוּן׃

11 Find them guilty,
O God,
May they fall through their plotting.
In the immensity of their crimes
Push them away.
Certainly, they rebelled against You!

יא הַאֲשִׁימֵם |
אֱלֹהִים
יִפְּלוּ מִמֹּעֲצוֹתֵיהֶם
בְּרֹב פִּשְׁעֵיהֶם
הַדִּיחֵמוֹ
כִּי מָרוּ בָךְ׃

12 But all who trust in You shall rejoice,
Eternally they will sing,
And You will shelter them.
And those who love Your name
Will exult in You.

יב וְיִשְׂמְחוּ כָל־חוֹסֵי בָךְ
לְעוֹלָם יְרַנֵּנוּ
וְתָסֵךְ עָלֵימוֹ
וְיַעְלְצוּ בְךָ
אֹהֲבֵי שְׁמֶךָ׃

13 Certainly, You
Will bless the just,
Eternal,
Like a large shield
You will surround him in grace

יג כִּי־אַתָּה
תְּבָרֵךְ צַדִּיק
יְהוָה
כַּצִּנָּה
רָצוֹן תַּעְטְרֶנּוּ׃

1. The נחילות are probably identical with the fifes (מחולות) associated with tambourines or drums both in the Song on the Sea (*Ex.* 15:20) and in *Ps.* 150, being round pipes of wood or reed. Fifes are used on extremely happy and extremely sorrowful occasions, so they are appropriate both for the lament (vv. 1-11) and the victory song (vv. 12-13).

2. There is some disagreement about whether הגג is a separate root, or simply an intensive form of the usual הגה "to think, to talk about".

3. The word כי here is emphatic. The sentence would make no sense if interpreted as an inference; if you already pray you suppose that you may be heard. So the sense is "only to You!".

4. The Rabbinic word ערכאות "courts of law" is commonly thought to derive from the Greek *archeion* However, a Greek word cannot really produce a Semitic ע (the Greek *arché* "government" appears correctly as ארכי in Galilean texts), so it is better to take the root ערך to mean "judicial proceedings". This also seems to be the meaning of the root in *Lev.* 27 where ערכו is money due by a kind of judicial proceeding, i.e., that can be collected by an officer of the court.

5. This description of God explains the difference between the monotheistic God and the pagan gods, which are personifications of the forces of nature and, therefore, amoral and destructive on occasion.
יגרך is spelled defectively even though the vowel in גור is long. The closing line can be translated "Never can a wicked man dwell with you", but regarding גר as abstract noun is preferable.

7. The איש דמים is not a "man of blood"; since murder is a capital crime it is clear that the murderer is condemned by God. The root here is דמה "imagination".

8. The initial ו is a *vaw* of contrast. As usual, ברב does not mean "plurality, the major part" but "immensity". In the Babylonian Talmud (*Berakot* 59b, *Ta`anit* 6b) the old prayer formula ברוב התשבחות is rejected because God is praised not only with a "majority of praise". This shows clearly that the Babylonian sages intended the prayers to be offered in the spoken language of the time, in which רוב means only "plurality", not in Biblical Hebrew, where it means "multitude, overwhelming mass". This latter interpretation seems to have been standard in Galilee all throughout Talmudic and Gaonic times, as shown by the Aschkenazic (Palestinian) version of the prayer נשמת which keeps רוב התשבחות in contrast to the Sephardic (Babylonian) text.

9. The meaning of שוררי is an old problem. It could mean "those who look at me"; in this case, to those who regard the poet as their inspiration. This would fit in well with the meaning "for the benefit of" attributed to most occurrences of למען preceding a noun but the meaning "because of (my/your) enemies" is certain in *Ps.* 8:3, 69:19. The sentence למען שוררי is repeated in a similar context in *Ps.* 27:11, it is acoustically similar to למען

צוררך of *Ps*. 8:3. Therefore, it is best to derive שרר from a meaning "to ambush" of the root שור attested to by *Hosea* 13:7 כְּנָמֵר עַל־דֶּרֶךְ אָשׁוּר "like a leopard I shall lie in ambush by the road" (or Ugarit/Canaanite שר "to destroy"..

10. הוות may derive from the Arabic *hawiya*, Ugaritic *hwy* "ardent desire"; Driver sees in the word Ugaritic *hwt* "bluster", possibly connected with Accadic *awātu* "word". Then the translation would be: "Nothing in his mouth is solid, their innards are just words, an open grave their throats." The switch between singular and plural is quite common in Hebrew.

11. The word מעצה does not mean "council" as in modern Hebrew but is an instrumental from עצה "the instrument of their counsel", i.e., their machinations.

12. The roots עלץ, עלז are interchangeable and mean a rejoicing in song. The Psalm ends with verse 13, the most lucky number, the number of divine attributes of mercy, *Ex*. 34:6-7.

Psalm 6

1 For the director in melodies
On the *sheminit*,
A Psalm of David.

א לַמְנַצֵּחַ בִּנְגִינוֹת
עַל־הַשְּׁמִינִית
מִזְמוֹר לְדָוִד׃

2 Eternal,
Do not chastise me in Your wrath
Nor punish me in Your anger.

ב יהוה
אַל־בְּאַפְּךָ תוֹכִיחֵנִי
וְאַל־בַּחֲמָתְךָ תְיַסְּרֵנִי׃

3 Favor me, Eternal,
For I am unfortunate,
Heal me, Eternal,
For my bones are in disorder.

ג חָנֵּנִי יהוה
כִּי אֻמְלַל אָנִי
רְפָאֵנִי יהוה
כִּי נִבְהֲלוּ עֲצָמָי׃

4 And my spirit
Has been stupefied very much,
But You, Eternal,
Until when?

ד וְנַפְשִׁי
נִבְהֲלָה מְאֹד
וְאַתָּה יהוה
עַד־מָתָי

5 Change my luck, Eternal,
Extricate my spirit,
Save me,
For your kindness's sake.

ה שׁוּבָה יהוה
חַלְּצָה נַפְשִׁי
הוֹשִׁיעֵנִי
לְמַעַן חַסְדֶּךָ׃

6 Truly, in death is no invoking You,
In the pit,
Who will give thanks to You?

ו כִּי אֵין בַּמָּוֶת זִכְרֶךָ
בִּשְׁאוֹל
מִי יוֹדֶה־לָּךְ׃

7 I am spent
In my worry,
Every night I am flooding
My couch;
With my tear
I am soaking my bed.

ז יָגַעְתִּי ׀
בְּאַנְחָתִי
אַשְׂחֶה בְכָל־לַיְלָה
מִטָּתִי
בְּדִמְעָתִי
עַרְשִׂי אַמְסֶה׃

8 My eye is dimmed from worry,
It left its place
Because of all my enemies.

ח עָשְׁשָׁה מִכַּעַס עֵינִי
עָתְקָה
בְּכָל־צוֹרְרָי׃

9 Depart from me
All evil doers.
Truly the Eternal has heard
The sound of my crying.

ט סוּרוּ מִמֶּנִּי
כָּל־פֹּעֲלֵי אָוֶן
כִּי־שָׁמַע יהוה
קוֹל בִּכְיִי׃

10 The Eternal has approved
My supplication,
The Eternal
Will accept my prayer.

י שָׁמַע יהוה
תְּחִנָּתִי
יהוה
תְּפִלָּתִי יִקָּח׃

11 All my enemies	יא יֵבֹשׁוּ ׀
Will be speechless	וְיִבָּהֲלוּ מְאֹד
And be much stupefied,	כָּל־אֹיְבָי
Their luck has turned,	יָשֻׁבוּ
They will be speechless in catastrophe.	יֵבֹשׁוּ רָגַע׃

1. Like the two preceding songs, this Psalm is a dirge followed by a victory song. It is not clear whether the *sheminit* is an eight-stringed lute or mini-harp or designates a song whose melody is restricted to one octave only, some kind of antique twelve-tone music.

3. It is difficult to find the correct English word for אמלל; its sense is given by the untranslatable Yiddish *nebbich*.
The two occurrences of נבהלו in vv. 3,4 cannot carry identical meanings. In most places, בהל means "to be terrified, to panic, act in a disorderly way out of panic". In classical Arabic, בהל means "to be cursed by God (and therefore unable to act)", the passive אנבהל means "to become stupid", see v. 11. (In modern Arabic, not relevant for us, the active means "to curse").

6. Death here means eternal death, having no part in the Future World, just as Life in most occurrences in the Psalms means Eternal Life. The pit is the place where the souls of sinners are destroyed.

7. מטה is a couch, also used for carrying the deceased to burial; ערש is a bed with a frame. אשחה means "I shall make swim", אמסה "I shall dissolve by soaking".

8. עתקה may alternatively may be translated as an Aramaism, "it aged".

10. שמע is more than "hear"; in Talmudic Hebrew it means "to understand, to accept". This is appropriate for the second appearance of the root here. In the Pentateuch, it also means "to accept discipline" (*Ex.* 24:7).

11. For the difficult verb בוש which in Hebrew has very many meanings, one may choose between the Accadic *bašu* "to be ashamed" or the Arabic בהת (derived by Nöldeke from an earlier בהת̇ corresponding to the Hebrew) "to be left speechless". Since the wicked probably will not feel shame, the second meaning is to be preferred.

In Arabic the passive of the verb בהל means "to become an imbecile"; that sense fits here.

The root רגע can mean 1) to be quiet, at ease, whole, 2) split, make a storm, enrage, 3) a very short time. Meanings 1) and 2) constitute *Gegensinn der Urworte* ("opposite meanings of archaic words"). Meaning 2) seems appropriate here, just as in *Ps.* 30:6: רֶגַע בְּאַפּוֹ חַיִּים בִּרְצוֹנוֹ "There is upheaval in His rage, Life in His pleasure", rather than "a second in His rage, Life in His pleasure" which makes no sense (and חיים does not mean "a life long"; in *Eccl.* 9:9 רְאֵה חַיִּים means "enjoy life"); it seems more important that the enemies of the poet be finished off once and for all rather than that they be vanquished in a moment. "In a moment" is expressed in Hebrew as כרגע (*Num.* 16:20).

Psalm 7

1 A *Shiggayon* by David Which he sang to the Eternal Following the words of Kush Ben Yemini.	א שִׁגָּיוֹן לְדָוִד אֲשֶׁר־שָׁר לַיהוָה עַל־דִּבְרֵי־כוּשׁ בֶּן־יְמִינִי׃
2 Eternal, my God, In You I trust, Help me from all my persecutors And save me.	ב יהוָה אֱלֹהַי בְּךָ חָסִיתִי הוֹשִׁיעֵנִי מִכָּל־רֹדְפַי וְהַצִּילֵנִי׃
3 Lest he tear me apart like a lion, Dismembering, And no one saves.	ג פֶּן־יִטְרֹף כְּאַרְיֵה נַפְשִׁי פֹּרֵק וְאֵין מַצִּיל׃
4 Eternal, my God, If I did do that, If there is crime on my hands,	ד יהוָה אֱלֹהַי אִם־עָשִׂיתִי זֹאת אִם־יֶשׁ־עָוֶל בְּכַפָּי׃
5 If I repaid My ally with evil, And stripped My companion empty,	ה אִם־גָּמַלְתִּי שׁוֹלְמִי רָע וָאֲחַלְּצָה צוֹרְרִי רֵיקָם׃
6 Then may the enemy pursue My person and catch it, Trample to the ground my life, And cause my liver To dwell in the dust, Selah.	ו יִרַדֹּף אוֹיֵב | נַפְשִׁי וְיַשֵּׂג וְיִרְמֹס לָאָרֶץ חַיָּי וּכְבוֹדִי | לֶעָפָר יַשְׁכֵּן סֶלָה׃
7 Rise, Eternal, \ In Your anger, Elevate Yourself Over my enemies' wrath, Awake over me The judgment You commanded.	ז קוּמָה יהוָה | בְּאַפֶּךָ הִנָּשֵׂא בְּעַבְרוֹת צוֹרְרָי וְעוּרָה אֵלַי מִשְׁפָּט צִוִּיתָ׃
8 Then an assembly of peoples Will surround You, And You will reside Very high over it.	ח וַעֲדַת לְאֻמִּים תְּסוֹבְבֶךָּ וְעָלֶיהָ לַמָּרוֹם שׁוּבָה׃
9 Eternal, Who judges nations,. Pass sentence for me, Eternal, According to my good deeds and my integrity.	ט יהוָה יָדִין עַמִּים שָׁפְטֵנִי יהוָה כְּצִדְקִי וּכְתֻמִּי עָלָי׃

10 May evil finish off
The wicked
But give basis to the just.
He who examines hearts
And loins
Is the just God.

י יִגְמָר־נָא רַע ׀
רְשָׁעִים
וּתְכוֹנֵן צַדִּיק
וּבֹחֵן לִבּוֹת
וּכְלָיוֹת
אֱלֹהִים צַדִּיק׃

11 My defense is by God,
The Savior
Of those straight of heart.

יא מָגִנִּי עַל־אֱלֹהִים
מוֹשִׁיעַ
יִשְׁרֵי־לֵב׃

12 God
Is a just judge
And a power
Who renders opinion every day!

יב אֱלֹהִים
שׁוֹפֵט צַדִּיק
וְאֵל
זֹעֵם בְּכָל־יוֹם׃

13 If one will not repent,
He will grind His sword,
He is spanning His bow
And making it ready.

יג אִם־לֹא יָשׁוּב
חַרְבּוֹ יִלְטוֹשׁ
קַשְׁתּוֹ דָרַךְ
וַיְכוֹנְנֶהָ׃

14 For Himself
He prepared deadly weapons,
His arrows
He will use against pursuers.

יד וְלוֹ
הֵכִין כְּלֵי־מָוֶת
חִצָּיו
לְדֹלְקִים יִפְעָל׃

15 Lo, by tort one does damage,
Is pregnant with sorrow,
And gives birth to a lie.

טו הִנֵּה יְחַבֶּל־אָוֶן
וְהָרָה עָמָל
וְיָלַד שָׁקֶר׃

16 A pit he dug
And excavated,
He fell
In the cut which he made.

טז בּוֹר כָּרָה
וַיַּחְפְּרֵהוּ
וַיִּפֹּל
בְּשַׁחַת יִפְעָל׃

17 May his effort turn on himself,
May his extortion descend
On his skull!

יז יָשׁוּב עֲמָלוֹ בְרֹאשׁוֹ
וְעַל־קָדְקֳדוֹ
חֲמָסוֹ יֵרֵד׃

18 I shall thank the Eternal for His equity;
I shall sing
The name of the Eternal Most High!

יח אוֹדֶה יְהוָה כְּצִדְקוֹ
וַאֲזַמְּרָה
שֵׁם יְהוָה עֶלְיוֹן׃

1. It is not known what a *shiggayon* means; probably it is a Penitential Psalm (in our case, a royal penitential psalm). The term might be cognate to Arabic סגא "to produce a wailing sound (camel)" or Accadic *šegum* "lament" (of a person whipped). The traditional identification of Kush ben Yemini with Saul has nothing to commend it; more reasonable is Ibn Ezra's conjecture that the "words of Kush ben Yemini refers to a well-known composition whose tune the poet is adopting.

3. Probably the best translation of the first clause would be "Lest he tear my breathing apart like a lion", referring to a method of killing often engaged by lions. It is not clear who the unnamed "he" is; from v. 6 it

seems that "he" is the agel of Death who also destroys the souls unless they are accepted by God into the "bundle of eternal life" (*1Sam*. 25:29).

5. שולמי is the one who is "wholly with me", צוררי is the one "bound to me, forming a bundle with me", root צרר; in v. 7 צוררי are "my enemies, those who cause me trouble" which is the more usual form from צור.

6. For the identification of the "enemy", cf. v. 3. כבוד is not "honor" but "the liver" as vital part whose destruction causes death; the same usage is still found in Rabbinic Hebrew (*Baba Meṣia`* 41a) where a vow "to donate the value of his כבוד" implies donation of the entire value of the person (*Lev*. 27) since a person cannot live without his liver (כבד). In the theory of temperaments, the liver is the seat of the soul of desires (Ibn Ezra on *Num*. 11:6).

8. The assembly of peoples will surround the presence of God in the Temple; עליה is translated by the Aramaic Targum as מטולתא "because of it" God will be recognized as residing in His heights; שובה is taken here from ישב "to dwell", not שוב "to return" (Ibn Ezra). The particle ל in למרום is emphatic, as in Arabic usage. V. 9 shows that the scope of the Psalm is national, not personal.

10. In its first occurrence, צדיק is a noun, describing a person, in the second occurrence it is an adjective, an attribute of God.

12. One might also translate "God judges the just". The second clause does not mean "God is angry every day" [although it is taken in this sense by the Talmud (*Berakhot* 7a).] He is a Power (original meaning of *el*) rendering His (judicial) opinion every day (following the primary meaning of זעם in Arabic).

14. דלק means to pursue (*Gen*. 31:36). Rashi declares that to be the original meaning of the root that more often means "to kindle, to burn". The meaning "to pursue" is similar to Arabic דלק "to attack with impetuosity" [the second meaning refers to Arabic ד̇לק "to light (a candelabrum)"].

15 עמל means "sorrow (caused by evil)"; it is a synonym of און "tort", as in *Ps*. 10:7 עָמָל וָאָוֶן (cf. also *Gen*. 41:51). Probably it is an intensive form of אמל, basis of אמלל "to feel badly, impotent"; similar meanings exist in Accadic and Arabic. In v. 17, the root עמל has the usual meaning "exertion".

16. There is probably an internal rhyme caused by the darkening of the *a* sound by the *`ayyin*: *wayyippōl baššaḥat yif`ål.* Note the use of repetitions at the start of verses 2,4 and the end of verses 14,16 (in the latter case with a switch in meaning from future-imperfect to past-perfect.).

Psalm 8

1 For the director, on the *Gittit*,
A Psalm of David.

א לַמְנַצֵּחַ עַל־הַגִּתִּית
מִזְמוֹר לְדָוִד׃

2 Eternal, our Master,
How mighty is Your name
On all the earth,
While spreading Your majesty
Over the Heavens!

ב יְהוָה אֲדֹנֵינוּ
מָה־אַדִּיר שִׁמְךָ
בְּכָל־הָאָרֶץ
אֲשֶׁר־תְּנָה הוֹדְךָ
עַל־הַשָּׁמָיִם׃

3 From the mouth of toddlers
And babies
You based strength,
On behalf of those bound to You,
To immobilize the enemy
And seeker of revenge.

ג מִפִּי עוֹלְלִים ׀
וְיֹנְקִים
יִסַּדְתָּ עֹז
לְמַעַן צוֹרְרֶיךָ
לְהַשְׁבִּית אוֹיֵב
וּמִתְנַקֵּם׃

4 When I contemplate Your sky
The work of Your fingers,
Moon and stars
Which You firmly put up.

ד כִּי־אֶרְאֶה שָׁמֶיךָ
מַעֲשֵׂי אֶצְבְּעֹתֶיךָ
יָרֵחַ וְכוֹכָבִים
אֲשֶׁר כּוֹנָנְתָּה׃

5 What is a human that You should consider him?
Or the common man
That You should care for him?

ה מָה־אֱנוֹשׁ כִּי־תִזְכְּרֶנּוּ
וּבֶן־אָדָם
כִּי תִפְקְדֶנּוּ׃

6 But You let him lack by a little
Being most powerful;
You crowned him with honor and splendor,

ו וַתְּחַסְּרֵהוּ מְּעַט
מֵאֱלֹהִים
וְכָבוֹד וְהָדָר תְּעַטְּרֵהוּ׃

7 You made him rule
Over the works of Your hands,
Everything
You put under his feet.

ז תַּמְשִׁילֵהוּ
בְּמַעֲשֵׂי יָדֶיךָ
כֹּל
שַׁתָּה תַחַת־רַגְלָיו׃

8 Herds of sheep and bulls, all of them,
And even
Beasts of the fields,

ח צֹנֶה וַאֲלָפִים כֻּלָּם
וְגַם
בַּהֲמוֹת שָׂדָי׃

9 Birds of the sky
And fish of the sea,
Crossing
Pathways of the oceans.

ט צִפּוֹר שָׁמַיִם
וּדְגֵי הַיָּם
עֹבֵר
אָרְחוֹת יַמִּים׃

10 Eternal, our Master,
How mighty is Your name
On all the earth!

י יְהוָה אֲדֹנֵינוּ
מָה־אַדִּיר שִׁמְךָ
בְּכָל־הָאָרֶץ׃

1. The *gitti*t probably is a musical instrument; it also could be a musical mode. This is one of the few songs without any lament.

2. תנה is a verbal noun, a participle, as recognized by Ibn Ezra, not a jussive; this precludes corruption in the text. The celebration of man's power over nature is only a celebration of God's might. As the Talmudim put it, engineering inventions are results of divine inspiration.

3. Here we take צררי in the sense described in *Ps.* 7:5, למען has the usual meaning of "for the benefit of", see the discussion of Ps. 5:9.

4. One contemplates the sky at night when the stars are visible, not during daytime when the sun's rays dominate everything.

5. בן אדם is the commoner, cf. *Ps*. 4:3. Compared to the universe, every human is a בן אדם.

6. The first *vaw* is a *vaw* of contrast, "but". In the second part, the construction ו..ו means "both" or "not only, but also". Note the symmetry of the stanza, with two *dagesh forte* each at the beginning and the end.

7. "Everything" seems to include the stars that are God's work (v. 4), but the list of earthly creations pointedly avoids mentioning insects and invertebrates, similar to *Gen*. 2:19 [in the interpretation of R. Yoḥanan ben Zakkai, *Gen. rabba* 17(4)] "The Eternal, God, forced from the earth all beast of the field and all birds of the sky and handed them over to man", meaning that the complexity of space exploration is easier than control of insects and worms.

8. Following Rashi, צנה is the same as צנא in *Num*. 32:24, "herds of sheep". The idea seems to be to contrast sheep, that are the most docile of domestic animals and whose existence is the herd, and bulls that are combative and unlikely to tolerate any rivals.
שׂדי may mean “mountain” and not “field”, as in Accadic *šadum* (and occasionally in Ugarit)..

9. The singular present participle עבר seems to refer to a collective. However, Ibn Ezra prefers this as a final reference to man, whom God has given mastery over nature, and who is able to cross the pathways of the oceans; in that case v. 8 and the first part of v. 9 are a parenthesis: "You let him rule over Your creation, all You gave under his feet (sheep, cattle, beast, bird, and fish), he is even crossing the seas."

Psalm 9

1 For the director
On *mut labben*
A Psalm of David.

א לַמְנַצֵּחַ
עַלְמוּת לַבֵּן
מִזְמוֹר לְדָוִד׃

2 I shall thank the Eternal
With all my heart,
I shall tell
All Your wonders.

ב **א**וֹדֶה יהוה
בְּכָל־לִבִּי
אֲסַפְּרָה
כָּל־נִפְלְאוֹתֶיךָ׃

3 I shall rejoice and exult in You,
I shall sing Your name, Most High.

ג אֶשְׂמְחָה וְאֶעֶלְצָה בָךְ
אֲזַמְּרָה שִׁמְךָ עֶלְיוֹן׃

4 As my enemies turn back,
They will stumble and be lost
Before You!

ד **בְּ**שׁוּב־אוֹיְבַי אָחוֹר
יִכָּשְׁלוּ וְיֹאבְדוּ
מִפָּנֶיךָ׃

5 Truly, You made
My case and my judgment,
You sat on the throne
As just judge.

ה כִּי־עָשִׂיתָ
מִשְׁפָּטִי וְדִינִי
יָשַׁבְתָּ לְכִסֵּא
שׁוֹפֵט צֶדֶק׃

6 You chastised peoples.
You destroyed the sinner,
You erased their name
Forever and ever.

ו **גָּ**עַרְתָּ גוֹיִם
אִבַּדְתָּ רָשָׁע
שְׁמָם מָחִיתָ
לְעוֹלָם וָעֶד׃

7 O enemy!
Ruins are finished forever.
Cities you have uprooted,
Their remembrance is lost.

ז **הָ**אוֹיֵב |
תַּמּוּ חֳרָבוֹת לָנֶצַח
וְעָרִים נָתַשְׁתָּ
אָבַד זִכְרָם הֵמָּה׃

8 But the Eternal
Resides eternally.
He establishes His throne for judgment.

ח וַיהוה
לְעוֹלָם יֵשֵׁב
כּוֹנֵן לַמִּשְׁפָּט כִּסְאוֹ׃

9 And He
Governs the land in justice,
Judges nations
In equity.

ט וְהוּא
יִשְׁפֹּט־תֵּבֵל בְּצֶדֶק
יָדִין לְאֻמִּים
בְּמֵישָׁרִים׃

10 The Eternal is refuge for the oppressed,
A refuge
For times of distress.

י **וִ**יהִי יהוה מִשְׂגָּב לַדָּךְ
מִשְׂגָּב
לְעִתּוֹת בַּצָּרָה׃

11 Those who know Your Name
Are trusting in You..
You never abandoned Your seekers, Eternal.

יא וְיִבְטְחוּ בְךָ
יוֹדְעֵי שְׁמֶךָ
כִּי לֹא־עָזַבְתָּ דֹרְשֶׁיךָ יהוה׃

12 Sing to the Eternal
Who resides in Zion,
Tell among the nations
His usual deeds.

יב **זַ**מְּרוּ לַיהוה
יֹשֵׁב צִיּוֹן
הַגִּידוּ בָעַמִּים
עֲלִילוֹתָיו׃

13 Truly, He Who requites blood
  Remembers them.
He does not forget
  The wail of the poor [meek].

יג כִּי־דֹרֵשׁ דָּמִים
אוֹתָם זָכָר
לֹא־שָׁכַח
צַעֲקַת עֲנִיִּים [עֲנָוִים]׃

14 Favor me, o Eternal,
See my plight
  Away from those who hate me,
Lift me up
  From the gates of Death.

יד חָנְנֵנִי יהוה
רְאֵה עָנְיִי
מִשֹּׂנְאָי
מְרוֹמְמִי
מִשַּׁעֲרֵי מָוֶת׃

15 That I may tell
  All your praises.
In the gates of Daughter Zion.
Let me rejoice
  In Your help.

טו לְמַעַן אֲסַפְּרָה
כָּל־תְּהִלָּתֶיךָ
בְּשַׁעֲרֵי בַת־צִיּוֹן
אָגִילָה
בִּישׁוּעָתֶךָ׃

16 The Gentiles are drowning
  In the ditch they made.
In this net which they concealed
  Their foot is caught.

טז טָבְעוּ גוֹיִם
בְּשַׁחַת עָשׂוּ
בְּרֶשֶׁת־זוּ טָמָנוּ
נִלְכְּדָה רַגְלָם׃

17 The Eternal is known
  By the judgment He made,
The malefactor is caught
  By the work of is own hand!
Higgayon Selah.

יז נוֹדַע | יהוה
מִשְׁפָּט עָשָׂה
בְּפֹעַל כַּפָּיו
נוֹקֵשׁ רָשָׁע
הִגָּיוֹן סֶלָה׃

18 The evildoers will return to the pit,
All Gentiles
  Who forget God!

יח יָשׁוּבוּ רְשָׁעִים לִשְׁאוֹלָה
כָּל־גּוֹיִם
שְׁכֵחֵי אֱלֹהִים׃

19 Truly, not forever
  Will the needy be forgotten,
Or the hope of the meek [poor]
  Be eternally lost.

יט כִּי לֹא לָנֶצַח
יִשָּׁכַח אֶבְיוֹן
תִּקְוַת עֲנִוִּים [עֲנִיִּים]
תֹּאבַד לָעַד׃

20 Rise, Eternal,
  A mortal should not be powerful.
Let Gentiles be judged
  before You.

כ קוּמָה יהוה
אַל־יָעֹז אֱנוֹשׁ
יִשָּׁפְטוּ גוֹיִם
עַל־פָּנֶיךָ׃

21 Set, o Eternal
  Mastery over them.
May Gentiles know;
They are mortals, Selah.

כא שִׁיתָה יהוה |
מוֹרָה לָהֶם
יֵדְעוּ גוֹיִם
אֱנוֹשׁ הֵמָּה סֶּלָה׃

1 . It is not known what *mut labbēn* is. The poem is the beginning of an alphabetic acrostic; most stanzas extend over two sentences. The letter ד is missing; but no alphabetic poem in Psalms contains a full alphabet with the exception of Ps. 119. The letter ג has only one verse. There is a problem with ה, since the verse starting with this letter ends in a seemingly superfluous המה and is followed by 4 verses starting with ו. It is not difficult to find verses starting with ו in Psalms, but the contents show that verses 7-9 form one unit and so do verses 10-11. Therefore, we take the stanza for ה to be 7-9, and verses 10 to 11 for ו. In the interpretation of the Talmud (*Megillah* 17b) given by a possible reading of Rashi's commentary (see *Diqduqe Sopherim ad loc.*), the alphabetic acrostic is reasonably complete since our Psalms 9 and 10 are considered to form one poem in the Septuagint and in a few Hebrew manuscripts as reported in the Yerushalmi (*Shabbat* 16(1)). Our division of

Psalms 9 and 10 follows Tosafot. Cassuto also argues for the split since Ps. 9 ends with a statement of victory and Ps. 10 begins again with a lament, as is common in the Davidic Psalms.

The prayer offered by the Psalm is somewhere between national and private.

4. יכשלו is read as a reflexive: May they (or they will) stumble over themselves.

7. The article in האויב is the vocative ה, as recognized by Qimḥi, cf. the use of הקהל "o Congregation", in *Num.* 15:15. There is no need to look for an exotic meaning of ערים, abandoned cities are parallel to "ruins". The last הֵמָּה is for contrast: "Those are whose remembrance is lost", i.e., both the ruined cities and the enemies who sacked them. In contrast "the Eternal is eternally throned" (v. 8). This emphasizes the unity of verses 7,8 (and their appendix, v. 9) as explained above.

8. The primary meaning of ישב is not "to dwell" but "to have as place of business", cf. *Gen.* 47:4 where the sons of Jacob say to Pharao "We came for temporary sojourn" (גור) ... "but now may we have Goshen as place of business" (ישב). Similarly, *Jud.* 4:2, where Sisera's headquarters are at Ḥaroshet Haggoyim (ישב). The meaning "to establish" for the root כנן is well established both in Hebrew and in Ugaritic. שפט means more "to govern" than "to judge"; some of the Biblical "Judges", while able to govern, were quite unfit to judge. The same meaning is found in Phoenician and Ugaritic. The word תבל for "world" appears only in poetic texts; in Accadic, *tebalu* is the opposite of *naru*, "streams of water". So תבל seems to be the equivalent of prosaic יבשה "dry land".

12. The word עלילות has many meanings. In the Pentateuch, it means "(false) accusations" but in Psalms and other poetic sources it seems to be related to Arabic עלי , one of whose meanings is " to act repeatedly" and to the Hebrew root עלה ,"to show supremacy". The meaning of vv. 12-13 is that the Eternal always acts to avenge the blood of the meek. It is not clear whether the Eternal resides in Zion or the resident of Zion sings and tells the Eternal's praises among the nations. Since more double duty clauses occur later in the poem, the ambiguity may be intentional but, in contrast to the later verses, here the Masoretic division of the verse declares that the Eternal resides in Zion.

13. In vv. 13,19 one reading is "the meek", the other "the poor, deprived" as *qere* and *ketib* . Probably the editors of Psalms found manuscripts giving both versions, by the usual rules the majority of sources is the *qere*.

In general, דרש means "to look after, to desire', only if applied to God does it mean "to exact punishment".

14. חננני is a unusual form, not shortened by the usual rules of grammar. משׂנאי is an example of a *mem privativum*, designating the absence of something. The poet is deprived even without the actions of people who hate him; since he implores God to lift him away from the gates of Death (meaning, as always in Psalms, Eternal Death), his deprivation is spiritual and does not need any haters.

15. Here the Masoretic punctuation established that "in the gates of daughter Zion" refers both to the preceding and the following clauses. Since the poet promises to praise God if he is saved from Eternal Death, Zion here is the Heavenly Zion.

16. The noun שחת is derived not from the verbal stem שחת "to destroy," but from שוח "to sink deep", and is synonym with Biblical Hebrew שׁוּחָה, Mishnaic Hebrew שִׁיחַ "a ditch".

17. If is not clear what *higgayon* means. It does not mean "logic" as in modern Hebrew, nor "spelling" as in Ugaritic, or "talking about, studying", as the root הגא means in some other places in the Bible. The Arabic הגא "to be the object of satire", may be a possible meaning since it may refer to the self-destruction of the evildoers described in vv. 16,17.

18. שאול, the pit, is the place of eternal silence, the place of destruction of the souls unfit for Eternal Life.

One could possibly but but unconvincingly translate "The evildoers should return to the pit".

19. The negation *la* refers to both clauses: not forever the needy will be forgotten, not forever the poor will be lost.

21. Here again, the clause יֵדְעוּ גוֹיִם "May Gentiles know" refers both to the preceding and the following clauses; this accounts for the unusual use of two major dividing accents in one short verse.

Psalm 10

1 Why, Eternal,
Are You standing far away,
Are You keeping aloof,
In times of danger?

א לָמָה יהוה
תַּעֲמֹד בְּרָחוֹק
תַּעְלִים
לְעִתּוֹת בַּצָּרָה׃

2 In haughtiness the wicked
Pursues the poor.
Let them be caught
By the plans they concocted.

ב בְּגַאֲוַת־רָשָׁע
יִדְלַק עָנִי
יִתָּפְשׂוּ |
בִּמְזִמּוֹת זוּ חָשָׁבוּ׃

3 Truly, the wicked praises
His own desires;
But he who blesses unlawful gain
Slanders
The Eternal.

ג כִּי־הִלֵּל רָשָׁע
עַל־תַּאֲוַת נַפְשׁוֹ
וּבֹצֵעַ בֵּרֵךְ
נִאֵץ |
יהוָה׃

4 The wicked,
His nose high,
Does not inquire.
There is no God
In all his plans.

ד רָשָׁע
כְּגֹבַהּ אַפּוֹ
בַּל־יִדְרֹשׁ
אֵין אֱלֹהִים
כׇּל־מְזִמּוֹתָיו׃

5 Powerful is his way [are his ways] any time;
Too elevated is Your judgment
Against him.
All his enemies
He blows away.

ה יָחִילוּ דְרָכָו [דְרָכָיו] | בְּכׇל־עֵת
מָרוֹם מִשְׁפָּטֶיךָ
מִנֶּגְדּוֹ
כׇּל־צוֹרְרָיו
יָפִיחַ בָּהֶם׃

6 He says in his heart,
"I shall not stumble,
For all generations
Without trouble."

ו אָמַר בְּלִבּוֹ
בַּל־אֶמּוֹט
לְדֹר וָדֹר
אֲשֶׁר לֹא־בְרָע׃

7 His mouth is full of
Curse,
Also deceit and damage.
Under his tongue
Are evil and tort.

ז אָלָה |
פִּיהוּ מָלֵא
וּמִרְמוֹת וָתֹךְ
תַּחַת לְשׁוֹנוֹ
עָמָל וָאָוֶן׃

8 He sits
In ambush in hamlets.
In secret
He will kill the innocent.
His eyes
Will discern the luckless.

ח יֵשֵׁב |
בְּמַאְרַב חֲצֵרִים
בַּמִּסְתָּרִים
יַהֲרֹג נָקִי
עֵינָיו
לְחֵלְכָה יִצְפֹּנוּ׃

9 He lies in ambush secretly,
Like a lion from his covert
He lies in ambush
To catch the poor.
He catches the poor
By drawing him into his net.

ט יֶאֱרֹב בַּמִּסְתָּר |
כְּאַרְיֵה בְסֻכֹּה
יֶאֱרֹב
לַחֲטוֹף עָנִי
יַחְטֹף עָנִי
בְּמׇשְׁכוֹ בְרִשְׁתּוֹ׃

10 And pounding [He pounded] the prostrate
The luckless.
Will fall into his power

י וְדָכָה [יִדְכֶּה] יָשֹׁחַ
וְנָפַל בַּעֲצוּמָיו
חֵלְכָּאִים [חֵיל כָּאִים]׃

11 He says in his heart
"God forgot;
He has hidden His face,
He will never see!"

יא אָמַר בְּלִבּוֹ
שָׁכַח אֵל
הִסְתִּיר פָּנָיו
בַּל־רָאָה לָנֶצַח׃

12 Arise, Eternal, Powerful,
Lift Your hand;
Do not forget the poor [meek].

יב קוּמָה יהוה אֵל
נְשָׂא יָדֶךָ
אַל־תִּשְׁכַּח עֲנִיִּים [עֲנָוִים]׃

13 Why
Does the wicked insult God,
Say in his heart,
"He will not care"?

יג עַל־מֶה |
נִאֵץ רָשָׁע | אֱלֹהִים
אָמַר בְּלִבּוֹ
לֹא תִּדְרֹשׁ׃

14 You see,
Truly, You
Are watching evil deeds and displeasure,
To give in Your hand.
To You
The luckless man surrenders himself,
The orphan
Whom You
Used to help.

יד רָאִתָה
כִּי־אַתָּה |
עָמָל וָכַעַס | תַּבִּיט
לָתֵת בְּיָדֶךָ
עָלֶיךָ
יַעֲזֹב חֵלֶכָה
יָתוֹם
אַתָּה |
הָיִיתָ עוֹזֵר׃

15 Break
The wicked's arm
And the criminal's,
You look for his crime, can it not be found?

טו שְׁבֹר
זְרוֹעַ רָשָׁע
וָרָע
תִּדְרוֹשׁ־רִשְׁעוֹ בַל־תִּמְצָא׃

16 The Eternal is King
For ever and ever.
The Gentiles will be lost
From His Land.

טז יהוה מֶלֶךְ
עוֹלָם וָעֶד
אָבְדוּ גוֹיִם
מֵאַרְצוֹ׃

17 Eternal, You heard the meek ones' desire;
Prepare their hearts,
Listen attentively with Your ear.

יז תַּאֲוַת עֲנָוִים שָׁמַעְתָּ יהוה
תָּכִין לִבָּם
תַּקְשִׁיב אָזְנֶךָ׃

18 To judge the orphan and downtrodden.
So the arrogant may not continue
To scare man
Away from the Land.

יח לִשְׁפֹּט יָתוֹם וָדָךְ
בַּל־יוֹסִיף עוֹד
לַעֲרֹץ אֱנוֹשׁ
מִן־הָאָרֶץ

3. Following Torczyner, in וּבֹצֵעַ בֵּרֵךְ we take the first word as subject and the second as verb; both words are participles, i.e., verbal nouns.

7. The unusual תֹּךְ is explained by the Arabic תכ "to cause damage".

8. חצר is an isolated manor surrounded by dependents' buildings, all surrounded by a fence or wall.

The unusual חלך appearing only in this Psalm is translated "the luckless", following all old authorities (Ibn Ḥayyuj, Dunash, Rashi) and Eliezer Ben Yehuda.

9. Ben Yehuda and Torczyner derive בסכה from a word סיך "underbrush".

15. The second clause in this verse is translated following Ibn Ezra.

16. The interpretation of the entire Psalm hinges on the reading of this verse. Since the Psalm ends with an acrostic formed by the last letters of the alphabet, and in the Septuagint Ps. 10 is part of Ps. 9, it is possible to see the "Land" as the Land of Israel, and the whole as a royal Psalm disguised as a private lament. However, this reading would imply a corruption and lacuna between the two parts of the alphabet. Also, the tenor of Ps. 10 is quite different from that of Ps. 9; in addition there is no Selah here, where it might be expected. It is therefore more reasonable to accept the two songs as different compositions, perhaps arranged together because of the rudimentary acrostics in both of them. In addition, verse 16 is a statement of fact, not a prayer. So it is better to follow the tradition of the Masoretic text and accept this Psalm as a private lament, independent of the preceding royal song. In this case, the Land is the Land of the Living, the Land of Eternal Life.

17. The usual translation of תאוה "desire, appetite" (cf. v.3) is not appropriate here. The proper translation should be derived, following J. Barth, from the Arabic תאוה "to groan". This meaning, therefore, may be an arabism, and not necessarily the meaning of colloquial Hebrew.

18. If עוד has the usual meaning of "still, continually", neither the second cesura nor the entire verse makes sense. Therefore, following Dahood, we take it from Ugaritic *g̅d*, Arabic עׄוד "to be arrogant".

The count of full syllables shows that the structure of this Psalm is different from Ps. 9; this supports our interpretation of the Land as the Land of Life.

Psalm 11

1. For the conductor, by David.
In the Eternal I am taking shelter.
How
Can you say to me:
Move
Your mountain, bird?

א לַמְנַצֵּחַ לְדָוִד
בַּיהוָה | חָסִיתִי
אֵיךְ
תֹּאמְרוּ לְנַפְשִׁי
נוּדִו [נוּדִי]
הַרְכֶם צִפּוֹר׃

2. Behold the wicked
Step on the bow,
Put their arrow firmly on the string,
To shoot from the darkness
At the straight-of-heart.

ב כִּי הִנֵּה הָרְשָׁעִים
יִדְרְכוּן קֶשֶׁת
כּוֹנְנוּ חִצָּם עַל־יֶתֶר
לִירוֹת בְּמוֹ־אֹפֶל
לְיִשְׁרֵי־לֵב׃

3. When the foundations
Are torn down,
The honest man
What can he do?

ג כִּי־הַשָּׁתוֹת
יֵהָרֵסוּן
צַדִּיק
מַה־פָּעָל׃

4. The Eternal
In His holy Hall,
The Eternal
On His heavenly Throne,
His eyes will see,
His eyelashes will examine
Mankind.

ד יְהוָה |
בְּהֵיכַל קָדְשׁוֹ
יְהוָה
בַּשָּׁמַיִם כִּסְאוֹ
עֵינָיו יֶחֱזוּ
עַפְעַפָּיו יִבְחֲנוּ
בְּנֵי אָדָם׃

5. The Eternal
Will examine the honest man;
But the wicked
And the lover of violence
Is hated by Him.

ה יְהוָה
צַדִּיק יִבְחָן
וְרָשָׁע
וְאֹהֵב חָמָס
שָׂנְאָה נַפְשׁוֹ׃

6. He will rain coals on the wicked,
Fire and sulphur,
And destructive storms
Are the portions of their cup.

ו יַמְטֵר עַל־רְשָׁעִים פַּחִים
אֵשׁ וְגָפְרִית
וְרוּחַ זִלְעָפוֹת
מְנָת כּוֹסָם׃

7. Truly, the Eternal is just,
He loves Righteousness.
The upright one
Will view His face.

ז כִּי־צַדִּיק יְהוָה
צְדָקוֹת אָהֵב
יָשָׁר
יֶחֱזוּ פָנֵימוֹ׃

A private Psalm, talking about eternal life or damnation.

1. נפשי means "my breathing person" or, in short, "me". The construction of the clause אֵיךְ תֹּאמְרוּ לְנַפְשִׁי נוּדִו [נוּדִי] הַרְכֶם צִפּוֹר׃ is difficult and therefore a preferred target of emendators. But the meaning, and the construction are clear if verses 1 and 2 are taken together. הַרְכֶם means "your (second person plural) mountain". This is the mountain of the people talking who are spanning the bow with their feet and putting the arrow on the bowstring to shoot the bird as soon as it appears. The meaning of the clause is that the enemies try to lure the poet into a trap, but he has discovered it in time. It is tempting to conjecture that the text, copied from Paleo-Hebrew

letters into "Hebrew" (Aramaic) letters when the difference between מ and ם was not developed, could be read as Arabic הרכ מצפר "poor idiot".

2. בְּמוֹ is amplification of בְּ.

3. This verse may be an introduction to v. 4, what will be the reaction of the Just, the Eternal, to the destruction of morality? But we have chosen "man" instead of "The Eternal" as the best reading.
The ה in מַה־פָּעָל is consonantal (as if written מַהּ), as seen from the following hard פּ.

5. צדיק may be a description of the just among men. Then the translation of the stanza would be:
The Eternal | Will discern the just || But both the wicked | And the lover of violence | He hates.

6. The identification of פחים with פחמים "coals" follows Rashi.

7. The priestly blessing, *Num.* 6:24-26, is alluded to here.

Psalm 12

1 For the conductor, on the *sheminit*,
A Psalm of David.

א לַמְנַצֵּ֥חַ עַֽל־הַשְּׁמִינִ֗ית
מִזְמ֥וֹר לְדָוִֽד׃

2 Help, Eternal,
For the pious are finished,
For the trustworthy have vanished
From mankind.

ב הוֹשִׁ֣יעָה יְ֭הוָה
כִּי־גָ֣מַר חָסִ֑יד
כִּֽי־פַ֥סּוּ אֱ֝מוּנִ֗ים
מִבְּנֵ֥י אָדָֽם׃

3 Men will
Tell lies
One to another,
Glib lips
Will talk with two hearts.

ג שָׁ֤וְא ׀
יְדַבְּרוּ֮
אִ֤ישׁ אֶת־רֵ֫עֵ֥הוּ
שְׂפַ֥ת חֲלָק֑וֹת
בְּלֵ֖ב וָלֵ֣ב יְדַבֵּֽרוּ

4 May the Eternal uproot
All glib lips,
The tongue
Speaking in boasts.

ד יַכְרֵ֣ת יְ֭הוָה
כָּל־שִׂפְתֵ֣י חֲלָק֑וֹת
לָ֝שׁ֗וֹן
מְדַבֶּ֥רֶת גְּדֹלֽוֹת׃

5 Those who say
"By our tongues we shall be mighty,
Our lips are with us;
Who is our lord?"

ה אֲשֶׁ֤ר אָֽמְר֨וּ ׀
לִלְשֹׁנֵ֣נוּ נַ֭גְבִּיר
שְׂפָתֵ֣ינוּ אִתָּ֑נוּ
מִ֖י אָד֣וֹן לָֽנוּ׃

6 From the robbing of the poor,
From the cry of the needy,
Now I shall arise
Says the Eternal
I will establish help
I shall make him pant.

ו מִשֹּׁ֥ד עֲנִיִּים֮
מֵֽאַנְקַ֪ת אֶבְי֫וֹנִ֥ים
עַתָּ֣ה אָ֭קוּם
יֹאמַ֣ר יְהוָ֑ה
אָשִׁ֥ית בְּ֝יֵ֗שַׁע
יָפִ֥יחַֽ לֽוֹ׃

7 The commands of the Eternal
Are pure saying,
Molten silver
In an earthen crucible,
Refined
Sevenfold.

ז אִֽמֲר֣וֹת יְהוָה֮
אֲמָר֪וֹת טְהֹ֫ר֥וֹת
כֶּ֣סֶף צָ֭רוּף
בַּעֲלִ֣יל לָאָ֑רֶץ
מְ֝זֻקָּ֗ק
שִׁבְעָתָֽיִם׃

8 You, Eternal, will guard them,
You will guard them
From this generation, forever.

ח אַתָּֽה־ יְהוָ֥ה תִּשְׁמְרֵ֑ם
תִּצְּרֶ֓נּוּ ׀
מִן־הַדּ֖וֹר ז֣וּ לְעוֹלָֽם׃

9 In circles
The wicked may stroll,
Given the elevation of vulgarity
By mankind.

ט סָבִ֗יב
רְשָׁעִ֥ים יִתְהַלָּכ֑וּן
כְּרֻ֥ם זֻ֝לּ֗וּת
לִבְנֵ֥י אָדָֽם׃

1. For *sheminit*, cf. *Ps.* 6.

2. חָסִיד is a collective. פסו is identical with אפסו "having no existence."

3. This Psalm has many plurals standing for abstracta, חלקות "glibness", גדולות "bragging", זלות "vulgarity". In modern Hebrew, abstracta are characterized by the ending ות throughout, but in Biblical Hebrew -וֹת is much more frequent.

7. אמר is not just "saying", but "commanding" as in the story of Creation; Arabic אמר "command, be a commander".
עליל means a crucible by the testimony of the Targum, this is the meaning accepted by all medieval commentators. The related word עלי means "the handle of the crucible". In לארץ the prefix is the ל of instrumentation.

9. זֻלּוּת is a noun from זלל "to be insignificant", in Arabic זל "stumble, commit an error or sin, being short-weight".

Psalm 13

1 For the conductor
A Psalm of David.

א לַמְנַצֵּחַ
מִזְמוֹר לְדָוִד׃

2 Until when, Eternal,
Will You totally forget me?
Until when
Will You hide Your face from me?

ב עַד־אָנָה יהוה
תִּשְׁכָּחֵנִי נֶצַח
עַד־אָנָה |
תַּסְתִּיר אֶת־פָּנֶיךָ מִמֶּנִּי׃

3 Until when shall I load my soul
With worries,
Sorrow in my heart, daily?
Until when
Will my foe triumph over me?

ג עַד־אָנָה אָשִׁית עֵצוֹת
בְּנַפְשִׁי
יָגוֹן בִּלְבָבִי יוֹמָם
עַד־אָנָה |
יָרוּם אֹיְבִי עָלָי׃

4 Look, please answer me
Eternal, my God,
Enlighten my eyes,
Lest I sleep in Death.

ד הַבִּיטָה עֲנֵנִי
יהוָה אֱלֹהָי
הָאִירָה עֵינַי
פֶּן־אִישַׁן הַמָּוֶת׃

5 Lest my foe may say, “I overcame him,”
My enemies rejoice,
When I stagger.

ה פֶּן־יֹאמַר אֹיְבִי יְכָלְתִּיו
צָרַי יָגִילוּ
כִּי אֶמּוֹט׃

6 As for me
I will trust in Your kindness.
My heart will rejoice in Your salvation.
I shall sing to the Eternal
Who truly has benefited me!

ו וַאֲנִי |
בְּחַסְדְּךָ בָטַחְתִּי
יָגֵל לִבִּי בִּישׁוּעָתֶךָ
אָשִׁירָה לַיהוָה
כִּי גָמַל עָלָי׃

3. עצות "counsels" never appear in the plural except in a derisive or derogatory way; a good counsel is always referred to in the singular; therefore the universally accepted translation is "worries".

The enemy are his own bad inclinations. The grace mentioned in v. 6 is not Calvin’s, but the psychological impetus needed by a split personality to chose the right path.

4. The request "light up my eye" refers to the early theoretical optics from Euclid through the Middle Ages, that vision is induced by optical rays emitted from the eye that scan the world. The verse proves the antiquity of that theory.

6. גמל is shorthand for גמל חסדים טובים, "He who dispenses positive benefits", in short, "who is a benefactor".

Psalm 53

א לַמְנַצֵּ֥חַ עַֽל־מָחֲלַ֗ת
מַשְׂכִּ֥יל לְדָוִֽד׃
ב אָ֘מַ֤ר נָבָ֣ל בְּ֭לִבּוֹ
אֵ֣ין אֱלֹהִ֑ים
הִֽ֝שְׁחִ֗יתוּ
וְהִֽתְעִ֥יבוּ עָ֝֗וֶל
אֵ֣ין עֹֽשֵׂה־טֽוֹב׃

ג אֱֽלֹהִ֗ים מִשָּׁמַיִם֮
הִשְׁקִ֪יף עַל־בְּנֵ֫י אָדָ֥ם
לִ֭רְאוֹת
הֲיֵ֣שׁ מַשְׂכִּ֑יל
דֹּ֝רֵ֗שׁ
אֶת־אֱלֹהִֽים׃

ד כֻּלּ֥וֹ סָג֘
יַחְדָּ֪ו נֶ֫אֱלָ֥חוּ
אֵ֣ין עֹֽשֵׂה־ט֑וֹב
אֵ֝֗ין
גַּ֣ם אֶחָֽד׃

ה הֲלֹ֥א יָדְע֗וּ
פֹּ֬עֲלֵ֬י אָ֗וֶן
אֹ֣כְלֵ֣י עַ֭מִּי
אָ֣כְלוּ לֶ֑חֶם
אֱ֝לֹהִ֗ים
לֹ֣א קָרָֽאוּ׃

ו שָׁ֤ם ׀
פָּֽחֲדוּ פַ֫חַד
לֹא־הָ֪יָה֫ פָ֥חַד
כִּֽי־אֱלֹהִ֗ים פִּ֭זַּר
עַצְמ֣וֹת חֹנָ֑ךְ
הֱ֝בִשֹׁ֗תָה
כִּֽי־אֱלֹהִ֥ים מְאָסָֽם׃

ז מִ֥י־יִתֵּ֣ן מִצִּיּוֹן֮
יְשֻׁ֫עֹ֥ת יִשְׂרָ֫אֵ֥ל
בְּשׁ֣וּב אֱ֭לֹהִים
שְׁב֣וּת עַמּ֑וֹ
יָגֵ֥ל יַ֝עֲקֹ֗ב
יִשְׂמַ֥ח יִשְׂרָאֵֽל׃

Psalm 14

א לַמְנַצֵּ֗חַ לְדָ֫וִ֥ד
אָ֘מַ֤ר נָבָ֣ל בְּ֭לִבּוֹ
אֵ֣ין אֱלֹהִ֑ים
הִֽ֝שְׁחִ֗יתוּ
הִֽתְעִ֥יבוּ עֲלִ֗ילָה
אֵ֣ין עֹֽשֵׂה־טֽוֹב׃

ב יהוה מִשָּׁמַיִם֮
הִשְׁקִ֪יף עַֽל־בְּנֵי־אָ֫דָ֥ם
לִ֭רְאוֹת
הֲיֵ֣שׁ מַשְׂכִּ֑יל
דֹּ֝רֵ֗שׁ
אֶת־אֱלֹהִֽים׃

ג הַכֹּ֥ל סָר֘
יַחְדָּ֪ו נֶ֫אֱלָ֥חוּ
אֵ֣ין עֹֽשֵׂה־ט֑וֹב
אֵ֝֗ין
גַּם־אֶחָֽד׃

ד הֲלֹ֥א יָדְע֗וּ
כָּל־פֹּ֬עֲלֵ֬י אָ֗וֶן
אֹכְלֵ֣י עַ֭מִּי
אָ֣כְלוּ לֶ֑חֶם
יהוה
לֹ֣א קָרָֽאוּ׃

ה שָׁ֤ם ׀
פָּ֣חֲדוּ פָ֑חַד
כִּֽי־אֱ֝לֹהִ֗ים
בְּד֣וֹר צַדִּֽיק׃
ו עֲצַת־עָנִ֥י תָבִ֑ישׁוּ
כִּ֖י יהוה מַחְסֵֽהוּ׃

ז מִ֥י־יִתֵּ֣ן מִצִּיּוֹן֮
יְשׁ֫וּעַ֥ת יִשְׂרָ֫אֵ֥ל
בְּשׁ֣וּב יהוה
שְׁב֣וּת עַמּ֑וֹ
יָגֵ֥ל יַ֝עֲקֹ֗ב
יִשְׂמַ֥ח יִשְׂרָאֵֽל׃

1 For the conductor, on Maḥalat,
A didactic song of David.
2 The despicable says in his heart:
"There is no God!"
They are corrupt,
Intending evil,
Nobody does good.

3 God from Heaven
Observes mankind,
To see
Whether someone intelligent
Seeks
God.

4 All are dross,
Together they went sour,
Nobody does good,
Not
A single one.

5 Don't they know
The evildoers,
Those consuming my people
Eating as food,
Who on God
Will not call,

6 Those
Trembling they will tremble
Where there was no fear,
For God
Dispersed
The bones of those camping against you.
You made them rot
For God despised them!

7 Who will present from Zion
The rescue of Israel,
When God turns around
The fortunes of His people;
Jacob will be jubilant,
Israel happy!

1 For the conductor, by David.

The despicable says in his heart
"There is no God!"
They are corrupt
Their principles are abominable,
Nobody does good.

2 The Eternal from Heaven
Observes mankind,
To see
If someone intelligent
Seeks
God.

3 All are deviates.
Together they went sour.
Nobody does good,
Not
A single one.

4 Don't they know,
All evildoers,
Those consuming my people,
Eating as food;
On the Eternal
They will not call.

5 Those
Trembling they will tremble,
For God is
In the dwelling of the just.

6 The counsel of the poor you insult,
But the Eternal is his refuge.

7 Who will present from Zion
The rescue of Israel,
When the Eternal turns around
The fortunes of His people
Jacob will be jubilant,
Israel happy!

14.1 עלילה cf. *Ps*. 9:12; it means *modus operandi.*

14.2 The ease by which "God" substitutes for the Tetragrammaton shows that the latter was pronounced with one short and two long syllables, even though the modern "adōnāy" seems to be excluded by 16:2.
דור is the same as Mishnaic Hebrew מדור "dwelling".

14:6 The original meaning of עני is not "poor" but "deprived".
53.6 The root is חנה "to encamp".

14,53: 7."When the Eternal turns around the fortunes of His people" does not mean "when He leads back the prisoners {exiles) of His people". This is *not* a song of return from exile, nor is Ps. 126. For other instances of שוב as "return to former status" cf. *Job* 42:10, *Jer.* 30:18, 33:7,10.

Psalm 15

1 A Psalm of David.
Eternal,
Who will abide in Your tent?
Who will dwell
On Your holy mountain?

א מִזְמוֹר לְדָוִד
יהוה
מִי־יָגוּר בְּאָהֳלֶךָ
מִי־יִשְׁכֹּן
בְּהַר קָדְשֶׁךָ׃

2 He who walks straight.
And acts honestly,
And talks truth
In his heart.

ב הוֹלֵךְ תָּמִים
וּפֹעֵל צֶדֶק
וְדֹבֵר אֱמֶת
בִּלְבָבוֹ׃

3 He did not spy out
For his tongue's sake,
He did not wrong his neighbor,
And shame
He did not put on his kin.

ג לֹא־רָגַל ׀
עַל־לְשֹׁנוֹ
לֹא־עָשָׂה לְרֵעֵהוּ רָעָה
וְחֶרְפָּה
לֹא־נָשָׂא עַל־קְרֹבוֹ׃

4 The despicable
Is contemptible in his eyes,
But those that fear the Eternal he honors,
He swears to his loss
And will not change.

ד נִבְזֶה ׀
בְּעֵינָיו נִמְאָס
וְאֶת־יִרְאֵי יהוה יְכַבֵּד
נִשְׁבַּע לְהָרַע
וְלֹא יָמִר׃

5 His money
He did not give on interest,
And bribes on behalf of the innocent
He did not take,
One, who does these things,
Never will he stumble!

ה כַּסְפּוֹ ׀
לֹא־נָתַן בְּנֶשֶׁךְ
וְשֹׁחַד עַל־נָקִי
לֹא־לָקָח
עֹשֵׂה אֵלֶּה
לֹא יִמּוֹט לְעוֹלָם׃

1. God's tent and His holy mountain refer to the heavenly Temple, the place where the souls of the just will dwell after death. It is therefore quite appropriate that most of the virtues of the just are enumerated in the past since these practices made him worthy to forever dwell in the Heavenly Halls.

3. רגל can mean either "to spy out", the translation chosen here; or "to exercise", i.e., "he did not exercise his tongue, did not do evil to his neighbor" as two parallel clauses. It is difficult to decide between the two meanings. For the first meaning, the use of the *qal* conjugation means that not even occasionally did he go hunting for information about other people.

5. The bribe-taker cannot be a judge, since for a judge to take bribes is a criminal offense It must be as a witness; he does not even accept payment for true testimony in behalf of an innocent person accused of a crime. עֹשֵׂה is a noun in construct state, "the doer of these".

Psalm 16

1 A Miktam by David
Preserve me, Almighty,
Truly in You I am taking refuge.

א מִכְתָּ֥ם לְדָוִ֑ד
שָֽׁמְרֵ֥נִי אֵ֝֗ל
כִּֽי־חָסִ֥יתִי בָֽךְ׃

2 Say to the Eternal:
You are my Master,
My good
Is only from You.

ב אָמַ֣רְתְּ לַֽ֭יהוה
אֲדֹנָ֣י אָ֑תָּה
ט֝וֹבָתִ֗י
בַּל־עָלֶֽיךָ׃

3 For the saints,
Those that are in the Land,
And the magnificent,
All my desire is to be with them.

ג לִ֭קְדוֹשִׁים
אֲשֶׁר־בָּאָ֣רֶץ הֵ֑מָּה
וְ֝אַדִּירֵ֗י
כָּל־חֶפְצִי־בָֽם׃

4 More pain to those
Who buy into strange cults;
Never could I pour their libations without blood,
I never could carry their names
On my lips.

ד יִרְבּ֣וּ עַצְּבוֹתָם֮
אַחֵ֪ר מָ֫הָ֥רוּ
בַּל־אַסִּ֣יךְ נִסְכֵּיהֶ֣ם מִדָּ֑ם
וּבַל־אֶשָּׂ֥א אֶת־שְׁ֝מוֹתָ֗ם
עַל־שְׂפָתָֽי׃

5 The Eternal
Is my portion and my cup;
You
Will lay out my lot.

ה יהוה
מְנָת־חֶלְקִ֥י וְכוֹסִ֑י
אַ֝תָּ֗ה
תּוֹמִ֥יךְ גּוֹרָלִֽי׃

6 The ropes fell for me
In pleasant places,
Also the inheritance
Pleases me.

ו חֲבָלִ֣ים נָֽפְלוּ־לִ֭י
בַּנְּעִמִ֑ים
אַף־נַ֝חֲלָ֗ת
שָֽׁפְרָ֥ה עָלָֽי׃

7 I shall praise the Eternal
Who has counseled me,
Also during night
My loins are instructing me.

ז אֲבָרֵ֗ךְ אֶת־יְ֭הוה
אֲשֶׁ֣ר יְעָצָ֑נִי
אַף־לֵ֝יל֗וֹת
יִסְּר֥וּנִי כִלְיוֹתָֽי׃

8 I always shall put the Eternal before me.
Certainly, on my right hand side
I shall not stagger.

ח שִׁוִּ֬יתִי יהוה֣ לְנֶגְדִּ֣י תָמִ֑יד
כִּ֥י מִֽ֝ימִינִ֗י
בַּל־אֶמּֽוֹט׃

9 Therefore
My heart is joyous,
My liver is jubilant,
Also my flesh
Shall rest in safety.

ט לָכֵ֤ן ׀
שָׂמַ֣ח לִ֭בִּי
וַיָּ֣גֶל כְּבוֹדִ֑י
אַף־בְּ֝שָׂרִ֗י
יִשְׁכֹּ֥ן לָבֶֽטַח׃

10 Certainly
You will not abandon my soul to the pit,
You will not let Your devout
See destruction.

י כִּ֤י ׀
לֹא־תַעֲזֹ֣ב נַפְשִׁ֣י לִשְׁא֑וֹל
לֹא־תִתֵּ֥ן חֲ֝סִידְךָ֗
לִרְא֥וֹת שָֽׁחַת׃

11 You will inform me	יא תּוֹדִיעֵנִי֮
Of the way of Life;	אֹרַח חַ֫יִּ֥ים
Filled with joys	שֹׂבַע שְׂ֭מָחוֹת
Before You,	אֶת־פָּנֶ֑יךָ
Pleasure forever is in Your right hand!.	נְעִמ֖וֹת בִּימִינְךָ֣ נֶֽצַח׃

A song about the future life; the Western Ashkenazic Psalm for mourners.

1. מכתם is a word of unknown etymology, maybe a parallel to מכתב "letter, document".

2. המה is an emphatic *those*. אדירים is Hebrew "mighty" or "glorious"; a construct state depending on a relative sentence is rare but not impossible.

4. מהר in the first conjugation means "to buy a bride", so it means "to buy into another family". The Septuagint translates "to be quick", but this acception is only found in the *pi`el* conjugation. The libations are certainly made to pagan deities, so "their names" are the names of these deities, which may not be pronounced (*Ex.* 23:13). Libations are made with wine, not blood; to sprinkle blood onto the altar is זרק, not נסך! Therefore, the blood is not the object of the libation, but the guilt incurred by pagan worship.

5. The lot is both the inheritance of and the random happenings to a person.

6. The ropes are those of the geometers who fix the boundaries of one's inheritance, following ancient Egyptian practice.

7. For כבד - כבוד, cf. *Ps*. 30:13. Also in the Talmud, *Bava meṣia`* 114a, כבוד is used for “liver”.

8. In the second line, the Hebrew also is elliptic. The meaning is: Certainly, [with Him] on my right side.

10. שחת is the destruction of the soul in the Pit, in contrast to the eternal Life of the pious celebrated in v. 11.

Psalm 17

1 A prayer by David.
Listen, Eternal, to sincerity,
Take note of my supplication,
Listen to my prayer
Disregard
Swindling lips.

א תְּפִלָּה לְדָוִד
שִׁמְעָה יהוה | צֶדֶק
הַקְשִׁיבָה רִנָּתִי
הַאֲזִינָה תְפִלָּתִי
בְּלֹא
שִׂפְתֵי מִרְמָה׃

2 From before You
May my judgment come,
Your eyes
May see probity.

ב מִלְּפָנֶיךָ
מִשְׁפָּטִי יֵצֵא
עֵינֶיךָ
תֶּחֱזֶינָה מֵישָׁרִים׃

3 You examined my heart
You visited me by night,
You melted me down, nothing to find.
Lewdness
Will not cross my mouth.

ג בָּחַנְתָּ לִבִּי |
פָּקַדְתָּ לַּיְלָה
צְרַפְתַּנִי בַל־תִּמְצָא
זַמֹּתִי
בַּל־יַעֲבָר־פִּי׃

4 Man’s actions
Against Your lips’ word?
I guarded
Against dissolute ways.

ד לִפְעֻלּוֹת אָדָם
בִּדְבַר שְׂפָתֶיךָ
אֲנִי שָׁמַרְתִּי
אָרְחוֹת פָּרִיץ׃

5 Support my shinbones
In Your courses,
Lest my steps would falter.

ה תָּמֹךְ אֲשֻׁרַי
בְּמַעְגְּלוֹתֶיךָ
בַּל־נָמוֹטּוּ פְעָמָי׃

6 I called on You,
Please hear me, Powerful,
Bend You ear to me,
Listen to my saying.

ו אֲנִי קְרָאתִיךָ
כִי־תַעֲנֵנִי אֵל
הַט־אָזְנְךָ לִי
שְׁמַע אִמְרָתִי׃

7 Distinguish Your pious,
Savior of shelter-seekers
From would-be tyrants,
By Your right hand.

ז הַפְלֵה חֲסָדֶיךָ
מוֹשִׁיעַ חוֹסִים
מִמִּתְקוֹמְמִים
בִּימִינֶךָ׃

8 Preserve me
Like a pupil of the eye,
Hide me
In Your wing’s shadow.

ח שָׁמְרֵנִי
כְּאִישׁוֹן בַּת־עָיִן
בְּצֵל כְּנָפֶיךָ
תַּסְתִּירֵנִי׃

9 Because of wickedness
So they hurled me;
My mortal enemies
Would encircle me.

ט מִפְּנֵי רְשָׁעִים
זוּ שַׁדּוּנִי
אֹיְבַי בְּנֶפֶשׁ
יַקִּיפוּ עָלָי׃

10 They closed their fat;
Their mouth
Talked in haughtiness.

י חֶלְבָּמוֹ סָּגְרוּ
פִּימוֹ
דִּבְּרוּ בְגֵאוּת׃

11 Our shinbones.
Now they surround me [us];
Their eyes they put
To bend to the ground.

יא אַשֻּׁרֵינוּ
עַתָּה סְבָבוּנִי [סְבָבוּנוּ]
עֵינֵיהֶם יָשִׁיתוּ
לִנְטוֹת בָּאָרֶץ׃

12 A simile: like a lion
Aching to tear,
Or a lion cub
Sitting in ambush.

יב דִּמְיֹנוֹ כְּאַרְיֵה
יִכְסוֹף לִטְרוֹף
וְכִכְפִיר
יֹשֵׁב בְּמִסְתָּרִים׃

13 Rise, o Eternal,
Forestall him,
Bring him to his knees,
Let my soul escape
From the wicked, by your sword.

יג קוּמָה יהוה
קַדְּמָה פָנָיו
הַכְרִיעֵהוּ
פַּלְּטָה נַפְשִׁי
מֵרָשָׁע חַרְבֶּךָ׃

14 From men, by Your hand, Eternal,
From men, permanently,
Separate them from life!
But those hidden with You
Fill their bellies.
May they be full with children,
And leave their leftovers
To their babies.

יד מִמְתִים יָדְךָ | יהוה
מִמְתִים מֵחֶלֶד
חֶלְקָם בַּחַיִּים
וּצְפִינְךָ [וּצְפוּנְךָ]
תְּמַלֵּא בִטְנָם
יִשְׂבְּעוּ בָנִים
וְהִנִּיחוּ יִתְרָם
לְעוֹלְלֵיהֶם׃

15 I, in sincerity,
May I see Your face,
May I be satiated in awakening
By Your image!

טו אֲנִי בְּצֶדֶק
אֶחֱזֶה פָנֶיךָ
אֶשְׂבְּעָה בְהָקִיץ
תְּמוּנָתֶךָ׃

A private Psalm, ending with an affirmation of eternal Life.

1. The acception "sincerity" for the root צדק is the main Arabic meaning; it is the opposite of "swindling lips". For רנה as prayer, song of prayer, cf. *1K.* 8:28, *Jer.* 7:16.

3.-4. זמתי is derived from זמה "lewd behavior". The word has to be read both as complement of the preceding and the start of the following clause.
The prefix ל in לִפְעֻלּוֹת אָדָם is for emphasis, corresponding to Arabic فَ.

5. מעגלה is a carriage trail or spur, a road from which one cannot deviate easily.

7. מִתְקוֹמְמִים are those who raise themselves over others.

14. מתים are men of military age. חלד, Arabic خلد, means "permanent, everlasting". חֶלְקָם is taken as a verbal form, equivalent to prosaic חַלֵּק אוֹתָם "split them off"; a similar meaning is found in Ugaritic.

15. The poet will be found worthy in heavenly court to see God's face, he will se His picture when he awakes after death. The poem is bracketed by the two expressions צדק.

2 Samuel 22

א וַיְדַבֵּר דָּוִד
לַיהוָה
אֶת־דִּבְרֵי
הַשִּׁירָה הַזֹּאת
בְּיוֹם הִצִּיל יְהוָה אֹתוֹ
מִכַּף כָּל־אֹיְבָיו
וּמִכַּף שָׁאוּל׃

ב וַיֹּאמַר
יְהוָה סַלְעִי וּמְצֻדָתִי
וּמְפַלְטִי־לִי׃
ג אֱלֹהֵי צוּרִי
אֶחֱסֶה־בּוֹ
מָגִנִּי
וְקֶרֶן יִשְׁעִי
מִשְׂגַּבִּי וּמְנוּסִי
מֹשִׁעִי
מֵחָמָס
תֹּשִׁעֵנִי׃

ד מְהֻלָּל
אֶקְרָא יְהוָה
וּמֵאֹיְבַי
אִוָּשֵׁעַ׃

ה כִּי אֲפָפֻנִי
מִשְׁבְּרֵי־מָוֶת
נַחֲלֵי בְלִיַּעַל
יְבַעֲתֻנִי׃

ו חֶבְלֵי שְׁאוֹל
סַבֻּנִי
קִדְּמֻנִי
מֹקְשֵׁי־מָוֶת׃

ז בַּצַּר־לִי
אֶקְרָא יְהוָה
וְאֶל־אֱלֹהַי
אֶקְרָא
וַיִּשְׁמַע מֵהֵיכָלוֹ קוֹלִי
וְשַׁוְעָתִי
בְּאָזְנָיו׃

ח וַתִּגְעַשׁ [וַיִּתְגָּעַשׁ] וַתִּרְעַשׁ
הָאָרֶץ
מוֹסְדוֹת הַשָּׁמַיִם
יִרְגָּזוּ
וַיִּתְגָּעֲשׁוּ
כִּי־חָרָה לוֹ׃

ט עָלָה עָשָׁן
בְּאַפּוֹ
וְאֵשׁ מִפִּיו
תֹּאכֵל

Psalm 18

א לַמְנַצֵּחַ ׀
לְעֶבֶד יְ׳ לְדָוִד
אֲשֶׁר דִּבֶּר ׀
לַיהוָה
אֶת־דִּבְרֵי
הַשִּׁירָה הַזֹּאת
בְּיוֹם ׀
הִצִּיל־יְהוָה אוֹתוֹ מִכַּף כָּל־אֹיְבָיו
וּמִיַּד שָׁאוּל׃

ב וַיֹּאמַר
אֶרְחָמְךָ יְהוָה חִזְקִי׃

ג יְהוָה ׀
סַלְעִי וּמְצוּדָתִי וּמְפַלְטִי
אֵלִי צוּרִי
אֶחֱסֶה־בּוֹ
מָגִנִּי וְקֶרֶן יִשְׁעִי
מִשְׂגַּבִּי׃

ד מְהֻלָּל
אֶקְרָא יְהוָה
וּמִן־אֹיְבַי
אִוָּשֵׁעַ׃

ה אֲפָפוּנִי חֶבְלֵי־מָוֶת
וְנַחֲלֵי בְלִיַּעַל יְבַעֲתוּנִי׃

ו חֶבְלֵי שְׁאוֹל סְבָבוּנִי
קִדְּמוּנִי
מוֹקְשֵׁי מָוֶת׃

ז בַּצַּר־לִי ׀
אֶקְרָא יְהוָה
וְאֶל־אֱלֹהַי אֲשַׁוֵּעַ
יִשְׁמַע מֵהֵיכָלוֹ קוֹלִי
וְשַׁוְעָתִי
לְפָנָיו ׀
תָּבוֹא בְאָזְנָיו׃

ח וַתִּגְעַשׁ וַתִּרְעַשׁ ׀
הָאָרֶץ
וּמוֹסְדֵי הָרִים יִרְגָּזוּ
וַיִּתְגָּעֲשׁוּ
כִּי־חָרָה לוֹ׃

ט עָלָה עָשָׁן ׀
בְּאַפּוֹ
וְאֵשׁ־מִפִּיו תֹּאכֵל
גֶּחָלִים.
בָּעֲרוּ מִמֶּנּוּ׃

י וַיֵּט שָׁמַיִם
וַיֵּרַד
וַעֲרָפֶל
תַּחַת רַגְלָיו׃

יא וַיִּרְכַּב עַל־כְּרוּב
וַיָּעֹף
וַיֵּדֶא
עַל־כַּנְפֵי־רוּחַ׃

יב יָשֶׁת חֹשֶׁךְ |
סִתְרוֹ
סְבִיבוֹתָיו סֻכָּתוֹ
חֶשְׁכַת־מַיִם
עָבֵי שְׁחָקִים׃

יג מִנֹּגַהּ נֶגְדּוֹ
עָבָיו עָבְרוּ
בָּרָד
וְגַחֲלֵי־אֵשׁ׃

יד וַיַּרְעֵם בַּשָּׁמַיִם |
יְהוָה
וְעֶלְיוֹן
יִתֵּן קֹלוֹ
בָּרָד
וְגַחֲלֵי־אֵשׁ׃

טו וַיִּשְׁלַח חִצָּיו
וַיְפִיצֵם
וּבְרָקִים רָב
וַיְהֻמֵּם׃

טז וַיֵּרָאוּ |
אֲפִיקֵי מַיִם
וַיִּגָּלוּ
מוֹסְדוֹת תֵּבֵל
מִגַּעֲרָתְךָ יְהוָה
מִנִּשְׁמַת
רוּחַ אַפֶּךָ׃

יז יִשְׁלַח מִמָּרוֹם
יִקָּחֵנִי
יַמְשֵׁנִי
מִמַּיִם רַבִּים׃

יח יַצִּילֵנִי
מֵאֹיְבִי עָז
וּמִשֹּׂנְאַי
כִּי־אָמְצוּ מִמֶּנִּי׃

גֶּחָלִים
בָּעֲרוּ מִמֶּנּוּ׃

י וַיֵּט שָׁמַיִם
וַיֵּרַד
וַעֲרָפֶל
תַּחַת רַגְלָיו׃

יא וַיִּרְכַּב עַל־כְּרוּב
וַיָּעֹף
וַיֵּרָא
עַל־כַּנְפֵי־רוּחַ׃

יב וַיָּשֶׁת חֹשֶׁךְ
סְבִיבֹתָיו
סֻכּוֹת
חַשְׁרַת־מַיִם
עָבֵי שְׁחָקִים׃

יג מִנֹּגַהּ
נֶגְדּוֹ
בָּעֲרוּ
גַּחֲלֵי־אֵשׁ׃

יד יַרְעֵם מִן־שָׁמַיִם
יְהוָה
וְעֶלְיוֹן
יִתֵּן קוֹלוֹ׃

טו וַיִּשְׁלַח חִצִּים
וַיְפִיצֵם
בָּרָק
וַיָּהְמם [וַיָּהֹם]׃

טז וַיֵּרָאוּ
אֲפִקֵי יָם
יִגָּלוּ
מֹסְדוֹת תֵּבֵל
בְּגַעֲרַת יְהוָה
מִנִּשְׁמַת
רוּחַ אַפּוֹ׃

יז יִשְׁלַח מִמָּרוֹם
יִקָּחֵנִי
יַמְשֵׁנִי
מִמַּיִם רַבִּים

יח יַצִּילֵנִי
מֵאֹיְבִי
עָז
מִשֹּׂנְאַי
כִּי אָמְצוּ
מִמֶּנִּי׃

יט יְקַדְּמ֥וּנִי בְיֽוֹם אֵידִ֑י
וַֽיְהִי יהוָ֖ה לְמִשְׁעָ֣ן לִֽי׃

יט יְקַדְּמֻ֖נִי
בְּי֣וֹם אֵידִ֑י
וַיְהִ֧י יהוָ֛ה מִשְׁעָ֖ן
לִֽי׃

כ וַיּוֹצִיאֵ֥נִי לַמֶּרְחָ֑ב
יְ֝חַלְּצֵ֗נִי
כִּ֘י חָ֥פֵֽץ בִּֽי׃

כ וַיֹּצֵ֥א לַמֶּרְחָ֖ב
אֹתִ֑י
יְחַלְּצֵ֖נִי
כִּֽי־חָ֥פֵֽץ בִּֽי׃

כא יִגְמְלֵ֣נִי יהוָ֣ה כְּצִדְקִ֑י
כְּבֹ֥ר יָ֝דַ֗י
יָשִׁ֥יב לִֽי׃

כא יִגְמְלֵ֥נִי יהוָ֖ה
כְּצִדְקָתִ֑י
כְּבֹ֥ר יָדַ֖י
יָשִׁ֥יב לִֽי׃

כב כִּֽי־שָׁ֭מַרְתִּי
דַּרְכֵ֣י יהוָ֑ה
לֹֽא־רָ֝שַׁ֗עְתִּי
מֵאֱלֹהָֽי׃

כב כִּ֥י שָׁמַ֖רְתִּי
דַּרְכֵ֣י יהוָ֑ה
וְלֹ֥א רָשַׁ֖עְתִּי
מֵאֱלֹהָֽי׃

כג כִּ֣י כָל־מִשְׁפָּטָ֣יו לְנֶגְדִּ֑י
וְ֝חֻקֹּתָ֗יו
לֹא־אָסִ֥יר מֶֽנִּי׃

כג כִּ֥י כָל־מִשְׁפָּטָ֖ו [מִשְׁפָּטָ֖יו]
לְנֶגְדִּ֑י
וְחֻקֹּתָ֖יו
לֹא־אָס֥וּר מִמֶּֽנָּה׃

כד וָאֱהִ֣י תָמִ֣ים עִמּ֑וֹ
וָ֝אֶשְׁתַּמֵּ֗ר
מֵעֲוֺנִֽי׃

כד וָאֶהְיֶ֥ה תָמִ֖ים
ל֑וֹ
וָאֶֽשְׁתַּמְּרָ֖ה
מֵעֲוֺנִֽי׃

כה וַיָּֽשֶׁב־יהוָ֣ה לִ֣י כְצִדְקִ֑י
כְּבֹ֥ר יָ֝דַ֗י
לְנֶ֣גֶד עֵינָֽיו׃

כה וַיָּ֧שֶׁב יהוָ֛ה לִ֖י
כְּצִדְקָתִ֑י
כְּבֹרִ֖י
לְנֶ֥גֶד עֵינָֽיו׃

כו עִם־חָסִ֥יד תִּתְחַסָּ֑ד
עִם־גְּבַ֥ר תָּ֝מִ֗ים
תִּתַּמָּֽם׃

כו עִם־חָסִ֖יד
תִּתְחַסָּ֑ד
עִם־גִּבּ֥וֹר תָּמִ֖ים
תִּתַּמָּֽם׃

כז עִם־נָבָ֥ר תִּתְבָּרָ֑ר
וְעִם־עִ֝קֵּ֗שׁ
תִּתְפַּתָּֽל

כז עִם־נָבָ֖ר
תִּתָּבָ֑ר
וְעִם־עִקֵּ֖שׁ
תִּתַּפָּֽל

כח כִּֽי־אַ֭תָּה
עַם־עָנִ֣י תוֹשִׁ֑יעַ
וְעֵינַ֖יִם רָמ֣וֹת תַּשְׁפִּֽיל׃

כח וְאֶת־עַ֥ם עָנִ֖י
תּוֹשִׁ֑יעַ
וְעֵינֶ֖יךָ
עַל־רָמִ֥ים תַּשְׁפִּֽיל׃

כט כִּֽי־אַ֭תָּה
תָּאִ֣יר נֵרִ֑י
יהוָ֥ה אֱ֝לֹהַ֗י
יַגִּ֥יהַּ חָשְׁכִּֽי׃

כט כִּֽי־אַתָּ֥ה נֵירִ֖י
יהוָ֑ה
וַיהוָ֖ה
יַגִּ֥יהַּ חָשְׁכִּֽי׃

ל כִּי בְכָה
אָרוּץ גְּדוּד
בֵּאלֹהַי
אֲדַלֶּג־שׁוּר׃

לא הָאֵל
תָּמִים דַּרְכּוֹ
אִמְרַת יהוה צְרוּפָה
מָגֵן הוּא
לְכֹל |
הַחוֹסִים בּוֹ׃

לב כִּי מִי אֱלוֹהַּ
מִבַּלְעֲדֵי יהוה
וּמִי־צוּר
זוּלָתִי אֱלֹהֵינוּ׃

לג הָאֵל
הַמְאַזְּרֵנִי חָיִל
וַיִּתֵּן תָּמִים דַּרְכִּי׃

לד מְשַׁוֶּה רַגְלַי
כָּאַיָּלוֹת
וְעַל בָּמֹתַי
יַעֲמִידֵנִי׃

לה מְלַמֵּד יָדַי
לַמִּלְחָמָה
וְנִחֲתָה קֶשֶׁת־נְחוּשָׁה
זְרוֹעֹתָי׃

לו וַתִּתֶּן־לִי
מָגֵן יִשְׁעֶךָ
וִימִינְךָ תִסְעָדֵנִי
וְעַנְוַתְךָ תַרְבֵּנִי׃

לז תַּרְחִיב צַעֲדִי תַחְתָּי
וְלֹא מָעֲדוּ
קַרְסֻלָּי

לח אֶרְדּוֹף אוֹיְבַי
וְאַשִּׂיגֵם
וְלֹא־אָשׁוּב
עַד־כַּלּוֹתָם׃

לט אֶמְחָצֵם
וְלֹא־יֻכְלוּ קוּם
יִפְּלוּ
תַּחַת רַגְלָי׃

ל כִּי בְכָה
אָרוּץ גְּדוּד
בֵּאלֹהַי
אֲדַלֶּג־שׁוּר׃

לא הָאֵל
תָּמִים דַּרְכּוֹ
אִמְרַת יהוה
צְרוּפָה
מָגֵן הוּא
לְכֹל
הַחֹסִים בּוֹ׃

לב כִּי מִי־אֵל
מִבַּלְעֲדֵי יהוה
וּמִי צוּר
מִבַּלְעֲדֵי אֱלֹהֵינוּ׃

לג הָאֵל מָעוּזִּי
חָיִל
וַיַּתֵּר תָּמִים
דַּרְכּוֹ [דַּרְכִּי]׃

לד מְשַׁוֶּה רַגְלָיו [רַגְלַי]
כָּאַיָּלוֹת
וְעַל בָּמוֹתַי
יַעֲמִדֵנִי׃

לה מְלַמֵּד יָדַי
לַמִּלְחָמָה
וְנִחַת קֶשֶׁת־נְחוּשָׁה
זְרֹעֹתָי׃

לו וַתִּתֶּן־לִי
מָגֵן יִשְׁעֶךָ
וַעֲנֹתְךָ
תַּרְבֵּנִי׃

לז תַּרְחִיב צַעֲדִי
תַּחְתֵּנִי
וְלֹא מָעֲדוּ
קַרְסֻלָּי׃

לח אֶרְדְּפָה אֹיְבַי
וָאַשְׁמִידֵם
וְלֹא אָשׁוּב
עַד־כַּלּוֹתָם׃

לט וָאֲכַלֵּם וָאֶמְחָצֵם
וְלֹא יְקוּמוּן
וַיִּפְּלוּ
תַּחַת רַגְלָי׃

מ וַתְּאַזְּרֵנִי חַיִל
לַמִּלְחָמָה
תַּכְרִיעַ קָמַי תַּחְתָּי׃

מא וְאֹיְבַי
תַּתָּה לִּי עֹרֶף
מְשַׂנְאַי
וָאַצְמִיתֵם׃

מב יְשַׁוְּעוּ וְאֵין מוֹשִׁיעַ
עַל־יְהוָה
וְלֹא עָנָם׃

מג וְאֶשְׁחָקֵם
כְּעָפָר עַל־פְּנֵי־רוּחַ
כְּטִיט חוּצוֹת אֲרִיקֵם׃

מד תְּפַלְּטֵנִי
מֵרִיבֵי עָם
תְּשִׂימֵנִי
לְרֹאשׁ גּוֹיִם
עַם לֹא־יָדַעְתִּי יַעַבְדוּנִי׃

מה לְשֵׁמַע אֹזֶן
יִשָּׁמְעוּ לִי
בְּנֵי־נֵכָר
יְכַחֲשׁוּ־לִי׃

מו בְּנֵי־נֵכָר יִבֹּלוּ
וְיַחְרְגוּ
מִמִּסְגְּרוֹתֵיהֶם׃

מז חַי־יְהוָה
וּבָרוּךְ צוּרִי
וְיָרוּם
אֱלוֹהֵי יִשְׁעִי׃

מה לְשֵׁמַע אֹזֶן
יִשָּׁמְעוּ לִי
בְּנֵי־נֵכָר
יְכַחֲשׁוּ־לִי׃

מ וַתַּאַזְרֵנִי חַיִל
לַמִּלְחָמָה
תַּכְרִיעַ קָמַי
תַּחְתֵּנִי׃

מא וְאֹיְבַי
תַּתָּה לִּי עֹרֶף
מְשַׂנְאַי
וָאַצְמִיתֵם׃

מב יִשְׁעוּ
וְאֵין מֹשִׁיעַ
אֶל־יְהוָה
וְלֹא־עָנָם׃

מג וְאֶשְׁחָקֵם
כַּעֲפַר־אָרֶץ
כְּטִיט־חוּצוֹת אֲדִקֵּם
אֶרְקָעֵם׃

מד וַתְּפַלְּטֵנִי
מֵרִיבֵי
עַמִּי
תִּשְׁמְרֵנִי
לְרֹאשׁ גּוֹיִם
עַם לֹא־יָדַעְתִּי
יַעַבְדֻנִי׃

מה בְּנֵי נֵכָר
יִתְכַּחֲשׁוּ־לִי
לִשְׁמוֹעַ אֹזֶן
יִשָּׁמְעוּ לִי׃

מו בְּנֵי נֵכָר
יִבֹּלוּ
וְיַחְגְּרוּ
מִמִּסְגְּרוֹתָם׃

מז חַי־יְהוָה
וּבָרוּךְ צוּרִי
וְיָרֻם
אֱלֹהֵי
צוּר יִשְׁעִי׃

מח הָאֵל
הַנֹּתֵן נְקָמֹת
לִי
וּמֹרִיד עַמִּים
תַּחְתֵּנִי׃

מט מְפַלְּטִי מֵאֹ֫יְבָ֥י
אַ֣ף מִן־֭קָמַי
תְּרוֹמְמֵ֑נִי
מֵאִ֥ישׁ ֝חָמָ֗ס
תַּצִּילֵֽנִי׃

נ עַל־כֵּ֤ן ׀
אוֹדְךָ֖ בַגּוֹיִ֥ם ׀ יְהוָ֑ה
וּלְשִׁמְךָ֥ אֲזַמֵּֽרָה׃

נא מַגְדִּל֮
יְשׁוּע֪וֹת מַ֫לְכּ֥וֹ
וְעֹ֣שֶׂה חֶ֤סֶד ׀
לִמְשִׁיח֗וֹ
לְדָוִ֥ד ֝וּלְזַרְע֗וֹ
עַד־עוֹלָֽם׃

מט וּמוֹצִיאִ֖י
מֵאֹיְבָ֑י
וּמִקָּמַי֙
תְּר֣וֹמְמֵ֔נִי
מֵאִ֥ישׁ חֲמָסִ֖ים
תַּצִּילֵֽנִי׃

נ עַל־כֵּ֛ן
אוֹדְךָ֥ יְהוָ֖ה
בַּגּוֹיִ֑ם
וּלְשִׁמְךָ֖ אֲזַמֵּֽרָה

נא מִגְדּ֖יל [מִגְד֖וֹל]
יְשׁוּע֣וֹת מַלְכּ֑וֹ
וְעֹֽשֶׂה־חֶ֧סֶד לִמְשִׁיח֛וֹ
לְדָוִ֥ד וּלְזַרְע֖וֹ
עַד־עוֹלָֽם׃

Psalm 18

1 For the Director,
By David,
The Eternal's servant,
Who spoke to the Eternal
The words
Of this song,
On the day the Eternal saved him from the palm of all his enemies
And from the hand of Saul.

2 And he said:
I love You, Eternal, my strength!

3 Eternal, my rock and my fortress and my refuge.
My God, my flint rock,
In Whom I shelter,
My shield and and horn of my help,
My stronghold.

4 I shall call to the Eternal,
To the Praiseworthy,
And I shall be helped
From my enemies.

5 Deadly groups envelope me
And evil torrents frighten me.

6 Hell's ropes surround me
Deadly traps
Are before me.

7 When I am in straits
I shall call to the Eternal,
And my God I beseech,
May He hear my voice in His palace
My supplication
Before Him shall reach His ears.

8 The earth
Then shook and trembled,
The roots of the mountains moved,
They shook
Because of His rage.

9 Smoke rose
In His nostrils,
Fire devours from His mouth
Embers
Scorch from Him.

2Samuel 22

David spoke to the Eternal the words of this song, on the day the Eternal saved him from the palm of all his enemies and from the palm of Saul.

2 He said:
Eternal,
My rock, and my fortress,
And my refuge!
3 My God, my flint rock,
In Whom I shelter,
My shield
And and horn of my help,
My stronghold
And my recourse,
My savior,
From oppression
He rescues me.

4 I shall call to the Eternal,
To the Praiseworthy,
And I shall be helped
From my enemies.

5 Deadly breakers
Envelope me
And evil torrents
Frighten me.

6 Hell's ropes
Surround me
Deadly traps
Are before me.

7 When I am in straits
I shall call to the Eternal,
And my God
I beseech,
May He hear my voice
In His palace
My supplication
In His ears.

8 The earth
Shook and quaked,
Heaven's foundations
Trembled.

9 Smoke rose
In His nostrils,
Fire devours
From His mouth
Embers
Scorch from Him.

10 He bent the heavens
    And descended
A dark cloud
    Under His feet.

11 He rode on a Cherub
    And flew
He soared
    On wings of wind.

12 He puts darkness
    His secret,
Around Himself as His tent,
The darkness of water
    Thick clouds of the sky.

13 From the radiance
    Which surround Him,
His clouds passed,
Hailstorm
    And fiery embers.

14 He thundered in heaven;
    The Eternal,
The Most High,
    Made heard His voice,
Hailstorm
    And fiery embers.

15 He sent His arrows
    And disperses them,
Powerful thunderbolts
    And confounded them.

16 There appeared
    Water streams,
Uncovered were bases of *terra firma*,
By Your angry shout, Eternal,
By the blowing
    Of Your anger's wind.

17 He sends up from high,
    He takes me,
He draws me up
    From mighty waters.

18 He saves me
From my enemy,
    The strong one,
And from my haters,
Those, much stronger
    Than myself.

10 He bent the heavens
    And descended
A dark cloud
    Under His feet.

11 He rode on a Cherub
    And flew
He appeared
    On wings of wind.

12 He puts darkness
    His surroundings,
    His tent,
The darkness of water
    Thick clouds of the sky.

13 From the radiance
    Which surround Him,
Fiery embers
    Burned.

14 He thundered in heaven,
    The Eternal.
The Most High,
    Made heard His voice.

15 He sent His arrows
    And disperses them,
Thunderbolt
    And confounded them.

16 There appeared
    Ocean streams,
Uncovered were
    Bases of *terra firma*,
By Your angry shout, Eternal,
By the blowing
    Of Your anger's wind.

17 He sends up from high,
    He takes me,
He draws me up
    From mighty waters.

18 He saves me
    From my enemy,
    The strong one,
From my haters,
Those, much stronger
    Than myself.

19 They preceded me on the day of my calamity,
But the Eternal was my support.

20 To vastness He leads me out,
He extricates me,
For He likes me.

21 The Eternal will reward me for my deserts,
For the purity of my hands
He will restore me.

22 Truly, I kept
The ways of the Eternal,
Never was I wicked
Against my God.

23 All His laws are always before me;
And His edicts
I shall not remove from me.

24 I shall be whole with Him,
And guard myself
From my criminality.

25 Then the Eternal will pay me back for my deserts,
For my hands' purity
Before His eyes.

26 With the pious You are graceful,
With a wholesome man
You act straightly.

27 With the pure You are pure,
With the devious
You are tricky.

28. Certainly, You
Will save a downtrodden people
But haughty eyes You will push low.

29 Certainly, You
Will light my candle,
The Eternal, my God
Will illuminate my darkness.

19 They preceded me
On the day of my calamity,
But the Eternal
Was support
For me.

20 To vastness
He leads me out,
He extricates me,
For He likes me.

21 The Eternal will reward me
For my deserts,
For the purity of my hands
He will restore me.

22 Truly I kept
The ways of the Eternal
Never was I wicked
Against my God.

23 All His laws
Are before me;
And His edicts
I shall not remove from me.

24 I shall be whole
With Him,
And guard myself
From my criminality.

25 Then the Eternal will pay back
To me
For my deserts,
For my purity
Before His eyes.

26 With the pious
You are graceful,
With a wholesome man
You act straightly.

27 With the pure
You are pure,
With the devious
You are tricky.

28 You will save,
Downtrodden people,
But Your eyes
You are lowering on the haughty.

29 Certainly, You are my Light,
Eternal.
And the Eternal
Will illuminate my darkness.

30 Certainly, with You
I shall overrun a trench,
And with my God
I shall jump over a wall.

31 The Power,
Perfect is His way,
The command of the Eternal is purified.
He is a shield
For all
Who trust in Him.

32 For Who is Almighty
Except the Eternal,
And Who is a rock
But our God?

33 The Power
Who girds me with strength,
And made my way upright.

34 He makes my feet like
Gazelles,
And on His Hills
He makes me stand.

35 He trains my hands
For war
And directed a snake-like bow
Into my.

36 You gave me
The shield of Your help,
Your right hand supported me,
Your force made me great.

37 You made my strides broad under me,
Never my ankles
Did stumble.
.

38 I shall pursue my enemics
And overtake them
And not return
Before finishing them.

39 I shall smash them
They never will be able to rise;
They shall fall
Under my feet.
.

40 You girded me with strength
For war.
Those who rise against me
You. will make prostrate under me

30 Certainly, with You
I shall overrun a trench,
And with my God
I shall jump over a wall.

31 The Power,
Perfect is His way,
The command of the Eternal
Is purified.
He is a shield
For all
Who trust in Him

32 For Who is a Power
Except the Eternal,
And Who is a rock
But our God?

33 The Power, my bulwark
Of strength,
And straightly opens
My [His] way.

34 He makes my [His] feet
Like gazelles,
And on His Hills
He makes me stand.

35 He trains my hand
For war,
And directed a snake-like bow
Into my hands.

36 You gave me
The shield of Your help,
Your force
Made me great.

37 You made my strides broad
Under me,
Never my ankles
Did stumble.

38 I shall pursue my enemies
And destroy them
And not return
Before finishing them.

39 I shall finish and smash them
They never will be able to rise;
They shall fall
Under my feet.

40 You girded me with strength
For war.
Those who rise against me
You will make prostrate under me.

41 And my enemies
You gave to me by the neck,
And my haters
I will force into silence.

42 They might pray, but no one helps,
To the Eternal
Who answers them not.

43 I shall grind them
Like dust in the wind,
Like street garbage I shall empty them out.

44 You let me escape
From the quarrels of the nation,
You installed me
As head of peoples,
A nation unknown to me shall serve me.

45 If they just hear by ear
They will obey me;
The foreigners
Will enthrone me.

46 Foreigners
Shall wilt,
They shall be confined
In their frames.

47 Hail to the Eternal,
Blessed be my Rock
And exalted
The God, my help.

48 The Power
Who gives vengeance to me,
Who subjugated peoples
Under me.

49 Who makes me escape from my enemies;
You will lift me up
Also before those who rise against me,
You saved me
From a criminal.

50 For this
I shall thank You among the Gentiles,
Eternal,
And shall sing to Your Name.

41 And my enemies
You gave to me
By the neck,
My haters
I will force into silence.

42 They look around,
but no one helps
To the Eternal
Who answers them not.

43 And I shall grind them
Like dust of the ground,
Like street garbage I shall crush them,
Flatten them.

44 You let me escape
From the quarrels of my nation,
You installed me
As head of peoples,
A nation unknown to me
Shall serve me.

45 Foreigners
Shall enthrone me;
If they just hear by ear
They will obey me.

46 Foreigners
Shall wilt,
They shall be confined
In their frames.

47 Hail to the Eternal,
Blessed be my Rock
And exalted
My God,
Rock of my help.

48 The Power
Who gives vengeance
To me,
Who subjugated peoples
Under me.

49 Who removes me
From my enemies,
From those who rise against me
You will lift me up,
You saved me
From criminal bands

50 For this
I shall thank You, Eternal,
Among the Gentiles,
And shall sing
To Your Name.

51 He increases
The fortunes
Of His king,
He shows love to His anointed,
To David and his descendants
Forever!

51 He is a tower
Of the fortunes of His king,
He shows love to His anointed,
To David and his descendants
Forever!

1 It is difficult to determine which of the two version is the older one. Since a note at the end of Ps. 72 declares the collection of Psalms 1 - 72 to be the diwan edited by David himself, and the version in Psalms is richer in internal rhymes and assonances, it is more likely that the court chronicles of the book of Samuel took a (probably earlier) version of the poem from the royal archives.

2. The verse is missing in Samuel and the metric structure of v. 3 is changed. The use of the root רחם in the meaning "to love" is an Aramaism.

5. Here חבל means "group", as in the expression חבל נביאים (1Sam. 10:5) "a band of prophets". In the next verse, the word has the standard meaning "rope". (Gesenius notes that in German "band" is “a rope” but “bande” a group of criminals).
8. ויתגעשו is a t-passive, not a reflexive.

15. "They" in verse 15 are the enemies of v. 4 or hell's messengers from v. 6, after the poets rescue by a volcanic eruption accompanied by an earthquake.

16. אפך means either "Your anger" or “Your nose”. For אפיק see Ps.43:3

21. For the root גמל, see Ps. 13:3.

27. ברר is not easily defined. From the context, it cannot have the meaning "to select" (which also would require a vocalization תִּתְבָּרֵר). Ben Yehuda/Torczyner see here a separate root נבר, most authors follow Ibn Ezra in declaring both נבר and תתברר derived from בר "pure", see Ps. 2:12. Arabic נבר "crier" is inappropriate. The parallel in *2Samuel* is explained by Y. Blau as the t-reflexive of the *hif'il* conjugation of בר; this would declare the version of Psalms as edited later to be more consistent with the usual normative grammar. A similar form is תֵּתַצַּב *Ex*. 2:4.

30. Here גְּדוּד has the meaning of Arabic גד "trench, pit".

31. As in *Deut.* 26:17-18, אמר means to command (the military); the Emir (Amir) is the commander. In Aramaic, דבר "to lead" has a similar meaning.

34. במתַי are "His hills", not "my hills".

35. The root of נחושה “snake like” (i.e., convex-concave-convex) is נחש “snake”. נחת is derive from Arabic נחו “to direct”. (Aron Pinsker).

35. Arabic ענוה “force”.

41. The Arabic meaning of אצמת is "to silence somebody".

45. There is a pun between שמע "listen" and שמע "keep discipline". In Ugaritic, Hebrew שׁ usually corresponds to *ṯ*, and כחת means "throne".

46. Ben Yehuda explains חרג as "escape with anguish"; Gesenius takes it as an Aramaism "to fear", related to Arabic חרג "to feel constricted (heart)". The parallel in Samuel has the common word חגר "to put on a belt"; this also indicates that the version of Psalms is the corrected later edition.

49. איש חמס is a collective, best translated as "organized crime".

Psalm 19

1 For the director,
A Psalm of David.

א לַמְנַצֵּחַ
מִזְמוֹר לְדָוִד׃

2 The heavens
Tell of the Powerful's glory
And His handiwork
Is proclaimed by the sky.

ב הַשָּׁמַיִם
מְסַפְּרִים כְּבוֹד־אֵל
וּמַעֲשֵׂה יָדָיו
מַגִּיד הָרָקִיעַ׃

3 One day to the next
Spouts information
And one night to the next
Recounts knowledge.

ג יוֹם לְיוֹם
יַבִּיעַ אֹמֶר
וְלַיְלָה לְּלַיְלָה
יְחַוֶּה־דָּעַת׃

4 Without telling
Nor with word;
Without
Their voices being heard.

ד אֵין אֹמֶר
וְאֵין דְּבָרִים
בְּלִי
נִשְׁמָע קוֹלָם׃

5 Over all the land
Goes out their talk
And to the end of dry land
Their words.
For the sun
He made a tent among them.

ה בְּכָל־הָאָרֶץ ׀
יָצָא קַוָּם
וּבקְצֵה תֵבֵל
מִלֵּיהֶם
לַשֶּׁמֶשׁ
שָׂם אֹהֶל בָּהֶם

6 And it, like a newlywed groom
Leaves its bridal chamber,
It enjoys like an athlete
To run its course.

ו וְהוּא כְּחָתָן
יֹצֵא מֵחֻפָּתוֹ
יָשִׂישׂ כְּגִבּוֹר
לָרוּץ אֹרַח׃

7 From the end of the heavens
Is its start.
It turns in at the other end;
Nothing is hidden
From its heat.

ז מִקְצֵה הַשָּׁמַיִם ׀
מוֹצָאוֹ
וּתְקוּפָתוֹ עַל־קְצוֹתָם
וְאֵין נִסְתָּר
מֵחַמָּתוֹ׃

8 The Eternal's teaching is perfect,
Restores the soul;
The Eternal's testimony is trustworthy,
Makes wise the silly.

ח תּוֹרַת יהוָה תְּמִימָה
מְשִׁיבַת נָפֶשׁ
עֵדוּת יהוָה נֶאֱמָנָה
מַחְכִּימַת פֶּתִי׃

9 The Eternal's statutes are straight,
Gladden the heart,
The Eternal's commandment is clear,
Enlightens the eye.

ט פִּקּוּדֵי יהוָה יְשָׁרִים
מְשַׂמְּחֵי־לֵב
מִצְוַת יהוָה בָּרָה
מְאִירַת עֵינָיִם׃

10 The fear of the Eternal is pure,
Standing forever
The Eternal's judgments are true,
Just all together.

י יִרְאַת יהוָה ׀ טְהוֹרָה
עוֹמֶדֶת לָעַד
מִשְׁפְּטֵי־ יהוָה אֱמֶת
צָדְקוּ יַחְדָּו.

11 Desirable more than gold
And masses of refined gold
Sweeter than nectar
And flowing honey.

יא הַֽנֶּחֱמָדִ֗ים מִ֭זָּהָב
וּמִפַּ֣ז רָ֑ב
וּמְתוּקִ֥ים מִ֝דְּבַ֗שׁ
וְנֹ֣פֶת צוּפִֽים׃

12 Also Your servant
Was careful about them,
In their observance
Is great consequence.

יב גַּֽם־עַ֭בְדְּךָ
נִזְהָ֣ר בָּהֶ֑ם
בְּ֝שָׁמְרָ֗ם
עֵ֣קֶב רָֽב׃

13 Errors, who can understand them?
From hidden sins cleanse me.

יג שְׁגִיא֥וֹת מִֽי־יָבִ֑ין
מִֽנִּסְתָּר֥וֹת נַקֵּֽנִי׃

14 Also from criminals
Save Your servant,
Do not let them rule over me,
Then I shall be faultless
And be cleansed
From great iniquity.

יד גַּ֤ם מִזֵּדִ֨ים ׀
חֲשֹׂ֬ךְ עַבְדֶּ֗ךָ
אַֽל־יִמְשְׁלוּ־בִ֭י
אָ֣ז אֵיתָ֑ם
וְ֝נִקֵּ֗יתִי
מִפֶּ֥שַׁע רָֽב׃

15 May my mouth's sayings be
Your pleasure,
And the thoughts of my heart before You,
Eternal,
My rock and my redeemer.

טו יִהְי֤וּ לְרָצ֨וֹן ׀
אִמְרֵי־פִ֡י
וְהֶגְי֣וֹן לִבִּ֣י לְפָנֶ֑יךָ
יְ֝הוָ֗ה
צוּרִ֥י וְגֹאֲלִֽי׃

11. דבש is any colloidal sweetener, either bee's honey or concentrated date juice. But נפת is only used for bee's honey, and in particular נֹ֣פֶת צוּפִֽים "flowing, floating bee's honey" freshly out of the honeycomb, so דבש here must mean something other than bee's honey.

Psalm 20

1 For the director,
A Psalm of David.

א לַמְנַצֵּחַ
מִזְמוֹר לְדָוִד׃

2 May the Eternal answer you,
On the day of distress,
May your shelter be
The Name
Of Jacob's God.

ב יַעַנְךָ יהוה
בְּיוֹם צָרָה
יְשַׂגֶּבְךָ
שֵׁם |
אֱלֹהֵי יַעֲקֹב׃

3 May He send your help from the Holiness,
And from Zion
Support you.

ג יִשְׁלַח־עֶזְרְךָ מִקֹּדֶשׁ
וּמִצִּיּוֹן
יִסְעָדֶךָּ׃

4 May He recognize all your flour offerings,
And may He turn your elevation offering into fat ashes, Selah.

ד יִזְכֹּר כָּל־מִנְחֹתֶךָ
וְעוֹלָתְךָ יְדַשְּׁנֶה סֶלָה׃

5 May He give you your heart's desire,
And fill all your counsels.

ה יִתֶּן־לְךָ כִלְבָבֶךָ
וְכָל־עֲצָתְךָ יְמַלֵּא׃

6 Let us rejoice in Your salvation,
In our God's name shall we be flagged,
May the Eternal fill
All your requests.

ו נְרַנְּנָה | בִּישׁוּעָתֶךָ
וּבְשֵׁם־אֱלֹהֵינוּ נִדְגֹּל
יְמַלֵּא יהוה
כָּל־מִשְׁאֲלוֹתֶיךָ

7 Now I know
That the Eternal saves
His anointed;
He answers him
From His holy Heaven,
With the strength of
His saving right arm.

ז עַתָּה יָדַעְתִּי
כִּי הוֹשִׁיעַ |
יהוה מְשִׁיחוֹ
יַעֲנֵהוּ
מִשְּׁמֵי קָדְשׁוֹ
בִּגְבֻרוֹת
יֵשַׁע יְמִינוֹ׃

8 There are these with chariots.
Those with horses,
But we
Will pray in the Name of the Eternal, our God.

ח אֵלֶּה בָרֶכֶב
וְאֵלֶּה בַסּוּסִים
וַאֲנַחְנוּ |
בְּשֵׁם־יְיָ אֱלֹהֵינוּ נַזְכִּיר׃

9 They
Went down and fell
But we rose
And will be encouraged.

ט הֵמָּה
כָּרְעוּ וְנָפָלוּ
וַאֲנַחְנוּ קַּמְנוּ
וַנִּתְעוֹדָד׃

10 Eternal, please save,
O King,
Answer us on the day of our calling.

י יהוה הוֹשִׁיעָה
הַמֶּלֶךְ
יַעֲנֵנוּ בְיוֹם־קָרְאֵנוּ׃

4. The עולה, the holocaust sacrifice, is totally burnt. Therefore, the verse cannot mean "let your offering be turned into ashes", it is turned into ashes automatically. The main meaning of דשן is either "fat" (like Arabic דסם) or "fertilizer"; "ashes" are called דשן only in connection with the Temple service. It seems rather that דשן here has the meaning it has in Mishnaic and Rabbinic Hebrew, *viz.*, either that some of the ashes are removed

from the altar in the ceremony called דִּשּׁוּן הַמִּזְבֵּחַ, which precedes all other Temple activities in the morning, or that the ashes are taken out to the appointed place from where they can be used as fertilizer. [In Second Temple practice, only the blood is sold by the Temple for commercial purposes]. The prayer is either that the addressee's sacrifice should be chosen by the Eternal to provide the ashes for this ceremony or that even the bones should be turned into ashes as sign of divine acceptance. Therefore, as in all other Psalms of the first two books, לדוד means "composed by David", not "addressed to David". The addressee is unknown, but he must be a close supporter of David's kingship.

Psalm 21

1 For the director,
A Psalm of David.

א לַמְנַצֵּחַ
מִזְמוֹר לְדָוִד׃

2 Eternal,
The king can rejoice in Your might,
And in Your help,
How much can he exult!

ב יהוה
בְּעָזְּךָ יִשְׂמַח־מֶלֶךְ
וּבִישׁוּעָתְךָ
מַה־יגיל [יָּגֶל] מְאֹד׃

3 You gave him
His heart's desire,
You did not withhold
The entreaty of his lips, Selah.

ג תַּאֲוַת לִבּוֹ
נָתַתָּה לּוֹ
וַאֲרֶשֶׁת שְׂפָתָיו
בַּל־מָנַעְתָּ סֶּלָה׃

4 Truly, You anticipate him
With blessings of the Good
You put on his head
A diadem of pure gold.

ד כִּי־תְקַדְּמֶנּוּ
בִּרְכוֹת טוֹב
תָּשִׁית לְרֹאשׁוֹ
עֲטֶרֶת פָּז׃

5 Life
He requested from You;
You gave to him
Length of days
Forever and ever.

ה חַיִּים ׀
שָׁאַל מִמְּךָ
נָתַתָּה לּוֹ
אֹרֶךְ יָמִים
עוֹלָם וָעֶד׃

6 Great is his honor
By Your help,
You settle on him
Splendor and majesty.

ו גָּדוֹל כְּבוֹדוֹ
בִּישׁוּעָתֶךָ
הוֹד וְהָדָר
תְּשַׁוֶּה עָלָיו׃

7 You put on him eternal blessing;
You gladden him in joy
Before You.

ז כִּי־תְשִׁיתֵהוּ בְרָכוֹת לָעַד
תְּחַדֵּהוּ בְשִׂמְחָה
אֶת־פָּנֶיךָ׃

8 Certainly, the king
Trusts in the Eternal,
And he will not stagger
In the love of the Supreme

ח11 כִּי־הַמֶּלֶךְ
בֹּטֵחַ בַּיהוָה
וּבְחֶסֶד עֶלְיוֹן
בַּל־יִמּוֹט׃

9 Your left hand will find
All Your enemies;
Your right hand will find Your haters.

ט תִּמְצָא יָדְךָ
לְכָל־אֹיְבֶיךָ
יְמִינְךָ תִּמְצָא שֹׂנְאֶיךָ׃

10 You will really turn them
Into a fiery oven
When You will take care of them.
The Eternal
In His rage will swallow them;
Fire will eat them.

י תְּשִׁיתֵמוֹ ׀
כְּתַנּוּר אֵשׁ
לְעֵת פָּנֶיךָ
יהוה
בְּאַפּוֹ יְבַלְּעֵם
וְתֹאכְלֵם אֵשׁ׃

11 You will wipe
  Their fruits from the Land,
And their seed
  From mankind.

יא פִּרְיָמוֹ
  מֵאֶרֶץ תְּאַבֵּד
וְזַרְעָם
  מִבְּנֵי אָדָם׃

12 For they tried evil against You;
They hatched a plan,
  They were impotent.

יב כִּי־נָטוּ עָלֶיךָ רָעָה
חָשְׁבוּ מְזִמָּה
  בַּל־יוּכָלוּ׃

13 Certainly,
  You will turn them into booty,
With Your bow
  Take aim at their faces.

יג כִּי
  תְּשִׁיתֵמוֹ שֶׁכֶם
בְּמֵיתָרֶיךָ
  תְּכוֹנֵן עַל־פְּנֵיהֶם׃

14 Be exalted, o Eternal, in Your might;
We shall sing and chant
  Of Your might!

יד רוּמָה יהוָה בְעֻזֶּךָ
נָשִׁירָה וּנְזַמְּרָה
  גְּבוּרָתֶךָ׃

6. Here שוה is a separate verb stem not associated with "to be equal" or "to pray"; it also appears in *Ps* 89:20: "I conferred help to the hero". It is the equivalent of Arabic אסוה "to settle of one's property on somebody", אסי "to leave property to somebody" (in some dialects also וסה).

10. The prefix כ here is emphatic, as recognized by Naḥmanides *Gen.* 39:19 when Potiphar's wife tells him כַּדְּבָרִים הָאֵלֶּה "these horrible things".
פָּנֶיךָ is a verbal form "when You turn".

13. שכם "booty" is from Jacob's blessing of Joseph, *Gen.* 48:22.

Psalm 22

1 For the director,
On "The Morning Hind",
A Psalm of David.

א לַמְנַצֵּחַ
עַל־אַיֶּלֶת הַשַּׁחַר
מִזְמוֹר לְדָוִד׃

2 My God, my Powerful,
Why did You abandon me?
Far from Him Who would help me.
The words of my roar.

ב אֵלִי אֵלִי
לָמָה עֲזַבְתָּנִי
רָחוֹק מִישׁוּעָתִי
דִּבְרֵי שַׁאֲגָתִי׃

3 My God,
I am calling by day.
But You will not answer,
And in the night
There is no quiet for me.

ג אֱלֹהַי
אֶקְרָא יוֹמָם
וְלֹא תַעֲנֶה
וְלַיְלָה
וְלֹא־דוּמִיָּה לִי׃

4 But You, Holy One,
Are throning
On the praises of Israel.

ד וְאַתָּה קָדוֹשׁ
יוֹשֵׁב
תְּהִלּוֹת יִשְׂרָאֵל׃

5 In You
Our fathers trusted;
They trusted
And You made them escape.

ה בְּךָ
בָּטְחוּ אֲבֹתֵינוּ
בָּטְחוּ
וַתְּפַלְּטֵמוֹ׃

6 To You they cried and went free,
In You they trusted and were not ashamed.

ו אֵלֶיךָ זָעֲקוּ וְנִמְלָטוּ
בְּךָ בָטְחוּ וְלֹא־בוֹשׁוּ׃

7 But I am a worm and not a man,
The most despicable of common men
And despised by the ruling class.

ז וְאָנֹכִי תוֹלַעַת וְלֹא־אִישׁ
חֶרְפַּת אָדָם
וּבְזוּי עָם׃

8 All who see me
Sneer at me,
They curl their lips,
They wag their heads.

ח כָּל־רֹאַי
יַלְעִגוּ לִי
יַפְטִירוּ בְשָׂפָה
יָנִיעוּ רֹאשׁ׃

9 "Turn to the Eternal, will He let him escape?
"Will He save him
"For truly He takes pleasure in him?"

ט גֹּל אֶל־יְהוָה יְפַלְּטֵהוּ
יַצִּילֵהוּ
כִּי חָפֵץ בּוֹ׃

10 Only You pushed me out of the belly,
You made me feel safe
On my mother's breasts.

י כִּי־אַתָּה גֹחִי מִבָּטֶן
מַבְטִיחִי
עַל־שְׁדֵי אִמִּי׃

11 Upon You
I was thrown from the womb,
From my mother's belly
You are my Power,

יא עָלֶיךָ
הָשְׁלַכְתִּי מֵרָחֶם
מִבֶּטֶן אִמִּי
אֵלִי אָתָּה׃

12 Do not go away from me,
For trouble is near,
Truly, nobody helps!

יב אַל־תִּרְחַק מִמֶּנִּי
כִּי־צָרָה קְרוֹבָה
כִּי־אֵין עוֹזֵר׃

13 Surrounding me
Are many bulls,
The strong-armed of Bashan encircle me,

יג סְבָבוּנִי
פָּרִים רַבִּים
אַבִּירֵי בָשָׁן כִּתְּרוּנִי׃

14 Wide they open their mouths on me;
A lion
Tears and roars.

יד פָּצוּ עָלַי פִּיהֶם
אַרְיֵה
טֹרֵף וְשֹׁאֵג׃

15 I was poured out like water,
Unfastened all my bones,
My heart was
Like wax,
Melted
In my bowels.

טו כַּמַּיִם נִשְׁפַּכְתִּי
וְהִתְפָּרְדוּ כָּל־עַצְמוֹתָי
הָיָה לִבִּי
כַּדּוֹנָג
נָמֵס
בְּתוֹךְ מֵעָי׃

16 Dry like a potsherd is
My force,
And my tongue
Glued to my palate,
You scatter me to dust of death.

טז יָבֵשׁ כַּחֶרֶשׂ |
כֹּחִי
וּלְשׁוֹנִי
מֻדְבָּק מַלְקוֹחָי
וְלַעֲפַר־מָוֶת תִּשְׁפְּתֵנִי׃

17 For dogs surround me,
A group of criminals
crush me
Like a lion,
My hands and feet.

יז כִּי־סְבָבוּנִי כְּלָבִים
עֲדַת מְרֵעִים
הִקִּיפוּנִי
כָּאֲרִי
יָדַי וְרַגְלָי׃

18 I am counting all my bones.
They observe,
Look at me.

יח אֲסַפֵּר כָּל־עַצְמוֹתָי
הֵמָּה יַבִּיטוּ
יִרְאוּ־בִי׃

19 They will split my clothes between them,
And for my garments
They will throw lots.

יט יְחַלְּקוּ בְגָדַי לָהֶם
וְעַל־לְבוּשִׁי
יַפִּילוּ גוֹרָל׃

20 But You, Eternal,
Do not remove Yourself,
My strength
Come quickly to my aid!

כ וְאַתָּה יהוה
אַל־תִּרְחָק
אֱיָלוּתִי
לְעֶזְרָתִי חוּשָׁה׃

21 Rescue my soul from the sword,
From the dog
My only one!

כא הַצִּילָה מֵחֶרֶב נַפְשִׁי
מִיַּד־כֶּלֶב
יְחִידָתִי׃

22 Save me
From the lion's mouth,
Answer me in face of buffaloes' horns!

כב הוֹשִׁיעֵנִי
מִפִּי אַרְיֵה
וּמִקַּרְנֵי רֵמִים עֲנִיתָנִי׃

23 I shall tell Your Name to my brethren,
Within the assembly I shall praise You.

כג אֲסַפְּרָה שִׁמְךָ לְאֶחָי
בְּתוֹךְ קָהָל אֲהַלְלֶךָּ׃

24 Those fearing the Eternal praise Him,
All seed of Jacob honor Him,
Dread Him
All seed of Israel!

כד יִרְאֵי יהוה | הַלְלוּהוּ
כָּל־זֶרַע יַעֲקֹב כַּבְּדוּהוּ
וְגוּרוּ מִמֶּנּוּ
כָּל־זֶרַע יִשְׂרָאֵל׃

25 For He did neither disdain nor abhor
The poor's prayer,
Nor did He hide His face from him,
But when he cries to Him for help, He hears.

כה כִּי לֹא־בָזָה וְלֹא שִׁקַּץ
עֱנוּת עָנִי
וְלֹא־הִסְתִּיר פָּנָיו מִמֶּנּוּ
וּבְשַׁוְּעוֹ אֵלָיו שָׁמֵעַ׃

26 From You is my fame.
In a great assembly
My vows I shall pay
Before those who fear Him.

כו מֵאִתְּךָ תְּהִלָּתִי
בְּקָהָל רָב
נְדָרַי אֲשַׁלֵּם
נֶגֶד יְרֵאָיו׃

27 May the meek eat and be satiated.
Praise the Eternal,
His seekers,
May your thoughts live eternally.

כז יֹאכְלוּ עֲנָוִים ׀ וְיִשְׂבָּעוּ
יְהַלְלוּ יהוה
דֹּרְשָׁיו
יְחִי לְבַבְכֶם לָעַד׃

28 They will adore;
All corners of the earth
Will turn to the Eternal.
All Gentile families
Will be prostrate before You.

כח יִזְכְּרוּ ׀
וְיָשֻׁבוּ אֶל־יהוה
כָּל־אַפְסֵי־אָרֶץ
וְיִשְׁתַּחֲווּ לְפָנֶיךָ
כָּל־מִשְׁפְּחוֹת גּוֹיִם׃

29 The Kingdom
Truly is the Eternal's
As well as dominion
Over the Gentiles.

כט כִּי לַיהוה
הַמְּלוּכָה
וּמֹשֵׁל
בַּגּוֹיִם׃

30 All fat ones of the earth
Eat and prostrate themselves,
Before Him they will fall on their knees
All who go down to dust,
But his soul
Will not survive.

ל אָכְלוּ וַיִּשְׁתַּחֲווּ ׀
כָּל־דִּשְׁנֵי־אֶרֶץ
לְפָנָיו יִכְרְעוּ
כָּל־יוֹרְדֵי עָפָר
וְנַפְשׁוֹ
לֹא חִיָּה׃

31 The seed who worship Him
Will be counted as the Lord's for ages.

לא זֶרַע יַעַבְדֶנּוּ
יְסֻפַּר לַאדֹנָי לַדּוֹר׃

32 They will come
And tell of His fairness,
To the people who will be born,
Because of what He has done.

לב יָבֹאוּ
וְיַגִּידוּ צִדְקָתוֹ
לְעַם נוֹלָד
כִּי עָשָׂה׃

1. Ayelet Haššahar seems to have been a known melody, similar to the references to a *laḥn* in medieval synagogal poetry.

7. We take עם to mean those enfranchised to vote, the landowners, whose assembly hall in Jerusalem was the בית העם and who in the later kingdom intervened every time there was a doubt about the royal succession.

8. יַפְטִירוּ really means "to cleave wide open", in connection with lips this is best done by curling the lips in a sneer.

17. We take נקף in the sense of Arabic נקפ "to break" (like the chick breaks the egg shell to be born.).

22. ראם seems to be Assyrian *rimu*, the wild ox which was hunted as big game.

21. There are two possible interpretations of the "dog". Either it is the mythical dog which eats the souls of

those who are not found worthy of the Future Life. [Dr. Eva Guggenheimer points out that this dog has close connection with the Greek Cerberus (Kerberos) and one might think that the Greek *kerb* comes from Semitic *kelb* with a change of the liquids *l,r*, so that Cerberus is simply "the dog".] Otherwise, "dog" could be the name of a weapon fashioned in imitation of dog's teeth. Dahood wants to see in this כלב a form of כילף "ax", Aramaic כולבא, but following the Arabic, where כלב is "dog" and כאלב "harpoon, enter-hook", it would probably better to translate "dog" in this interpretation as "halbert", a two-handled pole weapon. Most probably, the poet intended the expression to be ambiguous.

27. Everywhere in Biblical literature one thinks in the heart, not in the brain. So here the "hearts" are the "thoughts".

28. “Adore” for זכר is good Accadic style. For reasons of English grammar the last two lines have been interchanged.

30. In classical literature, and in the Orient to this day, a fat man is a rich man who can buy enough food. (בריא, in modern Hebrew "healthy", means "very fat" in Biblical Hebrew). He seems to restrict Eternal Life to voluntary worshippers of the Eternal.

Psalm 23

1 A Psalm of David.	א מִזְמוֹר לְדָוִד
The Eternal is my shepherd,	יְהוָה רֹעִי
I shall not want!	לֹא אֶחְסָר׃
2 In oases of luxuriant grasses	ב בִּנְאוֹת דֶּשֶׁא
He makes me lie down,	יַרְבִּיצֵנִי
He leads me to quiet waters.	עַל־מֵי מְנֻחוֹת יְנַהֲלֵנִי׃
3 He restores my soul,	ג נַפְשִׁי יְשׁוֹבֵב
He directs me on righteous paths	יַנְחֵנִי בְמַעְגְּלֵי־צֶדֶק
For His Name's sake.	לְמַעַן שְׁמוֹ׃
4 Even if I go in a most dark valley	ד גַּם כִּי־אֵלֵךְ בְּגֵיא צַלְמָוֶת
I shall not fear evil	לֹא־אִירָא רָע
For You are with me.	כִּי־אַתָּה עִמָּדִי
Your staff and Your support,	שִׁבְטְךָ וּמִשְׁעַנְתֶּךָ
They will console me!	הֵמָּה יְנַחֲמֻנִי׃
5 You will prepare for me	ה תַּעֲרֹךְ לְפָנַי ׀
A table	שֻׁלְחָן
Against of my tormentors!	נֶגֶד צֹרְרָי
You pomaded my head with oil,	דִּשַּׁנְתָּ בַשֶּׁמֶן רֹאשִׁי
My cup is overflowing.	כּוֹסִי רְוָיָה׃
6 Only	ו אַךְ ׀
Goodness and kindness will pursue me	טוֹב וָחֶסֶד יִרְדְּפוּנִי
All days of my life;	כָּל־יְמֵי חַיָּי
I shall dwell in the House of the Eternal	וְשַׁבְתִּי בְּבֵית־יְהוָה
Forever.	לְאֹרֶךְ יָמִים׃

2. דשא is "luxuriant vegetal growth", in particular "thick grass", parallel *disu* in Accadic.

3. צלמות has the meaning of Arabic צלמת "darkness; darkness of a moonless, starless night".

5. From Ugaritic myths it seems that the table is used to form a shield, to avoid backstabbing. The meaning of רוה is found well expressed in Arabic רוי "abundant water", רו "fertility, plenty". This is also the root underlying the proper name Ruth.

6. The translation assumes that "the House of the Eternal" is Paradise. If it were taken to be the Temple, one could as well translate "stay in" instead of "dwell". (See Notes to *Ps.* 30).

Psalm 24

1 Of David, a Psalm.
The Eternal's is
The earth and its fill,
The dry land
And its inhabitants.

א לְדָוִד מִזְמ֫וֹר
לַיהוה
הָאָרֶץ וּמְלוֹאָהּ
תֵּבֵל
וְיֹשְׁבֵי בָהּ׃

2 Certainly, He
Founded it on oceans,
And on streams
He built it up.

ב כִּי הוּא
עַל־יַמִּים יְסָדָהּ
וְעַל־נְהָרוֹת
יְכוֹנְנֶהָ׃

3 Who may ascend the Eternal's Mountain,
And who may stay
At His holy place?

ג מִי־יַעֲלֶה בְהַר יהוה
וּמִי־יָקוּם
בִּמְקוֹם קָדְשׁוֹ׃

4 He whose hands are clean and is pure of heart,
And who
Never desired vanity
And never swore by trickery.

ד נְקִי כַפַּיִם וּבַר־לֵבָב
אֲשֶׁר ׀
לֹא־נָשָׂא לַשָּׁוְא נַפְשִׁי
וְלֹא נִשְׁבַּע לְמִרְמָה׃

5 He will carry blessing
From the Eternal
And justification
From his saving God.

ה יִשָּׂא בְרָכָה
מֵאֵת יהוה
וּצְדָקָה
מֵאֱלֹהֵי יִשְׁעוֹ׃

6 That is
His seekers' dwelling,
Those who seek Your face,
Jacob, Selah.

ו זֶה
דּוֹר דֹּרְשָׁו
מְבַקְשֵׁי פָנֶיךָ
יַעֲקֹב סֶלָה׃

7 Lift, gates,
Your heads,
And be raised,
Eternal doors;
May He come,
The King of glory!

ז שְׂאוּ שְׁעָרִים ׀
רָאשֵׁיכֶם
וְהִנָּשְׂאוּ
פִּתְחֵי עוֹלָם
וְיָבוֹא
מֶלֶךְ הַכָּבוֹד׃

8 Who is He,
The King of glory?
The Eternal,
Strong and mighty,
The Eternal,
The mighty warrior!

ח מִי זֶה
מֶלֶךְ הַכָּבוֹד
יהוה
עִזּוּז וְגִבּוֹר
יהוה
גִּבּוֹר מִלְחָמָה׃

9 Lift, gates
Your heads,
And rise,
Eternal doors;
May He come,
The King of Glory!

ט שְׂאוּ שְׁעָרִים ׀
רָאשֵׁיכֶם
וּשְׂאוּ
פִּתְחֵי עוֹלָם
וְיָבֹא
מֶלֶךְ הַכָּבוֹד׃

10 Who now is He,
The King of glory?
The Eternal of Hosts,
He is the King of Glory, Selah!

י מִי הוּא זֶה
מֶלֶךְ הַכָּבוֹד
יהוה צְבָאוֹת
הוּא מֶלֶךְ הַכָּבוֹד סֶלָה׃

3. The Eternal's mountain is heavenly Paradise. Therefore the gates are those of Paradise and they are lifted, not turned open, like the main gates of many medieval castles and modern garage doors, and unlike the Temple doors.

4. The Ketib נָשָׂא נַפְשִׁי means "desire ardently", cf. Deut. 24:15. The reading נָשָׂא לַשָּׁוְא נַפְשִׁי could be related to Arabic נפס "evil eye", meaning "He never tried to use the vain evil eye", נַפְשִׁי being used as an adverb.

"To swear by trickery" is to swear with a mental reservation.

6. Taking דוֹר to mean דּוּר "dwelling".

Psalm 25

1 Of David.
You, Eternal,
I ardently desire.

א לְדָוִד
אֵלֶיךָ יהוה
נַפְשִׁי אֶשָּׂא׃

2 My God,
In You I trust,
May I not be put to shame;
May my enemies not triumph over me.

ב אֱלֹהַי
בְּךָ בָטַחְתִּי
אַל־אֵבוֹשָׁה
אַל־יַעַלְצוּ אֹיְבַי לִי׃

3 Nor should one of those who affirm You
Be put to shame;
Empty traitors
Will be put to shame.

ג גַּם כָּל־קֹוֶיךָ
לֹא יֵבֹשׁוּ
יֵבֹשׁוּ
הַבּוֹגְדִים רֵיקָם׃

4 Let me know,
Your ways, Eternal
Teach me
Your paths.

ד דְּרָכֶיךָ יהוה
הוֹדִיעֵנִי
אֹרְחוֹתֶיךָ
לַמְּדֵנִי׃

5 Instruct me in Your truth,
And teach me.
Truly, You are
My saving God.
For You I am hoping
All day long.

ה הַדְרִיכֵנִי בַאֲמִתֶּךָ |
וְלַמְּדֵנִי
כִּי־אַתָּה
אֱלֹהֵי יִשְׁעִי
אוֹתְךָ קִוִּיתִי
כָּל־הַיּוֹם׃

6 Eternal, remember Your mercy,
And Your love,
Truly existing from eternity.

ו זְכֹר־רַחֲמֶיךָ יהוה
וַחֲסָדֶיךָ
כִּי מֵעוֹלָם הֵמָּה׃

7 Do not mention the sins of my youth
And my offenses,
But in Your favor remember me
Because of Your goodness, Eternal.

ז חַטֹּאות נְעוּרַי |
וּפְשָׁעַי אַל־תִּזְכֹּר
כְּחַסְדְּךָ זְכָר־לִי־אַתָּה
לְמַעַן טוּבְךָ יהוה׃

8 Good and upright is the Eternal,
Hence He teaches sinners about the Road..

ח טוֹב וְיָשָׁר יהוה
עַל־כֵּן יוֹרֶה חַטָּאִים בַּדָּרֶךְ׃

9 He trains the meek
In law,
And teaches His way to the meek.

ט יַדְרֵךְ עֲנָוִים
בַּמִּשְׁפָּט
וִילַמֵּד עֲנָוִים דַּרְכּוֹ׃

10 All the Eternal's paths
Are love and truth
For the keepers of His covenant
And His testimonials.

י כָּל־אָרְחוֹת יהוה
חֶסֶד וֶאֱמֶת
לְנֹצְרֵי בְרִיתוֹ
וְעֵדֹתָיו׃

11 For Your Name's sake, Eternal,
Forgive my iniquity;
Truly, it is very great.

יא לְמַעַן־שִׁמְךָ יהוה
וְסָלַחְתָּ לַעֲוֹנִי
כִּי רַב־הוּא׃
יב מִי זֶה הָאִישׁ

12 Who is the man
Fearing the Eternal?
He will teach him
His preferred way.

יְרֵא יהוָה
יוֹרֶנּוּ
בְּדֶרֶךְ יִבְחָר׃

13 His soul
Will rest in comfort,
And his seed
Will inherit the earth.

יג נַפְשׁוֹ
בְּטוֹב תָּלִין
וְזַרְעוֹ
יִירַשׁ אָרֶץ׃

14 The Eternal's counsel
Is for those who fear Him.
His covenant
To inform them.

יד סוֹד יהוה
לִירֵאָיו
וּבְרִיתוֹ
לְהוֹדִיעָם׃

15 My eyes are always
On the Eternal,
Truly, He will free my feet from snares.

טו עֵינַי תָּמִיד
אֶל־יהוָה
כִּי הוּא־יוֹצִיא מֵרֶשֶׁת רַגְלָי׃

16 Turn to me and have mercy with me,
For I am alone and deprived.

טז פְּנֵה־אֵלַי וְחָנֵּנִי
כִּי־יָחִיד וְעָנִי אָנִי׃

17 My heart's distress is spreading,
From my straits
Take me out!

יז צָרוֹת לְבָבִי הִרְחִיבוּ
מִמְּצוּקוֹתַי
הוֹצִיאֵנִי׃

18 See my deprivation
And my toils,
And lift
All my sins.

יח רְאֵה־עָנְיִי
וַעֲמָלִי
וְשָׂא
לְכָל־חַטֹּאותָי׃

19 See my enemies, growing in number,
For they are hating me violent hate.

יט רְאֵה אוֹיְבַי כִּי־רָבּוּ
וְשִׂנְאַת חָמָס שְׂנֵאוּנִי׃

20 Please watch over my soul
And save me,
May I not be put to shame,
So much I seek refuge in You!

כ שָׁמְרָה נַפְשִׁי
וְהַצִּילֵנִי
אַל־אֵבוֹשׁ
כִּי־חָסִיתִי בָךְ׃

21 Integrity and uprightness will protect me;
Truly
I hope for You.

כא תֹּם־וָיֹשֶׁר יִצְּרוּנִי
כִּי
קִוִּיתִיךָ׃

22 God, rescue
Israel
From all
Their enemies.

כב פְּדֵה אֱלֹהִים
אֶת־יִשְׂרָאֵל
מִכֹּל
צָרוֹתָיו׃

1. For נשא נפשו see *Ps.* 24.

6. The best translation of חסד is "love, favor".

12. לין means to stay at a resting place.

14. סוד can mean either secret or "counsel, majesty, council".

18. ענה means "to deprive"; so עני is a person suffering from deprivation.

22. The Talmud (ברכות כב.) notes that in poetic texts צר enemy and צרה calamity are interchangeable.

Psalm 26

1 Of David.
Judge me, Eternal
Truly, I
Walked in my simplicity;
In the Eternal I trusted,
I shall not stumble.

א לְדָוִד
שָׁפְטֵנִי יהוה
כִּי־אֲנִי
בְּתֻמִּי הָלַכְתִּי
וּבַיהוָה בָּטַחְתִּי
לֹא אֶמְעָד׃

2 Test me, Eternal, and try me,
Purify my reins and my heart.

ב בְּחָנֵנִי יהוָה וְנַסֵּנִי
צָרוּפָה [צָרְפָה] כִלְיוֹתַי וְלִבִּי׃

3 Truly, Your love
Is before my eyes,
I am leading my life
With faith in You.

ג כִּי־חַסְדְּךָ
לְנֶגֶד עֵינָי
וְהִתְהַלַּכְתִּי
בַּאֲמִתֶּךָ׃

4 I did not sit
With men of frivolity,
And with those who have hidden secrets
I shall not come by.

ד לֹא־יָשַׁבְתִּי
עִם־מְתֵי־שָׁוְא
וְעִם־נַעֲלָמִים
לֹא אָבוֹא׃

5 I hate
The assembly of criminals,
And with wicked ones
I shall not sit.

ה שָׂנֵאתִי
קְהַל מְרֵעִים
וְעִם־רְשָׁעִים
לֹא אֵשֵׁב׃

6 I shall wash my hands in cleanliness,
When circling Your altar, Eternal.

ו אֶרְחַץ בְּנִקָּיוֹן כַּפָּי
וַאֲסֹבְבָה אֶת־מִזְבַּחֲךָ יהוָה׃

7 Declaiming
To the sound of thanksgiving,
And telling
All Your wonders.

ז לַשְׁמִעַ
בְּקוֹל תּוֹדָה
וּלְסַפֵּר
כָּל־נִפְלְאוֹתֶיךָ׃

8 Eternal, I love
Your House as shelter,
And the place
Of Your glory's Sanctuary.

ח יהוה אָהַבְתִּי
מְעוֹן בֵּיתֶךָ
וּמְקוֹם
מִשְׁכַּן כְּבוֹדֶךָ׃

9 Do not gather-in my soul with sinners,
Nor my life with men of blood guilt.

ט אַל־תֶּאֱסֹף עִם־חַטָּאִים נַפְשִׁי
וְעִם־אַנְשֵׁי דָמִים חַיָּי׃

10 In whose left hand is criminal intent
And their right hand
Is full of graft.

י אֲשֶׁר־בִּידֵיהֶם זִמָּה
וִימִינָם
מָלְאָה שֹּׁחַד׃

11 But I
Shall walk in my simplicity,
Redeem me, and have mercy with me!

יא וַאֲנִי
בְּתֻמִּי אֵלֵךְ
פְּדֵנִי וְחָנֵּנִי׃

12 My foot	יב רַגְלִי
Was standing straight.	עָמְדָה בְמִישׁוֹר
In assemblies	בְּמַקְהֵלִים
I shall worship the Eternal.	אֲבָרֵךְ יהוָה׃

2. The *ketib* is: "My reins and my heart are purified".

8. מָעוֹן usually is translated as "home", dwelling place", but this would be the house, not the dwelling space in the house. Therefore I prefer to connect the word to Arabic עון "Aid, help".

10. זִמָּה can have two meanings: "Action with criminal intent", from זמם , or "sexual perversion linked to idolatrous practices". The translation follows the first meaning but one should not exclude the second one.

12 אֲבָרֵךְ probably is intended to have a double meaning, "to bless, praise", or "to fall on one's knees", given a common etymology by Gesenius. The translation "to worship" is a compromise.

Psalm 27

1 Of David.	א לְדָוִד |
The Eternal	יְהוָה |
Is my light and my help;	אוֹרִי וְיִשְׁעִי
Whom shall I fear?	מִמִּי אִירָא
The Eternal is my life's stronghold,	יְהוָה מָעוֹז חַיַּי
Of whom shall I be afraid?	מִמִּי אֶפְחָד׃
2 With criminals	ב בִּקְרֹב עָלַי |
Coming close to me	מְרֵעִים
To eat my flesh,	לֶאֱכֹל אֶת־בְּשָׂרִי
My oppressors and my enemies,	צָרַי וְאֹיְבַי לִי
They stumbled and fell.	הֵמָּה כָשְׁלוּ וְנָפָלוּ׃
3 If a camp would	ג אִם־תַּחֲנֶה עָלַי |
Encamp against me	מַחֲנֶה
My heart shall not fear;	לֹא־יִירָא לִבִּי
If against me rise	אִם־תָּקוּם עָלַי
War,	מִלְחָמָה
In this	בְּזֹאת
I am trusting!	אֲנִי בוֹטֵחַ׃
4 One thing	ד אַחַת |
I am asking from the Eternal,	שָׁאַלְתִּי מֵאֵת־יהוה
This I shall seek;	אוֹתָהּ אֲבַקֵּשׁ
Dwelling in the Eternal's House	שִׁבְתִּי בְּבֵית־יהוה
All days of my Life,	כָּל־יְמֵי חַיַּי
To behold the Eternal's beauty	לַחֲזוֹת בְּנֹעַם־ יהוה
And to visit His Palace.	וּלְבַקֵּר בְּהֵיכָלוֹ׃
5 He surely will hide me in His hut	ה כִּי יִצְפְּנֵנִי | בְּסֻכֹּה
On the day of evil.	בְּיוֹם רָעָה
He will conceal me	יַסְתִּרֵנִי
In His secret tent;	בְּסֵתֶר אָהֳלוֹ
He will lift me	בְּצוּר
On a rock	יְרוֹמְמֵנִי׃
6 And now my head shall be lifted	ו וְעַתָּה יָרוּם רֹאשִׁי
Above my enemies around me;	עַל־אֹיְבַי סְבִיבוֹתַי
I shall sacrifice in His tent	וְאֶזְבְּחָה בְאָהֳלוֹ
Sacrifices of friendship;	זִבְחֵי תְרוּעָה
I shall sing and chant	אָשִׁירָה וַאֲזַמְּרָה
To the Eternal.	לַיהוָה׃
7 Listen, Eternal, to my calling voice,	ז שְׁמַע־יְהוָה קוֹלִי אֶקְרָא
Both favor me, and answer me.	וְחָנֵּנִי וַעֲנֵנִי׃
8 About You	
My heart says:	ח לְךָ |
Seek out His presence!	אָמַר לִבִּי
Your presence, Eternal, I am seeking.	בַּקְּשׁוּ פָנָי
	אֶת־פָּנֶיךָ יְהוָה אֲבַקֵּשׁ׃

9 Do not hide Your presence	ט אַל־תַּסְתֵּר פָּנֶיךָ	
From me,	מִמֶּנִּי
Do not bend your servant in anger,	אַל־תַּט־בְּאַף עַבְדֶּךָ
You were my succor.	עֶזְרָתִי הָיִיתָ
Do not abandon nor forsake me,	אַל־תִּטְּשֵׁנִי וְאַל־תַּעַזְבֵנִי
My helpful God.	אֱלֹהֵי יִשְׁעִי׃
10 Really my father and mother forsook me	י כִּי־אָבִי וְאִמִּי עֲזָבוּנִי
But the Eternal gathered me in.	וַיהוָה יַאַסְפֵנִי׃
11 Eternal, teach me Your way,	יא הוֹרֵנִי יהוה דַּרְכֶּךָ
Lead me	וּנְחֵנִי
On a straight path	בְּאֹרַח מִישׁוֹר
For those	לְמַעַן
Who observe me.	שׁוֹרְרָי׃
12 Do not give me	יב אַל־תִּתְּנֵנִי
To my oppressors' throat,	בְּנֶפֶשׁ צָרָי
For false witnesses rose against me	כִּי קָמוּ־בִי עֵדֵי־שֶׁקֶר
Inflating extortion.	וִיפֵחַ חָמָס׃
13 Perfectly I trust	יג לוּלֵא הֶאֱמַנְתִּי
To see the Eternal's goodness	לִרְאוֹת בְּטוּב־יהוה
In the Land of Life.	בְּאֶרֶץ חַיִּים׃
14 Pray to the Eternal,	יד קַוֵּה אֶל־יהוה
Strong	חֲזַק
And courageous be your heart,	וְיַאֲמֵץ לִבֶּךָ
And pray	וְקַוֵּה
To the Eternal!	אֶל־יהוה׃

2. The emphatic לי seems to mean: "oppressors and enemies perceived by me."

4. It is not clear whether the reference is to earthly life or eternal Life.

5. בקר may mean (a) to visit, (b) to be up early in the morning, (c) to investigate, audit. All three meaning might apply here.

6. תרועה can mean either "friendship" (*Num.* 23:21) or "trumpet blowing". The difference between זמר and שיר seems to be elucidated by Accadic, where *zamaru* is a formal temple chant with instrumental music, and *šar* a stanza in a longer composition.

12. נפש means, rather, "windpipe, breathing tube", but the English simile is the throat, meaning the place where his testimony is expressed in words.

14. Taking לולא from Accadic *lalu, lulu* "overwhelming fullness". The dots over the word may indicate a non-Hebrew word, since the Hebrew "lest, if not" does not make much sense here.

Psalm 28

1 By David.
I shall call,
Eternal, to You.
My rock,
Be not deaf to me,
Lest You be silent on my behalf
And I would be compared
To those descending into the Pit.

א לְדָוִד
אֵלֶיךָ יהוה |
אֶקְרָא
צוּרִי
אַל־תֶּחֱרַשׁ מִמֶּנִּי
פֶּן־תֶּחֱשֶׁה מִמֶּנִּי
וְנִמְשַׁלְתִּי
עִם־יוֹרְדֵי בוֹר׃

2 Listen to the sound of my supplications
When I appeal to You,
When I lift my hands
To Your holy Sanctuary.

ב שְׁמַע קוֹל תַּחֲנוּנַי
בְּשַׁוְּעִי אֵלֶיךָ
בְּנָשְׂאִי יָדַי
אֶל־דְּבִיר קָדְשֶׁךָ׃

3 Do not include me with criminals
And with evildoers,
Talkers of peace
With their friends
While evil is
In their hearts.

ג אַל־תִּמְשְׁכֵנִי עִם־רְשָׁעִים
וְעִם־פֹּעֲלֵי אָוֶן
דֹּבְרֵי שָׁלוֹם
עִם־רֵעֵיהֶם
וְרָעָה
בִּלְבָבָם׃

4 Give them according to their deeds
And their evil intentions;
According to their handiwork
Give to them,
Turn their acts back on them!

ד תֶּן־לָהֶם כְּפָעֳלָם
וּכְרֹעַ מַעַלְלֵיהֶם
כְּמַעֲשֵׂה יְדֵיהֶם
תֵּן לָהֶם
הָשֵׁב גְּמוּלָם לָהֶם׃

5 They never will understand
The deeds of the Eternal;
By His handiwork.
He will tear them down
And not build them up.

ה כִּי לֹא יָבִינוּ
אֶל־פְּעֻלֹּת יהוה
וְאֶל־מַעֲשֵׂה יָדָיו
יֶהֶרְסֵם
וְלֹא יִבְנֵם׃

6 Praised be the Eternal
For He heard
The voice of my supplications.

ו בָּרוּךְ יהוה
כִּי־שָׁמַע
קוֹל תַּחֲנוּנָי׃

7 The Eternal
Is my stronghold and my shield,
In Him my heart trusts and I will be helped;
My heart will exult
And I shall thank him with my song.

ז יהוה |
עֻזִּי וּמָגִנִּי
בּוֹ בָטַח לִבִּי וְנֶעֱזָרְתִּי
וַיַּעֲלֹז לִבִּי
וּמִשִּׁירִי אֲהוֹדֶנּוּ׃

8 The Eternal is my strength,
And He is the stronghold of help for His anointed.

ח יהוה עֹז־לָמוֹ
וּמָעוֹז יְשׁוּעוֹת מְשִׁיחוֹ הוּא׃

9 Please, help Your people,
And bless Your inheritance;
Shepherd and lift them
Forever.

ט הוֹשִׁיעָה | אֶת־עַמֶּךָ
וּבָרֵךְ ת־נַחֲלָתֶךָ
וּרְעֵם וְנַשְּׂאֵם
עַד־הָעוֹלָם׃

1. The Pit is the place of destruction of the souls unworthy of the Future Life. It is possible to parse the verse as
לְדָוִ֡ד \ אֵלֶ֡יךָ יְ֯י | \ אֶקְרָ֡א צ֘וּרִ֗י \ אַֽל־תֶּחֱרַ֗שׁ מִ֫מֶּ֥נִּי \ פֶּן־תֶּחֱשֶׁ֣ה מִמֶּ֑נִּי \ וְ֝נִמְשַׁ֗לְתִּי \ עִם־י֥וֹרְדֵי בֽוֹר׃

2. דְּבִיר is connected with Ethiopian *tabir* "innermost", also Aramaic דבר "to lead". It designated the centerpiece of the Tenple.

4. גמל means "to act correctly", it probably is used here ironically.

Psalm 29

1 A Psalm of David.	א מִזְמוֹר לְדָוִד
Give to the Eternal,	הָבוּ לַיהוה
O possessors of might,	בְּנֵי אֵלִים
Give to the Eternal	הָבוּ לַיהוה
Glory and strength!	כָּבוֹד וָעֹז׃
2 Give to the Eternal	ב הָבוּ לַיהוה
Glory of His Name,	כְּבוֹד שְׁמוֹ
Prostrate yourselves before the Eternal	הִשְׁתַּחֲווּ לַיהוה
In the splendor of the Sanctuary.	בְּהַדְרַת־קֹדֶשׁ׃
3 The Eternal's voice is over the waters,	ג קוֹל יהוה עַל־הַמָּיִם
The Powerful of Glory made thunder,	אֵל־הַכָּבוֹד הִרְעִים
The Eternal	יהוה
Over mighty waters.	עַל־מַיִם רַבִּים׃
4 The Eternal's voice in power,	ד קוֹל־יהוה בַּכֹּחַ
The Eternal's voice	קוֹל יהוה
In splendor.	בֶּהָדָר׃
5 The Eternal's voice	ה קוֹל יהוה
Shatters cedars;	שֹׁבֵר אֲרָזִים
The Eternal shattered	וַיְשַׁבֵּר יהוה
The cedars of Lebanon.	אֶת־אַרְזֵי הַלְּבָנוֹן׃
6 He made them dance like calves,	ו וַיַּרְקִידֵם כְּמוֹ־עֵגֶל
Lebanon and Antilebanon	לְבָנוֹן וְשִׂרְיֹן
Like young antelopes.	כְּמוֹ בֶן־רְאֵמִים׃
7 The Eternal's voice quarries	ז קוֹל־יהוה חֹצֵב
With shafts of fire.	לַהֲבוֹת אֵשׁ׃
8 The Eternal's voice	ח קוֹל יהוה
Makes the wilderness tremble,	יָחִיל מִדְבָּר
The Eternal makes tremble	יָחִיל יהוה
The wilderness of Qadesh.	מִדְבַּר קָדֵשׁ׃
9 The Eternal's voice	ט קוֹל יהוה ׀
Brings hinds into labor,	יְחוֹלֵל אַיָּלוֹת
And shaves off forests,	וַיֶּחֱשֹׂף יְעָרוֹת
And in His Hall	וּבְהֵיכָלוֹ
Everything	כֻּלּוֹ
Says "glory"!	אֹמֵר כָּבוֹד׃
10 The Eternal	י יהוה
Throned over the Deluge,	לַמַּבּוּל יָשָׁב
The Eternal sat	וַיֵּשֶׁב יהוה
As King always.	מֶלֶךְ לְעוֹלָם׃
11 The Eternal	יא יהוה עֹז
Will give strength to his people,	לְעַמּוֹ יִתֵּן
The Eternal	יהוה ׀
Will bless His people with peace.	יְבָרֵךְ אֶת־עַמּוֹ בַשָּׁלוֹם׃

Psalm 30

1 A Psalm,
Song of inauguration of the House, by David.

א מִזְמ֡וֹר
שִׁיר־חֲנֻכַּ֖ת הַבַּ֣יִת לְדָוִֽד׃

2 I will extol You, Eternal,
For You drew me up,
And You did not gladden my enemies over me.

ב אֲרוֹמִמְךָ֣ יהוה
כִּ֣י דִלִּיתָ֑נִי
וְלֹא־שִׂמַּ֖חְתָּ אֹיְבַ֣י לִֽי׃

3 Eternal, my God,
I prayed to You,
And You healed me.

ג יְהוָ֥ה אֱלֹהָ֑י
שִׁוַּ֥עְתִּי אֵ֝לֶ֗יךָ
וַתִּרְפָּאֵֽנִי׃

4 Eternal,
You raised my soul from a cavern
You enlivened me,
Lest I descend to the pit.

ד יהוה
הֶֽעֱלִ֣יתָ מִן־שְׁא֣וֹל נַפְשִׁ֑י
חִ֝יִּיתַ֗נִי
מיורדי־[מִיָּֽרְדִי] בֽוֹר׃

5 His pious, sing to the Eternal!
`And give thanks
To His holy renown!

ה זַמְּר֣וּ לַיהוָ֣ה חֲסִידָ֑יו
וְ֝הוֹד֗וּ
לְזֵ֣כֶר קָדְשֽׁוֹ׃

6 For upheaval
Is in His anger,
Life in His goodwill,
In the evening
One rests crying,
But the morning is song!

ו כִּ֤י רֶ֨גַע ׀
בְּאַפּוֹ֮
חַיִּ֪ים בִּרְצ֫וֹנ֥וֹ
בָּ֭עֶרֶב
יָלִ֥ין בֶּ֗כִי
וְלַבֹּ֥קֶר רִנָּֽה׃

7 But I
Said in my ease :
Never shall I stagger.

ז וַ֭אֲנִי
בַּל־אֶמּ֥וֹט לְעוֹלָֽם׃

8 Eternal, in Your goodwill
You gave me strength like a mountain,
But when You hid Your presence,
I was confounded.

ח יהוה בִּרְצוֹנְךָ֮
הֶעֱמַ֪דְתָּה לְֽהַרְרִ֫י עֹ֥ז
הִסְתַּ֥רְתָּ פָנֶ֗יךָ
הָיִ֥יתִי נִבְהָֽל׃

9 To You, Eternal, I shall call,
And to my Master
I beseech.

ט אֵלֶ֣יךָ יְהוָ֣ה אֶקְרָ֑א
וְאֶל־אֲ֝דֹנָ֗י
אֶתְחַנָּֽן׃

10 What gain is in my silence,
If I would go down to destruction?
Can dust praise You?
Can it tell Your truth?

י מַה־בֶּ֥צַע בְּדָמִי֮
בְּרִדְתִּ֫י אֶ֥ל־שָׁ֑חַת
הֲיוֹדְךָ֥ עָפָ֑ר
הֲיַגִּ֥יד אֲמִתֶּֽךָ׃

11 Listen, Eternal, and be gracious to me;
Eternal,
Be my help!

יא שְׁמַע־יְהוָ֥ה וְחָנֵּ֑נִי
יְ֝הוָ֗ה
הֱיֵֽה־עֹזֵ֥ר לִֽי׃

12 You turned my lament
Into a flute play for me,
You opened my sackcloth
And girded me with joy.

ב הָפַ֣כְתָּ מִסְפְּדִי֮
לְמָח֪וֹל לִ֥י
פִּתַּ֥חְתָּ שַׂקִּ֑י
וַתְּאַזְּרֵ֥נִי שִׂמְחָֽה׃

13 So that	יג לְמַעַן ׀
The liver shall sing to You	יְזַמֶּרְךָ֣ כָבוֹד
And never be silent.	וְלֹ֣א יִדֹּ֑ם
Eternal, my God,	יהוָ֥ה אֱ֝לֹהַ֗י
Forever I shall thank you.	לְעוֹלָ֥ם אוֹדֶֽךָּ׃

1. It is not clear which house is inaugurated. The contents do not fit for an inauguration of the Temple.

4. The *qere yâredî* is irregular, the *ketib yordî* is normative grammar. In masoretic prosody three syllables are needed in this word.
שאול here cannot be the Netherworld, since the poet is living. It is interpreted here as the mother's womb.

5. זכר is not only the remembrance but also how one is remembered by, as here by His name. The אזכרה mentioned in Wayyiqra is the declaration that the part of the Minḥa to be burned on the altar is taken in the Eternal's Name.

6. For רגע as "catastrophy" see Ps. 6:11.

12. מָחוֹל never is "dance"; it is what modern Herbrew calls חָלִיל "flute", i.e., "music instrument in the shape of a hollow round pipe". Miriam led the women with fifes and drums and the maidens of Shilo played flutes in the vineyards (nobody can engage in circular dance in a vineyard without destroying all its plants.)

13. כבוד usually means "honor, glory", but is used in the Talmud (*Bava meṣia*` 114a) as כבד "liver". In fact, "liver" here may mean "stomach" since it is motile similar to the heart.

Psalm 31

1 For the director,
A Psalm of David.

א לַמְנַצֵּחַ
מִזְמוֹר לְדָוִד׃

2 In You, Eternal, I am taking refuge,
Never shall I be disgraced,
In Your true friendship let me escape.

ב בְּךָ־יהוָה חָסִיתִי
אַל־אֵבוֹשָׁה לְעוֹלָם
בְּצִדְקָתְךָ פַלְּטֵנִי׃

3 Bend to me Your ear,
Rescue me soon,
Be for me a rock stronghold,
A fortified house,
To save me.

ג הַטֵּה אֵלַי ׀ אָזְנְךָ
מְהֵרָה הַצִּילֵנִי
הֱיֵה לִי ׀ לְצוּר־מָעוֹז
לְבֵית מְצוּדוֹת
לְהוֹשִׁיעֵנִי׃

4 For You are my crag and my fortress,
For Your Name's sake
Lead me and direct me!

ד כִּי־סַלְעִי וּמְצוּדָתִי אָתָּה
וּלְמַעַן שִׁמְךָ
תַּנְחֵנִי וּתְנַהֲלֵנִי׃

5 Get me out
From this trap
They hid for me,
For You
Are my stronghold!

ה תּוֹצִיאֵנִי
מֵרֶשֶׁת זוּ
טָמְנוּ לִי
כִּי־אַתָּה
מָעוּזִּי׃

6 Into Your hand
I deposit my spirit.
You redeemed me, Eternal,
True Power!

ו בְּיָדְךָ
אַפְקִיד רוּחִי
פָּדִיתָה אוֹתִי יהוה
אֵל אֱמֶת׃

7 I hate
Those who keep idle nothings;
But I
Am trusting in the Eternal.

ז שָׂנֵאתִי
הַשֹּׁמְרִים הַבְלֵי־שָׁוְא
וַאֲנִי
אֶל־יהוָה בָּטָחְתִּי׃

8 I shall celebrate and rejoice in Your love,
Since You saw
My deprivation,
You knew
My soul's sorrows.

ח אָגִילָה וְאֶשְׂמְחָה בְּחַסְדֶּךָ
אֲשֶׁר רָאִיתָ
אֶת־עָנְיִי
יָדַעְתָּ
בְּצָרוֹת נַפְשִׁי׃

9 But You did not extradite me
Into the hand of the foe,
You planted my feet in the wide space.

ט וְלֹא הִסְגַּרְתַּנִי
בְּיַד־אוֹיֵב
הֶעֱמַדְתָּ בַמֶּרְחָב רַגְלָי׃

10 Be gracious to me, Eternal,
For I am in straits,
My eye is darkened by worry,
My soul and my body.

י חָנֵּנִי יהוה
כִּי צַר־לִי
עָשְׁשָׁה בְכַעַס עֵינִי
נַפְשִׁי וּבִטְנִי׃

11 Certainly my life
Is ending in grief,
My years in groans,
By my sin my force is stumbling,
And my bones are rotting.

יא כִּי כָלוּ בְיָגוֹן
חַיַּי
וּשְׁנוֹתַי בַּאֲנָחָה
כָּשַׁל בַּעֲוֺנִי כֹחִי
וַעֲצָמַי עָשֵׁשׁוּ׃

12 Because of all my enemies I became a shame,
And for my neighbors
Even more,
A fear for my acquaintances.
Those who see me from the outside
Moved away from me.

יב מִכָּל־צֹרְרַי הָיִיתִי חֶרְפָּה
וְלִשְׁכֵנַי ׀
מְאֹד
וּפַחַד לִמְיֻדָּעָי
רֹאַי בַּחוּץ
נָדְדוּ מִמֶּנִּי׃

13 I am withering
Like a dead person.
I was
Like a ruined vessel.

יג נִשְׁכַּחְתִּי
כְּמֵת מִלֵּב
הָיִיתִי
כִּכְלִי אֹבֵד׃

14 Certainly, I heard
The slander of the many,
Terror all around,
They assembling against me together,
They planned to take my life.

יד כִּי שָׁמַעְתִּי ׀
דִּבַּת רַבִּים
מָגוֹר מִסָּבִיב
בְּהִוָּסְדָם יַחַד עָלַי
לָקַחַת נַפְשִׁי זָמָמוּ׃

15 But I,
In You I trust, Eternal,
I affirm
"You are my God."

טו וַאֲנִי ׀
עָלֶיךָ בָטַחְתִּי יהוה
אָמַרְתִּי
אֱלֹהַי אָתָּה׃

16 In Your hand are my seasons.
Save me from my enemies
And my pursuers.

טז בְּיָדְךָ עִתֹּתָי
הַצִּילֵנִי מִיַּד־אוֹיְבַי
וּמֵרֹדְפָי׃

17 Let Your presence shine
On Your servant,
Deliver me by Your kindness.

יז הָאִירָה פָנֶיךָ
עַל־עַבְדֶּךָ
הוֹשִׁיעֵנִי בְחַסְדֶּךָ׃

18 Eternal, do not let me be disgraced
For I call upon You,
The wicked shall be disgraced,
Silently, to the Pit.

ח יהוה אַל־אֵבוֹשָׁה
כִּי קְרָאתִיךָ
יֵבֹשׁוּ רְשָׁעִים
יִדְּמוּ לִשְׁאוֹל׃

19 Lying lips shall be muted,
That talk wantonly against the just,
In arrogance and contempt.

יט תֵּאָלַמְנָה שִׂפְתֵי שָׁקֶר
הַדֹּבְרוֹת עַל־צַדִּיק עָתָק
בְּגַאֲוָה וָבוּז׃

20 How immense is Your good
That You hid for those who fear You,
That You created
For those who rely on You,
In front of
Humankind

כ מָה רַב טוּבְךָ
אֲשֶׁר־צָפַנְתָּ לִּירֵאֶיךָ
פָּעַלְתָּ
לַחֹסִים בָּךְ
נֶגֶד
בְּנֵי אָדָם׃

21 Hide them
In the secret of Your presence,
From reversals of mankind,
Hide them in a hut,
From the quarrel of tongues.

.כא תַּסְתִּירֵם|
בְּסֵתֶר פָּנֶיךָ
מֵרֻכְסֵי אִישׁ
תִּצְפְּנֵם בְּסֻכָּה
מֵרִיב לְשֹׁנוֹת׃

22 Praised be the Eternal,
He showed me His wondrous kindness
In the fortified city.

כב בָּרוּךְ יהוה
כִּי־הִפְלִיא חַסְדּוֹ לִי
בְּעִיר מָצוֹר׃

23 And I
Had said in my hastiness:
"I am cut off
From before You!"
But now You heard
The voice of my supplications
When I prayed to You.

כג וַאֲנִי |
אָמַרְתִּי בְחָפְזִי
נִגְרַזְתִּי
מִנֶּגֶד עֵינֶיךָ
אָכֵן שָׁמַעְתָּ
קוֹל תַּחֲנוּנַי
בְּשַׁוְּעִי אֵלֶיךָ׃

24 Love the Eternal,
All His pious!
The Eternal guards
The faithful,
But He amply will pay back
Those acting in pride.

כד אֶהֱבוּ אֶת־יהוה כָּל־חֲסִידָיו
אֱמוּנִים
נֹצֵר יהוה
וּמְשַׁלֵּם עַל־יֶתֶר
עֹשֵׂה גַאֲוָה׃

25 Be strong
And may Your heart be stout,
All whose hope is
In the Eternal.

כה חִזְקוּ
וְיַאֲמֵץ לְבַבְכֶם
כָּל־הַמְיַחֲלִים
לַיהוה׃

2. Taking צדקה in the sense of the Arabic צדאקה, "true friendship".

3. A sentence without Etnaḥta.

7. "Idle nothings" are either idols or good luck charms kept by otherwise monotheistic people.

10. עשש appears only 3 times in Psalms and nowhere else in the Bible, two times here and once, in a direct parallel to v. 10, in Psalm 6. It seems that the same root in v. 11 has a different meaning. Rashi declares the word to mean "get dark", he also quotes Menaḥem ibn Saruq who connects the root with עש "moth", and gives the meaning "moth eaten", accepted also by Ibn Ezra. Rashi's own interpretation here and in Ps. 6 can be supported by Accadic *esesu* "to darken (sun, moon), to become dejected". I have chosen to adhere to the conventional translation "to become dark" for the first occurrence, based on Accadic. M. Lambert (REJ 39, p.302) derives the root (or better, one of the roots עשש) from Arabic עת̇ת̇ "to be putrid". Hebrew עש "moth" is Arabic עת̇ה, but the root עת̇ת̇ means "to eat (textiles by the moth), to importune somebody". I prefer that interpretation, following Menaḥem, for v. 11.

12 Reading צורר similar to Arabic צ̇רר "to cause damage".

13. The meaning of שכח as "withering" is well known from Ps. 137:5. מִלֵּב then means "(to be) without heart". The traditional translation "I was forgotten like a dead person, out of mind" does not fit into the context.

18. Taking דמו from דום "to be silent".

19. עתק is another multi-faceted word. In Gen. 12:8, the root means "to move, to transfer", as in Accadic *etequ* (talking about Abraham, coming from Accadic speaking Mesopotamia). In Aramaic, the root means "old". In

Arabic, it means "to get old" or "to be freed (slave)", i.e., to be a libertine. That last meaning seems to be the appropriate one here. It is not clear whether צדיק should be translated "just" , meaning the poet, or "Just", meaning God, צדיקו שך עולם.

21. רכש in Arabic is either "to overturn", used here, in contrast to "to bridle a camel" (Esther 8:14).

Psalm 32

1. Of David, a song of instruction.
Hail to him whose crime is forgiven,
Whose sin is covered up.

א לְדָוִד מַשְׂכִּיל
אַשְׁרֵי נְשׂוּי־פֶּשַׁע
כְּסוּי חֲטָאָה׃

2 Hail to the man
Whose felony the Eternal will not count
Since his spirit is without guile.

ב אַשְׁרֵי־אָדָם
לֹא יַחְשֹׁב יהוָה לוֹ עָוֺן
וְאֵין בְּרוּחוֹ רְמִיָּה׃

3 As long as I was silent,
My bones wasted,
During my roaring
All day long.

ג כִּי הֶחֱרַשְׁתִּי
בָּלוּ עֲצָמָי
בְּשַׁאֲגָתִי
כָּל־הַיּוֹם׃

4 Truly,
Day and night
Your hand is heavy on me
My juices are turned
Into summer dryness, Selah!

ד כִּי |
יוֹמָם וָלַיְלָה
תִּכְבַּד עָלַי יָדֶךָ
נֶהְפַּךְ לְשַׁדִּי
בְּחַרְבֹנֵי קַיִץ סֶלָה׃

5 I shall inform You of my sin,
My crime I did not cover up;
I said:
"I shall confess about my crimes
To the Eternal",
And You forgave the criminality of my sin, Selah!

ה חַטָּאתִי אוֹדִיעֲךָ
וַעֲוֺנִי לֹא־כִסִּיתִי
אָמַרְתִּי
אוֹדֶה עֲלֵי פְשָׁעַי
לַיהוָה
וְאַתָּה נָשָׂאתָ עֲוֺן חַטָּאתִי סֶלָה׃

6 About that
Everyone pious one should pray to You
At the time of finding;
Only that torrential
Great waters,
To him
Will not reach!

ו עַל־זֹאת
יִתְפַּלֵּל כָּל־חָסִיד | אֵלֶיךָ
לְעֵת מְצֹא
רַק לְשֵׁטֶף
מַיִם רַבִּים
אֵלָיו
לֹא יַגִּיעוּ׃

7 You
Are a hiding place for me,
From the enemy You will protect me,
Songs of escape
You will surround me with, Selah!.

ז אַתָּה |
סֵתֶר לִי
מִצַּר תִּצְּרֵנִי
רָנֵּי פַלֵּט
תְּסוֹבְבֵנִי סֶלָה׃

8 "I shall enlighten you
And shall teach you,
This way which you shall go,
I shall counsel upon you my eye.

ח אַשְׂכִּילְךָ |
וְאוֹרְךָ
בְּדֶרֶךְ־זוּ תֵלֵךְ
אִיעֲצָה עָלֶיךָ עֵינִי׃

9 Do not be
Like a horse, a mule,
Without understanding
By bit and bridle his gallop has to be braked,
No one
Could come near you!"

ט אַל־תִּהְיוּ |
כְּסוּס כְּפֶרֶד
אֵין הָבִין
בְּמֶתֶג־וָרֶסֶן עֶדְיוֹ לִבְלוֹם
בַּל
קְרֹב אֵלֶיךָ׃

10 Many sufferings are for the wicked;
But he who trusts in the Eternal,
Kindness
Will surround him.

י רַבִּים מַכְאוֹבִים לָרָשָׁע
וְהַבּוֹטֵחַ בַּיהוָה
חֶסֶד
יְסוֹבְבֶנּוּ׃

11 Rejoice in the Eternal and exult,
Just ones,
And chant,
All who are straight of heart!

יא שִׂמְחוּ בַיהוָה וְגִילוּ
צַדִּיקִים
וְהַרְנִינוּ
כָּל־יִשְׁרֵי־לֵב׃

4. Translating the word לשד, connected with honey (*Num.* 11:8), following Dunash and Rashi. One may connect this with Arabic לסד "to suckle dry".

3. Dr. Levoritz points out that the roaring (an animal sound, not human) is interior, that the poet is silent to the outer world, and that therefore he is wasting.

6. The use of ל in the sense of "that" in לשטף is an Aramaism.

9. Deriving עדי with Dahood from Ugaritic *$\bar{g}$d* "gallopping", same as Arabic אעדי.

Psalm 33

1 Rejoice, o just,
In the Eternal,
Praise is becoming
For the upright.

א רַנְּנוּ צַדִּיקִים
בַּיהוָה
לַיְשָׁרִים
נָאוָה תְהִלָּה׃

2 Thank the Eternal with the lute
With a ten-stringed harp,
Chant to Him.

ב הוֹדוּ לַיהוָה בְּכִנּוֹר
בְּנֵבֶל עָשׂוֹר
זַמְּרוּ־לוֹ׃

3 Sing to Him
A new song,
Play well
The trembling horn.

ג שִׁירוּ־לוֹ
שִׁיר חָדָשׁ
הֵיטִיבוּ נַגֵּן
בִּתְרוּעָה׃

4 Truly straightforward is the Eternal's word
And all His work
Is in faithfulness.

ד כִּי־יָשָׁר דְּבַר־יְהוָה
וְכָל־מַעֲשֵׂהוּ
בֶּאֱמוּנָה׃

5. He loves
Equity and justice;
The Eternal's love
Fills the land.

ה אֹהֵב
צְדָקָה וּמִשְׁפָּט
חֶסֶד יְהוָה
מָלְאָה הָאָרֶץ׃

6 By the Eternal's word
The Heavens were made,
And by the wind of His mouth
All their hosts

ו בִּדְבַר יהוה
שָׁמַיִם נַעֲשׂוּ
וּבְרוּחַ פִּיו
כָּל־צְבָאָם׃

7 The waters of the sea
He fills as in a dike,
He gives the depths into storehouses.

ז כֹּנֵס כַּנֵּד
מֵי הַיָּם
נֹתֵן בְּאֹצָרוֹת תְּהוֹמוֹת׃

8 Fear the Eternal
All the land,
Be in terror before Him
All inhabitants of the soil.

ח יִירְאוּ מֵיהוה
כָּל־הָאָרֶץ
מִמֶּנּוּ יָגוּרוּ
כָּל־יֹשְׁבֵי תֵבֵל׃

9 Certainly He spoke and it was;
He commanded
And it stood fast.

ט כִּי הוּא אָמַר וַיֶּהִי
הוּא־צִוָּה
וַיַּעֲמֹד׃

10 The Eternal thwarted
The counsel of Gentiles,
He annulled
The intentions of nations.

י יהוה
הֵפִיר עֲצַת גּוֹיִם
הֵנִיא
מַחְשְׁבוֹת עַמִּים׃

11 The Eternal's counsel
Will stay forever,
The thoughts of His heart
For all generations.

יא עֲצַת יהוה
לְעוֹלָם תַּעֲמֹד
מַחְשְׁבוֹת לִבּוֹ
לְדֹר וָדֹר׃

יב אַשְׁרֵי הַגּוֹי

12 Hail to the people
Whose God is the Eternal,
The nation
He chose as His inheritance.

אֲשֶׁר־יהוָה אֱלֹהָיו
הָעָם |
בָּחַר לְנַחֲלָה לוֹ׃

13 From Heaven
The Eternal viewed,
He saw
All of mankind.

יג מִשָּׁמַיִם
הִבִּיט יהוָה
רָאָה
אֶת־כָּל־בְּנֵי הָאָדָם׃

14 From His dwelling place He supervised
All earth dwellers.

יד מִמְּכוֹן־שִׁבְתּוֹ הִשְׁגִּיחַ
אֶל כָּל־יֹשְׁבֵי הָאָרֶץ׃

15 Who alone created their hearts
Who understands
All their doings.

טו הַיֹּצֵר יַחַד לִבָּם
הַמֵּבִין
אֶל־כָּל־מַעֲשֵׂיהֶם׃

16 No king
Can be saved by a large army,
The hero
Is not saved by great force.

טז אֵין הַמֶּלֶךְ
נוֹשָׁע בְּרָב־חָיִל
גִּבּוֹר
לֹא־יִנָּצֵל בְּרָב־כֹּחַ׃

17 The horse is deceptive
For victory,
In his great might
He will not escape.

יז שֶׁקֶר הַסּוּס
לִתְשׁוּעָה
וּבְרֹב חֵילוֹ
לֹא יְמַלֵּט׃

18 Behold, the eye of the Eternal
Is on those who fear Him,
Those who yearn for His love.

יח הִנֵּה עֵין יהוה
אֶל־יְרֵאָיו
לַמְיַחֲלִים לְחַסְדּוֹ׃

19 To save their souls from death,
To keep them alive
In famine.

יט לְהַצִּיל מִמָּוֶת נַפְשָׁם
וּלְחַיּוֹתָם
בָּרָעָב׃

20 Our soul
Waits for the Eternal,
Our help and our shield is He.

כ נַפְשֵׁנוּ
חִכְּתָה לַיהוָה
עֶזְרֵנוּ וּמָגִנֵּנוּ הוּא׃

21 Truly in Him
Our heart will rejoice,
For in His holy Name we trust.

כא כִּי־בוֹ
יִשְׂמַח לִבֵּנוּ
כִּי בְשֵׁם קָדְשׁוֹ בָטָחְנוּ׃

22 May Your love, Eternal, be over us,
As
We are yearning for You!

כב יְהִי־חַסְדְּךָ יהוָה עָלֵינוּ
כַּאֲשֶׁר
יִחַלְנוּ לָךְ׃

Psalm 34

1 By David.
When he disguised his mind
Before Abimelech
Who chased him away,
And he went.

א לְדָוִד
בְּשַׁנּוֹתוֹ אֶת־טַעְמוֹ
לִפְנֵי אֲבִימֶלֶךְ
וַיְגָרְשֵׁהוּ
וַיֵּלַךְ׃

2 I shall bless the Eternal all the time,
Always
His praise is in my mouth.

ב אֲבָרְכָה אֶת־יְהוָה בְּכָל־עֵת
תָּמִיד
תְּהִלָּתוֹ בְּפִי׃

3 In the Eternal
My soul glories itself,
May the meek hear and rejoice.

ג בַּיהוָה
תִּתְהַלֵּל נַפְשִׁי
יִשְׁמְעוּ עֲנָוִים וְיִשְׂמָחוּ׃

4 Greatly praise the Eternal with me,
Let us extol His name together.

ד גַּדְּלוּ לַיהוָה אִתִּי
וּנְרוֹמְמָה שְׁמוֹ יַחְדָּו׃

5 I sought the Eternal and He answered me,
And from all that I feared
He saved me.

ה דָּרַשְׁתִּי אֶת־יְהוָה וְעָנָנִי
וּמִכָּל־מְגוּרוֹתַי
הִצִּילָנִי׃

6 Gaze up to Him and shine,
Their faces
Never shall blush.

ו הִבִּיטוּ אֵלָיו וְנָהָרוּ
וּפְנֵיהֶם
אַל־יֶחְפָּרוּ׃

7 This poor man called
And the Eternal did hear,
From all his afflictions
He rescued him.

ז זֶה עָנִי קָרָא
וַיהוָה שָׁמֵעַ
וּמִכָּל־צָרוֹתָיו
הוֹשִׁיעוֹ׃

8 The Eternal's angel camps around those fearing Him
And extricates them.

ח חֹנֶה מַלְאַךְ־יְהוָה סָבִיב לִירֵאָיו
וַיְחַלְּצֵם׃

9 Understand and discern
That the Eternal is good,
Hail to the man
Who finds refuge in Him.

ט טַעֲמוּ וּרְאוּ
כִּי־טוֹב יְהוָה
אַשְׁרֵי הַגֶּבֶר
יֶחֱסֶה־בּוֹ׃

10 Fear the Eternal, His holy people,
Certainly there is no want
For those who fear Him.

י יְראוּ אֶת־יְהוָה קְדֹשָׁיו
כִּי אֵין מַחְסוֹר
לִירֵאָיו׃

11 Lion cubs
May be destitute and hungry
But the seekers of the Eternal
Will not miss anything good.

יא כְּפִירִים
רָשׁוּ וְרָעֵבוּ
וְדֹרְשֵׁי יְהוָה
לֹא־יַחְסְרוּ כָל־טוֹב׃

12 Come, sons,
Listen to me,
The fear of the Eternal
I shall teach you.

יב לְכוּ־בָנִים
שִׁמְעוּ־לִי
יִרְאַת יְהוָה
אֲלַמֶּדְכֶם׃

13 Who is the man
Who desires Life,
Who loves days
To see the Good?

יג מִי־הָאִישׁ
הֶחָפֵץ חַיִּים
אֹהֵב יָמִים
לִרְאוֹת טוֹב׃

14 Guard your tongue from evil
And your lips
From talking deceit.

יד נְצֹר לְשׁוֹנְךָ מֵרָע
וּשְׂפָתֶיךָ
מִדַּבֵּר מִרְמָה

15 Shun evil,
But do good,
Desire peace and pursue it.

טו סוּר מֵרָע
וַעֲשֵׂה־טוֹב
בַּקֵּשׁ שָׁלוֹם וְרָדְפֵהוּ׃

16 The Eternal's eyes
Are on the just ones,
And His ears
On their supplications.

טז עֵינֵי יהוה
אֶל־צַדִּיקִים
וְאָזְנָיו
אֶל־שַׁוְעָתָם׃

17 The Eternal's face is
Against evildoers
To exterminate their names from the Land.

יז פְּנֵי יהוה
בְּעֹשֵׂי רָע
לְהַכְרִית מֵאֶרֶץ זִכְרָם

18 Cry out, the Eternal is hearing,
From all their distress
He rescues them.

יח צָעֲקוּ וַיהוָה שָׁמֵעַ
וּמִכָּל־צָרוֹתָם
הִצִּילָם׃

19 The Eternal is close
To the broken hearted,
Those of crushed spirit He rescues.

יט קָרוֹב יהוה
לְנִשְׁבְּרֵי־לֵב
וְאֶת־דַּכְּאֵי־רוּחַ יוֹשִׁיעַ׃

20 Many are
The harms of the just one,
But from all of them
The Eternal will save him.

כ רַבּוֹת
רָעוֹת צַדִּיק
וּמִכֻּלָּם
יַצִּילֶנּוּ יהוה׃

21 He watches over all his bones,
Not one of them
Will be broken.

כא שֹׁמֵר כָּל־עַצְמוֹתָיו
אַחַת מֵהֵנָּה
לֹא נִשְׁבָּרָה׃

22 Wickedness kills the sinner;
The haters of the just will be found guilty.

כב תְּמוֹתֵת רָשָׁע רָעָה
וְשֹׂנְאֵי צַדִּיק יֶאְשָׁמוּ׃

23 The Eternal is redeeming
The soul of His servants.
Any who trust in Him
Never will be found guilty.

כג פּוֹדֶה יהוה
נֶפֶשׁ עֲבָדָיו
וְלֹא יֶאְשְׁמוּ
כָּל־הַחֹסִים בּוֹ׃

1. Like most alphabetic poems in Psalms, this is didactic. Except for the multiple alphabet in Ps. 119, no alphabet is complete. Here the ubiquitous letter ו is missing.

3. נפש as verbal stem means "to take a breath", it stands for "life" that distinguishes living things from inanimate material. Animals also have נפש , but for them it does not imply consciousness.

6. נהר as “shine, radiate” is an Aramaism.

7. שָׁמֵ֑עַ is the pausal form of past שָׁמַע.

13. The Good is eternal Life

14. As always, the Land is the place of the Future Life.

Psalm 35

1 Of David.
Eternal, please fight
Those who fight me,
Make war
Against those who war against me!

א לְדָוִ֨ד ׀
רִיבָ֣ה יְ֭הוָה
אֶת־יְרִיבַ֑י
לְ֝חַ֗ם
אֶת־לֹחֲמָֽי׃

2 Hold tight buckler and shield,
And arise
In my help.

ב הַחֲזֵ֣ק מָגֵ֣ן וְצִנָּ֑ה
וְ֝ק֗וּמָה
בְּעֶזְרָתִֽי׃

3 Arm javelin and socket
Against my pursuers;
Tell me:
"I am your succor."

ג וְהָ֘רֵ֤ק חֲנִ֣ית וּ֭סְגֹר
לִקְרַ֣את רֹדְפָ֑י
אֱמֹ֥ר לְ֝נַפְשִׁ֗י
יְשֻׁעָתֵ֥ךְ אָֽנִי׃

4 Those who plot against me,
Shall be aghast and ashamed.
They shall retreat and be confounded,
Those who plan
Evil for me.

ד יֵבֹ֣שׁוּ וְיִכָּלְמוּ֮
מְבַקְשֵׁ֪י נַ֫פְשִׁ֥י
יִסֹּ֣גוּ אָח֣וֹר וְיַחְפְּר֑וּ
חֹ֝שְׁבֵ֗י
רָעָתִֽי׃

5 May they be
Like chaff before the wind,
And the Eternal's angel pushes.

ה יִֽהְי֗וּ
כְּמֹ֥ץ לִפְנֵי־ר֑וּחַ
וּמַלְאַ֖ךְ יְהוָ֣ה דּוֹחֶֽה׃

6 May their path be
Darkness and destruction,
And the Eternal's angel
Pursues them.

ו יְהִֽי־דַרְכָּ֗ם
חֹ֥שֶׁךְ וַחֲלַקְלַקֹּ֑ת
וּמַלְאַ֥ךְ יְ֝הוָ֗ה
רֹדְפָֽם׃

7 For without cause they hid for me
Their trap in a pit-fall;
Without cause
They dug against me.

ז כִּֽי־חִנָּ֣ם טָֽמְנוּ־לִ֭י
שַׁ֣חַת רִשְׁתָּ֑ם
חִ֝נָּ֗ם
חָפְר֥וּ לְנַפְשִֽׁי׃

8 May catastrophe come over him,
Unforeseen,
His trap, hidden by himself, shall catch him,
May he fall into it
In catastrophe.

ח תְּבוֹאֵ֣הוּ שׁוֹאָה֮
לֹֽא־יֵ֫דָ֥ע
וְרִשְׁתּ֣וֹ אֲשֶׁר־טָמַ֣ן תִּלְכְּד֑וֹ
בְּ֝שׁוֹאָ֗ה
יִפָּל־בָּֽהּ׃

9 But I
Shall rejoice in the Eternal,
Will delight
In His rescue.

ט וְ֭נַפְשִׁי
תָּגִ֣יל בַּיהוָ֑ה
תָּ֝שִׂ֗ישׂ
בִּישׁוּעָתֽוֹ׃

10 All my bones shall say:
"Eternal,
Who is like You?
Savior of the deprived
From one stronger than him,
And the deprived and poor
From the one robbing him."

י כָּ֥ל עַצְמוֹתַ֨י ׀ תֹּאמַרְנָה֮
יְהוָ֗המִ֥י כָ֫מ֥וֹךָ
מַצִּ֣יל עָ֭נִי
מֵחָזָ֣ק מִמֶּ֑נּוּ
וְעָנִ֥י וְ֝אֶבְי֗וֹן
מִגֹּזְלֽוֹ׃

11 Dismembering witnesses
Do arise.
They interrogate me
About things I know nothing.

יא יְקוּמוּן
עֵדֵי חָמָס
אֲשֶׁר לֹא־יָדַעְתִּי
יִשְׁאָלוּנִי׃

12 They pay me back evil
For good,
They leave me deprived.

יב יְשַׁלְּמוּנִי רָעָה
תַּחַת טוֹבָה
שְׁכוֹל לְנַפְשִׁי׃

13 But as for me, when they were sick,
My garment was sackcloth;
I tormented myself by a fast,
But my prayer
Returned to my bosom.

יג וַאֲנִי | בַּחֲלוֹתָם
לְבוּשִׁי שָׂק
עִנֵּיתִי בַצּוֹם נַפְשִׁי
וּתְפִלָּתִי
עַל־חֵיקִי תָשׁוּב׃

14 As for a friend, one of my brothers,
I wandered about,
Like a mourner for his mother
Black I was, prostrate.

יד כְּרֵעַ כְּאָח לִי
הִתְהַלָּכְתִּי
כַּאֲבֶל־אֵם
קֹדֵר שַׁחוֹתִי׃

15 When I was limping
They rejoiced and assembled,
Muggers assembled against me,
I knew nothing,
They tore and were never quiet.

טו וּבְצַלְעִי
שָׂמְחוּ וְנֶאֱסָפוּ
נֶאֶסְפוּ עָלַי נֵכִים
וְלֹא יָדַעְתִּי
קָרְעוּ וְלֹא־דָמּוּ׃

16 Deviants
The mockers in a circle,
To gnash their teeth against me!

טז בְּחַנְפֵי
לַעֲגֵי מָעוֹג
חָרֹק עָלַי שִׁנֵּימוֹ׃

17 Master,
How much will You look at,
Please let recover my soul
From their sudden onslaught,
From those young lions
My only one.

יז אֲדֹנָי
כַּמָּה תִּרְאֶה
הָשִׁיבָה נַפְשִׁי
מִשֹּׁאֵיהֶם
מִכְּפִירִים
יְחִידָתִי׃

18 I shall thank You
In a great assembly,
Before a huge crowd I shall praise You.

יח אוֹדְךָ
בְּקָהָל רָב
בְּעַם עָצוּם אֲהַלְלֶךָּ׃

19 My enemies shall not gloat over me by lies,
Nor twinkle eyes
Those who hate me without cause

יט אַל־יִשְׂמְחוּ־לִי אֹיְבַי שֶׁקֶר
שֹׂנְאַי חִנָּם
יִקְרְצוּ־עָיִן׃

20 For they will not talk of peace,
About the quiet of the land.
They do design
Treacherous ideas.

כ כִּי לֹא שָׁלוֹם יְדַבֵּרוּ
וְעַל רִגְעֵי־אֶרֶץ
דִּבְרֵי מִרְמוֹת
יַחֲשֹׁבוּן׃

21 They widen their mouths against me;
They say,
"Hey, Hey,
Our eyes saw."

כא וַיַּרְחִיבוּ עָלַי פִּיהֶם
אָמְרוּ
הֶאָח | הֶאָח
רָאֲתָה עֵינֵינוּ׃

22 You saw, Eternal, Be not be silent; My Master, Do not be far from me!	כב רָאִיתָה יְהוָה אַל־תֶּחֱרַשׁ אֲדֹנָי אַל־תִּרְחַק מִמֶּנִּי׃
23 Awake and be roused For my judgment, My God and Master, to my suit.	כג הָעִירָה וְהָקִיצָה לְמִשְׁפָּטִי אֱלֹהַי וַאדֹנָי לְרִיבִי׃
24 Eternal, my God, Judge me according my deserts, Let them not gloat over me.	כד שָׁפְטֵנִי כְצִדְקְךָ יְהוָה אֱלֹהָי אַל־יִשְׂמְחוּ־לִי׃
25 They shall not say in their hearts: "Hey, us!" They shall not say: "We swallowed him up!"	כה אַל־יֹאמְרוּ בְלִבָּם הֶאָח נַפְשֵׁנוּ אַל־יֹאמְרוּ בִּלַּעֲנוּהוּ׃
26 Those who gloat over my calamity Shall be aghast and ashamed together, They shall wear shame and dishonor Who twist against me.	כו יֵבֹשׁוּ וְיַחְפְּרוּ ׀ יַחְדָּו שְׂמֵחֵי רָעָתִי יִלְבְּשׁוּ־בֹשֶׁת וּכְלִמָּה הַמַּגְדִּילִים עָלָי׃
27 Those desiring my justification Shall sing and enjoy, They will always say :"The Eternal shall be exalted He Who desires The well-being of His servant!"	כז יָרֹנּוּ וְיִשְׂמְחוּ חֲפֵצֵי צִדְקִי וְיֹאמְרוּ תָמִיד יִגְדַּל יְהוָה הֶחָפֵץ שְׁלוֹם עַבְדּוֹ׃
28 And my tongue Shall pronounce Your justice, All day long Your praise!	כח וּלְשׁוֹנִי תֶּהְגֶּה צִדְקֶךָ כָּל־הַיּוֹם תְּהִלָּתֶךָ׃

3. The word סגור was considered problematic and a preferred target of textual emendators until it appeared in the war-scroll from Qumran (5:7) with the clear meaning of "socket of the javelin". When Nebuchadnezzar exiled all חרש ומסגר (2Kings 24:14), he did not take "manufacturers and plumbers" as these words denote in modern Hebrew, but the "makers of javelins and their sockets", i.e., all the makers of infantry weapons.

7. שחת is a pit-fall used to trap animals.

8. שואה is a sudden, unforeseen disaster; possibly a tornado or hurricane, but also all other kind of catastrophe.

9. נפש "breathing", is not only "soul" but also "person, personality", and, for humans, "consciousness". All these meanings are used in this Psalm at different places.

10. This is one of two occurrences in the Masoretic Bible where כל "all" is pronounced *kal* and not *kol;* the other occurrence is Proverbs 19:7

11. Reading חמס parallel to Arabic חׄמס "to tear into pieces".

12. A person may be left childless, not a soul. Here the reference is to Arabic תׄכל "to be deprived of a friend".

15. In modern Hebrew, נכים are "handicapped, disabled persons". This meaning is derived from our verse here, 6if the word is taken from the Arabic stem נכא ,נכי "to be wounded". But it is better to consider the word pure Hebrew, from the root הכה "to hit"; they are hit-men or muggers.

16. With H. L. Fleischer, I see in the Hebrew חנף the equivalent of the identical root in Arabic, meaning "To be contorted (in Arabic mostly: legs or feet), to turn to one side".

26. גדל in Hebrew means not only "to grow" but also "to braid, to twist" (cf. Deut. 22:12). Mary Magdalen appears in the Talmud as *Miryam, megaddela naša* "Miryam, the braider of women's hair" (*Ḥagiga* 4b).

Psalm 36

1 For the Director,
By the servant of the Eternal, By David.

א לַמְנַצֵּחַ ׀
לְעֶבֶד־יְהוָֹה לְדָוִד׃

2 Crime inspires the wicked
In his heart,
No fear of God
Before his eyes.

ב נְאֻם־פֶּשַׁע לָרָשָׁע
בְּקֶרֶב לִבִּי
אֵין־פַּחַד אֱלֹהִים
לְנֶגֶד עֵינָיו׃

3 Very smooth it is before him in his eyes,
To find his hateful felony.

ג כִּי־הֶחֱלִיק אֵלָיו בְּעֵינָיו
לִמְצֹא עֲוֺנוֹ לִשְׂנֹא׃

4 Words of his mouth
Are evil and deceit
He has stopped thinking of betterment.

ד דִּבְרֵי־פִיו
אָוֶן וּמִרְמָה
חָדַל לְהַשְׂכִּיל לְהֵיטִיב׃

5 On his couch he invents
Evil;
He embarks
On the no-good way;
Wickedness
He does not disdain.

ה אָוֶן ׀
יַחְשֹׁב עַל־מִשְׁכָּבוֹ
יִתְיַצֵּב
עַל־דֶּרֶךְ לֹא־טוֹב
רָע
לֹא יִמְאָס׃

6 Eternal,
In the Heaven is Your love,
Your truth
Reaches to the skies.

ו יהוה
בְּהַשָּׁמַיִם חַסְדֶּךָ
אֱמוּנָתְךָ
עַד־שְׁחָקִים׃

7 Your salvation is like mighty mountains,
Your justice
A great abyss,
You save man and animal, Eternal.

ז צִדְקָתְךָ ׀ כְּהַרְרֵי־אֵל
מִשְׁפָּטֶיךָ
תְּהוֹם רַבָּה
אָדָם וּבְהֵמָה תוֹשִׁיעַ יְיָ׃

8 God, how precious is Your love.
And mankind
Is taking shelter
In the shadow of Your wings.

ח מַה־יָּקָר חַסְדְּךָ אֱלֹהִים
וּבְנֵי אָדָם
בְּצֵל כְּנָפֶיךָ
יֶחֱסָיוּן׃

9 They drink their fill
From Your house's fat,
And the river of Your delicacies waters them.

ט יִרְוְיֻן
מִדֶּשֶׁן בֵּיתֶךָ
וְנַחַל עֲדָנֶיךָ תַשְׁקֵם׃

10 Truly, with You
Is the fountain of Life,
In Your brightness
We shall see light.

י כִּי־עִמְּךָ
מְקוֹר חַיִּים
בְּאוֹרְךָ
נִרְאֶה־אוֹר׃

11 Draw Your love
Over those who know You,
And Your salvation
Over the ones straight of heart.

יא מְשֹׁךְ חַסְדְּךָ
לְיֹדְעֶיךָ
וְצִדְקָתְךָ
לְיִשְׁרֵי־לֵב׃

12 Do not let me be overtaken	יב אַל־תְּבוֹאֵנִי
By the foot of pride,	רֶגֶל גַּאֲוָה
The hand of the wicked	וְיַד־רְשָׁעִים
Shall not chase me away.	אַל־תְּנִדֵנִי׃
13 There they will fall.	יג שָׁם נָפְלוּ
The perpetrators of evil,	פֹּעֲלֵי אָוֶן
They will be pushed,	דֹּחוּ
And will not be able to rise.	וְלֹא־יָכְלוּ קוּם׃

2. For י (in לבי) as suffix of the third person singular possessive, cf. *Ps*. 24:4.

5. חשב means not only thinking, but thinking new thoughts, inventing (Ex. 31:4).

6. The form בְּהַשָּׁמַיִם, in contrast to the compressed form בַּשָּׁמַיִם is otherwise found only in Rabbinic Hebrew. It emphasizes the definite article, the poet talks of the ideal, not the physical, Heaven.

10. It would be easy to translate: "In Your light, we see the light", but this not being a repetitive use of a clause, we should look for related meanings in cognate languages. Therefore, I prefer to link the first occurrence of אור to Accadic *uru, ulu* "the luxuriance of oil", or also Arabic אור "intensity of fire".

Psalm 37

1 By David.
Do not get inflamed about evildoers,
Do not be envious
Of workers of crimes.

א לְדָוִ֨ד ׀
אַל־תִּתְחַ֥ר בַּמְּרֵעִ֑ים
אַל־תְּ֝קַנֵּ֗א
בְּעֹשֵׂ֥י עַוְלָֽה׃

2 For like grass
Soon they will dry up
And like the green meadow
They will wilt.

ב כִּ֣י כֶ֭חָצִיר
מְהֵרָ֣ה יִמָּ֑לוּ
וּכְיֶ֥רֶק דֶּ֝֗שֶׁא
יִבּוֹלֽוּן׃

3 Trust in the Eternal
And do good,
Dwell in the Land
And observe in faith.

ג בְּטַ֣ח בַּ֭יהוה
וַעֲשֵׂה־ט֑וֹב
שְׁכָן־אֶ֝֗רֶץ
וּרְעֵ֥ה אֱמוּנָֽה׃

4 Enjoy yourself in the Eternal,
And He will give to you
Your heart's desires.

ד וְהִתְעַנַּ֥ג עַל־יהוָ֑ה
וְיִֽתֶּן־לְ֝ךָ֗
מִשְׁאֲלֹ֥ת לִבֶּֽךָ׃

5 Roll over to the Eternal your ways,
Trust in Him
And He will act

ה גּ֣וֹל עַל־יהוָ֣ה דַּרְכֶּ֑ךָ
וּבְטַ֥ח עָ֝לָ֗יו
וְה֣וּא יַעֲשֶֽׂה׃
6

6 And make your salvation shine like light
And your right
Like noontime.

ו וְהוֹצִ֣יא כָא֣וֹר צִדְקֶ֑ךָ
וּ֝מִשְׁפָּטֶ֗ךָ
כַּֽצָּהֳרָֽיִם׃

7 Be silent in the Eternal,
And hope in Him,
Do not get inflamed
About one who succeeds,
The man
Executing tricks.

ז דּ֤וֹם ׀ לַיהוה
וְהִתְח֬וֹלֵֽל ל֗וֹ
אַל־תִּ֭תְחַר
בְּמַצְלִ֣יחַ דַּרְכּ֑וֹ
בְּ֝אִ֗ישׁ
עֹשֶׂ֥ה מְזִמּֽוֹת׃

8 Let up from rage,
Abandon fury,
Do not get inflamed
Surely to harm.

ח הֶ֣רֶף מֵ֭אַף
וַעֲזֹ֣ב חֵמָ֑ה
אַל־תִּ֝תְחַ֗ר
אַךְ־לְהָרֵֽעַ׃

9 For evildoers will be cut off,
But those who hope for the Eternal,
They will inherit the Land.

ט כִּֽי־מְרֵעִ֥ים יִכָּרֵת֑וּן
וְקֹוֵ֥י יהוה
הֵ֝֗מָּה יִֽירְשׁוּ־אָֽרֶץ׃

10 In a little while
There is no wicked one,
You watch his place and he is no more.

י וְע֣וֹד מְ֭עַט
וְאֵ֣ין רָשָׁ֑ע
וְהִתְבּוֹנַ֖נְתָּ עַל־מְקוֹמ֣וֹ וְאֵינֶֽנּוּ׃

11 But the meek will inherit the Land,
They will enjoy themselves
In immense peace.

יא וַעֲנָוִ֥ים יִֽירְשׁוּ־אָ֑רֶץ
וְ֝הִתְעַנְּג֗וּ
עַל־רֹ֥ב שָׁלֽוֹם׃

12 The wicked plots
Against the just
And gnashes his teeth against him.

יב זֹמֵם רָשָׁע
לַצַּדִּיק
וְחֹרֵק עָלָיו שִׁנָּיו׃

13 The Almighty laughs at him,
For He saw
That his day will come.

יג אֲדֹנָי יִשְׂחַק־לוֹ
כִּי־רָאָה
כִּי־יָבֹא יוֹמוֹ׃

14 The wicked ones drew
A sword
And stepped on their bow
To fell
The deprived and downtrodden,
To slaughter
Those of straight ways.

יד חֶרֶב |
פָּתְחוּ רְשָׁעִים
וְדָרְכוּ קַשְׁתָּם
לְהַפִּיל
עָנִי וְאֶבְיוֹן
לִטְבוֹחַ
יִשְׁרֵי־דָרֶךְ׃

15 Their sword
Shall come into their own hearts
And their bows
Shall be broken.

טו חַרְבָּם
תָּבוֹא בְלִבָּם
וְקַשְּׁתוֹתָם
תִּשָּׁבַרְנָה׃

16 A little is better
For the just
Than riches
For the mighty wicked.

טז טוֹב מְעַט
לַצַּדִּיק
מֵהֲמוֹן
רְשָׁעִים רַבִּים׃

17 Certainly the arms of the wicked ones
Will be broken,
For the Eternal sustains the just.

יז כִּי זְרוֹעוֹת רְשָׁעִים
תִּשָּׁבַרְנָה
וְסוֹמֵךְ צַדִּיקִים יהוה׃

18 The Eternal understands
The days of the simple ones;
Their legacy
Will endure forever.

יח יוֹדֵעַ יהוה
יְמֵי תְמִימִם
וְנַחֲלָתָם
לְעוֹלָם תִּהְיֶה׃

19 They will not be ashamed
In times of distress,
But in days of famine they will be sated.

יט לֹא־יֵבֹשׁוּ
בְּעֵת רָעָה
וּבִימֵי רְעָבוֹן יִשְׂבָּעוּ׃

20 But the wicked ones will be lost
The enemies of the Eternal,
Like the pride of fresh meadows
Will be finished, in smoke finished.

כ כִּי רְשָׁעִים | יֹאבֵדוּ
וְאֹיְבֵי יהוה
כִּיקַר כָּרִים
כָּלוּ בֶעָשָׁן כָּלוּ׃

21 The wicked borrows
And will not repay
But the just
Grants and gives.

כא לֹוֶה רָשָׁע
וְלֹא יְשַׁלֵּם
וְצַדִּיק
חוֹנֵן וְנוֹתֵן׃

22 Certainly, those who bless him
Will inherit the Land
But those who curse him
Will be cut off.

כב כִּי מְבֹרָכָיו
יִרְשׁוּ אָרֶץ
וּמְקֻלָּלָיו
יִכָּרֵתוּ׃

23 From the Eternal
The steps of man are well founded.
His path he will choose.

כג מֵיהוה
מִצְעֲדֵי־גֶבֶר כּוֹנָנוּ
וְדַרְכּוֹ יֶחְפָּץ׃

24 When he falls, he will not be carried off;
Certainly the Eternal
Supports his hand.

כד כִּי־יִפֹּל לֹא־יוּטָל
כִּי־יְיָ
סוֹמֵךְ יָדוֹ׃

25 I was a lad,
Now I am old,
But I never saw
A virtuous man abandoned
And his seed
Begging for bread

כה נַעַר ׀ הָיִיתִי
גַּם־זָקַנְתִּי
וְלֹא־רָאִיתִי
צַדִּיק נֶעֱזָב
וְזַרְעוֹ
מְבַקֶּשׁ־לָחֶם׃

26 All day long
He grants and lends out
And his seed
Is a blessing.

כו כָּל־הַיּוֹם
חוֹנֵן וּמַלְוֶה
וְזַרְעוֹ
לִבְרָכָה׃

27 Turn from evil
And do good,
Then you will dwell for eternity.

כז סוּר מֵרָע
וַעֲשֵׂה־טוֹב
וּשְׁכֹן לְעוֹלָם׃

28 Truly, the Eternal
Loves justice,
He will not abandon His pious,
Forever they are protected;
But the wickeds' seed will be felled.

כח כִּי יהוֹה ׀
אֹהֵב מִשְׁפָּט
וְלֹא־יַעֲזֹב אֶת־חֲסִידָיו
לְעוֹלָם נִשְׁמָרוּ
וְזֶרַע רְשָׁעִים נִכְרָת׃

29 The just will inherit the Land
And eternally dwell in it.

כט צַדִּיקִים יִירְשׁוּ־אָרֶץ
וְיִשְׁכְּנוּ לָעַד עָלֶיהָ׃

30 The mouth of the righteous
Articulates wisdom,
His tongue
Is to speak justice.

ל פִּי־צַדִּיק
יֶהְגֶּה חָכְמָה
וּלְשׁוֹנוֹ
תְּדַבֵּר מִשְׁפָּט׃

31 The teachings of his God are in his heart,
Never will his steps stumble.

לא תּוֹרַת אֱלֹהָיו בְּלִבּוֹ
לֹא תִמְעַד אֲשֻׁרָיו׃

32 The criminal watches out
For the just
And desires
To kill him.

לב צוֹפֶה רָשָׁע
לַצַּדִּיק
וּמְבַקֵּשׁ
לַהֲמִיתוֹ׃

33 The Eternal
Will not abandon him to his hand
And will not find him guilty
When he is judged.

לג יהוה
לֹא־יַעַזְבֶנּוּ בְיָדוֹ
וְלֹא יַרְשִׁיעֶנּוּ
בְּהִשָּׁפְטוֹ׃

34 Call on the Eternal,
Keep to His way,
Then He will raise you,
To inherit the Land,
You will witness the extinction of the wicked.

לד קַוֵּה אֶל־יהוֹה ׀
וּשְׁמֹר דַּרְכּוֹ
וִירוֹמִמְךָ
לָרֶשֶׁת אָרֶץ
בְּהִכָּרֵת רְשָׁעִים תִּרְאֶה׃

35 I saw
A powerfully wicked one
Spreading out his roots
Like an original tree, lushly green;

לה רָאִיתִי
רָשָׁע עָרִיץ
וּמִתְעָרֶה
כְּאֶזְרָח רַעֲנָן׃

36 But he passed
And is no more,
I was looking for him
But he was not to be found.

לו וַיַּעֲבֹר
וְהִנֵּה אֵינֶנּוּ
וָאֲבַקְשֵׁהוּ
וְלֹא נִמְצָא׃

37 Watch uprightness,
Look out for straightness,
Then peace is a man's finality.

לז שְׁמָר־תָּם
וּרְאֵה יָשָׁר
כִּי־אַחֲרִית לְאִישׁ שָׁלוֹם׃

38 But the sinners
Will be destroyed together,
The finality of the wicked is extinction.

לח וּפֹשְׁעִים
נִשְׁמְדוּ יַחְדָּו
אַחֲרִית רְשָׁעִים נִכְרָתָה׃

39 The victory of the just
Is from the Eternal,
Their stronghold
In times of distress.

לט וּתְשׁוּעַת צַדִּיקִים
מֵיהוָה
מָעוּזָּם
בְּעֵת צָרָה׃

40 The Eternal will help them, make them escape,
Make them escape from the wicked,
And save them,
For they trusted in Him!

מ וַיַּעְזְרֵם יהוה וַיְפַלְּטֵם
יְפַלְּטֵם מֵרְשָׁעִים
וְיוֹשִׁיעֵם
כִּי חָסוּ בוֹ׃

Like all alphabetic poems, this one is didactic and more a collection of wisdom sayings. The alphabetic groups mostly appear in pairs of two verses.

1. חרה means to make a fire to grill something; חררה is bread made over the grill in contrast to פת made in the oven. The modern meaning of מתחרה "to compete" comes from this Psalm.

14. The use of the verb פתח in the sense "to draw the sword" is an Accadism.

16. המון "a lot" in the sense of "money" is found also Prov. 5:9. רבים does double duty, both for "money" and "wicked" (Ibn Ezra). A money-belt is called המין in Aramaic, Arabic, and Farsi.

20. כר is a word for a meadow of young grasses.

25. Instead of "I never saw", A. Berliner suggests Mishnaic "I never could understand". But v. 26 negates this interpretation.

29. It is clear from this verse that the Land is the Land of the Living, the place of Eternal Life.

32. Verse 33 shows that here the "wicked" is Satan.

35. אזרח has been defined by Menaḥem ibn Saruq and all following authors as "something or somebody growing in the soil in which it was originally planted", meaning for humans "indigenous" and for trees "not transplanted". For our verse here one might think also of Arabic זָרוּח "small hill".

Psalm 38

1 A Psalm by David, to remember.

א מִזְמ֖וֹר לְדָוִ֣ד לְהַזְכִּֽיר׃

2 Eternal,
Do not reform me in Your anger,
Nor in Your wrath punish me!

ב יהוה
אַל־בְּקֶצְפְּךָ֥ תוֹכִיחֵ֑נִי
וּבַחֲמָתְךָ֥ תְיַסְּרֵֽנִי׃

3 Certainly, Your arrows
Stuck in me,
Your hand rested on me.

ג כִּֽי־חִ֭צֶּיךָ
נִ֣חֲתוּ בִ֑י
וַתִּנְחַ֖ת עָלַ֣י יָדֶֽךָ׃

4 Nothing is whole in my flesh
Because of Your rage,
No peace is in my bones
Because of my sin.

ד אֵין־מְתֹ֣ם בִּ֭בְשָׂרִי
מִפְּנֵ֣י זַעְמֶ֑ךָ
אֵין־שָׁל֥וֹם בַּ֝עֲצָמַ֗י
מִפְּנֵ֥י חַטָּאתִֽי׃

5 Truly, my sins
Passed over my head,
Like a heavy load
They are more than I can bear.

ה כִּ֣י עֲ֭וֺנֹתַי
עָבְר֣וּ רֹאשִׁ֑י
כְּמַשָּׂ֥א כָ֝בֵ֗ד
יִכְבְּד֥וּ מִמֶּֽנִּי׃

6 My sores
Stink, they fester,
Because of
My folly.

ו הִבְאִ֣ישׁוּ נָ֭מַקּוּ
חַבּוּרֹתָ֑י
מִ֝פְּנֵ֗י
אִוַּלְתִּֽי׃

7 I cringe, I am flattened completely.
All day long
I am roving in gloom.

ז נַעֲוֵ֣יתִי שַׁחֹ֣תִי עַד־מְאֹ֑ד
כָּל־הַ֝יּ֗וֹם
קֹדֵ֥ר הִלָּֽכְתִּי׃

8 Truly, my kidneys
Are full of burning,
Nothing is whole
In my flesh!

ח כִּֽי־כְ֭סָלַי
מָלְא֣וּ נִקְלֶ֑ה
וְאֵ֥ין מְ֝תֹ֗ם
בִּבְשָׂרִֽי׃

9 I am weakened and totally crushed;
I am shouting
The neighing of my heart!

ט נְפוּג֣וֹתִי וְנִדְכֵּ֣יתִי עַד־מְאֹ֑ד
שָׁ֝אַ֗גְתִּי
מִֽנַּהֲמַ֥ת לִבִּֽי׃

10 Almighty,
Before You is all my desire,
And my sighing
Is not hidden from You!

י אֲֽדֹנָ֗י
נֶגְדְּךָ֥ כָל־תַּאֲוָתִ֑י
וְ֝אַנְחָתִ֗י
מִמְּךָ֥ לֹא־נִסְתָּֽרָה׃

11 My heart is intensely burning,
My force has left me,
The light of my eyes also
Is not with me.

יא לִבִּ֣י סְ֭חַרְחַר
עֲזָבַ֣נִי כֹחִ֑י
א֥וֹר עֵינַ֥י גַּם־הֵ֝֗ם
אֵ֣ין אִתִּֽי׃

12 My lovers
And friends
Are stopped opposite my plagues,
But my relatives
Stand at a distance.

יב אֹהֲבַ֨י ׀
וְרֵעַ֗י
מִנֶּ֣גֶד נִגְעִ֣י יַעֲמֹ֑דוּ
וּ֝קְרוֹבַ֗י
מֵרָחֹ֥ק עָמָֽדוּ׃

13 Those who are out to get me;
Put up traps.
Those who want my downfall
Are spreading falsehoods.
Treachery
They ponder all day long!

יג וַיְנַקְשׁ֤וּ ׀
מְבַקְשֵׁ֬י נַפְשִׁ֗י
וְדֹרְשֵׁ֣י רָ֭עָתִי
דִּבְּר֣וּ הַוּ֑וֹת
וּ֝מִרְמ֗וֹת
כָּל־הַיּ֥וֹם יֶהְגּֽוּ׃

14 But I am like a deaf man
Who cannot hear,
And like a dumb person
Who will not open his mouth!

יד וַאֲנִ֣י כְ֭חֵרֵשׁ
לֹ֣א אֶשְׁמָ֑ע
וּ֝כְאִלֵּ֗ם
לֹ֣א יִפְתַּח־פִּֽיו׃

15 I shall be like a man
Who cannot hear,
And in whose mouth are no
Reproofs.

טו וָאֱהִ֗י כְּ֭אִישׁ
אֲשֶׁ֣ר לֹא־שֹׁמֵ֑עַ
וְאֵ֥ין בְּ֝פִ֗יו
תּוֹכָחֽוֹת׃

16 Truly, in You, Eternal, I hope,
You will answer,
Almighty, my God.

טז כִּֽי־לְךָ֣ יהוָ֣ה הוֹחָ֑לְתִּי
אַתָּ֥ה תַ֝עֲנֶ֗ה
אֲדֹנָ֥י אֱלֹהָֽי׃

17 Truly, I said:
"Lest they should gloat over me,
When my feet totter
They would triumph over me!".

יז כִּֽי־אָ֭מַרְתִּי
פֶּן־יִשְׂמְחוּ־לִ֑י
בְּמ֥וֹט רַ֝גְלִ֗י
עָלַ֥י הִגְדִּֽילוּ׃

18 Truly, I
Am ready for limping,
And my suffering
Always is before me!

יח כִּֽי־אֲ֭נִי
לְצֶ֣לַע נָכ֑וֹן
וּמַכְאוֹבִ֖י
נֶגְדִּ֣י תָמִֽיד׃

19 Certainly, I shall confess my crime;
I shall be afraid
Because of my sin.

יט כִּֽי־עֲוֺנִ֥י אַגִּ֑יד
אֶ֝דְאַ֗ג
מֵֽחַטָּאתִֽי׃

20 My enemies
Are powerful in life,
And numerous
My lying enemies.

כ וְ֭אֹיְבַי
חַיִּ֣ים עָצֵ֑מוּ
וְרַבּ֖וּ
שֹׂנְאַ֣י שָֽׁקֶר׃

21 Those who repay evil
For good;
Accuse me
For my pursuit of Good.

כא וּמְשַׁלְּמֵ֣י רָ֭עָה
תַּ֣חַת טוֹבָ֑ה
יִ֝שְׂטְנ֗וּנִי
תַּ֣חַת רָֽדְופִי [רָֽדְפִי] ־טֽוֹב׃

22 Do not abandon me, Eternal,
My God,
Do not withdraw from me!

כב אַל־תַּעַזְבֵ֣נִי יהוָ֑ה
אֱ֝לֹהַ֗י
אַל־תִּרְחַ֥ק מִמֶּֽנִּי׃

23 Help me quickly,
Almighty,
My salvation!

כג ח֥וּשָׁה לְעֶזְרָתִ֑י
אֲ֝דֹנָ֗י
תְּשׁוּעָתִֽי׃

Psalm 39

1 For Yedutun the director,
A Psalm by David.

א לַמְנַצֵּחַ לִידִיתוּן [לִידוּתוּן]
מִזְמוֹר לְדָוִד׃

2 I said,
I shall watch my ways,
Not to sin with my tongue,
I shall keep a muzzle for my mouth,
As long as the wicked is my adversary.

ב אָמַרְתִּי
אֶשְׁמְרָה דְרָכַי
מֵחֲטוֹא בִלְשׁוֹנִי
אֶשְׁמְרָה לְפִי מַחְסוֹם
בְּעֹד רָשָׁע לְנֶגְדִּי׃

3 I shall remain dumb, silent,
I shall be quiet, absent any good,
My pain is disabling.

ג נֶאֱלַמְתִּי דוּמִיָּה
הֶחֱשֵׁיתִי מִטּוֹב
וּכְאֵבִי נֶעְכָּר׃

4 Hot is my heart inside me,
When I talk, fire burns,
When I spoke
With my tongue!

ד חַם־לִבִּי |
בְּקִרְבִּי
בַּהֲגִיגִי תִבְעַר־אֵשׁ
דִּבַּרְתִּי
בִּלְשׁוֹנִי

5 Eternal, let me know my end,
The measure of my days, what it is,
May I know
How deficient I am?

ה הוֹדִיעֵנִי יהוה | קִצִּי
וּמִדַּת יָמַי מַה־הִיא
אֵדְעָה
מֶה־חָדֵל אָנִי׃

6 Only a few hand-breadths
You gave as my days,
My duration is nothing before You,
Every man is but totally vapor
Even if erect, Selah.

ו הִנֵּה טְפָחוֹת |
נָתַתָּה יָמַי
וְחֶלְדִּי כְאַיִן נֶגְדֶּךָ
אַךְ־כָּל־הֶבֶל כָּל־אָדָם
נִצָּב סֶלָה׃

7 Only in deep darkness man ambles,
Only vapor excites them,
He amasses
Not knowing who will collect it.

ז אַךְ־בְּצֶלֶם | יִתְהַלֶּךְ־אִישׁ
אַךְ־הֶבֶל יֶהֱמָיוּן
יִצְבֹּר
וְלֹא־יֵדַע מִי־אֹסְפָם׃

8 And now, what did I hope, Almighty?
My prayer
Is but to You!

ח וְעַתָּה מַה־קִּוִּיתִי אֲדֹנָי
תּוֹחַלְתִּי
לְךָ הִיא׃

9 Save me from all my misdeeds,
Do not put upon me
The shame of a knave.

ט מִכָּל־פְּשָׁעַי הַצִּילֵנִי
חֶרְפַּת נָבָל
אַל־תְּשִׂימֵנִי

10 I have become dumb,
I cannot open my mouth,
Certainly, You have wrought.

י נֶאֱלַמְתִּי
לֹא אֶפְתַּח־פִּי
כִּי אַתָּה עָשִׂיתָ׃

11 Lift from me Your plague;
From the blow of Your fist
I am finished.

א הָסֵר מֵעָלַי נִגְעֶךָ
מִתִּגְרַת יָדְךָ
אֲנִי כָלִיתִי׃

12 As correction for crime
You punish man,
His desirable parts melt like a moth;
Every man is only vapor, Selah.

יב בְּתוֹכָחוֹת עַל־עָוֺן ׀
יִסַּרְתָּ אִישׁ
וַתֶּמֶס כָּעָשׁ חֲמוּדוֹ
אַךְ הֶבֶל כָּל־אָדָם סֶלָה׃

13 Eternal, listen to my prayer,
Please hear my supplication,
Be not be silent to my tears;
For I am a stranger with You,
A sojourner,
Like all my forefathers.

יג שִׁמְעָה־תְפִלָּתִי ׀ יהוה
וְשַׁוְעָתִי ׀ הַאֲזִינָה
אֶל־דִּמְעָתִי אַל־תֶּחֱרַשׁ
כִּי גֵר אָנֹכִי עִמָּךְ
תּוֹשָׁב
כְּכָל־אֲבוֹתָי׃

14 Turn away from me, so I can recover
.Before I go and am no more.

יד הָשַׁע מִמֶּנִּי וְאַבְלִיגָה
בְּטֶרֶם אֵלֵךְ וְאֵינֶנִּי׃

This Psalm is remarkable for its many rhymes at major caesuras. In contrast to most Davidic Psalms which start as a wail and end as a song, this one starts as a song and ends as a wail.

3. עכר has many meanings. The main Biblical Hebrew meaning is "to destroy"; here we derive it from Syriac "to hinder" (Rabbinical Hebrew and Arabic "muddy").

6. חלד taken here similar to Arabic חׄלד "indefinite duration, being eternal".

7. Taking צלם intermediary between צל "shadow", צלמות "very deep shadow".

14. Taking בלג in the Arabic sense "to be of good cheer, to be brilliant"; the translations of Rashi and Ibn Ezra "to become strong" are not supported by the parallel *Amos* 5:9 and contradicted by the Aramaic Targum.

Psalm 40

1 For the Director,
A Psalm by David.

א לַמְנַצֵּחַ
לְדָוִד מִזְמוֹר׃

2 I intently cried to the Eternal,
He turned to me
And heard my supplication.

ב קַוֹּה קִוִּיתִי יְהוָה
וַיֵּט אֵלַי
וַיִּשְׁמַע שַׁוְעָתִי׃

3 He lifted me
From the roaring pit,
From the miry clay,
He put my feet on a rock,
Made my strides firm.

ג וַיַּעֲלֵנִי ׀
מִבּוֹר שָׁאוֹן
מִטִּיט הַיָּוֵן
וַיָּקֶם עַל־סֶלַע רַגְלַי
כּוֹנֵן אֲשֻׁרָי׃

4 He put in my mouth
A new song,
A praise for our God.
May the many see and fear,
And trust
In the Eternal.

ד וַיִּתֵּן בְּפִי ׀
שִׁיר חָדָשׁ
תְּהִלָּה לֵאלֹהֵינוּ
יִרְאוּ רַבִּים וְיִירָאוּ
וְיִבְטְחוּ
בַּיהוָה׃

5 Hail to the man
Who puts his confidence
In the Eternal,
Who did not turn to the monstrous
And deviant falsehood.

ה אַשְׁרֵי־הַגֶּבֶר
אֲשֶׁר־שָׂם יְיָ
מִבְטַחוֹ
וְלֹא־פָנָה אֶל־רְהָבִים
וְשָׂטֵי כָזָב׃

6 You did great things, You,
Eternal, my God,
Your wonders and intentions regarding us,
Nothing
Is comparable to You.
I might tell and proclaim,
They are too mighty
To be recounted!

ו רַבּוֹת עָשִׂיתָ ׀ אַתָּה ׀
יְהוָה אֱלֹהַי
נִפְלְאֹתֶיךָ וּמַחְשְׁבֹתֶיךָ אֵלֵינוּ
אֵין ׀
עֲרֹךְ אֵלֶיךָ
אַגִּידָה וַאֲדַבֵּרָה
עָצְמוּ
מִסַּפֵּר׃

7 You never desired bloody and flour offerings.
Ears
You dug out in me.
You did not ask for
Holocaust and purification-offering.

ז זֶבַח וּמִנְחָה ׀ לֹא־חָפַצְתָּ
אָזְנַיִם
כָּרִיתָ לִּי
עוֹלָה וַחֲטָאָה
לֹא שָׁאָלְתָּ׃

8 Then I said:
Here I am coming,
In a scroll of the ledger book
My account is written up.

ח אָז אָמַרְתִּי
הִנֵּה־בָאתִי
בִּמְגִלַּת־סֵפֶר
כָּתוּב עָלָי׃

9 To do Your will, My God, is what I desire, For
Your teachings
Are in my bowels.

ט לַעֲשׂוֹת רְצוֹנְךָ אֱלֹהַי חָפָצְתִּי
וְתוֹרָתְךָ
בְּתוֹךְ מֵעָי׃

10 I did announce justice
In a large assembly.
Behold, my lips
I shall not confine,
Eternal,
You do know.

י בִּשַּׂרְתִּי צֶדֶק |
בְּקָהָל רָב
הִנֵּה שְׂפָתַי
לֹא אֶכְלָא
יהוה
אַתָּה יָדָעְתָּ׃

11 I did not cover up Your justice
Within my heart,
Your faith and salvation I proclaimed,
I did not conceal Your love and truth
Before a large crowd!

יא צִדְקָתְךָ לֹא־כִסִּיתִי |
בְּתוֹךְ לִבִּי
אֱמוּנָתְךָ וּתְשׁוּעָתְךָ אָמָרְתִּי
לֹא־כִחַדְתִּי חַסְדְּךָ וַאֲמִתְּךָ
לְקָהָל רָב׃

12 You, Eternal,
Do not lock Your mercy out of my reach;
May Your kindness and truth
Always protect me.

יב אַתָּה יהוה
לֹא־תִכְלָא רַחֲמֶיךָ מִמֶּנִּי
חַסְדְּךָ וַאֲמִתְּךָ
תָּמִיד יִצְּרוּנִי׃

13 Evil ones
Gang up against me
Without number.
My sins have caught up with me,
I can no longer see;
They are more than my head's hairs,
Therefore I lost courage.

יג כִּי אָפְפוּ עָלַי |
רָעוֹת
עַד־אֵין מִסְפָּר
הִשִּׂיגוּנִי עֲוֺנֹתַי
וְלֹא־יָכֹלְתִּי לִרְאוֹת
עָצְמוּ מִשַּׂעֲרוֹת רֹאשִׁי
וְלִבִּי עֲזָבָנִי׃

14 May it please You, Eternal,
To save me.
Eternal,
Please hasten to my help.

יד רְצֵה־יהוה
לְהַצִּילֵנִי
יהוה
לְעֶזְרָתִי חוּשָׁה׃

15 Those who are after my life to destroy it
Shall be ashamed and disgraced
Separately;.
They shall turn back
And be dishonored
Who desire
A bad end for me.

טו יֵבֹשׁוּ וְיַחְפְּרוּ |
יַחַד
מְבַקְשֵׁי נַפְשִׁי לִסְפּוֹתָהּ
יִסֹּגוּ אָחוֹר
וְיִכָּלְמוּ
חֲפֵצֵי
רָעָתִי׃

16 Those shall be desolate
Because of their shame,
Who say about me:
"Hey, Hey!"

טז יָשֹׁמּוּ
עַל־עֵקֶב בָּשְׁתָּם
הָאֹמְרִים לִי
הֶאָח | הֶאָח׃

17 May all your seekers
Rejoice and enjoy;
May they always say
The Eternal is great,
The lovers
Of your salvation.

יז יָשִׂישׂוּ וְיִשְׂמְחוּ |
בְּךָ כָּל־מְבַקְשֶׁיךָ
יֹאמְרוּ תָמִיד
יִגְדַּל יְהוָה
אֹהֲבֵי
תְּשׁוּעָתֶךָ׃

18 But I	יח וַאֲנִ֤י ׀
Am deprived and poor.	עָנִ֪י וְאֶבְי֫וֹן
May the Eternal think of me.	אֲדֹנָ֢י יַחֲשָׁ֫ב לִ֥י
You are my help and succour,	עֶזְרָתִ֣י וּמְפַלְטִ֣י אַ֑תָּה
My God	אֱ֝לֹהַ֗י
Do not tarry.	אַל־תְּאַחַֽר׃

1. Arabic קוה "to cry" is more appropriate in the context than common "hope".

5. רהב is mainly a sea monster but stands also for all kinds of mythical pagan monstrosities. Line 2 and 3 are switched for the English.

6. A "but" is implied in line 6.

7. חטאה is not חטאת ; it is restricted to bloody sacrifices, excluding, for example, the Red Cow.

8. The סופר appears in Kings as minister of defense, or better, as quartermaster general who keeps all lists connected with the army and its needs, who forms the soldiers into army divisions (*2K*. 25:19). So the root ספרdoes not primarily denote a book, something written, but an account book. The scribe who writes documents, שטר, is the שוטר.

15. It seems that here יחד does not mean "collectively" but "singly", in the sense of Arabic וחד.

16. אֹ֝הֲבֵ֗י תְּשׁוּעָתֶ֑ךָ were translated reluctantly as "lovers" of Your salvation. It looks as if it were better to refer to Arabic אהב "to prepare": "May those who are prepared for Your salvation always say . . .." (Remember the many faces of the root, in particular the אהבה of the daughters of Jerusalem, *Cant*. 3:10: "leather" (Ugaritic), "raw leather" (Arabic).)

Psalm 41

1 For the director,
A Psalm of David.

א לַמְנַצֵּחַ
מִזְמוֹר לְדָוִד׃

2 Hail to him
Who is thoughtful of the needy,
On the day of misfortune
The Eternal will let him escape.

ב אַשְׁרֵי
מַשְׂכִּיל אֶל־דָּל
בְּיוֹם רָעָה
יְמַלְּטֵהוּ יהוה׃

3 The Eternal
Will preserve and vitalize him,
He will be made fortunate in the Land;
Do will not give him
Into the throat of his enemies.

ג יהוה ׀
יִשְׁמְרֵהוּ וִיחַיֵּהוּ
יְאֻשַּׁר [וְאֻשַּׁר] בָּאָרֶץ
וְאַל־תִּתְּנֵהוּ
בְּנֶפֶשׁ אֹיְבָיו׃

4 The Eternal will support him
On the sick-bed;
Every one of his couches
You turned over in his sickness.

ד יהוה יִסְעָדֶנּוּ
עַל־עֶרֶשׂ דְּוָי
כָּל־מִשְׁכָּבוֹ
הָפַכְתָּ בְחָלְיוֹ׃

5 I said:
"Eternal, be gracious to me,
Heal my soul
Though I sinned against You!"

ה אֲנִי־אָמַרְתִּי
יהוה חָנֵּנִי
רְפָאָה נַפְשִׁי
כִּי־חָטָאתִי לָךְ׃

6 My enemies
Discuss bad news that happen to me::
"When will he die
And his name be lost?"

ו אוֹיְבַי
יֹאמְרוּ רַע לִי
מָתַי יָמוּת
וְאָבַד שְׁמוֹ׃

7 And when he comes to visit
He speaks lies;
He is collecting evil
To spread when he goes abroad.

ז וְאִם־בָּא לִרְאוֹת ׀
שָׁוְא יְדַבֵּר לִבּוֹ
יִקְבָּץ־אָוֶן לוֹ
יֵצֵא לַחוּץ יְדַבֵּר׃

8 Together
They whisper about me,
All my haters;
About me
They plan evil for me.

ח יַחַד
עָלַי יִתְלַחֲשׁוּ
כָּל־שֹׂנְאָי
עָלַי ׀
יַחְשְׁבוּ רָעָה לִי׃

9 "A noxious substance
Will be poured into him
And when he lies down
He will never get up!"

ט דְּבַר־בְּלִיַּעַל
יָצוּק בּוֹ
וַאֲשֶׁר שָׁכַב
לֹא־יוֹסִיף לָקוּם׃

10 My friend also,
Whom I trusted,
He who eats my bread,
Twisted deceit about me!

י גַּם אִישׁ־שְׁלוֹמִי ׀
אֲשֶׁר־בָּטַחְתִּי בוֹ
אוֹכֵל לַחְמִי
הִגְדִּיל עָלַי עָקֵב׃

11 But You, Eternal,
Be gracious to me and let me stand up;
Then I shall pay them back.

יא וְאַתָּה יהוה
חָנֵּנִי וַהֲקִימֵנִי
וַאֲשַׁלְּמָה לָהֶם׃

12 By this I shall know
That really You are pleased with me,
When my enemy will not trumpet over me..

יב בְּזֹאת יָדַעְתִּי
כִּֽי־חָפַצְתָּ בִּי
כִּי לֹֽא־יָרִיעַ אֹיְבִי עָלָֽי׃

13 As for me in my simplicity
You supported me,
And made me stand forever firmly before You.

יג וַאֲנִי בְּתֻמִּי
תָּמַכְתָּ בִּי
וַתַּצִּיבֵנִי לְפָנֶיךָ לְעוֹלָֽם׃

14 Praised be the Eternal,
The God of Israel,
From Eternity
To Eternity,
Amen, Amen.

יד בָּרוּךְ יהוה ׀
אֱלֹהֵי יִשְׂרָאֵל
מֵֽהָעוֹלָם
וְעַד הָעוֹלָם
אָמֵן ׀ וְאָמֵֽן׃

3. Here, the translator has a dilemma. Taking תתנהו as second person singular masculine, one has an unexplained (but not unheard-of), isolated change from indirect to direct speech. Alternatively, the word could be third person singular feminine and represent one of the few places in the Bible where God is addressed in the feminine (cf. *Num.* 11:15). The last line should really read "windpipe" instead of "throat", another meaning of the ubiquitous נפש.

5. An example of the כי of contrast, which also is a כי of emphasis.

14. The last verse is the conclusion of the first book of Psalms; it is not part of the Psalm.

Book Two

Psalm 42

1 For the director,
A *maskil* by the Qoraḥides.

א לַמְנַצֵּחַ
מַשְׂכִּיל לִבְנֵי־קֹרַח׃

2 Like a hind
Yearning for wadis,
So my soul yearns for You, God!

ב כְּאַיָּל
תַּעֲרֹג עַל־אֲפִיקֵי־מָיִם
כֵּן נַפְשִׁי תַעֲרֹג אֵלֶיךָ אֱלֹהִים׃

3 My soul is thirsting
For God,
For the living Power,
When may I come
And appear
Before God's presence?

ג צָמְאָה נַפְשִׁי |
לֵאלֹהִים
לְאֵל חָי
מָתַי אָבוֹא
וְאֵרָאֶה
פְּנֵי אֱלֹהִים׃

4 My tear was bread for me
Day and night,
When it was said to me every day:
"Where is your God?"

ד הָיְתָה־לִּי דִמְעָתִי לֶחֶם
יוֹמָם וָלָיְלָה
בֶּאֱמֹר אֵלַי כָּל־הַיּוֹם
אַיֵּה אֱלֹהֶיךָ׃

5 This I shall remember
And pour out my soul:
When I was passing under cover,
Was toddling,
To God's house
With sounds of joy and thanksgiving,
In festive throng!

ה אֵלֶּה אֶזְכְּרָה |
וְאֶשְׁפְּכָה עָלַי | נַפְשִׁי
כִּי אֶעֱבֹר | בַּסָּךְ
אֶדַּדֵּם
עַד־בֵּית אֱלֹהִים
בְּקוֹל־רִנָּה וְתוֹדָה
הָמוֹן חוֹגֵג׃

6 Why are you dejected,
My soul,
And are flustered about me?
Hope in God,
Truly I shall still thank Him
For the salvation of His presence!

ו מַה־תִּשְׁתּוֹחֲחִי |
נַפְשִׁי
וַתֶּהֱמִי עָלָי
הוֹחִילִי לֵאלֹהִים
כִּי־עוֹד אוֹדֶנּוּ
יְשׁוּעוֹת פָּנָיו׃

7 My God, inside me
My soul is dejected.
Therefore I shall call on You,
Away from the land of the Jordan
And the Ḥermon's heights,
From a low hill!

ז אֱלֹהַי עָלַי
נַפְשִׁי תִשְׁתּוֹחָח
עַל־כֵּן אֶזְכָּרְךָ
מֵאֶרֶץ יַרְדֵּן
וְחֶרְמוֹנִים
מֵהַר מִצְעָר׃

8 One abyss calls to the other
By the thunder of Your currents.
All Your breakers and waves
Passed over me!

ח תְּהוֹם אֶל־תְּהוֹם קוֹרֵא
לְקוֹל צִנּוֹרֶיךָ
כָּל־מִשְׁבָּרֶיךָ וְגַלֶּיךָ
עָלַי עָבָרוּ׃

9 By day	ט יוֹמָם |
The Eternal commands His kindness,	יְצַוֶּה יהוה | חַסְדּוֹ
And by night	וּבַלַּיְלָה
His song is with me,	שִׁירֹה [שִׁירוֹ] עִמִּי
A prayer	תְּפִלָּה
To the Power who keeps me alive!	לְאֵל חַיָּי׃
10 May I say	י אוֹמְרָה |
To the Power, my rock,	לְאֵל סַלְעִי
Why did You forget me?	לָמָה שְׁכַחְתָּנִי
Why do I have to walk in a black mood	לָמָּה־קֹדֵר אֵלֵךְ
Under enemy's pressure?"	בְּלַחַץ אוֹיֵב׃
11 With murder in my bones	יא בְּרֶצַח | בְּעַצְמוֹתַי
My oppressors are insulting me	חֵרְפוּנִי צוֹרְרָי
By saying to me all day long:	בְּאָמְרָם אֵלַי כָּל־הַיּוֹם
"Where is your God?"	אַיֵּה אֱלֹהֶיךָ׃
12 My soul,	יב מַה־תִּשְׁתּוֹחֲחִי |
Why are you dejected	נַפְשִׁי
And are flustered about me?	וּמַה־תֶּהֱמִי עָלָי
Hope in God	הוֹחִילִי לֵאלֹהִים
Certainly I shall still thank Him,	כִּי־עוֹד אוֹדֶנּוּ
My salvation	יְשׁוּעֹת פָּנַי
And my God.	וֵאלֹהָי׃

In the entire second Book of Psalms, the prevailing Name of the Deity is "God", not "Eternal"; see Pss. 14/53.

1. The בני קרח are not "the sons of Qoraḥ" (or Korach) but of the family; they are the group of poets and singers lead by Heman, the grandson of the prophet Samuel and descendant of the Pentateuchal Qoraḥ, of the family of Qehat (Kehat), in the eighteenth generation (1Chron. 6:16 ff.). These were the court poets of David, together with the groups led by Asaph of the family of Gershon, and Eitan of the family of Merari (loc. cit. 24, 29). Therefore, "the sons of Korach" are simply the poets from the family of Kehat, whose official composition were incorporated in the Diwan of the poems from David's court.

משכיל refers to the Temple service, *2 Chr.* 30:22.

2. The root ערג appears only here and in *Joel* 1:20 where also it refers to animals suffering from the disappearance of water from prairie streams in the heat of the summer. On the meager basis of lexical evidence, one cannot decide whether the word means "whining" or "to be thirsty for water", or even Arabic ערג "to stay in a place", meaning that the hind will prefer to stay in the wadi in the faint hope that water will appear there. The Septuagint translated here *epipoyei* "pines", and in Joel *anebleqan* "to look up with longing". The Aramaic Targum Jonathan to Joel translates מסברא "hopes" but the anonymous Targum to Psalms, influenced by the Syriac Peshitto, has מרגג "lusts" or "trembles". Ibn Janaḥ and Qimḥi declare ערג to mean the sound of hinds, comparable to גער as sound of donkeys. So your guess about the exact meaning of the root is as good as mine and everybody else's. אפיק is a wadi, the bed of a brook or river that regularly runs dry in summer. I am taking the word as an *af'el* form of the Aramaic פוק "to exit", meaning "a conduit for moving things out". The Aramaic אפקא means "deportation, banishment". In *Job* 40:18 it is said of Behemoth that עֲצָמָיו אֲפִיקֵי נְחוּשָׁה "his bones are bronze tubing", so אפיק is a conduit, also a river bed, ready to discharge water if necessary but not regularly filled with water.

5. The contracted form אדדם is short for אדדה אִתָּם, "I shall walk like a toddler with them". The root דדה in this sense is well attested to in Rabbinical Hebrew (e.g., *Sabb.* 128b).

6. תשתוחחי means verbally "you (f.) will lie down flat both on your face and body".

7. The meaning of the root זכר here is the Accadic “to call out, mention.” In the geographic references, the prefix in מארץ, מהר is taken as the *mem* of privation to indicate the absence of the object. חרמונים is a superlative, "the highest Ḥermon". Instead of in the harsh landscape East of Jerusalem, the poet locates himself in the pleasant foothills to the West.

8. צנור is really a pipe, a water or sewage pipe, used here for sudden currents in the ocean.

11. Targum and the classical commentators all read the verse meaning that the enemies intend to murder the poet, but the verse does not say this and any murderer is attempting to damage organs and soft parts and not bones.

12. Instead of "My salvation and my God" one might also translate "By the salvation of His presence, of my GOD", taking the suffix in פני as third person singular possessive (cf. *Ps*. 24:4).

Psalm 43

1 Judge for me, God,
Fight my fight
Against an impious nation;
Let me escape from a man of deceit and evil.

א שָׁפְטֵנִי אֱלֹהִים ׀
וְרִיבָה רִיבִי
מִגּוֹי לֹא־חָסִיד
מֵאִישׁ־מִרְמָה וְעַוְלָה תְפַלְּטֵנִי׃

2 For You are
The God of my refuge;
Why did You neglect me?
Why do I have to wander in black mood
Under the enemy's pressure?

ב כִּי־אַתָּה ׀
אֱלֹהֵי מָעוּזִּי
לָמָה זְנַחְתָּנִי
לָמָּה־קֹדֵר אֶתְהַלֵּךְ
בְּלַחַץ אוֹיֵב׃

3 Send Your light and Your truth,
They shall guide me,
They shall bring me to Your holy mountain
And Your dwelling place.

ג שְׁלַח־אוֹרְךָ וַאֲמִתְּךָ
הֵמָּה יַנְחוּנִי
יְבִיאוּנִי אֶל־הַר־קָדְשְׁךָ
וְאֶל־מִשְׁכְּנוֹתֶיךָ׃

4 I shall come
To God's altar,
To the Power,
The joy of my age,
I shall thank You with the lute,
God, my Power.

ד וְאָבוֹאָה ׀
אֶל־מִזְבַּח אֱלֹהִים
אֶל־אֵל
שִׂמְחַת גִּילִי
וְאוֹדְךָ בְכִנּוֹר
אֱלֹהִים אֱלֹהָי׃

5 Why are you deject,
My soul,
And are flustered?
Hope for God,
Certainly I shall still thank Him,
My Salvation
And my God.

ה מַה־תִּשְׁתּוֹחֲחִי ׀
נַפְשִׁי
וּמַה־תֶּהֱמִי עָלָי
הוֹחִילִי לֵאלֹהִים
כִּי־עוֹד אוֹדֶנּוּ
יְשׁוּעֹת פָּנַי
וֵאלֹהָי׃

This Psalm is either the continuation of or a part of the preceding Psalm, given the verbal repetitions in verses 2 and 5.

Psalm 44

1 For the director, a *maskil* by the Qoraḥides.

לַמְנַצֵּחַ לִבְנֵי־קֹרַח מַשְׂכִּיל׃ א

2 God,
We heard with our ears,
Our fathers told us:
Deeds You worked in their days,
In ancient days.

אֱלֹהִים ׀ ב
בְּאָזְנֵינוּ שָׁמַעְנוּ
אֲבוֹתֵינוּ סִפְּרוּ־לָנוּ
פֹּעַל־פָּעַלְתָּ בִימֵיהֶם
בִּימֵי קֶדֶם׃

3 You,
Your hand,
You did uproot peoples
And settled them,
You broke nations
And sent them away.

אַתָּה ׀ ג
יָדְךָ
גּוֹיִם הוֹרַשְׁתָּ
וַתִּטָּעֵם
תָּרַע לְאֻמִּים
וַתְּשַׁלְּחֵם׃

4 For not with their sword
Did they inherit the land;
Their arms did not help them,
But Your right hand and Your left arm
And the light of Your presence;
So much You liked them.

כִּי לֹא בְחַרְבָּם ד
יָרְשׁוּ־אָרֶץ
וּזְרוֹעָם
לֹא־הוֹשִׁיעָה לָּמוֹ
כִּי־יְמִינְךָ וּזְרוֹעֲךָ
וְאוֹר פָּנֶיךָ
כִּי רְצִיתָם׃

5 You are my King, o God,
Commander
Of the salvation of Jacob.

אַתָּה־הוּא מַלְכִּי אֱלֹהִים ה
צַוֵּה
יְשׁוּעוֹת יַעֲקֹב׃

6 With You
We gore our oppressors,
In Your name
We trample over our attackers.

בְּךָ ו
צָרֵינוּ נְנַגֵּחַ
בְּשִׁמְךָ
נָבוּס קָמֵינוּ

7 Certainly, I shall not rely on my bow,
And my sword
Will not save me.

כִּי לֹא בְקַשְׁתִּי אֶבְטָח ז
וְחַרְבִּי
לֹא תוֹשִׁיעֵנִי׃

8 But truly You saved us
From our oppressors,
And our haters You put to shame.

כִּי הוֹשַׁעְתָּנוּ ח
מִצָּרֵינוּ
וּמְשַׂנְאֵינוּ הֱבִישׁוֹתָ׃

9 God
We praise every day,
To Your name
We forever give thanks, Selah.

בֵּאלֹהִים ט
הִלַּלְנוּ כָל־הַיּוֹם
וְשִׁמְךָ ׀
לְעוֹלָם נוֹדֶה סֶלָה׃

10 But You have neglected us
And made us ashamed,
You will not accompany
Our armies.

אַף־זָנַחְתָּ י
וַתַּכְלִימֵנוּ
וְלֹא־תֵצֵא
בְּצִבְאוֹתֵינוּ

11 You turned us back
Before the oppressor,
And our haters
Plunder for themselves.

יא תְּשִׁיבֵנוּ אָחוֹר
מִנִּי־צָר
וּמְשַׂנְאֵינוּ
שָׁסוּ לָמוֹ׃

12 You delivered us
Like sheep, as food;
And among the nations
You scattered us!

יב תִּתְּנֵנוּ
כְּצֹאן מַאֲכָל
וּבַגּוֹיִם
זֵרִיתָנוּ׃

13 You sold Your people not for wealth,
You did not go high
In their sale price!

יג תִּמְכֹּר עַמְּךָ בְלֹא־הוֹן
וְלֹא־רִבִּיתָ
בִּמְחִירֵיהֶם׃

14 You made us a shame
Among our neighbors,
Scorn and a spittle
For our surroundings.

יד תְּשִׂימֵנוּ חֶרְפָּה
לִשְׁכֵנֵינוּ
לַעַג וָקֶלֶס
לִסְבִיבוֹתֵינוּ׃

15 You made us a byword
Among the peoples,
A head-shake
Among the nations!

טו תְּשִׂימֵנוּ מָשָׁל
בַּגּוֹיִם
מְנוֹד־רֹאשׁ
בַּל־אֻמִּים׃

16 Every day
My shame is before me,
The disgrace of my face overwhelms me.

טז כָּל־הַיּוֹם
כְּלִמָּתִי נֶגְדִּי
וּבֹשֶׁת פָּנַי כִּסָּתְנִי׃

17 Before the voice
Of the insulter and blasphemer,
Because of the enemy
Bent on private revenge.

יז מִקּוֹל
מְחָרֵף וּמְגַדֵּף
מִפְּנֵי אוֹיֵב
וּמִתְנַקֵּם׃

18 All this came over us
But we did not forget You,
We did not become untrue
To Your covenant.

יח כָּל־זֹאת בָּאַתְנוּ
וְלֹא שְׁכַחֲנוּךָ
וְלֹא־שִׁקַּרְנוּ
בִּבְרִיתֶךָ׃

19 Our heart did not retreat
Nor our steps deviate
From Your way!

יט לֹא־נָסוֹג אָחוֹר לִבֵּנוּ
וַתֵּט אֲשֻׁרֵינוּ
מִנִּי אָרְחֶךָ׃

20 You certainly pounded us
At the place of jackals,
You covered us with deep darkness!

כ כִּי דִכִּיתָנוּ
בִּמְקוֹם תַּנִּים
וַתְּכַס עָלֵינוּ בְצַלְמָוֶת׃

21 Did we forget
The Name of our God,
And lifted our hands
To a strange power?

כא אִם־שָׁכַחְנוּ
שֵׁם אֱלֹהֵינוּ
וַנִּפְרֹשׂ כַּפֵּינוּ
לְאֵל זָר׃

22 May God
Check this out,
Truly He knows
The secrets of the heart.

כב הֲלֹא אֱלֹהִים
יַחֲקָר־זֹאת
כִּי־הוּא יֹדֵעַ
תַּעֲלֻמוֹת לֵב׃

23 Truly, for You	כג כִּֽי־עָלֶיךָ
We are killed every day,	הֹרַגְנוּ כָל־הַיּוֹם
And considered	נֶחְשַׁבְנוּ
Like sheep for slaughter.	כְּצֹאן טִבְחָה׃
24 Be roused,	כד עוּרָה ׀
Why do You sleep, Almighty,	לָמָּה תִישַׁן ׀ אֲדֹנָי
Please awake,	הָקִיצָה
Do not forever abandon.	אַל־תִּזְנַח לָנֶצַח׃
25 Why are You hiding Your face,	כה לָמָּה פָנֶיךָ תַסְתִּיר
Forget our deprivation and oppression?	תִּשְׁכַּח עָנְיֵנוּ וְלַחֲצֵנוּ׃
26 Truly our soul lies flat in the dust,	כו כִּי שָׁחָה לֶעָפָר נַפְשֵׁנוּ
Our bellies are glued to the ground.	דָּבְקָה לָאָרֶץ בִּטְנֵנוּ׃
27 Please arise,	כז קוּמָה
Please be our help,	עֶזְרָתָה לָּנוּ
Redeem us	וּפְדֵנוּ
For the sake of Your kindness!	לְמַעַן חַסְדֶּךָ׃

3. Taking the root רעע of תרע in its Rabbinic Hebrew sense "to be shaky, ready to disintegrate".

4. In line 3 the accents are ◌֣֗ ◌֣֓.

5 The imperative צוה is read as a noun.

14 קלס is read as Arabic “spittle, fluid which is spit out”.

Psalm 45

1 For the director, on Shoshanim
By the Qorahides,
A *maskil*,
A wedding song.

א לַמְנַצֵּ֥חַ עַל־שֹׁשַׁנִּ֗ים
לִבְנֵי־קֹ֑רַח
מַ֝שְׂכִּ֗יל
שִׁ֣יר יְדִידֹֽת׃

2 My heart swarms
Of beauty.
I shall present
My work to the king,
My tongue
Is the pen
Of a skilled secretary.

ב רָ֘חַ֤שׁ לִבִּ֨י ׀
דָּ֘בָ֤ר ט֗וֹב
אֹמֵ֣ר אָ֭נִי
מַעֲשַׂ֣י לְמֶ֑לֶךְ
לְ֝שׁוֹנִ֗י
עֵ֤ט ׀
ס֬וֹפֵ֬ר מָהִֽיר׃

3 You are most beautiful
Among men,
Elegance is poured
Over your lips,
Therefore God blessed you forever.

ג יָפְיָפִ֡יתָ
מִבְּנֵ֬י אָדָ֗ם
ה֣וּצַק חֵ֭ן
בְּשִׂפְתוֹתֶ֑יךָ
עַל־כֵּ֤ן בֵּרַכְךָ֖ אֱלֹהִ֣ים לְעוֹלָֽם׃

4 Hero, gird your sword on your hips,
Your dignity
And your majesty.

ד חֲג֣וֹר חַרְבְּךָ֣ עַל־יָרֵ֣ךְ גִּבּ֑וֹר
ה֝וֹדְךָ֗
וַהֲדָרֶֽךָ׃

5 Your majesty,
Good luck! ride,
For truth
And justice for the meek;
Your right hand will guide you to awesome deeds!

ה וַהֲדָרְךָ֨ ׀
צְלַ֬ח רְכַ֗ב
עַֽל־דְּבַר־אֱ֭מֶת
וְעַנְוָה־צֶ֑דֶק
וְתוֹרְךָ֖ נוֹרָא֣וֹת יְמִינֶֽךָ׃

6 Your arrows are sharpened
(Nations
Will fall under you,)
Into the heart
Of the king's enemies.

ו חִצֶּ֗יךָ שְׁנ֫וּנִ֥ים
עַ֭מִּים
תַּחְתֶּ֣יךָ יִפְּל֑וּ
בְּ֝לֵ֗ב
אוֹיְבֵ֥י הַמֶּֽלֶךְ׃

7 Your throne, by God,
Forever,
Is a straight scepter,
The scepter of your reign.

ז כִּסְאֲךָ֣ אֱ֭לֹהִים
עוֹלָ֣ם וָעֶ֑ד
שֵׁ֥בֶט מִ֝ישֹׁ֗ר
שֵׁ֣בֶט מַלְכוּתֶֽךָ׃

8 You loved justice
And hated evil,
Therefore
God, your Master
Anointed you
With oil of happiness
In preference to your fellows.

ח אָהַ֣בְתָּ צֶּדֶק֮
וַתִּשְׂנָ֫א רֶ֥שַׁע
עַל־כֵּ֤ן ׀
מְשָׁחֲךָ֡
אֱלֹהִ֣ים אֱ֭לֹהֶיךָ
שֶׁ֣מֶן שָׂשׂ֑וֹן
מֵֽחֲבֵרֶֽיךָ׃

9 Myrrh, and Aloe, Cassia
All your vestments,
From palaces of ivory
Instruments gladden you.

ט מֹר וַאֲהָלוֹת קְצִיעוֹת
כָּל־בִּגְדֹתֶיךָ
מִן־הֵיכְלֵי שֵׁן
מִנִּי שִׂמְּחוּךָ׃

10 Princesses
Visit you,
The queen stands at your right hand side
With Ophir gold!

י בְּנוֹת מְלָכִים
בִּיקְּרוֹתֶיךָ
נִצְּבָה שֵׁגַל לִימִינְךָ
בְּכֶתֶם אוֹפִיר׃

11 Listen, daughter, and see,
Bend your ear,
Forget your clan
And your father's house,

יא שִׁמְעִי־בַת וּרְאִי
וְהַטִּי אָזְנֵךְ
וְשִׁכְחִי עַמֵּךְ
וּבֵית אָבִיךְ׃

12 So the king may desire your beauty,
For he is your lord,
Bow down before him!

יב וְיִתְאָו הַמֶּלֶךְ יָפְיֵךְ
כִּי הוּא אֲדֹנַיִךְ
וְהִשְׁתַּחֲוִי־לוֹ׃

13 With Tyrian bushels
As gift
The richest of the nation
Will beg for an audience with you.

יג וּבַת־צֹר |
בְּמִנְחָה
פָּנַיִךְ יְחַלּוּ
עֲשִׁירֵי עָם׃

14 All the inner finery of the princess:
Her garments inlaid with golden threads.

יד כָּל־כְּבוּדָּה בַת־מֶלֶךְ פְּנִימָה
מִמִּשְׁבְּצוֹת זָהָב לְבוּשָׁהּ׃

15 In embroidery
She will be brought to the king,
The maidens after her,
Her companions,
Are brought to you.

טו לִרְקָמוֹת
תּוּבַל לַמֶּלֶךְ
בְּתוּלוֹת אַחֲרֶיהָ
רֵעוֹתֶיהָ
מוּבָאוֹת לָךְ׃

16 They will be conveyed
With joy and song,
They will enter
The king's palace.

טז תּוּבַלְנָה
בִּשְׂמָחֹת וָגִיל
תְּבֹאֶינָה
בְּהֵיכַל מֶלֶךְ׃

17 In place of your fathers
Will be your sons,
Make them rulers
Everywhere in the land.

יז תַּחַת אֲבֹתֶיךָ
יִהְיוּ בָנֶיךָ
תְּשִׁיתֵמוֹ לְשָׂרִים
בְּכָל־הָאָרֶץ׃

18 I shall make Your Name mentioned
In every generation,
For nations will praise You
Forever and ever!

יח אַזְכִּירָה שִׁמְךָ
בְּכָל־דֹּר וָדֹר
עַל־כֵּן עַמִּים יְהוֹדֻךָ
לְעֹלָם וָעֶד

1. Shoshanim "lilies" seems to the name of a fixed melody for wedding songs.

3. For סופר cf. *Ps*. 40:8.

8,10. It is difficult to find the distinction between ששון and שמחה; on basis of Accadic one might speculate that

ששון has an element of spontaneity whereas שמחה implies material well-being, well-feeling. A high-class courtesan is called *samḥu* in Accadic, as verb the word means "to live in splendor and abundance".

10. שגל is what is meant by Middle High German *quëne* “the wedded wife and mother”.

9. מִנִּי is construct of מִינִּים ”musical instruments”.

11. Since עם "people" also can mean "clan, family", it is not implied that the bride is a foreigner. In fact, if she were a foreigner then the marriage would be the token of a political alliance and the princess should not forget her origins.

12. A *bat* is equal to an *epha* (Ezech. 45:11), a volume of approximately 40 gallons. For the pun on *bat* see v.14.

14. Here I am following M. Dahood who remarks rightly that in *2Kings* 23:7 the women do not weave houses but dresses for Astarthe, compare Arabic בת "to cut"; it probably is a fashioned dress, in contrast to a shapeless שמלה. So בת means "daughter, a measure, dress, house".

Psalm 46

1 For the director, by the Qoraḥides,
A song on *Alamot.*

א לַמְנַצֵּחַ לִבְנֵי־קֹרַח
עַל־עֲלָמוֹת שִׁיר׃

2 God is for us
Refuge and strength,
Help in distress,
Easily found.

ב אֱלֹהִים לָנוּ
מַחֲסֶה וָעֹז
עֶזְרָה בְצָרוֹת
נִמְצָא מְאֹד׃

3 Thus we shall not fear
When earth turns over,
When mountains shake
In the heart of the Sea.

ג עַל־כֵּן לֹא־נִירָא
בְּהָמִיר אָרֶץ
וּבְמוֹט הָרִים
בְּלֵב יַמִּים׃

4 Its waters are agitated, fermenting.
Mountains quake in His haughtiness, Selah!

ד יֶהֱמוּ יֶחְמְרוּ מֵימָיו
יִרְעֲשׁוּ הָרִים בְּגַאֲוָתוֹ סֶלָה׃

5 The brook: Its spring heads
Gladden the city of God,
The sanctuary,
Dwelling of the Most High!

ה נָהָר פְּלָגָיו
יְשַׂמְּחוּ עִיר־אֱלֹהִים
קְדֹשׁ
מִשְׁכְּנֵי עֶלְיוֹן׃

6 God is in its midst,
It will not reel,
God will help it,
Towards morning.

ו אֱלֹהִים בְּקִרְבָּהּ
בַּל־תִּמּוֹט
יַעְזְרֶהָ אֱלֹהִים
לִפְנוֹת בֹּקֶר׃

7 Nations are agitated,
Kingdoms stagger,
He sounds His voice,
The earth is shaking.

ז הָמוּ גוֹיִם
מָטוּ מַמְלָכוֹת
נָתַן בְּקוֹלוֹ
תָּמוּג אָרֶץ׃

8 The Eternal of hosts is with us.
Our refuge
Is Jacob's God, Selah.

ח יהוָה צְבָאוֹת עִמָּנוּ
מִשְׂגָּב־לָנוּ
אֱלֹהֵי יַעֲקֹב סֶלָה׃

9 Go and see
The Eternal's actions,
Who places destruction in the land.

ט לְכוּ־חֲזוּ
מִפְעֲלוֹת יהוָה
אֲשֶׁר־שָׂם שַׁמּוֹת בָּאָרֶץ׃

10 He silences wars
To the end of the earth,
Breaks the bow
And chops up the spear;
Chariots
He burns in fire!

י מַשְׁבִּית מִלְחָמוֹת
עַד־קְצֵה הָאָרֶץ
קֶשֶׁת יְשַׁבֵּר
וְקִצֵּץ חֲנִית
עֲגָלוֹת
יִשְׂרֹף בָּאֵשׁ׃

11 Refrain and know
That I am God,
Exalted over peoples,
Exalted over the earth!

יא הַרְפּוּ וּדְעוּ
כִּי־אָנֹכִי אֱלֹהִים
אָרוּם בַּגּוֹיִם
אָרוּם בָּאָרֶץ׃

12 The Eternal of hosts is with us.	יב יְהוָ֣ה צְבָא֣וֹת עִמָּ֑נוּ
Our refuge	מִשְׂגָּֽב־לָ֝נוּ
Is Jacob's God, Selah.	אֱלֹהֵ֖י יַעֲקֹ֣ב סֶֽלָה׃

1. `*Alamot* might be an Elamitic melody but cf. *Ps*. 48:15.

3. One might also translate "When mountains shake (fall) Into the middle of the sea." It is not very clear what "When earth turns over" means; it could be a big earthquake or an exchange of the old for a new earth (*Jes*. 66:22). The entire Psalm is full of imagery of the "Day of the Lord" found in the later prophets.

5.and 6. The new flow of water which will signify the final redemption of Jerusalem is a common prophetic concept, cf. *Is*. 33:21-22, 66:12, *Zach*. 14:8, *Joel* 4:18, *Ezech*. 40:2, 47. The fourth line has an unusual construct state with a dividing accent; this shows that the poetic-musical meaning of the accents overrides grammatical and syntactic concerns. The somewhat disjointed diction of the stanza can be explained by taking נהר "The brook!" as a kind of heading, the rest is quite regular with 1 2 1 2 stresses per line.

7. From the many proposed variants of the meaning of מוג we chose the Arabic "to be agitated", said of the ocean; an image that connects with the first part of the Psalm. One also might translate "melts" with Ibn Ezra.

9. The destruction seemingly is the elimination of all war industries.

Psalm 47

1 For the director,
A psalm of the Qorahides.

א לַמְנַצֵּ֬חַ ׀
לִבְנֵי־קֹ֬רַח מִזְמֽוֹר׃

2 All nations
Clap your hands,
Blow the trumpet for God,
With a joyful sound.

ב כָּֽל־הָעַמִּים
תִּקְעוּ־כָ֑ף
הָרִיעוּ לֵֽאלֹהִים
בְּק֣וֹל רִנָּֽה׃

3 For the Eternal, Most High and Awesome, Is
overlord
Over all earth.

ג כִּֽי־יְהוָ֣ה עֶלְי֣וֹן נוֹרָ֑א
מֶ֥לֶךְ גָּ֝ד֗וֹל
עַל־כָּל־הָאָֽרֶץ

4 He would subdue nations under us,
And tribes
Under our feet.

ד יַדְבֵּ֣ר עַמִּ֣ים תַּחְתֵּ֑ינוּ
וּ֝לְאֻמִּ֗ים
תַּ֣חַת רַגְלֵֽינוּ׃

5 He would select our heritage,
The pride of Jacob that he loves, Selah.

ה יִבְחַר־לָ֥נוּ אֶת־נַחֲלָתֵ֑נוּ
אֶ֥ת גְּא֨וֹן יַעֲקֹ֖ב אֲשֶׁר־אָהֵ֣ב סֶֽלָה׃

6 God rose
On trumpet sound,
The Eternal
By the sound of the horn.

ו עָלָ֣ה אֱ֭לֹהִים
בִּתְרוּעָ֑ה
יְ֝הוָ֗ה
בְּק֣וֹל שׁוֹפָֽר׃

7 Sing to God, sing!
Sing to our King, sing!

ז זַמְּר֣וּ אֱלֹהִ֣ים זַמֵּ֑רוּ
זַמְּר֖וּ לְמַלְכֵּ֣נוּ זַמֵּֽרוּ׃

8 For King of all earth is God,
Sing a didactic song!

ח כִּ֤י מֶ֖לֶךְ כָּל־הָאָ֥רֶץ אֱלֹהִ֗ים
זַמְּר֥וּ מַשְׂכִּֽיל׃

9 God is king
Over the Gentiles,
God
Sits
On His holy throne.

ט מָלַ֣ךְ אֱ֭לֹהִים
עַל־גּוֹיִ֑ם
אֱ֝לֹהִ֗ים
יָשַׁ֤ב ׀
עַל־כִּסֵּ֬א קָדְשֽׁוֹ׃

10 The nobles of nations
Assemble,
The people
Of Abraham's God.
Certainly God's
Are the shields of the land,
Most high.

י נְדִ֘יבֵ֤י עַמִּ֨ים ׀
נֶאֱסָ֗פוּ
עַ֭ם
אֱלֹהֵ֣י אַבְרָהָ֑ם
כִּ֣י לֵ֭אלֹהִים
מָֽגִנֵּי־אֶ֝֗רֶץ
מְאֹ֣ד נַעֲלָֽה׃

5 This verse contains one of 5 occurrences of accented אֶ֥ת in the Bible, instead of normal אֶת.

10 Following Ibn Ezra, one could also translate the second part of the verse as: "In God's hand - Are the rulers of the earth - Most high!" In both cases, the final clause refers to the first, not the second clause of the part.

Psalm 48

1 A song, a Psalm
Of the Qorahides.

א שִׁ֥יר מִ֝זְמ֗וֹר
לִבְנֵי־קֹֽרַח׃

2 The Eternal is great and much praised
In God's city,
His holy mountain.

ב גָּ֘ד֤וֹל יהוָ֣ה וּמְהֻלָּ֣ל מְאֹ֑ד
בְּעִ֥יר אֱ֝לֹהֵ֗ינוּ
הַר־קָדְשֽׁוֹ׃

3 Beautiful mountaintop,
Delight of all the earth,
Mount Zion
The North side,
The capital
Of a great King.

ג יְפֵ֥ה נוֹף֮
מְשׂ֢וֹשׂ כָּל־הָ֫אָ֥רֶץ
הַר־צִ֭יּוֹן
יַרְכְּתֵ֣י צָפ֑וֹן
קִ֝רְיַ֗ת
מֶ֣לֶךְ רָֽב׃

4 In its palaces, God
Is known as refuge.

ד אֱלֹהִ֥ים בְּ֝אַרְמְנוֹתֶ֗יהָ
נוֹדַ֥ע לְמִשְׂגָּֽב׃

5 Behold, kings
Assembled,
Together crossed over.

ה כִּֽי־הִנֵּ֣ה הַ֭מְּלָכִים
נֽוֹעֲד֑וּ
עָבְר֥וּ יַחְדָּֽו׃

6 They saw,
Were much astonished,
Were disturbed, acted rashly.

ו הֵ֣מָּה רָ֭אוּ
כֵּ֣ן תָּמָ֑הוּ
נִבְהֲל֥וּ נֶחְפָּֽזוּ׃

7 Trembling
Gripped them there,
Pains
Like a woman in labor.

ז רְ֭עָדָה
אֲחָזָ֣תַם שָׁ֑ם
חִ֝֗יל
כַּיּוֹלֵֽדָה׃

8 By an East wind
You break
Ore ships.

ח בְּר֖וּחַ קָדִ֑ים
תְּ֝שַׁבֵּ֗ר
אֳנִיּ֥וֹת תַּרְשִֽׁישׁ׃

9 As we heard,
So we saw,
In the city of the Eternal of Hosts,
In our God's city,
May God establish it firmly forever, Selah.

ט כַּאֲשֶׁ֤ר שָׁמַ֨עְנוּ ׀
כֵּ֤ן רָאִ֗ינוּ
בְּעִ֣יר יהוָ֣ה צְ֭בָאוֹת
בְּעִ֣יר אֱלֹהֵ֑ינוּ
אֱלֹהִ֨ים יְכוֹנְנֶ֖הָ עַד־עוֹלָ֣ם סֶֽלָה׃

10 God, we imagine Your kindness
Inside
Of Your Temple.

י דִּמִּ֣ינוּ אֱלֹהִ֣ים חַסְדֶּ֑ךָ
בְּ֝קֶ֗רֶב
הֵיכָלֶֽךָ׃

11 Appropriate to Your name,God,
Is Your praise,
To the ends of the earth
Truth
Fills Your right hand.

יא כְּשִׁמְךָ֤ אֱלֹהִ֗ים
כֵּ֣ן תְּ֭הִלָּתְךָ
עַל־קַצְוֵי־אֶ֑רֶץ
צֶ֝֗דֶק
מָלְאָ֥ה יְמִינֶֽךָ׃

2 Let Mount Zion	יב יִשְׂמַח ׀
Rejoice.	הַר־צִיּוֹן
Jubilate,	תָּגֵלְנָה
Daughters of Judah,	בְּנוֹת יְהוּדָה
About	לְמַעַן
Your justice.	מִשְׁפָּטֶיךָ׃
13 Walk around Zion,	יג סֹבּוּ צִיּוֹן
Make a complete tour around it,	וְהַקִּיפוּהָ
Count	סִפְרוּ
Its towers.	מִגְדָּלֶיהָ׃
14 Consider	יד שִׁיתוּ לִבְּכֶם ׀
Its walls,	לְחֵילָה
Climb its palaces,	פַּסְּגוּ אַרְמְנוֹתֶיהָ
So it shall be told	לְמַעַן תְּסַפְּרוּ
To a later generation.	לְדוֹר אַחֲרוֹן׃
15 Truly, He	טו כִּי זֶה ׀
Is God, our Mighty One,	אֱלֹהִים אֱלֹהֵינוּ
Forever;	עוֹלָם וָעֶד
He	הוּא
Will lead us beyond death.	יְנַהֲגֵנוּ עַל־מוּת

3. The common interpretation of Mishnaic נוף is "beautiful landscape, beautiful foliage" but it seems better to follow both here and in the Talmud (e.g., *Qidd.* 40b) the corresponding Arabic ניף "to be elevated, high", accepted in the dictionaries of Levy and Gesenius. The translation of Qimḥi, "best of all climates", is unconvincing. Mount Zion in North-West of the City of David.

8. Usually, a storm in Israel comes from the West; the Hamsin winds from the Eastern desert usually do not reach hurricane strength. But the extraordinary phenomenon of a hurricane from the East plays a great role in Biblical history, so in the passage through the Red Sea (*Ex*. 14:21) and in the recital of the catastrophe setting the stage for the book of *Job* (1:19).

10. This usage "to imagine" of the verb דמה is unjustifiably restricted to Rabbinic Hebrew by the dictionaries.

11. The verb פסג is a hapax, so its meaning is anybody's guess. The noun פסגה traditionally means "peak, acme", so פסג is taken to mean "climb high". Ibn Ezra's "admire their heights" is a conjecture.

Psalm 49

1 For the director,
By the Qorahides, a Psalm.

א לַמְנַצֵּ֬חַ ׀
לִבְנֵי־קֹ֬רַח מִזְמֽוֹר׃

2 Hear this, all nations,
Listen,
All soil dwellers!

ב שִׁמְעוּ־זֹ֭את
כָּל־הָעַמִּ֑ים
הַ֝אֲזִ֗ינוּ
כָּל־יֹ֥שְׁבֵי חָֽלֶד׃

3 Both lowly men
And important ones,
Together,
Rich and poor.

ג גַּם־בְּנֵ֣י אָ֭דָם
גַּם־בְּנֵי־אִ֑ישׁ
יַ֝֗חַד
עָשִׁ֥יר וְאֶבְיֽוֹן׃

4 My mouth
Shall speak wisdom,
The studies of my heart are for insight.

ד פִּ֭י
יְדַבֵּ֣ר חָכְמ֑וֹת
וְהָג֖וּת לִבִּ֣י תְבוּנֽוֹת׃

5 I shall bend my ear to the parable,
I shall begin on the lute
My simile.

ה אַטֶּ֣ה לְמָשָׁ֣ל אָזְנִ֑י
אֶפְתַּ֥ח בְּ֝כִנּ֗וֹר
חִידָתִֽי׃

6 Why shall I be afraid
In the days of evil,
The sin of my heels surround me?

ו לָ֣מָּה אִ֭ירָא
בִּ֣ימֵי רָ֑ע
עֲוֺ֖ן עֲקֵבַ֣י יְסוּבֵּֽנִי׃

7 Those who trust their power
And in their great riches
Take pride!

ז הַבֹּטְחִ֥ים עַל־חֵילָ֑ם
וּבְרֹ֥ב עָ֝שְׁרָ֗ם
יִתְהַלָּֽלוּ׃

8 Ha,
No man can truly redeem,
Nor pay to God his weregild.

ח אָ֗ח
לֹא־פָדֹ֣ה יִפְדֶּ֣ה אִ֑ישׁ
לֹא־יִתֵּ֖ן לֵאלֹהִ֣ים כָּפְרֽוֹ׃

9 Too expensive
Is their ransom;
He ceases forever.

ט וְ֭יֵקַר
פִּדְי֥וֹן נַ֝פְשָׁ֗ם
וְחָדַ֥ל לְעוֹלָֽם׃

10 When they might have lived eternally,
Never see destruction.

י וִיחִי־ע֥וֹד לָנֶ֑צַח
לֹ֖א יִרְאֶ֣ה הַשָּֽׁחַת׃

11 Behold,
The wise will die,
Together the lazy and brutish vanish,
And leave their power to others.

יא כִּ֤י יִרְאֶ֨ה ׀
חֲכָ֘מִ֤ים יָמ֗וּתוּ
יַ֤חַד כְּסִ֣יל וָבַ֣עַר יֹאבֵ֑דוּ
וְעָזְב֖וּ לַאֲחֵרִ֣ים חֵילָֽם׃

12 Their grave is their house
Forever,
Their dwelling
For all generations
That is their reputation
On earth.

יב קִרְבָּ֤ם בָּ֥תֵּ֨ימוֹ ׀
לְֽעוֹלָ֗ם
מִ֭שְׁכְּנֹתָם
לְדֹ֣ר וָדֹ֑ר
קָֽרְא֥וּ בִ֝שְׁמוֹתָ֗ם
עֲלֵ֣י אֲדָמֽוֹת׃

13 But a man
Cannot stay in splendor,
He is compared to silent animals.

יג וְאָדָ֣ם בִּיקָ֣ר
בַּל־יָלִ֑ין
נִמְשַׁ֖ל כַּבְּהֵמ֣וֹת נִדְמֽוּ׃

14 That is the way
Of those who indulge in sloth,
Their future
Is willed by their mouths, Selah.

יד זֶ֣ה דַ֭רְכָּם
כֵּ֣סֶל לָ֑מוֹ
וְאַחֲרֵיהֶ֓ם ׀
בְּפִיהֶ֖ם יִרְצ֣וּ סֶֽלָה׃

15 Like sheep
They descend into the deep,
Death will shepherd them,
The straightforward rule them
Like cattlemen,
And their humors [rocks]
To be worn out in the deep,
Not being a dwelling place for him.

טו כַּצֹּ֤אן ׀
לִשְׁא֢וֹל שַׁ֫תּוּ
מָ֤וֶת יִֽרְעֵ֗ם
וַיִּרְדּ֤וּ בָ֨ם יְשָׁרִ֨ים ׀
לַבֹּ֗קֶר
וְצִירָם [וְֽצוּרָם֙]
לְבַלּ֥וֹת שְׁא֗וֹל
מִזְּבֻ֥ל לֽוֹ׃

16 But God
Will redeem my soul
From the deep,
Certainly He will take me up, Selah!

טז אַךְ־אֱלֹהִ֗ים
יִפְדֶּ֣ה נַ֭פְשִׁי
מִֽיַּד־שְׁא֑וֹל
כִּ֖י יִקָּחֵ֣נִי סֶֽלָה׃

17 Do not be afraid
When a man gets rich,
When he increases
The reputation of his house,

יז אַל־תִּ֭ירָא
כִּֽי־יַעֲשִׁ֣ר אִ֑ישׁ
כִּֽי־יִ֝רְבֶּ֗ה
כְּב֣וֹד בֵּיתֽוֹ׃

18 For in his death
He cannot take anything with him,
His reputation will not follow him!

יח כִּ֤י לֹ֣א בְ֭מוֹתוֹ
יִקַּ֣ח הַכֹּ֑ל
לֹא־יֵרֵ֖ד אַחֲרָ֣יו כְּבוֹדֽוֹ׃

19 For his soul
Already in his lifetime is cursed,
But you can be praised
For you will have it good.

יט כִּֽי־נַ֭פְשׁוֹ
בְּחַיָּ֣יו יְבָרֵ֑ךְ
וְ֝יוֹדֻ֗ךָ
כִּי־תֵיטִ֥יב לָֽךְ׃

20 While you will come
To his fathers place,
For eternity
They will not see light.

כ תָּ֭בוֹא
עַד־דּ֣וֹר אֲבוֹתָ֑יו
עַד־נֵ֝֗צַח
לֹ֣א יִרְאוּ־אֽוֹר׃

21 A man in splendor	כא אָדָ֣ם בִּ֭יקָר
Cannot understand:	וְלֹ֣א יָבִ֑ין
He is compared	נִמְשַׁ֖ל
To silent animals.	כַּבְּהֵמ֣וֹת נִדְמֽוּ׃

6 It is best to translate the traditional "heel" for עקב rather than adopt "pursuer" (Rashi) or "deceiver" (Ben Yehuda).

8 Taking with Ibn Janaḥ אח as short form of the exclamation האח rather than a difficult to place "brother". כסיל here (and elsewhere) as well as כסל in v. 14 are taken in the sense of the Arabic "sloth, do-nothingness".

12 Following Ibn Ezra I am identifying קרבם and קברם for the translation.

13 Deriving נדמו from דמם 'to be silent"; it also could mean "like extinct animals".

15 Translating the Ketib צירם "juice, fish sauce", in Rabbinic Hebrew. Perhaps one may see in צורם "their rock" a poetic shortening of צורתם "their form, shape". Instead of בֹּקֶר we read בּוֹקֵר "cattleman". The essence of the last two clauses is the theology often repeated in Psalms that the bad guys are annihilated in death without a chance of a future life. On the other hand, the eternal Life of the good people, celebrated in vv. 16, 20, is automatically a life of eternal bliss.

Psalm 50

1 A psalm of Asaph.
Power,
God,
The Eternal
Spoke and summoned the earth
From sunrise
To its setting.

א מִזְמוֹר לְאָסָף
אֵל |
אֱלֹהִים
יהוה
דִּבֶּר וַיִּקְרָא־אָרֶץ
מִמִּזְרַח־שֶׁמֶשׁ
עַד־מְבֹאוֹ׃

2 From Zion, the perfection of beauty,
God appears.

ב מִצִּיּוֹן מִכְלַל־יֹפִי
אֱלֹהִים הוֹפִיעַ׃

3 Our God will come, He will not be silent,
Fire consumes before Him
And His surroundings
Are very stormy.

ג יָבֹא אֱלֹהֵינוּ וְאַל־יֶחֱרַשׁ
אֵשׁ־לְפָנָיו תֹּאכֵל
וּסְבִיבָיו
נִשְׂעֲרָה מְאֹד

4 He will summon heaven above
And the earth
To the lawsuit against His people.

ד יִקְרָא אֶל־הַשָּׁמַיִם מֵעָל
וְאֶל־הָאָרֶץ
לָדִין עַמּוֹ

5 Assemble for Me My pious ones,
Entering My covenant by bloody sacrifice.

ה אִסְפוּ־לִי חֲסִידָי
כֹּרְתֵי בְרִיתִי עֲלֵי־זָבַח׃

6 The heavens will proclaim His truth,
For God
Is the judge, Selah.

ו וַיַּגִּידוּ שָׁמַיִם צִדְקוֹ
כִּי־אֱלֹהִים
שֹׁפֵט הוּא סֶלָה

7 Listen, my people,
I shall speak,
Israel,
I shall inform against you,
I am God, your Powerful.

ז שִׁמְעָה עַמִּי | וַאֲדַבֵּרָה
יִשְׂרָאֵל
וְאָעִידָה בָּךְ
אֱלֹהִים אֱלֹהֶיךָ אָנֹכִי

8 Not about your sacrifices
Shall I admonish you,
Your holocausts always are before me.

ח לֹא עַל־זְבָחֶיךָ
אוֹכִיחֶךָ
וְעוֹלֹתֶיךָ לְנֶגְדִּי תָמִיד׃

9 I will not take a bull from your house
Nor from your corrals
Bell-wethers,

ט לֹא־אֶקַּח מִבֵּיתְךָ פָר
מִמִּכְלְאֹתֶיךָ
עַתּוּדִים

10 For I own all beasts of the woods,
The animals
On bull mountains.

י כִּי־לִי כָל־חַיְתוֹ־יָעַר
בְּהֵמוֹת
בְּהַרְרֵי־אָלֶף׃

11 I know
All mountain birds,
The vermin of the field
Is with me.

יא יָדַעְתִּי
כָּל־עוֹף הָרִים
וְזִיז שָׂדַי
עִמָּדִי׃

12 If I were hungry, I would not tell you, For I own the globe And its contents.	יב אִם־אֶרְעַב לֹא־אֹמַר לָךְ כִּי לִי תֵבֵל וּמְלֹאָהּ׃
13 Would I eat The meat of bullocks, Drink the blood of bell-wethers?	יג הַאוֹכַל בְּשַׂר אַבִּירִים וְדַם עַתּוּדִים אֶשְׁתֶּה׃
14 Sacrifice to God in thanksgiving, Pay your vows to the Most High.	יד זְבַח לֵאלֹהִים תּוֹדָה וְשַׁלֵּם לְעֶלְיוֹן נְדָרֶיךָ׃
15 Then call upon Me On the day of distress, I shall extricate you So you shall honor Me.	טו וּקְרָאֵנִי בְּיוֹם צָרָה אֲחַלֶּצְךָ וּתְכַבְּדֵנִי׃
16 But to the wicked Says God: How can you Talk about My laws, Carry My covenant on your lips?	טז וְלָרָשָׁע ׀ אָמַר אֱלֹהִים מַה־לְּךָ לְסַפֵּר חֻקָּי וַתִּשָּׂא בְרִיתִי עֲלֵי־פִיךָ
17 For you Hated instruction And threw My words behind you.	יז וְאַתָּה שָׂנֵאתָ מוּסָר וַתַּשְׁלֵךְ דְּבָרַי אַחֲרֶיךָ׃
18 When you saw a thief You were his willing receiver, You put your lot with adulterers.	יח אִם־רָאִיתָ גַנָּב וַתִּרֶץ עִמּוֹ וְעִם מְנָאֲפִים חֶלְקֶךָ׃
19 Your mouth You freed for evil, And your tongue You yoked onto deceit.	יט פִּיךָ שָׁלַחְתָּ בְרָעָה וּלְשׁוֹנְךָ תַּצְמִיד מִרְמָה׃
20 You sit down To talk against your brother, You spread slander Against your mother's son.	כ תֵּשֵׁב בְּאָחִיךָ תְדַבֵּר בְּבֶן־אִמְּךָ תִּתֶּן־דֹּפִי׃
21 These you did And I shall be silent? You invented That I should be like You? I shall admonish and proceed against you.	כא אֵלֶּה עָשִׂיתָ ׀ וְהֶחֱרַשְׁתִּי דִּמִּיתָ הֱיוֹת אֶהְיֶה כָמוֹךָ אוֹכִיחֲךָ וְאֶעֶרְכָה לְעֵינֶיךָ׃
22 Understand this, You who forget God, Lest I shall tear you up And nobody can save.	כב בִּינוּ־נָא זֹאת שֹׁכְחֵי אֱלוֹהַּ פֶּן־אֶטְרֹף וְאֵין מַצִּיל

23 He who sacrifices in thanksgiving is honoring
me,
He is on the way.
I shall let him see
God's salvation!

כג זֹבֵחַ תּוֹדָה יְכַבְּדָנְנִי
שָׂם דֶּרֶךְ
אַרְאֶנּוּ
בְּיֵשַׁע אֱלֹהִים

4. For the meaning of ערך see *Ps*. 5:4.

7. Deriving עד with Barth from a root cognate with Arabic عَدَّ "to know".

10. בהמות could also mean "the Behemoth" (*Job* 40:15-24).

11. זיז here is taken in the sense of the same word in Aramaic, "vermin". (In Arabic, the meaning is "cicadae"). It should be noted that in the story of creation, Man is not given rule over worms and insects, only over vertebrates (*Gen.* 2:20). So God's mastery of invertebrates is His real sign of power. (H. Guggenheimer, Magie et Dialectique, *Diogène* 60 (1967), 93-97).

Psalm 51

1 For the director,
A psalm of David.

א לַמְנַצֵּחַ
מִזְמוֹר לְדָוִד׃

2 When the prophet Nathan
Came to him
After he came
To Bathseba.

ב בְּבוֹא־אֵלָיו
נָתָן הַנָּבִיא
אֲשֶׁר־בָּא
אֶל־בַּת־שָׁבַע׃

3 Pardon me, God, in Your kindness,
By Your immense mercy
Wipe off my crimes.

ג חָנֵּנִי אֱלֹהִים כְּחַסְדֶּךָ
כְּרֹב רַחֲמֶיךָ
מְחֵה פְשָׁעָי׃

4 Repeatedly
Cleanse me from my sin;
From my transgression purify me.

ד הֶרֶבה [הֶרֶב]
כַּבְּסֵנִי מֵעֲוֺנִי
וּמֵחַטָּאתִי טַהֲרֵנִי׃

5 Truly, my crimes
I recognize,
My transgression is always before me.

ה כִּי־פְשָׁעַי
אֲנִי אֵדָע
וְחַטָּאתִי נֶגְדִּי תָמִיד׃

6 Towards You alone I sinned,
I did
The evil in Your eyes,
Therefore You are just in Your sentence,
Justified in Your judging.

ו לְךָ לְבַדְּךָ | חָטָאתִי
וְהָרַע בְּעֵינֶיךָ עָשִׂיתִי
לְמַעַן־תִּצְדַּק בְּדָבְרֶךָ
תִּזְכֶּה בְשָׁפְטֶךָ׃

7 Truly I was created in sin,
And in guilt
My mother was in heat for me.

ז הֵן־בְּעָווֹן חוֹלָלְתִּי
וּבְחֵטְא
יֶחֱמַתְנִי אִמִּי׃

8 Truly, truth
You demand innermost,
And in what is hidden
You teach me wisdom.

ח הֵן־אֱמֶת
חָפַצְתָּ בַטֻּחוֹת
וּבְסָתֻם
חָכְמָה תוֹדִיעֵנִי׃

9 Sprinkle me with hyssop and I shall be pure,
Cleanse me
So I shall be whiter than snow.

ט תְּחַטְּאֵנִי בְאֵזוֹב וְאֶטְהָר
תְּכַבְּסֵנִי
וּמִשֶּׁלֶג אַלְבִּין׃

10 Let me hear
Joy and rejoicing,
Let exult
The bones You crushed.

י תַּשְׁמִיעֵנִי
שָׂשׂוֹן וְשִׂמְחָה
תָּגֵלְנָה
עֲצָמוֹת דִּכִּיתָ׃

11 Hide Your face
From my transgressions
And erase all my sins.

יא הַסְתֵּר פָּנֶיךָ
מֵחֲטָאָי
כָּל־עֲוֺנֹתַי מְח

12 God, Create in me
A pure heart
And rejuvenate in me
A firm spirit.

יב לֵב טָהוֹר
בְּרָא־לִי אֱלֹהִים
וְרוּחַ נָכוֹן
חַדֵּשׁ בְּקִרְבִּי׃

13 Do not throw me away from before You,
Your holy spirit
Do not take from me.

יג אַל־תַּשְׁלִיכֵנִי מִלְּפָנֶיךָ
וְרוּחַ קָדְשְׁךָ
אַל־תִּקַּח מִמֶּנִּי׃

14 Return to me
The joy of Your salvation,
Support me in noble spirit.

יד הָשִׁיבָה לִּי
שְׂשׂוֹן יִשְׁעֶךָ
וְרוּחַ נְדִיבָה תִסְמְכֵנִי׃

15 I shall teach Your worship to criminals,
And sinners
Will return to You.

טו אֲלַמְּדָה פֹשְׁעִים דְּרָכֶיךָ
וְחַטָּאִים
אֵלֶיךָ יָשׁוּבוּ׃

16 Save me from Silence,
O God,
My Power of my salvation,
My tongue shall sing
Of Your equity.

טז הַצִּילֵנִי מִדָּמִים ׀
אֱלֹהִים
אֱלֹהֵי תְּשׁוּעָתִי
תְּרַנֵּן לְשׁוֹנִי
צִדְקָתֶךָ׃

17 My Master,
Open my lips,
Then my mouth
Will tell Your praise.

יז אֲדֹנָי
שְׂפָתַי תִּפְתָּח
וּפִי
יַגִּיד תְּהִלָּתֶךָ׃

18 For
You desire neither sacrifice nor gift,
A holocaust
Is not pleasurable to You.

יח כִּי ׀
לֹא־תַחְפֹּץ זֶבַח וְאֶתֵּנָה
עוֹלָה
לֹא תִרְצֶה׃

19 A broken spirit
Is sacrifice for God.
A broken and crushed heart
God
Will not despise.

יט זִבְחֵי אֱלֹהִים
רוּחַ נִשְׁבָּרָה
לֵב־נִשְׁבָּר וְנִדְכֶּה
אֱלֹהִים
לֹא תִבְזֶה׃

20 In Your pleasure, please favor
Zion,
Build
The walls of Jerusalem.

כ הֵיטִיבָה בִרְצוֹנְךָ
אֶת־צִיּוֹן
תִּבְנֶה
חוֹמוֹת יְרוּשָׁלָם׃

21 Then You will desire honest sacrifices,
Holocaust and total offering,
Then bulls may be brought on Your altar.

כא אָז תַּחְפֹּץ זִבְחֵי־צֶדֶק
עוֹלָה וְכָלִיל
אָז יַעֲלוּ עַל־מִזְבַּחֲךָ פָרִים.

We hear the poet's opinion that voluntary sacrifices are acceptable only as the sacrifice of a broken spirit. Since his sin with Bathseba was not inadvertent, he was barred from bringing an obligatory cleansing sacrifice.

Psalm 52

1 For the director,
    A didactic poem by David.

א לַמְנַצֵּחַ
מַשְׂכִּיל לְדָוִד׃

2 When Doeg the Edomite
    Came
    And told Saul
And said to him:
David came
    To the house of Ahimelekh.

ב בְּבוֹא ׀
דּוֹאֵג הָאֲדֹמִי
וַיַּגֵּד לְשָׁאוּל
וַיֹּאמֶר לוֹ
בָּא דָוִד
אֶל־בֵּית אֲחִימֶלֶךְ׃

3 Why do you boast in wickedness,
    Strong man,
Powerful abomination
    All day long.

ג מַה־תִּתְהַלֵּל בְּרָעָה
הַגִּבּוֹר
חֶסֶד אֵל
כָּל־הַיּוֹם׃

4 Corruption
    You plan for your tongue,
Like a honed razor
    Doing mischief.

ד הַוּוֹת
תַּחְשֹׁב לְשׁוֹנֶךָ
כְּתַעַר מְלֻטָּשׁ
עֹשֵׂה רְמִיָּה׃

5 You prefer evil over goodness,
Lies
    Over straight talk, Selah.

ה אָהַבְתָּ רָּע מִטּוֹב
שֶׁקֶר ׀
מִדַּבֵּר צֶדֶק סֶלָה

6 You love to swallow all,
Tongue of trickery.

ו אָהַבְתָּ כָל־דִּבְרֵי־בָלַע
לְשׁוֹן מִרְמָה׃

7 But God
    Will demolish you forever,
Will excise and remove you from the Tent,
Uproot you from the Land of Life, Selah.

ז גַּם־אֵל
יִתָּצְךָ לָנֶצַח
יַחְתְּךָ וְיִסָּחֲךָ מֵאֹהֶל
וְשֵׁרֶשְׁךָ מֵאֶרֶץ חַיִּים סֶלָה׃

8 The just will see and they will fear,
And gloat over him.

ח וְיִרְאוּ צַדִּיקִים וְיִירָאוּ
וְעָלָיו יִשְׂחָקוּ׃

9 Behold the man
    Who does not make God his stronghold,
Who trusts
    In his immense riches
Becomes impudent
    In his corruption.

ט הִנֵּה הַגֶּבֶר
לֹא־יָשִׂים אֱלֹהִים מָעוּזּוֹ
וַיִּבְטַח
בְּרֹב עָשְׁרוֹ
יָעֹז
בְּהַוָּתוֹ׃

10 But I am
    Like a greening olive tree
    In God's House,
I am trusting in God's kindness
    Forever and ever..

י וַאֲנִי ׀
כְּזַיִת רַעֲנָן
בְּבֵית אֱלֹהִים
בָּטַחְתִּי בְחֶסֶד אֱלֹהִים
עוֹלָם וָעֶד׃

11 I shall thank You forever
    For what You did,

יא אוֹדְךָ לְעוֹלָם
כִּי עָשִׂיתָ

And shout Your name: The Very Good	וַאֲקַוֶּה שִׁמְךָ כִי־טוֹב
In front of Your pious.	נֶגֶד חֲסִידֶיךָ׃

3. The second root חסד in Hebrew is either equivalent to Aramaic "insult, abomination" or to Arabic "envy".

7. The Tent here probably is not the terrestrial but the heavenly Temple, situated in the Land of Life.

8. An intended pun on the weak roots ראה “to see” and ירא “to fear”.

11. Arabic קוה “to cry, shout”

Psalm 53 see under Psalm 14

Psalm 54

1 For the director, in melodies
A didactic song by David.

א לַמְנַצֵּחַ בִּנְגִינֹת
מַשְׂכִּיל לְדָוִד׃

2 When the people of Siph came
And told Saul:
Here David
Is hiding with us.

ב בְּבוֹא הַזִּיפִים
וַיֹּאמְרוּ לְשָׁאוּל
הֲלֹא־דָוִד
מִסְתַּתֵּר עִמָּנוּ׃

3 God,
In Your Name help me;
In Your might judge me.

ג אֱלֹהִים
בְּשִׁמְךָ הוֹשִׁיעֵנִי
וּבִגְבוּרָתְךָ תְדִינֵנִי׃

4 God,
Listen to my prayer,
Bend Your ear
To may mouth's saying.

ד אֱלֹהִים
שְׁמַע תְּפִלָּתִי
הַאֲזִינָה
לְאִמְרֵי־פִי׃

5 Certainly strangers
Rose against me,
And strongmen
Desired my life,
Did not consider God over them, Selah.

ה כִּי זָרִים ׀
קָמוּ עָלַי
וְעָרִיצִים
בִּקְשׁוּ נַפְשִׁי
לֹא שָׂמוּ אֱלֹהִים לְנֶגְדָּם סֶלָה׃

6 Therefore, God
Be helping me
Almighty,
Be supporting my life.

ו הִנֵּה אֱלֹהִים
עֹזֵר לִי
אֲדֹנָי
בְּסֹמְכֵי נַפְשִׁי׃

7 The evil may rebound
Against those who observe me;
In Your truth
Squeeze them.

ז יָשׁוּב [יָשִׁיב] הָרַע
לְשֹׁרְרָי
בַּאֲמִתְּךָ
הַצְמִיתֵם׃

8 I shall sacrifice to You willingly,
I shall thank Your name, Eternal, which is good,

ח בִּנְדָבָה אֶזְבְּחָה־לָּךְ
אוֹדֶה שִּׁמְךָ יְיָ כִּי־טוֹב׃

9 Since from all trouble
You saved me,
And my enemies'
Saw mine eye.

ט כִּי מִכָּל־צָרָה
הִצִּילָנִי
וּבְאֹיְבַי
רָאֲתָה עֵינִי׃

9 My enemies' downfall or punishment.

Psalm 55

1 For the director, in melodies,
A didactic song by David.

א לַמְנַצֵּחַ בִּנְגִינֹת
מַשְׂכִּיל לְדָוִד׃

2 Listen, o God,
To my prayer,
Nor disregard
My supplication.

ב הַאֲזִינָה אֱלֹהִים
תְּפִלָּתִי
וְאַל־תִּתְעַלַּם
מִתְּחִנָּתִי

3 Please take notice of me, and answer me,
I am rambling in my talk and neighing.

ג הַקְשִׁיבָה לִּי וַעֲנֵנִי
אָרִיד בְּשִׂיחִי וְאָהִימָה׃

4 By the noise of the enemy,
The creaking of the wicked,
They load me down with iniquity
And attack me with wrath.

ד מִקּוֹל אוֹיֵב
מִפְּנֵי עָקַת רָשָׁע
כִּי־יָמִיטוּ עָלַי אָוֶן
וּבְאַף יִשְׂטְמוּנִי

5 My heart
Trembles within me,
Terrors of Death
Fell on me.

ה לִבִּי
יָחִיל בְּקִרְבִּי
אֵימוֹת מָוֶת
נָפְלוּ עָלָי׃

6 Fear and shaking
Overcomes me,
I am covered
With shudder.

ו יִרְאָה וָרַעַד
יָבֹא בִי
וַתְּכַסֵּנִי
פַּלָּצוּת׃

7 I said:
Who might give me wings
Like a dove,
I would fly away to dwell.

ז וָאֹמַר
מִי־יִתֶּן־לִּי אֵבֶר
כַּיּוֹנָה
אָעוּפָה וְאֶשְׁכֹּנָה׃

8 Then
I would wander far away,
Stay in the wilderness, Selah.

ח הִנֵּה
אַרְחִיק נְדֹד
אָלִין בַּמִּדְבָּר סֶלָה׃

9 Quickly, I would seek shelter
From the wild winds and storms.

ט אָחִישָׁה מִפְלָט לִי
מֵרוּחַ סֹעָה מִסָּעַר׃

10 Swallow up, Master,
Their cleft tongue,
For I saw violence and strife in the city.

י בַּלַּע אֲדֹנָי
פַּלַּג לְשׁוֹנָם
כִּי־רָאִיתִי חָמָס וְרִיב בָּעִיר׃

11 Day and night
They surround it on its walls,
Iniquity and worry in its midst.

יא יוֹמָם וָלַיְלָה
יְסוֹבְבֻהָ עַל־חוֹמֹתֶיהָ
וְאָוֶן וְעָמָל בְּקִרְבָּהּ

12 Corruption is in its midst,
From its public places will not depart
Violence and deceit.

יב הַוּוֹת בְּקִרְבָּהּ
וְלֹא־יָמִישׁ מֵרְחֹבָהּ
תֹּךְ וּמִרְמָה׃

13 For a no-enemy slanders me; I could bear,
A non-hater
Twists around me
Could I hide from him?

יג כִּ֤י לֹֽא־אוֹיֵ֥ב יְחָרְפֵ֗נִי וְאֶ֫שָּׂ֥א
לֹֽא־מְשַׂנְאִ֖י
עָלַ֣י הִגְדִּ֑יל
וְאֶסָּתֵ֥ר מִמֶּֽנּוּ׃

14 But you, a human of my worth,
My commander
And my acquaintance.

יד וְאַתָּ֣ה אֱנ֣וֹשׁ כְּעֶרְכִּ֑י
אַ֝לּוּפִ֗י
וּמְיֻדָּעִֽי

15 Together
We used to have sweet counsel,
In God's House
We used to go with emotion.

טו אֲשֶׁ֣ר יַ֭חְדָּו
נַמְתִּ֣יק ס֑וֹד
בְּבֵ֥ית אֱ֝לֹהִ֗ים
נְהַלֵּ֥ךְ בְּרָֽגֶשׁ׃

16 Desolation on them!
May they descend alive to the Pit,
True evil is in their dwelling, in themselves.

טז יַשִּׁ֤ימָ֨וֶת ׀ [יַשִּׁ֣יא מָ֣וֶת] ׀ עָלֵ֗ימוֹ
יֵרְד֣וּ שְׁא֣וֹל חַיִּ֑ים
כִּֽי־רָע֖וֹת בִּמְגוּרָ֣ם בְּקִרְבָּֽם׃

17 But I,
To God I shall call,
The Eternal
Will save me.

יז אֲ֭נִי
אֶל־אֱלֹהִ֣ים אֶקְרָ֑א
וַ֝יהוָ֗ה
יוֹשִׁיעֵֽנִי׃

18 Evening, morning, and noontime
I am uttering and wailing,
And He will hear my voice.

יח עֶ֤רֶב וָבֹ֣קֶר וְ֭צָהֳרַיִם
אָשִׂ֣יחָה וְאֶהֱמֶ֑ה
וַיִּשְׁמַ֥ע קוֹלִֽי׃

19 He redeemed my soul for peace
From my confidant,
For the majority
Were with me.

יט פָּדָ֬ה בְשָׁל֣וֹם נַ֭פְשִׁי
מִקֲּרָב־לִ֑י
כִּֽי־בְ֝רַבִּ֗ים
הָי֥וּ עִמָּדִֽי׃

20 May the Powerful hear
And subdue them,
He who thrones from eternity,
Atrophy, no change is with them,
For they did not fear God.

כ יִשְׁמַ֤ע ׀ אֵ֨ל ׀
וְֽיַעֲנֵ֗ם
וְיֹ֤שֵׁ֥ב קֶ֗דֶם
סֶ֫לָה אֲשֶׁ֤ר אֵ֣ין חֲלִיפ֣וֹת לָ֑מוֹ
וְלֹ֖א יָרְא֣וּ אֱלֹהִֽים׃

21 He sent his hand
Against his confederates,
Desecrated his covenant.

כא שָׁלַ֣ח יָ֭דָיו
בִּשְׁלֹמָ֗יו
חִלֵּ֥ל בְּרִיתֽוֹ׃

22 More slippery
Than butter is his mouth,
While intending a fight,
His words are softer than oil,
They are brass knuckles.

כב חָלְק֤וּ ׀
מַחְמָאֹ֬ת פִּ֗יו
וּֽקֲרָב־לִ֫בּ֥וֹ
רַכּ֣וּ דְבָרָ֣יו מִשֶּׁ֑מֶן
וְהֵ֣מָּה פְתִחֽוֹת׃

23 Throw your burden
On the Eternal,
Then He will provide for you,
He will never let reel
The just one.

כג הַשְׁלֵ֤ךְ עַל־יְהוָ֨ה ׀
יְהָבְךָ֮
וְה֪וּא יְכַ֫לְכְּלֶ֥ךָ
לֹא־יִתֵּ֖ן לְעוֹלָ֥ם מ֗וֹט
לַצַּדִּֽיק׃

24 But You, God, fell them	כד וְאַתָּה אֱלֹהִים ׀ תּוֹרִדֵם ׀
To the Pit of destruction.	לִבְאֵר שַׁחַת
Men of bloodshed and trickery	אַנְשֵׁי דָמִים וּמִרְמָה
Will not live out half their days.	לֹא־יֶחֱצוּ יְמֵיהֶם
But I	וַאֲנִי
Shall trust in You.	אֶבְטַח־בָּךְ׃

3. Following E. Täubler, I am taking אריד from the root רוד "rambling".

7. אבר "member" is really the bird's flight arm and flight muscle.

16. The Ketib is ישימות"desolation", the Qere ישא מות also derives the verb (first word) from שמם "to be desolate".

20. This Selah cannot be the musical note since it follows a dividing accent,; it is read as Arabic של whose principal meaning is "atrophy" (of a limb).

23. יהבך is traditionally translated as "your burden". The Aramaic verb יהב means "to give", so as noun it must be something (a load) put on somebody by, or with the help of, another person.

22. Comparing the hapax פְּתִחוֹת with Arabic פתחה which means, among other things, "finger-knuckles" as weapons.

Psalm 56

1 For the director,
On *yonat 'elem reḥoqim*
Mikhtam by David,
When the Philistines seized him at Gat.

א לַמְנַצֵּחַ ׀
עַל־יוֹנַת אֵלֶם רְחֹקִים
לְדָוִד מִכְתָּם
בֶּאֱחֹז אֹתוֹ פְלִשְׁתִּים בְּגַת

2 Be gracious to me, God,
For men aspire against me,
All day long
They push me, fighting.

ב חָנֵּנִי אֱלֹהִים
כִּי־שְׁאָפַנִי אֱנוֹשׁ
כָּל־הַיּוֹם
לֹחֵם יִלְחָצֵנִי׃

3 Those who stare at me aspire against me
All day long,
The majority fight against me, Exalted One.

ג שָׁאֲפוּ שׁוֹרְרַי
כָּל־הַיּוֹם
כִּי־רַבִּים לֹחֲמִים לִי מָרוֹם

4 The day when I fear,
I
Shall trust in You.

ד יוֹם אִירָא
אֲנִי
אֵלֶיךָ אֶבְטָח׃

5 Of God
I praise His word,
In God I trust,
I shall not fear.
What may flesh do to me?

ה בֵּאלֹהִים
אֲהַלֵּל דְּבָרוֹ
בֵּאלֹהִים בָּטַחְתִּי
לֹא אִירָא
מַה־יַּעֲשֶׂה בָשָׂר לִי

6 All day long
Those who talk against me conspire,
All their thoughts are of evil.

ו כָּל־הַיּוֹם
דְּבָרַי יְעַצֵּבוּ
עָלַי כָּל־מַחְשְׁבֹתָם לָרָע׃

7 They fear,
They hide, they
Are those who watch my heels
While hoping for my soul.

ז יָגוּרוּ ׀
יִצְפִּינוּ [יִצְפּוֹנוּ] הֵמָּה
עֲקֵבַי יִשְׁמֹרוּ
כַּאֲשֶׁר קִוּוּ נַפְשִׁי׃

8 Let them escape into guilt,
In wrath
Nations
Bring down, o God.

ח עַל־אָוֶן פַּלֶּט־לָמוֹ
בְּאַף
עַמִּים ׀
הוֹרֵד אֱלֹהִים׃

9 My swaying
You wrote down,
You, please put my tear into Your water-skin,
Behold,
In your book.

ט נֹדִי
סָפַרְתָּה
אָתָּה שִׂימָה דִמְעָתִי בְנֹאדֶךָ
הֲלֹא
בְּסִפְרָתֶךָ׃

10 Then
My enemies will turn backwards,
On the day I shall call;
By this I will have known
That God is with me.

י אָז ׀
יָשׁוּבוּ אוֹיְבַי אָחוֹר
בְּיוֹם אֶקְרָא
זֶה־יָדַעְתִּי
כִּי־אֱלֹהִים לִי

11 I shall praise the Word	יא בֵּֽאלֹהִים
Of God,	אֲהַלֵּל דָּבָר
I shall praise the Word	בַּיי
Of the Eternal.	אֲהַלֵּל דָּבָר׃
12 In God I trust,	יב בֵּאלֹהִים בָּטַחְתִּי
I shall not fear!	לֹא אִירָא
What may man do to me?	מַה־יַּעֲשֶׂה אָדָם לִי׃
13 To You, o God, are my vows	יג עָלַי אֱלֹהִים נְדָרֶיךָ
I shall pay thanksgiving to You!	אֲשַׁלֵּם תּוֹדֹת לָךְ׃
14 For You saved my soul	יד כִּי הִצַּלְתָּ נַפְשִׁי
From Death,	מִמָּוֶת
Nay, my feet from being pushed,	הֲלֹא רַגְלַי מִדֶּחִי
That I can wander	לְהִתְהַלֵּךְ
Before God	לִפְנֵי אֱלֹהִים
In the light	בְּאוֹר
Of Life!	הַחַיִּים׃

1. It seems that "the silent dove at far-away places", was a known melody.

6. Reading דּוֹבְרַי "those who are talking" for the meaning of דְּבָרַי ("my words).

14. Clearly, Death and Life here mean eternal death and eternal life.

Psalm 57

1 For the director, "do not destroy",
Of David, a *mikhtam*
When he was fleeing before Saul
In the cave.

א לַמְנַצֵּחַ אַל־תַּשְׁחֵת
לְדָוִד מִכְתָּם
בְּבָרְחוֹ מִפְּנֵי־שָׁאוּל
בַּמְּעָרָה׃

2 Be gracious to me, o God,
Be gracious,
Truly in You
Is my soul seeking shelter.
I shall take shelter in Your wings' shadow
Until
Evil passes.

ב חָנֵּנִי אֱלֹהִים ׀
חָנֵּנִי
כִּי בְךָ
חָסָיָה נַפְשִׁי
וּבְצֵל־כְּנָפֶיךָ אֶחְסֶה
עַד
יַעֲבֹר הַוּוֹת׃

3 I shall call
To most high God,
To the Power
Who completes for me.

ג אֶקְרָא
לֵאלֹהִים עֶלְיוֹן
לָאֵל
גֹּמֵר עָלָי׃

4 He sends from Heaven and saves me,
Disgrace to who aspires against me, Selah!
God will send
His kindness and His fidelity.

ד יִשְׁלַח מִשָּׁמַיִם ׀ וְיוֹשִׁיעֵנִי
חֵרֵף שֹׁאֲפִי סֶלָה
יִשְׁלַח אֱלֹהִים
חַסְדּוֹ וַאֲמִתּוֹ׃

5 My life is
Amongst lions,
I will lie down amongst flares,
Amongst people whose teeth
Are spear and arrows,
And their tongue
A pointed sword.

ה נַפְשִׁי ׀
בְּתוֹךְ לְבָאִם
אֶשְׁכְּבָה לֹהֲטִים
בְּנֵי־אָדָם שִׁנֵּיהֶם
חֲנִית וְחִצִּים
וּלְשׁוֹנָם
חֶרֶב חַדָּה׃

6 Be exalted over Heaven, God,
Over all earth is Your splendor.

ו רוּמָה עַל־הַשָּׁמַיִם אֱלֹהִים
עַל כָּל־הָאָרֶץ כְּבוֹדֶךָ׃

7 A snare
They prepared for my steps,
I am bent;
They dug a trench before me,
They fell into it, Selah.

ז רֶשֶׁת ׀
הֵכִינוּ לִפְעָמַי
כָּפַף נַפְשִׁי
כָּרוּ לְפָנַי שִׁיחָה
נָפְלוּ בְתוֹכָהּ סֶלָה׃

8 My heart is steadfast, God,
My heart is steadfast,
I will sing
And make music.

ח נָכוֹן לִבִּי אֱלֹהִים
נָכוֹן לִבִּי
אָשִׁירָה
וַאֲזַמֵּרָה׃

9 Rise, my spirit, rise,
Harp and lute,
I will raise early in the morning.

ט עוּרָה כְבוֹדִי עוּרָה
הַנֵּבֶל וְכִנּוֹר
אָעִירָה שָּׁחַר׃

10 I shall thank You amongst nations,
Master,
I will compose chants about You
Among races.

י אוֹדְךָ בָעַמִּים ׀
אֲדֹנָי
אֲזַמֶּרְךָ
בַּל־אֻמִּים׃

11 Because Your kindness is great onto Heaven
And Your fidelity onto the skies.

יא כִּי־גָדֹל עַד־שָׁמַיִם חַסְדֶּךָ
וְעַד־שְׁחָקִים אֲמִתֶּךָ׃

12 Be exalted over Heaven, God,
Over all earth is Your splendor.

יב רוּמָה עַל־שָׁמַיִם אֱלֹהִים
עַל כָּל־הָאָרֶץ כְּבוֹדֶךָ׃

Psalm 58

1 For the director, "do not destroy",
A *mikhtam* by David.

א לַמְנַצֵּחַ אַל־תַּשְׁחֵת
לְדָוִד מִכְתָּם׃

2 Is it true that
Justice in secret
You pronounce,
That you judge in rectitude
Simple people?

ב הַאֻמְנָם
אֵלֶם צֶדֶק
תְּדַבֵּרוּן
מֵישָׁרִים תִּשְׁפְּטוּ
בְּנֵי אָדָם׃

3 Even in the heart
They do evil,
Over the land
Your oppressive hands
You spread.

ג אַף־בְּלֵב
עוֹלֹת תִּפְעָלוּן
בָּאָרֶץ
חֲמַס יְדֵיכֶם
תְּפַלֵּסוּן׃

4 The wicked are pervert from the womb,
They err from the belly,
The speakers of lies.

ד זֹרוּ רְשָׁעִים מֵרָחֶם
תָּעוּ מִבֶּטֶן
דֹּבְרֵי כָזָב׃

5 Their wrath
Is like snake venom,
Like a deaf python
He plugs his ear.

ה חֲמַת־לָמוֹ
כִּדְמוּת חֲמַת־נָחָשׁ
כְּמוֹ־פֶתֶן חֵרֵשׁ
יַאְטֵם אָזְנוֹ׃

6 So it shall not hear
The voice of snake-charmers,
.Conjurers of ingenious conjuring.

ו אֲשֶׁר לֹא־יִשְׁמַע
לְקוֹל מְלַחֲשִׁים
חוֹבֵר חֲבָרִים מְחֻכָּם׃

7 God,
Break down their teeth in their mouth.
Eternal,
Demolish
The molars of young lions.

ז אֱלֹהִים
הֲרָס־שִׁנֵּימוֹ בְּפִימוֹ
מַלְתְּעוֹת כְּפִירִים
נְתֹץ ׀
יְהוָה׃

8 Let them melt away like water,
Let them disappear,
When He draws His arrow [arrows]
Really, they will be wilting!

ח יִמָּאֲסוּ כְמוֹ־מַיִם
יִתְהַלְּכוּ־לָמוֹ
יִדְרֹךְ חִצָּו [חִצָּיו]
כְּמוֹ יִתְמֹלָלוּ׃

9 Like a snail
They shall go fluid,
Like a still-born mole,
Never seeing the sun.

ט כְּמוֹ שַׁבְּלוּל
תֶּמֶס יַהֲלֹךְ
נֵפֶל אֵשֶׁת
בַּל־חָזוּ שָׁמֶשׁ׃

10 Before
Their thorn-bushes produce caper-berries,
When they are fresh, full of anger,
He blows them away in a storm!

י בְּטֶרֶם ׀
יָבִינוּ סִּירֹתֵיכֶם אָטָד
כְּמוֹ־חַי כְּמוֹ־חָרוֹן
יִשְׂעָרֶנּוּ׃

11 The just will rejoice	יא יִשְׂמַח צַדִּיק
That he saw vengeance,	כִּי־חָזָה נָקָם
His steps he will wash	פְּעָמָיו יִרְחַץ
In the blood of the wicked,	בְּדַם הָרָשָׁע׃
12 Then mankind will say:	יב וְיֹאמַר אָדָם
The just produces fruit,	אַךְ־פְּרִי לַצַּדִּיק
Really there is a God,	אַךְ יֵשׁ־אֱלֹהִים
Judge on the earth.	שֹׁפְטִים בָּאָרֶץ׃

8. All medieval commentators (such as Raski, Ibn Ezra, Qinḥi) are of the opinion that ימאסו is not passive of מאס "to be an object of abhorrence, to be despicable", but is a secondary form of מסס "to melt". Nevertheless, the use of the unusual form shows that the poet intended a pun.

9. The Targum translates נפל אשת "like a still-birth or a mole".

10. סיר is either a pot or a dry twig from a thorny bush, see the pun Eccl. 7:6. The Torczyner-Bernhard-Cohn translation is: "Before one notices it, your pots will be full of poison thorns", but אטד is not documented to mean poison thorns; the RV version "before your pots can feel the thorns" makes no sense unless it means "before the heat of (rapidly burning and rapidly dying out) thorns can heat the pot." Dahood declares the Hebrew to be unintelligible, but it is unintelligible only to prosaic minds. I am following here the translation of Ibn Ezra in the name of Rav Hay Gaon, who declares אטד here not to be a thorn bush but a fruit of the spiny caper bush, in Hebrew usually אביונה. This translation implies that in Rav Hay Gaon's Babylonian Aramaic there still was surviving the meaning "to give" of Accadic *byn* (*banu.)* Therefore, יבינו here is an Accadism, meaning “they will give, produce" and not a meaningless Hebrew "they will understand".

Psalm 59

1 For the director, "do not destroy",
A *mikhtam* by David,
When Saul sent
And they were watching the house
To kill him.

א לַמְנַצֵּ֣חַ אַל־תַּשְׁחֵת֮
לְדָוִ֪ד מִ֫כְתָּ֥ם
בִּשְׁלֹ֥חַ שָׁא֑וּל
וַֽיִּשְׁמְר֥וּ אֶת־הַ֝בַּ֗יִת
לַהֲמִיתֽוֹ׃

2 Save me from my enemies,
My God,
Protect me from those who rise against me.

ב הַצִּילֵ֣נִי מֵאֹיְבַ֣י ׀
אֱלֹהָ֑י
מִּֽמִּתְקוֹמְמַ֥י תְּשַׂגְּבֵֽנִי׃

3 Save me
From evil doers
And from men of bloodshed
Rescue me.

ג הַ֭צִּילֵנִי
מִפֹּ֣עֲלֵי אָ֑וֶן
וּֽמֵאַנְשֵׁ֥י דָ֝מִ֗ים
הוֹשִׁיעֵֽנִי׃

4 For they lie in ambush
For me,
Strong ones attack me,
For no crime nor sin on my part, o Eternal.

ד כִּ֤י הִנֵּ֪ה אָֽרְב֡וּ
לְנַפְשִׁ֗י
יָג֣וּרוּ עָלַ֣י עַזִּ֑ים
לֹֽא־פִשְׁעִ֖י וְלֹא־חַטָּאתִ֣י יהוה׃

5 Without help,
While they run and prepare,
Please, rise for me and see.

ה בְּֽלִי־עָ֭וֺן
יְרוּצ֣וּן וְיִכּוֹנָ֑נוּ
ע֖וּרָה לִקְרָאתִ֣י וּרְאֵֽה׃

6 But You, Eternal, God of Hosts,
God of Israel,
Awake
To punish all Gentiles,
Do not favor any evil traitor, Selah.

ו וְאַתָּ֤ה יהוה־אֱלֹהִ֥ים ׀ צְבָא֡וֹת
אֱלֹ֘הֵ֤י יִשְׂרָאֵ֗ל
הָקִ֗יצָה
לִפְקֹ֥ד כָּל־הַגּוֹיִ֑ם
אַל־תָּ֝חֹ֗ן כָּל־בֹּ֥גְדֵי אָ֣וֶן סֶֽלָה׃

7 They assemble in the evening,
Growl like dogs,
And encircle the city.

ז יָשׁ֣וּבוּ לָ֭עֶרֶב
יֶהֱמ֥וּ כַכָּ֗לֶב
וִ֘יס֥וֹבְבוּ עִֽיר׃

8 Behold,
They pronounce with their mouths,
Swords
On their lips,
Who really listens?

ח הִנֵּ֤ה ׀
יַבִּ֘יע֤וּן בְּפִיהֶ֗ם
חֲ֭רָבוֹת
בְּשִׂפְתוֹתֵיהֶ֑ם
כִּ֥י מִ֣י שֹׁמֵֽעַ׃

9 But You, Eternal,
Will laugh at them,
Will scoff
At all Gentiles.

ט וְאַתָּ֣ה יהוה
תִּשְׂחַק־לָ֑מוֹ
תִּ֝לְעַ֗ג
לְכָל־גּוֹיִֽם׃

10 O Mighty,
I am waiting for You,
For God
Is my refuge.

י עֻזּ֗וֹ
אֵלֶ֥יךָ אֶשְׁמֹ֑רָה
כִּ֥י אֱ֝לֹהִ֗ים
מִשְׂגַּבִּֽי׃

11 My kind God precedes me,
God
Will prefer me over my enemies.

יא אֱלֹהֵי חַסְדּוֹ [חַסְדִּי] יְקַדְּמֵנִי
אֱלֹהִים
יַרְאֵנִי בְשֹׁרְרָי׃

12 Do not kill them,
Lest my people will wilt,
Shake them by Your power
And bring them down,
Our shield, Master.

יב אַל־תַּהַרְגֵם |
פֶּן־יִשְׁכְּחוּ עַמִּי
הֲנִיעֵמוֹ בְחֵילְךָ
וְהוֹרִידֵמוֹ
מָגִנֵּנוּ אֲדֹנָי׃

13 Their mouths' sin, the their lips' word,
Will have them caught in their pride,
They talk of incantation and witchcraft.

יג חַטַּאת פִּימוֹ דְּבַר־שְׂפָתֵימוֹ
וְיִלָּכְדוּ בִגְאוֹנָם
וּמֵאָלָה וּמִכַּחַשׁ יְסַפֵּרוּ׃

14 Finish them off in rage,
Finish them, annihilate them,
They shall know that God
Rules over Jacob
To the ends of the earth, Selah.

יד כַּלֵּה בְחֵמָה
כַּלֵּה וְאֵינֵמוֹ
וְיֵדְעוּ כִּי־אֱלֹהִים
מֹשֵׁל בְּיַעֲקֹב
לְאַפְסֵי הָאָרֶץ סֶלָה׃

15 Let them assemble in the evening,
Growl like dogs,
And encircle the city.

טו וְיָשֻׁבוּ לָעֶרֶב
יֶהֱמוּ כַכָּלֶב
וִיסוֹבְבוּ עִיר׃

16 They
Move to feed
As long as they are not full
And will rest in the night.

טז הֵמָּה
יְנוּעוּן [יְנִיעוּן] לֶאֱכֹל
אִם־לֹא יִשְׂבְּעוּ
וַיָּלִינוּ׃

17 But I
Shall sing of Your strength,
In the morning chanting of Your grace,
For You were refuge to me,
And shelter,
On my day of trouble.

יז וַאֲנִי |
אָשִׁיר עֻזֶּךָ
וַאֲרַנֵּן לַבֹּקֶר חַסְדֶּךָ
כִּי־הָיִיתָ מִשְׂגָּב לִי
וּמָנוֹס
בְּיוֹם צַר־לִי׃

18 My might,
I shall make music for You,
For God is my refuge,
My kind God.

יח עֻזִּי
אֵלֶיךָ אֲזַמֵּרָה
כִּי־אֱלֹהִים מִשְׂגַּבִּי
אֱלֹהֵי חַסְדִּי׃

1. The second part of the verse seems to be inappropriate since the Psalm is the prayer of a king for his people, not that of an individual being fugitive in his own land.

5. עון is translated as Arabic "help" *`aûn.*

7-15. יָשׁוּבוּ לָעֶרֶב is read by Torczyner to mean "Let them assemble in the prairie (עֲרָבָה).

10. עזו is the equivalent of עזי in v. 18, it cannot be translated "his strength" since there is no third person to which the expression can refer. One has only the choice of either explaining the suffix *u* as a dialectal form of the first person singular suffix or seeing (with M. Dahood) in עזו an archaic form עז "strength" in the nominative. For the first alternative speaks the general tendency in classical poetry to avoid identical repetitions in refrains (cf. the addition of a *v* of contrast in v. 15.)

11. The *ketib* חסדו would have to be translated “in His kindness”.

ראה is taken not as the basic meaning “to see” but as either Rabbinic Hebrew “to understand, to accept as valid”, or Arabic “to judge”. The שורר is Accadic *šaru* “enemy” (from the Tel El-Amarna texts).

Psalm 60

1 For the director,
On Shushan Edut
A didactic *mikhtam* by David.

א לַמְנַצֵּחַ
עַל־שׁוּשַׁן עֵדוּת
מִכְתָּם לְדָוִד לְלַמֵּד׃

2 When he attacked
Aram between the Two Rivers
And Aram Sobah
And Joab returned
And smote Edom in the Salt Valley,
Twelve thousand.

ב בְּהַצּוֹתוֹ ׀
אֶת אֲרַם נַהֲרַיִם
וְאֶת־אֲרַם צוֹבָה
וַיָּשָׁב יוֹאָב
וַיַּךְ אֶת־אֱדוֹם בְּגֵיא־מֶלַח
שְׁנֵים עָשָׂר אָלֶף׃

3 God,
You had abandoned us, breached us, You were angry with us,
You had turned us away.

ג אֱלֹהִים
זְנַחְתָּנוּ פְרַצְתָּנוּ
אָנַפְתָּ
תְּשׁוֹבֵב לָנוּ׃

4 You made the earth tremble, and split it,
Its weak broken parts are certainly bent!

ד הִרְעַשְׁתָּה אֶרֶץ פְּצַמְתָּהּ
רְפָה שְׁבָרֶיהָ כִי־מָטָה׃

5 You showed Your people the hard way,
You let us drink
Poison wine.

ה הִרְאִיתָה עַמְּךָ קָשָׁה
הִשְׁקִיתָנוּ
יַיִן תַּרְעֵלָה׃

6 You gave those who fear You a banner
To assemble under
Against
Archery, Selah.

ו נָתַתָּה לִּירֵאֶיךָ נֵּס
לְהִתְנוֹסֵס
מִפְּנֵי
קֹשֶׁט סֶלָה׃

7 So that
Your beloved ones may be extricated; Help with Your right hand and answer us [me].

ז לְמַעַן
יֵחָלְצוּן יְדִידֶיךָ
הוֹשִׁיעָה יְמִינְךָ וַעֲנֵנוּ [וַעֲנֵנִי]׃

8 God
Spoke in His holy place; I shall rejoice.
I shall take Sichem as my part
And shall measure the valley of Sukkot.

ח אֱלֹהִים ׀
דִּבֶּר בְּקָדְשׁוֹ אֶעְלֹזָה
אֲחַלְּקָה שְׁכֶם
וְעֵמֶק סֻכּוֹת אֲמַדֵּד׃

9 Mine is Gilead
And mine is Manasseh,
Ephraim
Is my main stronghold,
Judah
My lawgiver's staff.

ט לִי גִלְעָד ׀
וְלִי מְנַשֶּׁה
וְאֶפְרַיִם
מָעוֹז רֹאשִׁי
יְהוּדָה
מְחֹקְקִי׃

10 Moab
Is my washing bowl,
Over Edom
I shall throw my shoe,
To me
Philistia will get friendly.

י מוֹאָב ׀
סִיר רַחְצִי
עַל־אֱדוֹם
אַשְׁלִיךְ נַעֲלִי
עָלַי
פְּלֶשֶׁת הִתְרֹעָעִי׃

11 Who will bring me
To the city in the rock,
Who will guide me into Edom?

יא מִ֤י יֹבִלֵ֗נִי
עִ֣יר מָצ֑וֹר
מִ֖י נָחַ֣נִי עַד־אֱדֽוֹם׃

12 Will You, God, not abandon us?
Should God not march
With our armies?

יב הֲלֹא־אַתָּ֣ה אֱלֹהִ֣ים זְנַחְתָּ֑נוּ
וְלֹא־תֵצֵ֥א אֱ֝לֹהִ֗ים
בְּצִבְאוֹתֵֽינוּ׃

13 Give us help from the oppressor,
For vanity
Is the help of man.

יג הָֽבָה־לָּ֣נוּ עֶזְרָ֣ת מִצָּ֑ר
וְ֝שָׁ֗וְא
תְּשׁוּעַ֥ת אָדָֽם׃

14 We shall be valiant in God,
For He
Will trample down our oppressors.

יד בֵּאלֹהִ֥ים נַעֲשֶׂה־חָ֑יִל
וְ֝ה֗וּא
יָב֥וּס צָרֵֽינוּ׃

3. Joab's big strategic mistake (*2Sam.* 10:8-9) which led him into a trap between several enemy armies is ascribed to God's anger; the same thought appears in the description of the Egyptians drowning in the Red Sea since they ran into the water, not away from it, and Sisera's defeat when he put his horses and chariots within running distance of 10’000 men racing down from Mt. Tabor.

6. Normally, without special divine protection, against archers one would disperse, not assemble, one's troops. קשט is a secondary form, also found in Targumic Aramaic, of קשת "archery."

7. The *Ketib* “us” seems to make even more sense than the *Qere* “me”.

Psalms 61

1 For the director, on *neginat*, by David

א לַמְנַצֵּחַ עַל־נְגִינַת לְדָוִד׃

2 Listen, God,
To my entreaty,
Be attentive
To my prayer.

ב שִׁמְעָה אֱלֹהִים
רִנָּתִי
הַקְשִׁיבָה
תְּפִלָּתִי׃

3 From the end of the earth
I am calling to You,
When I am fainting
On a high rock, lead me away from it.

ג מִקְצֵה הָאָרֶץ ׀
אֵלֶיךָ אֶקְרָא
בַּעֲטֹף לִבִּי
בְּצוּר־יָרוּם מִמֶּנִּי תַנְחֵנִי׃

4 For You were my shelter,
A fortified tower
Against the enemy.

ד כִּי־הָיִיתָ מַחְסֶה לִי
מִגְדַּל־עֹז
מִפְּנֵי אוֹיֵב׃

5 May I live in Your Tent
Forever,
May I find shelter in Your wings' secret,
Selah.

ה אָגוּרָה בְאָהָלְךָ
עוֹלָמִים
אֶחֱסֶה בְסֵתֶר כְּנָפֶיךָ סֶּלָה׃

6 Surely You, God,
Listened to my vows,
You did prepare the reward
Of those who fear Your name.

ו כִּי־אַתָּה אֱלֹהִים
שָׁמַעְתָּ לִנְדָרָי
נָתַתָּ יְרֻשַּׁת
יִרְאֵי שְׁמֶךָ׃

7 Years You will add to the king's days,
His years,
As in previous generations.

ז יָמִים עַל־יְמֵי־מֶלֶךְ תּוֹסִיף
שְׁנוֹתָיו
כְּמוֹ־דֹר וָדֹר׃

8 May he eternally dwell
Before God,
Kindness and truth
Prepared to guard him.

ח יֵשֵׁב עוֹלָם
לִפְנֵי אֱלֹהִים
חֶסֶד וֶאֱמֶת
מַן יִנְצְרֻהוּ׃

9 Verily, I shall sing to Your name forever, While
I pay my vows
Daily.

ט כֵּן אֲזַמְּרָה שִׁמְךָ לָעַד
לְשַׁלְּמִי נְדָרַי
יוֹם ׀ יוֹם׃

1. *Neginat* seems to be a musical instrument.

8. מן is taken as a verb, from the root מנה "to appoint, to count".

Psalm 62

1 For the director, on Yedutun
A Psalm of David.

א לַמְנַצֵּחַ עַל־יְדוּתוּן
מִזְמוֹר לְדָוִד׃

2 Only to God
Is my soul silent.
From Him
Is my salvation.

ב אַךְ אֶל־אֱלֹהִים
דּוּמִיָּה נַפְשִׁי
מִמֶּנּוּ
יְשׁוּעָתִי׃

3 Only He is my rock
And my salvation,
My refuge
I shall not reel very much.

ג אַךְ־הוּא צוּרִי
וִישׁוּעָתִי
מִשְׂגַּבִּי
לֹא־אֶמּוֹט רַבָּה׃

4 Until when
Will you pounce upon a man
Will you all want to be murderers,
Like a leaning wall,
A fence
Pushed in?

ד עַד־אָנָה ׀
תְּהוֹתְתוּ עַל־אִישׁ
תְּרָצְּחוּ כֻלְּכֶם
כְּקִיר נָטוּי
גָּדֵר
הַדְּחוּיָה׃

5 Only from his elevation
They counseled to overthrow;
They desire lies,
They bless with the mouth
But in their innards
They curse, Selah.

ה אַךְ מִשְּׂאֵתוֹ ׀
יָעֲצוּ לְהַדִּיחַ
יִרְצוּ כָזָב
בְּפִיו יְבָרֵכוּ
וּבְקִרְבָּם
יְקַלְלוּ־סֶלָה׃

6 My soul be silent
Only to God.
My hope
Certainly, is from Him.

ו אַךְ לֵאלֹהִים
דּוֹמִּי נַפְשִׁי
כִּי־מִמֶּנּוּ
תִּקְוָתִי׃

7 Only He is my rock
And my salvation,
My refuge,
I shall not reel.

ז אַךְ־הוּא צוּרִי
וִישׁוּעָתִי
מִשְׂגַּבִּי
לֹא אֶמּוֹט׃

8 On God
Is my safety and honor.
The rock of my strength, my shelter
Is God.

ח עַל־אֱלֹהִים
יִשְׁעִי וּכְבוֹדִי
צוּר־עֻזִּי מַחְסִי
בֵּאלֹהִים׃

9 Trust in Him at all times,
People, pour out your hearts before Him.
God is our refuge, Selah.

ט בִּטְחוּ בוֹ בְכָל־עֵת ׀
עָם שִׁפְכוּ לְפָנָיו לְבַבְכֶם
אֱלֹהִים מַחֲסֶה־לָּנוּ סֶלָה׃

10 By contrast,	י אַ֤ךְ ׀
Vapor are lowly men,	הֶ֥בֶל בְּנֵי־אָדָם֮
A lie the upper classes,	כָּזָ֪ב בְּנֵ֫י אִ֥ישׁ
To rise on scales;	בְּמֹאזְנַ֥יִם לַעֲל֑וֹת
They	הֵ֝֗מָּה
All are of vapor.	מֵהֶ֥בֶל יָֽחַד׃
11 Do not count on oppression,	יא אַל־תִּבְטְח֣וּ בְעֹשֶׁק֮
Do not come to nought by robbery; Do	וּבְגָזֵ֪ל אַל־תֶּ֫הְבָּ֥לוּ
not take notice of	חַ֤יִל ׀
Might	כִּֽי־יָנ֑וּב
When it bears fruit.	אַל־תָּשִׁ֥יתוּ לֵֽב׃
12 Once	יב אַחַ֤ת ׀
Did God speak,	דִּבֶּ֬ר אֱלֹהִ֗ים
These two I did understand:	שְׁתַּֽיִם־ז֥וּ שָׁמָ֑עְתִּי
That the power	כִּ֥י עֹ֝֗ז
is God's.	לֵאלֹהִֽים׃
13 Yours, Master, is kindness,	יג וּלְךָֽ־אֲדֹנָ֥י חָ֑סֶד
Certainly You will reward everyone according to his deeds!	כִּֽי־אַ֨תָּ֥ה תְשַׁלֵּ֖ם לְאִ֣ישׁ כְּֽמַעֲשֵֽׂהוּ׃

1. The meaning "for Yedutun" is not clear, it might be that Yedutun is not only the name of a musician but also of a musical instrument.

4. The vocalization of Ben Asher תְּרָצְּח֡וּ means "will be intent on murdering" as t-passive of the *pael* conjugation; the vocalization of Ben Naftali תְּרַצְּחוּ would mean "you will murder". The root רצח could also have the Arabic meaning "to break". The different forms are רוצח "murderer", מרצח "habitual murderer", מרצח "intent on murdering" (Abba Bendavid, Tarbiz 26, p. 384 ff.) The root הות of תהותתו is explained by Ben Yehuda as "to gang up against somebody" from the Arabic הוש (defined by Brelot as "being agitated (crowd)"), הות "to descend to the bottom of a ravine", but the better interpretation seems to be that of Y. Blau who sees in הות a secondary root of הוה, Arabic הוי "to fall down (object), to pounce upon the prey (falcon)", cf. *Job* 37:6.

Psalm 63

1 A psalm of David
When he was
In the wilderness of Judah.

א מִזְמ֥וֹר לְדָוִ֑ד
בִּ֝הְיוֹת֗וֹ
בְּמִדְבַּ֥ר יְהוּדָֽה׃

2 God,
You are my Power, I long for You,
My soul
Is thirsting for You,
My flesh desires You
In a parched and thirsty land without water.

ב אֱלֹהִ֤ים ׀
אֵלִ֥י אַתָּ֗ה אֲֽשַׁ֫חֲרֶ֥ךָּ
צָמְאָ֬ה לְךָ֨ ׀
נַפְשִׁ֗י
כָּמַ֣הּ לְךָ֣ בְשָׂרִ֑י
בְּאֶֽרֶץ־צִיָּ֖ה וְעָיֵ֣ף בְּלִי־מָֽיִם׃

3 Truly,
I had a vision of You in the Sanctuary,
To see Your power
And splendor.

ג כֵּ֭ן
בַּקֹּ֣דֶשׁ חֲזִיתִ֑יךָ
לִרְא֥וֹת עֻ֝זְּךָ֗
וּכְבוֹדֶֽךָ׃

4 For Your kindness is better
Than Life,
My lips shall praise You.

ד כִּי־ט֣וֹב חַ֭סְדְּךָ
מֵֽחַיִּ֗ים
שְׂפָתַ֥י יְשַׁבְּחֽוּנְךָ׃

5 Truly, I shall praise You with my life,
To Your Name
I shall lift my hands.

ה כֵּ֣ן אֲבָרֶכְךָ֣ בְחַיָּ֑י
בְּ֝שִׁמְךָ֗
אֶשָּׂ֥א כַפָּֽי׃

6 As with fat and oil
My soul will be filled,
With singing lips.
My mouth will glorify.

ו כְּמ֤וֹ חֵ֣לֶב וָ֭דֶשֶׁן
תִּשְׂבַּ֣ע נַפְשִׁ֑י
וְשִׂפְתֵ֥י רְ֝נָנ֗וֹת
יְהַלֶּל־פִּֽי׃

7 When I remember You on my couch,
During the nightly watch
I shall think about You.

ז אִם־זְכַרְתִּ֥יךָ עַל־יְצוּעָ֑י
בְּ֝אַשְׁמֻר֗וֹת
אֶהְגֶּה־בָּֽךְ׃

8 For You were my help
And in Your wings' shadow I shall sing!

ח כִּֽי־הָיִ֣יתָ עֶזְרָ֣תָה לִּ֑י
וּבְצֵ֖ל כְּנָפֶ֣יךָ אֲרַנֵּֽן׃

9 My soul is glued to You:
Me
Supported Your right hand.

ט דָּבְקָ֣ה נַפְשִׁ֣י אַחֲרֶ֑יךָ
בִּ֝֗י
תָּמְכָ֥ה יְמִינֶֽךָ׃

10 But they for sudden catastrophe
Are after me,
May they end up
In the deepest of the Land.

י וְהֵ֗מָּה לְ֭שׁוֹאָה
יְבַקְשׁ֣וּ נַפְשִׁ֑י
יָ֝בֹ֗אוּ
בְּתַחְתִּיּ֥וֹת הָאָֽרֶץ׃

11 May He mash them by the sword,
May they be the portion of jackals.

יא יַגִּירֻ֥הוּ עַל־יְדֵי־חָ֑רֶב
מְנָ֖ת שֻׁעָלִ֣ים יִהְיֽוּ׃

12 But the king	יב וְהַמֶּלֶךְ
Will rejoice in God,	יִשְׂמַח בֵּאלֹהִים
May exult himself	יִתְהַלֵּל
Every one who swears by Him,	כָּל־הַנִּשְׁבָּע בּוֹ
For the mouth of the spreaders of lies	כִּי יִסָּכֵר
Will be dammed up.	פִּי דוֹבְרֵי־שָׁקֶר׃

2. It seems that Ibn Gabirol, in his prayer for the Day of Atonement starting with the first two lines of this verse, considered the *revia* as dividing *revia gadol*.
עיף has a meaning of "thirsty", Rashi *Deut.* 25:18.

Psalm 64

1 For the director,
A psalm of David.

א לַמְנַצֵּחַ
מִזְמוֹר לְדָוִד׃

2 Listen, God, to my voice, my talk:
From the dread of the foe
Protect my life.

ב שְׁמַע אֱלֹהִים קוֹלִי בְשִׂיחִי
מִפַּחַד אוֹיֵב
תִּצֹּר חַיָּי׃

3 Hide me
From the council of miscreants,
From the assembly
Of evil doers,

ג תַּסְתִּירֵנִי
מִסּוֹד מְרֵעִים
מֵרִגְשַׁת
פֹּעֲלֵי אָוֶן׃

4 Who sharpened their tongues like a sword,
Who press their arrows
With poison,

ד אֲשֶׁר שָׁנְנוּ כַחֶרֶב לְשׁוֹנָם
דָּרְכוּ חִצָּם
דָּבָר מָר׃

5 To shoot the simple one from ambush.
Suddenly they shoot him
And are not afraid.

ה לִירוֹת בַּמִּסְתָּרִים תָּם
פִּתְאֹם יֹרֻהוּ
וְלֹא יִירָאוּ׃

6 They strengthen themselves
For evil deed,
They tell
To hide snares,
They say:
Who will see us?

ו יְחַזְּקוּ־לָמוֹ ׀
דָּבָר רָע
יְסַפְּרוּ
לִטְמוֹן מוֹקְשִׁים
אָמְרוּ
מִי יִרְאֶה־לָּמוֹ׃

7 They look for evil
We finished!
Exceedingly ingenious
From the inner of a man
And the depth of the heart.

ז יַחְפְּשׂוּ עוֹלֹת
תַּמְנוּ
חֵפֶשׂ מְחֻפָּשׂ
וְקֶרֶב אִישׁ
וְלֵב עָמֹק׃

8 God shoots them
Suddenly, by an arrow,
Permanent shall be
Their wounds.

ח וַיֹּרֵם אֱלֹהִים
חֵץ פִּתְאוֹם
הָיוּ
מַכּוֹתָם׃

9 He makes them stumble by their tongues,
Every one who considers them
Will shake his head.

ט וַיַּכְשִׁילֻהוּ עָלֵימוֹ לְשׁוֹנָם
יִתְנֹדְדוּ
כָּל־רֹאֵה בָם׃

10 May all mankind fear
And tell
The deed of God,
And understand His work.

י וַיִּירְאוּ כָּל־אָדָם
וַיַּגִּידוּ
פֹּעַל אֱלֹהִים
וּמַעֲשֵׂהוּ הִשְׂכִּילוּ

11 May the just rejoice in the Eternal
And take refuge in Him,
And all those of a straight heart
Exult themselves.

: יא יִשְׂמַח צַדִּיק בַּיהוה
וְחָסָה בוֹ
וְיִתְהַלְלוּ
כָּל־יִשְׁרֵי־לֵב

Psalm 65

1 For the director, a psalm,
A song of David.

א לַמְנַצֵּחַ מִזְמוֹר
לְדָוִד שִׁיר׃

2 Perpetual praise is for You, God in Zion,
And to You
Vows are paid.

ב לְךָ דֻמִיָּה תְהִלָּה אֱלֹהִים בְּצִיּוֹן
וּלְךָ
יְשֻׁלַּם־נֶדֶר׃

3 He Who hears prayer,
To You
All flesh should come.

ג שֹׁמֵעַ תְּפִלָּה
עָדֶיךָ
כָּל־בָּשָׂר יָבֹאוּ׃

4 Talking of sins
Overwhelms me.
Our crimes,
May You cover them up.

ד דִּבְרֵי עֲוֺנֹת
גָּבְרוּ מֶנִּי
פְּשָׁעֵינוּ
אַתָּה תְכַפְּרֵם׃

5 Hail to him
Whom You select and bring close,
Who may dwell in Your courtyard;
May we be filled
With the good of Your House,
The Sanctuary
Of Your Temple!

ה אַשְׁרֵי ׀
תִּבְחַר וּתְקָרֵב
יִשְׁכֹּן חֲצֵרֶיךָ
נִשְׂבְּעָה
בְּטוּב בֵּיתֶךָ
קְדֹשׁ
הֵיכָלֶךָ׃

6 Fearsome One,
Answer us in truth,
God of our salvation,
Fortress of all ends of the earth
And the far Seas,

ו נוֹרָאוֹת ׀
בְּצֶדֶק תַּעֲנֵנוּ
אֱלֹהֵי יִשְׁעֵנוּ
מִבְטָח כָּל־קַצְוֵי־אֶרֶץ
וְיָם רְחֹקִים׃

7 Who by His force founds mountains,
Girded
In might,

ז מֵכִין הָרִים בְּכֹחוֹ
נֶאְזָר
בִּגְבוּרָה׃

8 Who silences
The roar of the seas,
The roar of their waves
And of multitudes of nations.

ח מַשְׁבִּיחַ ׀
שְׁאוֹן יַמִּים
שְׁאוֹן גַּלֵּיהֶם
וַהֲמוֹן לְאֻמִּים׃

9 The dwellers of the fringes
Feared
Your signs,
Those who exit at sunrise or sunset You make sing.

ט וַיִּירְאוּ ׀
יֹשְׁבֵי קְצָוֹת
מֵאוֹתֹתֶיךָ
מוֹצָאֵי־בֹקֶר וָעֶרֶב תַּרְנִין׃

10 May You remember the land
And drench it
To make it very rich;
By a stream of God
Full of water,
Give substance to their grain
So solidly You will prepare it.

י פָּקַדְתָּ הָאָרֶץ ׀
וַתְּשֹׁקְקֶהָ
רַבַּת תַּעְשְׁרֶנָּה
פֶּלֶג אֱלֹהִים
מָלֵא מָיִם
תָּכִין דְּגָנָם
כִּי־כֵן תְּכִינֶהָ

11 Its furrows make fertile,
Flatten its glebes,
Make it fat by soft rains,
Bless its growth.

יא תְּלָמֶיהָ רַוֵּה
נַחֵת גְּדוּדֶהָ
בִּרְבִיבִים תְּמֹגְגֶנָּה
צִמְחָהּ תְּבָרֵךְ׃

12 You crowned
The year by Your goodness;
And Your first-fruits
Let drip with fat.

יב עִטַּרְתָּ
שְׁנַת טוֹבָתֶךָ
וּמַעְגָּלֶיךָ
יִרְעֲפוּן דָּשֶׁן׃

13 Let drip
The oases in the wilderness,
Then joy
The hills will gird.

יג יִרְעֲפוּ
נְאוֹת מִדְבָּר
וְגִיל
גְּבָעוֹת תַּחְגֹּרְנָה

14 May the pasturages be full
With sheep,
And the valleys clothed in grain,
They will jubilate
And sing!

יד לָבְשׁוּ כָרִים ׀
הַצֹּאן
וַעֲמָקִים יַעַטְפוּ־בָר
יִתְרוֹעֲעוּ
אַף־יָשִׁירוּ׃

2. Taking דמיה in the sense of Arabic דום "permanence, perpetuity".

9. Sun and stars exit at sunrise and sunset.

12. מעגל is translated as “first fruits” from Arabic עגל “to be in a hurry”, מעגל “precocious”.

Psalm 66

1 For the director, a song, a psalm.
Show admiration for God,
All the earth!

א לַמְנַצֵּחַ שִׁיר מִזְמוֹר
הָרִיעוּ לֵאלֹהִים
כָּל־הָאָרֶץ׃

2 Sing the glory of His name,
Look out for the glory
That is His praise.

ב זַמְּרוּ כְבוֹד־שְׁמוֹ
שִׂימוּ כָבוֹד
תְּהִלָּתוֹ׃

3 Say to God:
How awesome are Your works;
Because of Your great might
Your enemies must dissemble before You.

ג אִמְרוּ לֵאלֹהִים
מַה־נּוֹרָא מַעֲשֶׂיךָ
בְּרֹב עֻזְּךָ
יְכַחֲשׁוּ־לְךָ אֹיְבֶיךָ׃

4 All the earth
Should prostrate themselves before You
And make music to You;
Make music to Your name, Selah.

ד כָּל־הָאָרֶץ ׀
יִשְׁתַּחֲווּ לְךָ
וִיזַמְּרוּ־לָךְ
יְזַמְּרוּ שִׁמְךָ סֶלָה׃

5 Go and see
God's deeds,
His awesome deeds
For mankind.

ה לְכוּ וּרְאוּ
מִפְעֲלוֹת אֱלֹהִים
נוֹרָא עֲלִילָה
עַל־בְּנֵי אָדָם׃

6 He turned the Sea
Into dry land,
Through the river
They went by foot;
There
We rejoiced in Him.

ו הָפַךְ יָם ׀
לְיַבָּשָׁה
בַּנָּהָר
יַעַבְרוּ בְרָגֶל
שָׁם
נִשְׂמְחָה־בּוֹ׃

7 He rules in His power
Eternally,
His eyes
Watch the Gentiles,
The rebellious,
Lest they should rise, Selah.

ז מֹשֵׁל בִּגְבוּרָתוֹ ׀
עוֹלָם
עֵינָיו
בַּגּוֹיִם תִּצְפֶּינָה
הַסּוֹרְרִים ׀
אַל־יָרִימוּ [יָרוּמוּ] לָמוֹ סֶלָה׃

8 Peoples, praise
Our God,
Express
By voice His praise.

ח בָּרְכוּ עַמִּים ׀
אֱלֹהֵינוּ
וְהַשְׁמִיעוּ
קוֹל תְּהִלָּתוֹ׃

9 He deposits our souls
Into Life,
He did not let our feet reel.

ט הַשָּׂם נַפְשֵׁנוּ
בַּחַיִּים
וְלֹא־נָתַן לַמּוֹט רַגְלֵנוּ׃

10 Truly, You tried us, God,
You melted us down
As one melts down silver.

י כִּי־בְחַנְתָּנוּ אֱלֹהִים
צְרַפְתָּנוּ
כִּצְרָף־כָּסֶף׃

11 You brought us into a bulwark,
You put a tight belt around our loins.

יא הֲבֵאתָנוּ בַמְּצוּדָה
שַׂמְתָּ מוּעָקָה בְמָתְנֵינוּ׃

12 You grafted sickness on our heads,
We came into fire and water
Then You let us out
Into abundance.

יב הִרְכַּבְתָּ אֱנוֹשׁ לְרֹאשֵׁנוּ
בָּאנוּ־בָאֵשׁ וּבַמַּיִם
וַתּוֹצִיאֵנוּ
לָרְוָיָה׃

13 I shall come to Your house with holocausts,
I shall pay my vows to You,

יג אָבוֹא בֵיתְךָ בְעוֹלוֹת
אֲשַׁלֵּם לְךָ נְדָרָי׃

14 What my lips sputtered out,
And my mouth said
When I was in straights.

יד אֲשֶׁר־פָּצוּ שְׂפָתָי
וְדִבֶּר־פִּי
בַּצַּר־לִי׃

15 The choicest holocausts I shall offer You
With the burnt smell of bucks;
I shall bring cattle with rams, Selah.

טו עֹלוֹת מֵחִים אַעֲלֶה־לָּךְ
עִם־קְטֹרֶת אֵילִים
אֶעֱשֶׂה בָקָר עִם־עַתּוּדִים סֶלָה׃

16 Come, listen, and let me tell,
All who fear God,
What He did for me.

טז לְכוּ שִׁמְעוּ וַאֲסַפְּרָה
כָּל־יִרְאֵי אֱלֹהִים
אֲשֶׁר עָשָׂה לְנַפְשִׁי׃

17 To Him my mouth appealed,
Magnificating
Under my tongue.

יז אֵלָיו פִּי־קָרָאתִי
וְרוֹמַם
תַּחַת לְשׁוֹנִי׃

18 Wickedness
If I had seen in my heart,
The Almighty would not have heard.

יח אָוֶן
אִם־רָאִיתִי בְלִבִּי
לֹא יִשְׁמַע | אֲדֹנָי׃

19 However
God heard,
He responded
To my prayer's voice.

יט אָכֵן
שָׁמַע אֱלֹהִים
הִקְשִׁיב
קוֹל תְּפִלָּתִי׃

20 Praised be God,
Who did not remove my prayer and His grace
From me.

כ בָּרוּךְ אֱלֹהִים
אֲשֶׁר לֹא־הֵסִיר תְּפִלָּתִי וְחַסְדּוֹ
מֵאִתִּי׃

9. "Life" is life everlasting after death.

Psalm 67

1 For the director, in melodies,
A Psalm, a song.

א לַמְנַצֵּ֥חַ בִּנְגִינֹ֗ת
מִזְמ֥וֹר שִֽׁיר׃

2 God
May He merciful to us and bless us,
May His face shine over us, Selah,

ב אֱֽלֹהִ֗ים
יְחָנֵּ֥נוּ וִיבָרְכֵ֑נוּ
יָ֤אֵ֥ר פָּנָ֖יו אִתָּ֣נוּ סֶֽלָה׃

3 To have Your way known on the earth,
Among all Gentiles
Your salvation.

ג לָדַ֣עַת בָּאָ֣רֶץ דַּרְכֶּ֑ךָ
בְּכָל־גּ֝וֹיִ֗ם
יְשׁוּעָתֶֽךָ׃

4 Let nations praise You,
God,
May they praise You,
All nations.

ד יוֹד֖וּךָ עַמִּ֥ים ׀
אֱלֹהִ֑ים
י֝וֹד֗וּךָ
עַמִּ֥ים כֻּלָּֽם׃

5 Peoples shall rejoice and sing,
Because You judge nations plainly,
And peoples
You lead on the earth, Selah

ה יִ֥שְׂמְח֥וּ וִירַנְּנ֗וּ לְאֻ֫מִּ֥ים
כִּֽי־תִשְׁפֹּ֣ט עַמִּ֣ים מִישֹׁ֑ר
וּלְאֻמִּ֓ים ׀
בָּאָ֖רֶץ תַּנְחֵ֣ם סֶֽלָה׃

6 Let nations praise You,
God,
May they praise You,
All nations.

ו יוֹד֖וּךָ עַמִּ֥ים ׀
אֱלֹהִ֑ים
י֝וֹד֗וּךָ
עַמִּ֥ים כֻּלָּֽם׃

7 May the earth
Give its produce,
Bless us,
God, our power.

ז אֶ֭רֶץ
נָתְנָ֣ה יְבוּלָ֑הּ
יְ֝בָרְכֵ֗נוּ
אֱלֹהִ֥ים אֱלֹהֵֽינוּ׃

8 May God bless us,
And may fear Him
All the ends of the earth!

ח יְבָרְכֵ֥נוּ אֱלֹהִ֑ים
וְיִֽירְא֥וּ א֝וֹת֗וֹ
כָּל־אַפְסֵי־אָֽרֶץ׃

Psalm 68

1 For the director, by David
A Psalm, a song.

א לַמְנַצֵּחַ לְדָוִד
מִזְמוֹר שִׁיר׃

2 When God arises,
His enemies disperse,
His haters flee
From before Him.

ב יָקוּם אֱלֹהִים
יָפוּצוּ אוֹיְבָיו
וְיָנוּסוּ מְשַׂנְאָיו
מִפָּנָיו׃

3 Like the drifting of smoke they drift,
Like the melting of wax
Before fire,
So the evildoers are lost
Before God.

ג כְּהִנְדֹּף עָשָׁן תִּנְדֹּף
כְּהִמֵּס דּוֹנַג
מִפְּנֵי־אֵשׁ
יֹאבְדוּ רְשָׁעִים
מִפְּנֵי אֱלֹהִים׃

4 But the just
Rejoice, jubilate,
Before God,
They are suddenly filled with joy.

ד וְצַדִּיקִים
יִשְׂמְחוּ יַעַלְצוּ
לִפְנֵי אֱלֹהִים
וְיָשִׂישׂוּ בְשִׂמְחָה׃

5 Sing to God.,
Chant to His name,
Prepare a way
For the Rider on clouds;
His name is YH,
And jubilate before Him.

ה שִׁירוּ | לֵאלֹהִים
זַמְּרוּ שְׁמוֹ
סֹלּוּ
לָרֹכֵב בָּעֲרָבוֹת
בְּיָהּ שְׁמוֹ
וְעִלְזוּ לְפָנָיו׃

6 The father of orphans
And judge for widows,
God
In His holy abode.

ו אֲבִי יְתוֹמִים
וְדַיַּן אַלְמָנוֹת
אֱלֹהִים
בִּמְעוֹן קָדְשׁוֹ׃

7 God
Installs bachelors as heads of family,
He delivers the bound ones
In ingenious ways;
But the deviant
Will dwell in aridity.

ז אֱלֹהִים |
מוֹשִׁיב יְחִידִים | בַּיְתָה
מוֹצִיא אֲסִירִים
בַּכּוֹשָׁרוֹת
אַךְ־סוֹרְרִים
שָׁכְנוּ צְחִיחָה׃

8 God, when You went out
Before Your people,
When You stepped out in the desert, Selah,

ח אֱלֹהִים בְּצֵאתְךָ
לִפְנֵי עַמֶּךָ
בְּצַעְדְּךָ בִישִׁימוֹן סֶלָה׃

:

9 The earth trembled,
The skies dripped,
Before God,
The One of Sinai,
Before God,
The God of Israel.

ט אֶרֶץ רָעָשָׁה |
אַף־שָׁמַיִם נָטְפוּ
מִפְּנֵי אֱלֹהִים
זֶה סִינַי
מִפְּנֵי אֱלֹהִים
אֱלֹהֵי יִשְׂרָאֵל

10 God, pour down
A gift of rain,
Your inheritance and Your dominion
You built solidly.

י גֶּשֶׁם נְדָבוֹת
תָּנִיף אֱלֹהִים
נַחֲלָתְךָ וְנִלְאָה
אַתָּה כוֹנַנְתָּהּ׃

11 Your tribe dwelt there;
In Your goodness You prepared them for riches,
o God.

יא חַיָּתְךָ יָשְׁבוּ־בָהּ
תָּכִין בְּטוֹבָתְךָ לֶעָנִי אֱלֹהִים׃

12 The Almighty gives His command,
Proclamations
To His mighty army.

יב אֲדֹנָי יִתֶּן־אֹמֶר
הַמְבַשְּׂרוֹת
צָבָא רָב׃

13 The kings of armies
Scatter, scatter,
And the local field
Distributes spoils.

יג מַלְכֵי צְבָאוֹת
יִדֹּדוּן יִדֹּדוּן
וּנְוַת בַּיִת
תְּחַלֵּק שָׁלָל׃

14 If they lie down
In the troughs,
Dove's wings
Plated with silver
And its flight arms
With greenish fine gold.

יד אִם־תִּשְׁכְּבוּן
בֵּין שְׁפַתָּיִם
כַּנְפֵי יוֹנָה
נֶחְפָּה בַכֶּסֶף
וְאֶבְרוֹתֶיהָ
בִּירַקְרַק חָרוּץ׃

15 When the All-ruler breaks in His kings
It snows on the Black Mountain.

טו בְּפָרֵשׂ שַׁדַּי מְלָכִים בָּהּ
תַּשְׁלֵג בְּצַלְמוֹן

16 Mountain of God,
Mount Bashan,
M Hilly ountain,
Mount Bashan.

טז הַר־אֱלֹהִים
הַר־בָּשָׁן
הַר־גַּבְנֻנִּים
הַר־בָּשָׁן׃

17 Why do you lie in wait,
Hilly mountains,
Against the mountain
Which God desired as His throne?
Certainly, the Eternal
Will throne forever.

יז לָמָּה ׀ תְּרַצְּדוּן
הָרִים גַּבְנֻנִּים
הָהָר
חָמַד אֱלֹהִים לְשִׁבְתּוֹ
אַף־יְיָ
יִשְׁכֹּן לָנֶצַח׃

18 The chariot of God,
Two myriads thousands of officers,
The Almighty is high
In his Sanctuary, Sinai.

יח רֶכֶב אֱלֹהִים
רִבֹּתַיִם אַלְפֵי שִׁנְאָן
אֲדֹנָי בָם
סִינַי בַּקֹּדֶשׁ׃

19 You ascended the heights,
You caught a captive,
You took gifts
For mankind;
Even among the rebellious
God YH will reside.

יט עָלִיתָ לַמָּרוֹם ׀
שָׁבִיתָ שֶּׁבִי
לָקַחְתָּ מַתָּנוֹת
בָּאָדָם
וְאַף סוֹרְרִים
לִשְׁכֹּן ׀ יָהּ אֱלֹהִים׃

20 Praised be the Almighty,
Day
By day He loads upon us,
The God of our salvation, Selah.

כ בָּר֥וּךְ אֲדֹנָ֗י
י֤וֹם ׀
י֥וֹם יַעֲמָס־לָ֑נוּ
הָאֵ֥ל יְֽשׁוּעָתֵ֣נוּ סֶֽלָה׃

21 The Power is for us
The Power of our deliverance;
The Eternal Almighty
From Death
Leads away.

כא הָאֵ֤ל ׀ לָנוּ֮
אֵ֪ל לְֽמוֹשָׁ֫ע֥וֹת
וְלֱיהוִ֥ה אֲדֹנָ֑י
לַ֝מָּ֗וֶת
תּוֹצָאֽוֹת׃

22 Certainly God will crush
The head of His enemies,
The hairy skull
Parading
In his sins.

כב אַךְ־אֱלֹהִ֗ים יִמְחַץ֮
רֹ֤אשׁ אֹ֫יְבָ֥יו
קָדְקֹ֥ד שֵׂעָ֑ר
מִ֝תְהַלֵּ֗ךְ
אֲדֹנָי בַּאֲשָׁמָֽיו׃

23 The Almighty says:
I will rescue from the sea monster,
I will rescue
From the depths of the sea.

כג אָמַ֣ר
מִבָּשָׁ֣ן אָשִׁ֑יב
אָ֝שִׁ֗יב
מִֽמְּצֻל֥וֹת יָֽם׃

24 So that
Your feet will wallow in blood;
Your dogs' tongue
Will take part of your enemies.

כד לְמַ֤עַן ׀
תִּֽמְחַ֣ץ רַ֭גְלְךָ בְּדָ֑ם
לְשׁ֥וֹן כְּלָבֶ֗יךָ
מֵאוֹיְבִ֥ים מִנֵּֽהוּ

25 Behold your procession, God,
The procession of my God, my King, in the Sanctuary.

כה רָא֣וּ הֲלִיכוֹתֶ֣יךָ אֱלֹהִ֑ים
הֲלִיכ֓וֹת אֵלִ֖י מַלְכִּ֣י בַקֹּֽדֶשׁ׃

26 Singers precede
After musicians,
In the midst of girls
Drumming.
27 With choirs
Praise God,
The Eternal,
By the voice of Israel.

כו קִדְּמ֣וּ שָׁ֭רִים
אַחַ֣ר נֹגְנִ֑ים
בְּת֥וֹךְ עֲ֝לָמ֗וֹת
תּוֹפֵפֽוֹת׃

כז בְּֽ֭מַקְהֵלוֹת
בָּרְכ֣וּ אֱלֹהִ֑ים
יהוה
מִמְּק֥וֹר יִשְׂרָאֵֽל׃

28 There Benjamin, the young,
Rules them;
The princes of Judah
With their shouts,
The princes of Zebulun,
The princes of Naphtali.

כח שָׁ֤ם בִּנְיָמִ֨ן ׀ צָעִ֡יר
רֹדֵ֗ם
שָׂרֵ֣י יְ֭הוּדָה
רִגְמָתָ֑ם
שָׂרֵ֥י זְ֝בֻל֗וּן
שָׂרֵ֥י נַפְתָּלִֽי׃

29 God, please command Your power;
Please fortify, o God,
That
What You had done with us.

כט צִוָּ֣ה אֱ֭לֹהֶיךָ עֻזֶּ֑ךָ
עוּזָּ֥ה אֱלֹהִ֑ים
ז֝֗וּ
פָּעַ֥לְתָּ לָּֽנוּ׃

30 From Your Temple,
Over Jerusalem.
Kings will bring gifts to You.

ל מֵהֵיכָלֶךָ
עַל־יְרוּשָׁלִָם
לְךָ יוֹבִילוּ מְלָכִים שָׁי׃

31 Rebuke the wild animal of lances,
The assembly of buffaloes,
Among the calves of peoples,
Trampling in desire of money!
He scattered nations,
Which like battles.

לא גְּעַר חַיַּת קָנֶה
עֲדַת אַבִּירִים |
בְּעֶגְלֵי עַמִּים
מִתְרַפֵּס בְּרַצֵּי־כָסֶף
בִּזַּר עַמִּים
קְרָבוֹת יֶחְפָּצוּ׃

32 They will bring bronze wares
From Egypt;
The Sudan will pay directly
To God.

לב יֶאֱתָיוּ חַשְׁמַנִּים
מִנִּי מִצְרָיִם
כּוּשׁ תָּרִיץ יָדָיו
לֵאלֹהִים׃

33 Kingdoms of the earth,
Sing to God,
Make music to the Almighty, Selah,

לג מַמְלְכוֹת הָאָרֶץ
שִׁירוּ לֵאלֹהִים
זַמְּרוּ אֲדֹנָי סֶלָה׃

34 To the rider
In eternal heavens;
With His voice He surely proclaims
The voice of authority.

לד לָרֹכֵב
בִּשְׁמֵי שְׁמֵי־קֶדֶם
הֵן־יִתֵּן בְּקוֹלוֹ
קוֹל עֹז׃

35 Proclaim God's glory,
His pride over Israel,
And His might
In the skies!

לה תְּנוּ עֹז לֵאלֹהִים
עַל־יִשְׂרָאֵל גַּאֲוָתוֹ
וְעֻזּוֹ
בַּשְּׁחָקִים׃

36 God is awesome from His Sanctuary.
The Power of Israel
He gives
Force and backbone to the people.
God be praised.

לו נוֹרָא אֱלֹהִים מִמִּקְדָּשֶׁיךָ
אֵל יִשְׂרָאֵל
הוּא נֹתֵן
עֹז וְתַעֲצֻמוֹת לָעָם
בָּרוּךְ אֱלֹהִים

A particularly complicated and dark poem.

4. The many synonyms for "joy" in Hebrew create a problem. Arabic and Ugaritic are of no great help here. On the basis of Accadic, it seems that שׂוש has an element of surprise whereas שמח contains the meaning of well-being, richness.

5. עלץ, עלז are different forms of the same root.

7. The translation of כושרות follows Ibn Ezra whose opinion now can be supported by Ugaritic כתֿר.

10. For נלאה we choose the Accadic root *leu* "to be strong, powerful" (surmised to be the root of the Babylonian name Leah) instead of common Semitic ליא "to feel sick, weak". Naturally, one could see in נחלה a form of נחלה "sick" (cf. the punctuation אֲמִתּוֹ for אֲמָתּוֹ in *Ps*. 91:4), and translate the last two lines: "Your sick and weak You put on his feet again".

11. Taking עני as equivalent of Arabic عَنِيَ "to be rich". חיה here is not "wild animal" but "clan, group", cf. *1Sam.* 18:18, *2Sam.* 23,13 (following Ben Yehuda, E. Täubler.)

13. Deriving ידדון from Arabic דּאדּא "to walk unsteadily" or דּאד "to scatter".

18. As noted by Mandelkern, the soft ב in בם after a consonantal י shows that the word is not the usual בָּם "in them", but is best explained as a verb form derived from the root במה "to be high, to erect".

23. (Cf. also v. 16) בשן here is in the sea, Ugaritic *bt`* and Accadic *basmu* "sea monster, Hydra", related to Hebrew פתן "python".

24. In contrast to v. 22, מחץ here is not the common Hebrew 'to smash" but is derived from Arabic "to run" (said of a gazelle)

27. Taking מקר to be derived from the root קרה "to call" by an instrumental mem.

28. רגם means "noise, roaring thunder" in Accadic which also appears as a secondary meaning of the root in Ugaritic.

29. Here and in the following, each successive appearance of עוז refers to another meaning of the many-faceted root.

31. The first line is translated following Ibn Ezra; one might also translate (cf. v. 11) "troops of lancers" but the following lines all follow the animal simile. The double meaning is probably the inspiration for the entire sequence of images.

32. Egyptian חסמן means "brass, bronze" (Gunkel). The penultimate line is translated using the Rabbinical meaning of הריץ “to deliver (payment, communication)”.

Psalm 69

1 For the Director,
"On lilies", by David.

א לַמְנַצֵּחַ |
עַל־שׁוֹשַׁנִּים לְדָוִד׃

2 Save me, God,
Because water threatens my life!

ב הוֹשִׁיעֵנִי אֱלֹהִים
כִּי בָאוּ מַיִם עַד־נָפֶשׁ׃

3 I am drowning
In the mire of deep
Where there is no foothold;
I came in deepest waters
And a flash-flood carried me away!

ג טָבַעְתִּי |
בִּיוֵן מְצוּלָה
וְאֵין מָעֳמָד
בָּאתִי בְמַעֲמַקֵּי־מַיִם
וְשִׁבֹּלֶת שְׁטָפָתְנִי׃

4 I became tired from crying,
My throat is hoarse,
My eyes are finished
While I am waiting
For my God.

ד יָגַעְתִּי בְקָרְאִי
נִחַר גְּרוֹנִי
כָּלוּ עֵינַי
מְיַחֵל
לֵאלֹהָי׃

5 More
Than the hairs on my head
Are those who hate me for nothing.
My oppressors became powerful,
My lying enemies!
What I did not rob
I have to return.

ה רַבּוּ |
מִשַּׂעֲרוֹת רֹאשִׁי
שֹׂנְאַי חִנָּם
עָצְמוּ מַצְמִיתַי
אֹיְבַי שֶׁקֶר
אֲשֶׁר לֹא־גָזַלְתִּי
אָז אָשִׁיב׃

6 God,
You know
My folly;
My sins
Are not hidden from you.

ו אֱלֹהִים
אַתָּה יָדַעְתָּ
לְאִוַּלְתִּי
וְאַשְׁמוֹתַי
מִמְּךָ לֹא־נִכְחָדוּ׃

7 May Your callers not be ashamed by me
Almighty, Eternal of Hosts,
May Your petitioners not be disgraced by me
God
Of Israel!

ז אַל־יֵבֹשׁוּ בִי | קֹוֶיךָ
אֲדֹנָי יהוה צְבָאוֹת
אַל־יִכָּלְמוּ בִי מְבַקְשֶׁיךָ
אֱלֹהֵי
יִשְׂרָאֵל׃

8 Only because of You
I carried shame,
Disgrace covered my face.

ח כִּי־עָלֶיךָ
נָשָׂאתִי חֶרְפָּה
כִּסְּתָה כְלִמָּה פָנָי׃

9 Queer
I was for my brothers,
A stranger
For my mother's sons.

ט מוּזָר
הָיִיתִי לְאֶחָי
וְנָכְרִי
לִבְנֵי אִמִּי׃

10 Truly, zeal for Your House ate me up
And Your insulters' insults
Fell on me.

י כִּי־קִנְאַת בֵּיתְךָ אֲכָלָתְנִי
וְחֶרְפּוֹת חוֹרְפֶיךָ
נָפְלוּ עָלָי׃

11 I cried out my soul in fast,
It became my profession.

יא וָאֶבְכֶּה בַצּוֹם נַפְשִׁי
וַתְּהִי לַחֲרָפוֹת לִי׃

12 I exchanged my garments for sackcloth,
I became a tale for them.

יב וָאֶתְּנָה לְבוּשִׁי שָׂק
וָאֱהִי לָהֶם לְמָשָׁל׃

13 Talking about me are
Those who sit at the gate
And singing
The drinkers of liquor.

יג יָשִׂיחוּ בִי
יֹשְׁבֵי שָׁעַר
וּנְגִינוֹת
שׁוֹתֵי שֵׁכָר׃

14 But I am praying to You,
Eternal,
At a time of goodwill.
God, in Your enormous grace,
Answer me
With Your true salvation!

יד וַאֲנִי תְפִלָּתִי־לְךָ ׀
יהוה
עֵת רָצוֹן
אֱלֹהִים בְּרָב־חַסְדֶּךָ
עֲנֵנִי
בֶּאֱמֶת יִשְׁעֶךָ׃

15 Rescue me from the mud,
Do not let me drown.
I shall be rescued from my haters
And from deepest waters.

טו הַצִּילֵנִי מִטִּיט
וְאַל־אֶטְבָּעָה
אִנָּצְלָה מִשֹּׂנְאַי
וּמִמַּעֲמַקֵּי־מָיִם׃

16 A flash-flood
May not sweep me away
The deep may not swallow me,
The Pit’s mouth may not close upon me.

טז אַל־תִּשְׁטְפֵנִי ׀
שִׁבֹּלֶת מַיִם
וְאַל־תִּבְלָעֵנִי מְצוּלָה
וְאַל־תֶּאְטַר־עָלַי בְּאֵר פִּיהָ׃

17 Answer me, Eternal,
Truly Your kindness is good.
In the immensity of Your mercy
Turn to me!

יז עֲנֵנִי יהוה
כִּי־טוֹב חַסְדֶּךָ
כְּרֹב רַחֲמֶיךָ
פְּנֵה אֵלָי׃

18 Do not hide Your presence
From Your servant
Because I am in straits;
Answer me soon!

יח וְאַל־תַּסְתֵּר פָּנֶיךָ
מֵעַבְדֶּךָ
כִּי־צַר־לִי
מַהֵר עֲנֵנִי׃

19 Please bring deliverance quickly to my soul,
Redeem me because of my enemies.

יט קָרְבָה אֶל־נַפְשִׁי גְאָלָהּ
לְמַעַן אֹיְבַי פְּדֵנִי

20 You know
My insults, my shame
And my disgrace.
Before You
Are all my oppressors!

כ אַתָּה יָדַעְתָּ
חֶרְפָּתִי וּבָשְׁתִּי
וּכְלִמָּתִי
נֶגְדְּךָ
כָּל־צוֹרְרָי׃

21 Shame
Broke my heart, and I fell ill;
I hoped for sympathy but there was none;
And I found no
Consolers.

כא חֶרְפָּה ׀
שָׁבְרָה לִבִּי וָאָנוּשָׁה
וָאֲקַוֶּה לָנוּד וָאַיִן
וְלַמְנַחֲמִים
וְלֹא מָצָאתִי

22 They gave poison into my food
And for my thirst
They made me drink vinegar.

כב וַיִּתְּנוּ בְּבָרוּתִי רֹאשׁ
וְלִצְמָאִי
יַשְׁקוּנִי חֹמֶץ׃

23 May their table be a snare before them
And their peace offerings a trap.

כג יְהִי שֻׁלְחָנָם לִפְנֵיהֶם לְפָח
וְלִשְׁלוֹמִים לְמוֹקֵשׁ׃

24 May their eyes darken
So they cannot see
And their loins
In a permanent tremor.

כד תֶּחְשַׁכְנָה עֵינֵיהֶם
מֵרְאוֹת
וּמָתְנֵיהֶם
תָּמִיד הַמְעַד׃

25 Pour Your wrath over them
Let Your burning wrath
Overtake them!

כה שְׁפָךְ־עֲלֵיהֶם זַעְמֶךָ
וַחֲרוֹן אַפְּךָ
יַשִּׂיגֵם׃

26 Their strongholds may become desolate;
In their tents
Nobody shall dwell!

כו תְּהִי־טִירָתָם נְשַׁמָּה
בְּאָהֳלֵיהֶם
אַל־יְהִי יֹשֵׁב׃

27 Truly they ran after what You Yourself had smitten
They gossip about the pain of those You had wounded.

כז כִּי־אַתָּה אֲשֶׁר־הִכִּיתָ רָדָפוּ
וְאֶל־מַכְאוֹב חֲלָלֶיךָ יְסַפֵּרוּ׃

28 Heap guilt
Upon their transgressions,
They shall not come
Into Your justification

כח תְּנָה־עָוֺן
עַל־עֲוֺנָם
וְאַל־יָבֹא
בְּצִדְקָתֶךָ׃

29 They shall be erased
From the book of Life
And with the just one
They shall not be inscribed

כט יִמָּחוּ
מִסֵּפֶר חַיִּים
וְעִם צַדִּיקִים
אַל־יִכָּתֵבוּ׃

30 But I
Am poor and hurting;
Your help, God, will be my refuge.
666

ל וַאֲנִי
עָנִי וְכוֹאֵב
יְשׁוּעָתְךָ אֱלֹהִים תְּשַׂגְּבֵנִי׃

31 I shall praise the name of God in song
And magnify Him in thanksgiving.

לא אֲהַלְלָה שֵׁם־אֱלֹהִים בְּשִׁיר
וַאֲגַדְּלֶנּוּ בְתוֹדָה׃

32 It will please the Eternal
Better than a bovine bull,
Horned, split-hoofed.

לב וְתִיטַב לַיי
מִשּׁוֹר פָּר
מַקְרִן מַפְרִיס

33 The meek see, rejoice;
The God-seekers,
May your spirits revive.

לג רָאוּ עֲנָוִים יִשְׂמָחוּ
דֹּרְשֵׁי אֱלֹהִים
וִיחִי לְבַבְכֶם׃

34 Certainly, the Eternal listens to the needy,
And His prisoners
He did not disdain.

לד כִּי־שֹׁמֵעַ אֶל־אֶבְיוֹנִים יהוה
וְאֶת־אֲסִירָיו
לֹא בָזָה׃

35 Praise Him,	לה יְֽהַלְל֗וּהוּ
Sky and earth,	שָׁמַ֥יִם וָאָ֑רֶץ
Oceans	יַ֝מִּ֗ים
And all that swarms in them.	וְֽכָל־רֹמֵ֥שׂ בָּֽם׃
36 Certainly God	לו כִּ֤י אֱלֹהִ֨ים ׀
Will save Zion,	י֘וֹשִׁ֤יעַ צִיּ֗וֹן
And rebuilds	וְ֭יִבְנֶה
The cities of Judah.	עָרֵ֣י יְהוּדָ֑ה
They shall dwell there	וְיָ֥שְׁבוּ שָׁ֝֗ם
And inherit it.	וִירֵשֽׁוּהָ׃
37 Then the descendants of His servants	לז וְזֶ֣רַע עֲ֭בָדָיו
Will succeed to it,	יִנְחָל֑וּהָ
And the lovers of His name	וְאֹהֲבֵ֥י שְׁ֝מ֗וֹ
Shall reside in it.	יִשְׁכְּנוּ־בָֽהּ׃

11. Hebrew חרף corresponds to Arabic חׄרפ "to be demented, senile" in v. 10 but to חרפ "earn the upkeep of one's family" in v. 11.

16. Compare the hapax אטר to Arabic אטר"enclose, curve around".
In the translation, the order of the lines has been changed twice to accommodate English syntax.

21. Cf. Job 2:11.

22. Rabbinic הבראה is "food necessary for sustenance".

Psalm 70

1 For the director
By David, to memorize.

2 God, to my rescue,
Eternal,
Hasten to my help!

3 Those who are after my life
Shall be ashamed and disgraced;
They shall turn back
And be dishonored,
Those who desire
Evil for me.

4 They shall return
Because of their shame,
Those who say:
"Hey, Hey!"

5 Delight and rejoice they shall be
All in You, all Your seekers;
They shall always say:
“God be exalted",
The lovers of
Your salvation.

6 But I
Am deprived and downtrodden
God, be quick for me,
You are my help and refuge.
Eternal
Do not tarry.

א לַמְנַצֵּחַ
לְדָוִד לְהַזְכִּיר׃

ב אֱלֹהִים לְהַצִּילֵנִי
יְיָ
לְעֶזְרָתִי חוּשָׁה׃

ג יֵבֹשׁוּ וְיַחְפְּרוּ
מְבַקְשֵׁי נַפְשִׁי
יִסֹּגוּ אָחוֹר
וְיִכָּלְמוּ
חֲפֵצֵי
רָעָתִי׃

ד יָשׁוּבוּ
עַל־עֵקֶב בָּשְׁתָּם
הָאֹמְרִים
הֶאָח ׀ הֶאָח׃

ה יָשִׂישׂוּ וְיִשְׂמְחוּ ׀
בְּךָ כָּל־מְבַקְשֶׁיךָ
וְיֹאמְרוּ תָמִיד
יִגְדַּל אֱלֹהִים
אֹהֲבֵי
יְשׁוּעָתֶךָ׃

ו וַאֲנִי ׀
עָנִי וְאֶבְיוֹן
אֱלֹהִים חוּשָׁה־לִּי
עֶזְרִי וּמְפַלְטִי אַתָּה
יהוה
אַל־תְּאַחַר׃

A second version of the last verses of Psalm 40.

Psalm 71

1 In You I trust, Eternal,
Never may I come to shame.

א בְּךָֽ־יְהֹוָ֥ה חָסִ֑יתִי
אַל־אֵב֥וֹשָׁה לְעוֹלָֽם׃

2 In Your equity
Save me and let me escape,
Bend Your ear to me
And deliver me.

ב בְּצִדְקָתְךָ֗
תַּצִּילֵ֥נִי וּֽתְפַלְּטֵ֑נִי
הַטֵּֽה־אֵלַ֥י אָ֝זְנְךָ֗
וְהוֹשִׁיעֵֽנִי׃

3 Be for me
A rock dwelling,
Always to come to.
Please give orders to deliver me
Because You are my crag and my fortress.

ג הֱ‍ֽיֵה לִ֨י ׀
לְצ֥וּר מָע֡וֹן
לָב֗וֹא תָּמִ֗יד
צִוִּ֥יתָ לְהוֹשִׁיעֵ֑נִי
כִּֽי־סַלְעִ֖י וּמְצוּדָתִ֣י אָֽתָּה׃

4 My God, let me escape
From the hand of the evildoer,
From the palm of the criminal and oppressor.

ד אֱֽלֹהַ֗י פַּ֭לְּטֵנִי
מִיַּ֣ד רָשָׁ֑ע
מִכַּ֖ף מְעַוֵּ֣ל וְחוֹמֵֽץ׃

5 Because You are my hope,
Almighty, Eternal,
My shelter since my youth.

ה כִּֽי־אַתָּ֥ה תִקְוָתִ֑י
אֲדֹנָ֥י יֱ֝הֹוִ֗ה
מִבְטַחִ֥י מִנְּעוּרָֽי׃

6 Upon You
I was leaning for support from the womb;
From my mother's belly
Your were my guide,
Always my praise is directed to You.

ו עָלֶ֤יךָ ׀
נִסְמַ֬כְתִּי מִבֶּ֗טֶן
מִמְּעֵ֣י אִ֭מִּי
אַתָּ֣ה גוֹזִ֑י
בְּךָ֖ תְהִלָּתִ֣י תָמִֽיד׃

7 A sign
I was for the many;
But You
Are my strong refuge.

ז כְּ֭מוֹפֵת
הָיִ֣יתִי לְרַבִּ֑ים
וְ֝אַתָּ֗ה
מַחֲסִי־עֹֽז׃

8 My mouth shall be filled
With Your praise,
Every day
In Your glory.

ח יִמָּ֣לֵא פִ֭י
תְּהִלָּתֶ֑ךָ
כָּל־הַ֝יּ֗וֹם
תִּפְאַרְתֶּֽךָ׃

9 Do not throw me out
In old age,
When my forces diminish
Do not abandon me.

ט אַל־תַּ֭שְׁלִיכֵנִי
לְעֵ֣ת זִקְנָ֑ה
כִּכְל֥וֹת כֹּ֝חִ֗י
אַל־תַּעַזְבֵֽנִי׃

10 Certainly my enemies gave orders about me,
Those who watch me
Take counsel together,

י כִּֽי־אָמְר֣וּ אוֹיְבַ֣י לִ֑י
וְשֹׁמְרֵ֥י נַ֝פְשִׁ֗י
נוֹעֲצ֥וּ יַחְדָּֽו׃

11 Saying,
God has abandoned him,
Pursue and grab him
Because he has no assist.

יא לֵאמֹר
אֱלֹהִים עֲזָבוֹ
רִדְפוּ וְתִפְשׂוּהוּ
כִּי אֵין מַצִּיל׃

12 God,
Do not remove Yourself from me;
My God,
Be quick to my help!

יב אֱלֹהִים
אַל־תִּרְחַק מִמֶּנִּי
אֱלֹהַי
לְעֶזְרָתִי חִישָׁה [חוּשָׁה]׃

13 Ashamed, finished, shall be
My opponents;
Clothed in shame shall be
And in disgrace,
Those who desire
My downfall.

יג יֵבֹשׁוּ יִכְלוּ
שֹׂטְנֵי נַפְשִׁי
יַעֲטוּ חֶרְפָּה
וּכְלִמָּה
מְבַקְשֵׁי
רָעָתִי׃

14 But I
Will always hope;
I will add
More to all Your praise!

יד וַאֲנִי
תָּמִיד אֲיַחֵל
וְהוֹסַפְתִּי
עַל־כָּל־תְּהִלָּתֶךָ׃

15 My mouth
Shall tell Your justice,
Every day
Your helping acts,
Even though I cannot know their number.

טו פִּי ׀
יְסַפֵּר צִדְקָתֶךָ
כָּל־הַיּוֹם
תְּשׁוּעָתֶךָ
כִּי לֹא יָדַעְתִּי סְפֹרוֹת׃

16 When I come to old age,
Almighty, Eternal,
I shall remember Your unique justice.

טז אָבוֹא בִּגְבֻרוֹת
אֲדֹנָי יֱהוִה
אַזְכִּיר צִדְקָתְךָ לְבַדֶּךָ׃

17 God,
You taught me from my youth;
And still
I am proclaiming Your wonders!

יז אֱלֹהִים
לִמַּדְתַּנִי מִנְּעוּרָי
וְעַד־הֵנָּה
אַגִּיד נִפְלְאוֹתֶיךָ׃

18 And at old age and white hair,
God, do not abandon me
So I may tell Your power to the generation,
To every one comes
Your might.

יח וְגַם עַד־זִקְנָה ׀ וְשֵׂיבָה
אֱלֹהִים אַל־תַּעַזְבֵנִי
עַד־אַגִּיד זְרוֹעֲךָ לְדוֹר
לְכָל־יָבוֹא
גְּבוּרָתֶךָ׃

19 Your equity, God, reach very high;
Where You did great deeds,
God,
Who is like You?

יט וְצִדְקָתְךָ אֱלֹהִים עַד־מָרוֹם
אֲשֶׁר־עָשִׂיתָ גְדֹלוֹת
אֱלֹהִים
מִי כָמוֹךָ׃

20 You showed me
Troubles, many and evil;
You returned and revived me,
And from the Netherworld
You returned and lifted me up.

כ אֲשֶׁר הִרְאִיתַנוּ [הִרְאִיתַנִי] ׀
צָרוֹת רַבּוֹת וְרָעוֹת
תָּשׁוּב תְּחַיֵּינוּ [תְּחַיֵּינִי]
וּמִתְּהֹמוֹת הָאָרֶץ
תָּשׁוּב תַּעֲלֵנִי׃

21 You increased	כא תֶּ֤רֶב ׀
My exuberance,	גְּֽדֻלָּתִ֗י
And You turned to console me.	וְתִסֹּ֥ב תְּֽנַחֲמֵֽנִי׃
22 So I also	כב גַּם־אֲנִ֤י ׀
Will thank You with stringed instruments,	א֘וֹדְךָ֤ בִכְלִי־נֶ֗בֶל
Declare Your truth, My God,	אֲמִתְּךָ֥ אֱלֹהָ֑י
I shall sing to You with the lute,	אֲזַמְּרָ֣ה לְךָ֣ בְכִנּ֑וֹר
Wholly One	קְ֝ד֗וֹשׁ
Of Israel!	יִשְׂרָאֵֽל׃
23 My lips shall chant,	כג תְּרַנֵּ֣נָּה שְׂ֭פָתַי
Truly I shall sing to You,	כִּ֣י אֲזַמְּרָה־לָּ֑ךְ
For my soul	וְ֝נַפְשִׁ֗י
Which You redeemed.	אֲשֶׁ֣ר פָּדִֽיתָ׃
24 My tongue also all day	כד גַּם־לְשׁוֹנִ֗י כָּל־֭הַיּוֹם
Shall meditate Your equity.	תֶּהְגֶּ֣ה צִדְקָתֶ֑ךָ
Clearly those came to shame, came to disgrace	כִּֽי־בֹ֥שׁוּ כִֽי־חָ֝פְר֗וּ
Who desire evil for me.	מְבַקְשֵׁ֥י רָעָתִֽי׃

1. The first three verses are a variant of *Ps.* 31:2-4.

4. Following Rashi, identifying חמץ (*ḥomeṣ*) as a form of חמס (*ḥomes*) meaning “acting by illegal force”.

6. Deriving גוזי from גוז "pass by, pass to the other side" (*Nu.* 11:31, *Ps.* 90:10), following the Targum and Arabic. Similar wording is in *Ps.* 22:10-11.

20. The Ketib is plural in the entire verse.

21. If the word גדלתי would mean “greatness”, the *u* would have to be long and the ל without dagesh. The punctuation without dagesh, while ungrammatical (Hebrew nouns that start with sheva always have the second vowel long) is an indication of another meaning, compare ערום in *Gen.* 2:25,3:1 The meaning here is taken from Arabic גד̇ל "to be exuberant". Cf. J. Barth, Die Nominalbildung in den semitischen Sprachen (Berlin, 1889), 55 ff.

Psalm 72

1 For Solomon.
  God, Your laws
  Give to the king;
Your equity to the king's son.

א לִשְׁלֹמֹה ׀
  אֱלֹהִים מִשְׁפָּטֶיךָ
  לְמֶלֶךְ תֵּן
וְצִדְקָתְךָ לְבֶן־מֶלֶךְ׃

2 He shall judge Your people in equity,
And Your deprived ones by the law.

ב יָדִין עַמְּךָ בְצֶדֶק
וַעֲנִיֶּיךָ בְמִשְׁפָּט׃

3 The mountains may carry peace for the people,
And hills
  Equity.

ג יִשְׂאוּ הָרִים שָׁלוֹם לָעָם
וּגְבָעוֹת
  בִּצְדָקָה׃

4 He shall judge the deprived of the people,
Save
  The sons of the downtrodden
And suppress extortion.

ד יִשְׁפֹּט ׀
עֲנִיֵּי־עָם יוֹשִׁיעַ
לִבְנֵי אֶבְיוֹן
וִידַכֵּא עוֹשֵׁק׃

5 They shall fear You with the sun
And before the moon
  For all generations.

ה יִירָאוּךָ עִם־שָׁמֶשׁ
וְלִפְנֵי יָרֵחַ
  דּוֹר דּוֹרִים׃

6 He shall be
  Like rain on fleece-wool,
Like showers
  Dropping to the earth.

ו יֵרֵד
  כְּמָטָר עַל־גֵּז
כִּרְבִיבִים
  זַרְזִיף אָרֶץ׃

7 In his days the just may bloom,
Immense peace
  Without moon-periods.

ז יִפְרַח־בְּיָמָיו צַדִּיק
וְרֹב שָׁלוֹם
  עַד־בְּלִי יָרֵחַ׃

8 He shall rule
  From Sea to Sea,
From the Euphrates
  To the ends of the earth.

ח וְיֵרְדְּ
  מִיָּם עַד־יָם
וּמִנָּהָר
  עַד־אַפְסֵי־אָרֶץ׃

9 Before him
  Desert animals will bow,
His enemies
  Will lick dust.

ט לְפָנָיו
  יִכְרְעוּ צִיִּים
וְאֹיְבָיו
  עָפָר יְלַחֵכוּ׃

10 The kings of Tarsis and the islands
  Will proffer gifts,
The kings of Sheba and Saba
  Will offer donations.

י מַלְכֵי תַרְשִׁישׁ וְאִיִּים
  מִנְחָה יָשִׁיבוּ
מַלְכֵי שְׁבָא וּסְבָא
  אֶשְׁכָּר יַקְרִיבוּ׃

11 All kings will be prostrate before him;
All peoples
  Will serve him,

יא וְיִשְׁתַּחֲווּ־לוֹ כָל־מְלָכִים
כָּל־גּוֹיִם
  יַעַבְדוּהוּ׃

12 Because he will rescue	יב כִּֽי־יַצִּיל
The imploring downtrodden,	אֶבְיוֹן מְשַׁוֵּעַ
And the deprived	וְעָנִי
Who has no help.	וְאֵין־עֹזֵר לוֹ׃
13 He will have mercy	יג יָחֹס
On the poor and downtrodden;	עַל־דַּל וְאֶבְיוֹן
He will save families of the downtrodden.	וְנַפְשׁוֹת אֶבְיוֹנִים יוֹשִׁיעַ׃
14 From crime and oppression	יד מִתּוֹךְ וּמֵחָמָס
He will liberate them,	יִגְאַל נַפְשָׁם
Their blood will be important in his eyes.	וְיֵיקַר דָּמָם בְּעֵינָיו
15 So he will live and receive	טו וִיחִי וְיִתֶּן־לוֹ
From the gold of Sheba;	מִזְּהַב שְׁבָא
Prayers for him always.	וְיִתְפַּלֵּל בַּעֲדוֹ תָמִיד
All day	כָּל־הַיּוֹם
They will bless him.	יְבָרֲכֶנְהוּ׃
16 There will be abundant grain	טז יְהִי פִסַּת־בַּר ׀
In the land,	בָּאָרֶץ
Up to the mountain tops.	בְּרֹאשׁ הָרִים
Its produce will rustle like the Lebanon,	יִרְעַשׁ כַּלְּבָנוֹן פִּרְיוֹ
It will sprout in the city	וְיָצִיצוּ מֵעִיר
Like the earth's grass.	כְּעֵשֶׂב הָאָרֶץ׃
17 His name may stand	יז יְהִי שְׁמוֹ ׀
Forever;	לְעוֹלָם
Before the sun	לִפְנֵי שֶׁמֶשׁ
May his name bear fruit.	יִנֵּין [יִנּוֹן] שְׁמוֹ
One shall praise oneself in him;	וְיִתְבָּרְכוּ בוֹ
All peoples shall declare him fortunate.	כָּל־גּוֹיִם אַשְׁרוּהוּ׃
18 Praised be	יח בָּרוּךְ
The Eternal, God,	יְהוָה אֱלֹהִים
Israel's God,	אֱלֹהֵי יִשְׂרָאֵל
Who alone performs wonders,	עֹשֵׂה נִפְלָאוֹת לְבַדּוֹ
19 And praised be	יט וּבָרוּךְ ׀
The name of His glory forever,	שֵׁם כְּבוֹדוֹ לְעוֹלָם
And may His glory fill	וְיִמָּלֵא כְבוֹדוֹ
All the land,	אֶת־כָּל־הָאָרֶץ
Amen and Amen!	אָמֵן ׀ וְאָמֵן׃
20 End of the prayers	כ כָּלּוּ תְפִלּוֹת
Of David	דָּוִד
Son of Isay.	בֶּן־יִשָׁי׃

9. By *Is*. 13:21, צי is an animal living in the desert or in deserted ruins.

10. Tarsis seems to have been a generic Phoenician name for ports from which ore and metal was shipped. Sheba was in today's Yemen; Saba seems to have been on the other side of the Red Sea, today's Erythrea.

14. Taking נפשות as short for נפשות ביתם "everybody in their families".

15. There is an extra syllable in יברכנהו, probably for reasons of meter and melody.

17. The root יהו is taken to mean "to be in a permanent state", as in Talmudic Hebrew. Tradition takes the third and fourth lines to mean "Before the sun his name is Yinnon"; hence Yinnon is one of the names of the Messiah.

18. The last three verses are not part of the poem; vv. 18,19 are the doxology at the end of Book 2 of Psalms and v. 20 the end of the official Diwan produced by David (this seems to be Ibn Ezra's opinion).

20. The root of תפלה is פלל; the dagesh stands for the lost letter of the stem, this forces the preceding long vowel to become short. One might translate "aspirations, hopes of David", cf. *Gen.* 48:11.

Book Three

Psalm 73

1 A Psalm of Asaph.
God is totally good for Israel,
For the pure of heart.`

א מִזְמ֗וֹר לְאָ֫סָ֥ף
אַ֤ךְ ט֣וֹב לְיִשְׂרָאֵ֣ל אֱלֹהִ֑ים
לְבָרֵ֥י לֵבָֽב׃

2 But I, almost,
My feet were bent,
Like nothing,
My limbs were spilled.

ב וַאֲנִ֗י כִּ֭מְעַט
נָטָ֣וּי [נָטָ֣יוּ] רַגְלָ֑י
כְּ֝אַ֗יִן
שֻׁפְּכָ֥ה [שֻׁפְּכ֥וּ] אֲשֻׁרָֽי׃

3 For I was jealous
Of hooligans;
I gazed upon the peace of evildoers.

ג כִּֽי־קִ֭נֵּאתִי
בַּהוֹלְלִ֑ים
שְׁל֖וֹם רְשָׁעִ֣ים אֶרְאֶֽה׃

4 For there is no choking in their deaths,
And their bodies are fat.

ד כִּ֤י אֵ֣ין חַרְצֻבּ֣וֹת לְמוֹתָ֑ם
וּבָרִ֥יא אוּלָֽם׃

5 They do not toil like lowly people,
And among upper class men
They are not stricken.

ה בַּעֲמַ֣ל אֱנ֣וֹשׁ אֵינֵ֑מוֹ
וְעִם־אָ֝דָ֗ם
לֹ֣א יְנֻגָּֽעוּ׃

6 Therefore,
Pride is their necklace,
A wrap-around
Of theirs are ill-gotten gains.

ו לָ֭כֵן
עֲנָקַ֣תְמוֹ גַאֲוָ֑ה
יַעֲטָף־שִׁ֝֗ית
חָמָ֥ס לָֽמוֹ׃

7 Their eyes pop out from fat,
They transgress
The artful works of the heart.

ז יָ֭צָא מֵחֵ֣לֶב עֵינֵ֑מוֹ
עָ֝בְר֗וּ
מַשְׂכִּיּ֥וֹת לֵבָֽב׃

8 They are rotting
And talking about evil oppression;
They will talk without the Most High.

ח יָמִ֤יקוּ ׀
וִידַבְּר֣וּ בְרָ֣ע עֹ֑שֶׁק
מִמָּר֥וֹם יְדַבֵּֽרוּ׃

9 They put their mouths against Heaven
And their tongues
Cruise the land.

ט שַׁתּ֣וּ בַשָּׁמַ֣יִם פִּיהֶ֑ם
וּ֝לְשׁוֹנָ֗ם
תִּֽהֲלַ֥ךְ בָּאָֽרֶץ׃

10 Indeed
They turn people into pebbles
And all water
They suck up for themselves.

י לָכֵ֤ן
יָשִׁ֣יב [יָשׁ֣וּב] עַמּ֣וֹ הֲלֹ֑ם
וּמֵ֥י מָ֝לֵ֗א
יִמָּ֥צוּ לָֽמוֹ׃

11 They say:
How can God know?
Does the Highest have knowledge?

יא וְאָמְר֗וּ
אֵיכָ֥ה יָדַֽע־אֵ֑ל
וְיֵ֖שׁ דֵּעָ֣ה בְעֶלְיֽוֹן׃

12 Behold, so are the evildoers.
And those who forget eternity
Achieve power.

יב הִנֵּה־אֵ֥לֶּה רְשָׁעִ֑ים
וְשַׁלְוֵ֥י ע֝וֹלָ֗ם
הִשְׂגּוּ־חָֽיִל׃

13 Woe, for nothing
Did I keep my heart pure,
And washed my palms in innocence.

יג אַךְ־רִיק
זִכִּיתִי לְבָבִי
וָאֶרְחַץ בְּנִקָּיוֹן כַּפָּי׃

14 Only to be smitten
Every day,
And be corrected
In the.
mornings

יד וָאֱהִי נָגוּעַ
כָּל־הַיּוֹם
וְתוֹכַחְתִּי
לַבְּקָרִים׃

15 If I said:
"I shall tell how",
I would betray Your sons'
generation.

טו אִם־אָמַרְתִּי
אֲסַפְּרָה כְמוֹ
הִנֵּה דוֹר
בָּנֶיךָ בָגָדְתִּי׃

16 I ponder
To know that;
It is worrisome in my eyes.

טז וָאֲחַשְּׁבָה
לָדַעַת זֹאת
עָמָל הִיא [הוּא] בְעֵינָי׃

17 Until I come
To God's sanctuary,
To understand
Their end.

יז עַד־אָבוֹא
אֶל־מִקְדְּשֵׁי־אֵל
אָבִינָה
לְאַחֲרִיתָם׃

18 Woe, on slippery ground
You will put them,
Throw them down
To sudden catastrophe.

יח אַךְ בַּחֲלָקוֹת
תָּשִׁית לָמוֹ
הִפַּלְתָּם
לְמַשּׁוּאוֹת׃

19 How they will be desolate suddenly
They come to an end, they are finished
In stupidity,

יט אֵיךְ הָיוּ לְשַׁמָּה כְרָגַע
סָפוּ תַמּוּ
מִן־בַּלָּהוֹת׃

20 Like a dream after awakening.
Master,
In the City
You will despise their image.

כ כַּחֲלוֹם מֵהָקִיץ
אֲדֹנָי
בָּעִיר |
צַלְמָם תִּבְזֶה׃

21 When
My heart sours
And my reins
Give me sharp pain,

כא כִּי
יִתְחַמֵּץ לְבָבִי
כִלְיוֹתַי
אֶשְׁתּוֹנָן׃

22 I am ignorant,
Without knowledge.
Beastly
I was with You.

כב וַאֲנִי־בַעַר
וְלֹא אֵדָע
בְּהֵמוֹת
הָיִיתִי עִמָּךְ׃

23 But I am always with You,
You grasped
My right hand.

כג וַאֲנִי תָמִיד עִמָּךְ
אָחַזְתָּ
בְּיַד־יְמִינִי׃

24 With Your counsel You led me,
To lasting
Honor You take me.

כד בַּעֲצָתְךָ תַנְחֵנִי
וְאַחַר
כָּבוֹד תִּקָּחֵנִי׃

25 What will I have in Heaven?	כה מִי־לִ֥י בַשָּׁמָ֑יִם
With You	וְעִמְּךָ֗
I have no desires on the earth	לֹא־חָפַ֥צְתִּי בָאָֽרֶץ׃
26 Finished is my flesh and heart!	כו כָּלָ֥ה שְׁאֵרִ֗י וּלְבָ֫בִ֥י
My heart's rock and my part is	צוּר־לְבָבִ֥י וְחֶלְקִ֑י
God forever.	אֱלֹהִ֥ים לְעוֹלָֽם׃
27 Truly, those far from You will be ruined.	כז כִּֽי־הִנֵּ֣ה רְחֵקֶ֣יךָ יֹאבֵ֑דוּ
You annihilate	הִ֝צְמַ֗תָּה
Every one who strays from You.	כָּל־זוֹנֶ֥ה מִמֶּֽךָּ׃
28 But for me,	כח וַאֲנִ֤י ׀
The closeness to God is good for me.	קִֽרֲבַ֥ת אֱלֹהִ֗ים לִ֫י־ט֥וֹב
I put	שַׁתִּ֤י ׀
My refuge in the Almighty Eternal,	בַּאדֹנָ֣י יְהוִ֣ה מַחְסִ֑י
To tell	לְ֝סַפֵּ֗ר
All Your messages.	כָּל־מַלְאֲכוֹתֶֽיךָ׃

4. Deriving the hapax חרצבות from Arabic حرب "to tighten a rope".
אולם is read as from Ugaritic 'ul "body", Arabic אלי "to be stout, fat".

10. הלם means "to smash with a hammer", from a rock this gives pebbles.

11. Meaning, does God care about the deeds of humans?

12. Following Dahood, deriving שלו from Aramaic שלא, שלי "to forget". Instead of "eternity" one might translate "The Eternal".

15. דור is a group living together.

19. Taking בלהות in the sense of Arabic בלה "to lose one's mind, mental capabilities".

Psalm 74

1 A didactic poem by Asaph.
Why, God,
Did You permanently abandon,
Did Your anger blow smoke
Against the sheep of Your pasture?

א מַשְׂכִּיל לְאָסָף
לָמָה אֱלֹהִים
זָנַחְתָּ לָנֶצַח
יֶעְשַׁן אַפְּךָ
בְּצֹאן מַרְעִיתֶךָ׃

2 Remember Your assembly
That You acquired of old,
That You saved,
The tribe of Your inheritance;
Mount Zion,
This One,
On which You dwelt.

ב זְכֹר עֲדָתְךָ ׀
קָנִיתָ קֶּדֶם
גָּאַלְתָּ
שֵׁבֶט נַחֲלָתֶךָ
הַר־צִיּוֹן
זֶה ׀
שָׁכַנְתָּ בּוֹ׃

3 Lift Your steps
Over total destruction,
All the enemy's evil done in the Sanctuary.

ג הָרִימָה פְעָמֶיךָ
לְמַשֻּׁאוֹת נֶצַח
כָּל־הֵרַע אוֹיֵב בַּקֹּדֶשׁ׃

4 Your adversaries roared
At Your places of assembly;
They erected all their standards.

ד שָׁאֲגוּ צֹרְרֶיךָ
בְּקֶרֶב מוֹעֲדֶךָ
שָׂמוּ אוֹתֹתָם אֹתוֹת׃

5 May they be recorded
As attackers of the Sublime
In the thicket of wood
With axes.

ה יִוָּדַע
כְּמֵבִיא לְמָעְלָה
בִּסֲבָךְ־עֵץ
קַרְדֻּמּוֹת׃

6 And now
Its carvings all together
They smash
With hatches and planes.

ו וְעַתְּ [וְעַתָּה]
פִּתּוּחֶיהָ יָּחַד
בְּכַשִּׁיל וְכֵילַפֹּת
יַהֲלֹמוּן׃

7 They put fire
To Your sanctuary,
They desecrated Your name's abode
To the ground.

ז שִׁלְחוּ בָאֵשׁ
מִקְדָּשֶׁךָ
לָאָרֶץ
חִלְּלוּ מִשְׁכַּן־שְׁמֶךָ׃

8 They said in their heart,
Destructive together,
They burned all of God's assembly places in the land.

ח אָמְרוּ בְלִבָּם
נִינָם יָחַד
שָׂרְפוּ כָל־מוֹעֲדֵי־אֵל בָּאָרֶץ׃

9 We did not see
Signs for us,
There is no prophet any more,
Neither is with us
One who knows what to count.

ט אוֹתֹתֵינוּ
לֹא רָאִינוּ
אֵין־עוֹד נָבִיא
וְלֹא־אִתָּנוּ
יֹדֵעַ עַד־מָה׃

10 Until when, o God,
May the attacker blaspheme,
May the enemy slander Your eternal name?

י עַד־מָתַי אֱלֹהִים
יְחָרֶף צָר
יְנָאֵץ אוֹיֵב שִׁמְךָ לָנֶצַח׃

11 Why do You restrain Your left hand
And Your right hand?
Destroy out of Your bosom.

יא לָמָּה תָשִׁיב יָדְךָ
וִימִינֶךָ
מִקֶּרֶב חוקך [חֵיקְךָ] כַלֵּה׃

12 And God
Is King from before creation,
He works victory
On earth.

יב וֵאלֹהִים
מַלְכִּי מִקֶּדֶם
פֹּעֵל יְשׁוּעוֹת
בְּקֶרֶב הָאָרֶץ׃

13 The Sea You scattered in Your power,
You broke the heads of the sea-monsters
On the water.

יג אַתָּה פוֹרַרְתָּ בְעָזְּךָ יָם
שִׁבַּרְתָּ רָאשֵׁי תַנִּינִים
עַל־הַמָּיִם׃

14 You smashed
The heads of Leviathan,
You gave it as food
To desert dwellers.

יד אַתָּה רִצַּצְתָּ
רָאשֵׁי לִוְיָתָן
תִּתְּנֶנּוּ מַאֲכָל
לְעָם לְצִיִּים׃

15 You broke open
Source and brook;
You made dry up
Wild rivers.

טו אַתָּה בָקַעְתָּ
מַעְיָן וָנָחַל
אַתָּה הוֹבַשְׁתָּ
נַהֲרוֹת אֵיתָן׃

16 Yours is the day,
Yours also night;
You prepared
Light and sun.

טז לְךָ יוֹם
אַף־לְךָ לָיְלָה
אַתָּה הֲכִינוֹתָ
מָאוֹר וָשָׁמֶשׁ׃

17 You fixed
All borders of earth;
Summer and winter,
You created them.

יז אַתָּה הִצַּבְתָּ
כָּל־גְּבוּלוֹת אָרֶץ
קַיִץ וָחֹרֶף
אַתָּה יְצַרְתָּם׃

18 Remember that, Enemy,
Blasphemer against the Eternal,
Despicable people,
Who slander Your name.

יח זְכָר־זֹאת אוֹיֵב
חֵרֵף | יְיָ
וְעַם־נָבָל
נִאֲצוּ שְׁמֶךָ׃

19 Do not abandon to armies
The people You taught;
The souls of Your poor
Do not forget forever.

יט אַל־תִּתֵּן לְחַיַּת
נֶפֶשׁ תּוֹרֶךָ
חַיַּת עֲנִיֶּיךָ
אַל־תִּשְׁכַּח לָנֶצַח׃

20 Look upon the covenant
For they filled the dark places on earth
As oases of violence.

כ הַבֵּט לַבְּרִית
כִּי־מָלְאוּ מַחֲשַׁכֵּי־אֶרֶץ
נְאוֹת חָמָס׃

21 The downtrodden shall not stay ashamed,
The poor and needy
Shall praise Your name.

כא אַל־יָשֹׁב דַּךְ נִכְלָם
עָנִי וְאֶבְיוֹן
יְהַלְלוּ שְׁמֶךָ׃

22 Arise, o God,
Fight Your fight!
Remember the despicable's blaspheming
Every day.

כב קוּמָה אֱלֹהִים
רִיבָה רִיבֶךָ
זְכֹר חֶרְפָּתְךָ מִנִּי־נָבָל
כָּל־הַיּוֹם׃

23 Do not forget
Your attackers' voice;
The hum of those who rise against You
Ascends always.

כג אַל־תִּשְׁכַּח
קוֹל צֹרְרֶיךָ
שְׁאוֹן קָמֶיךָ
עֹלֶה תָמִיד׃

8. The root of נינם is ינה "violent", following Ibn Janaḥ and Ibn Ezra. Rashi translates it as "their rulers", from ינון, *Ps.* 72:17.

9. עד as adverb is read as Arabic "number, enumerate".

15. נהרות איתן correspond to נחל איתן (*Deut.* 21:4), "uncultivable riverbed" (*Sifri* #207, R. Saadya Gaon, Rashi).

19. The pun on חיה depends on the multiple meaning of the word. Here we follow Rashi who derives the meaning of חיה "mobilized army" from *2Sam.* 23:11; the acception "soul" is quite frequent in Psalms. The first occurrence of חית is an archaic absolute state, the second one is a construct state. חיה means also "wild beast"; Torczyner-Cohn translate: "Do not abandon to the wild animal the soul of Your turtle dove."

The translation of תּוֹרֶךָ "those who You taught" already is in the Targum.

Psalm 75

1 For the director, "destroy not",
A Psalm, song of Asaph.

א לַמְנַצֵּחַ אַל־תַּשְׁחֵת
מִזְמוֹר לְאָסָף שִׁיר׃

2 We thank You,
God,
We thank,
Your Name is so close;
They tell
Your wonders.

ב הוֹדִינוּ לְּךָ ׀
אֱלֹהִים
הוֹדִינוּ
וְקָרוֹב שְׁמֶךָ
סִפְּרוּ
נִפְלְאוֹתֶיךָ

3 Certainly
I shall fix a term;
I
Will judge honestly.

ג כִּי
אֶקַּח מוֹעֵד
אֲנִי
מֵישָׁרִים אֶשְׁפֹּט׃

4 Dissolving
Were the earth and all its inhabitants;
I made its pillars firm, Selah.

ד נְמוֹגִים
אֶרֶץ וְכָל־יֹשְׁבֶיהָ
אָנֹכִי תִכַּנְתִּי עַמּוּדֶיהָ סֶּלָה׃

5 I said to the hoodlums:
Do not hoot,
And to the wicked:
Do not raise a horn!

ה אָמַרְתִּי לַהוֹלְלִים
אַל־תָּהֹלּוּ
וְלָרְשָׁעִים
אַל־תָּרִימוּ קָרֶן׃

6 Do not raise your horn against the Most High,
Talking with libertine neck.

ו אַל־תָּרִימוּ לַמָּרוֹם קַרְנְכֶם
תְּדַבְּרוּ בְצַוָּאר עָתָק׃

7 Certainly, neither from sunrise
Nor from sunset,
And neither
From prairie nor mountains,

ז כִּי לֹא מִמּוֹצָא
וּמִמַּעֲרָב
וְלֹא
מִמִּדְבַּר הָרִים׃

8 Only God is the judge,
This one He brings down
And that one He lifts up.

ח כִּי־אֱלֹהִים שֹׁפֵט
זֶה יַשְׁפִּיל
וְזֶה יָרִים׃

9 Truly, a cup is in the Eternal's Hand,
Fermenting wine
Full to mix
From which He pours.
Only its dregs
Will squeeze out, drink,
All
The wicked of the earth.

ט כִּי כוֹס בְּיַד־יהוה
וְיַיִן חָמַר ׀
מָלֵא מֶסֶךְ
וַיַּגֵּר מִזֶּה
אַךְ־שְׁמָרֶיהָ
יִמְצוּ יִשְׁתּוּ
כֹּל
רִשְׁעֵי־אָרֶץ׃

10 But I
Shall tell forever;
I shall make music
To Jacob's God.

י וַאֲנִי
אַגִּיד לְעֹלָם
אֲזַמְּרָה
לֵאלֹהֵי יַעֲקֹב׃

11 And I shall knock down all wickeds' horns. יא וְכָל־קַרְנֵ֣י רְשָׁעִ֣ים אֲגַדֵּ֑עַ
Uplifted shall be תְּ֝רוֹמַ֗מְנָה
The horns of the just. קַרְנ֥וֹת צַדִּֽיק׃

Psalm 76

1 To the director, in melodies,
A Psalm, song of Asaph.

א לַמְנַצֵּחַ בִּנְגִינֹת
מִזְמוֹר לְאָסָף שִׁיר׃

2 God is understood in Judah;
In Israel
His Name is great.

ב נוֹדָע בִּיהוּדָה אֱלֹהִים
בְּיִשְׂרָאֵל
גָּדוֹל שְׁמוֹ׃

3 His hut is in Salem,
His abode in Zion.

ג וַיְהִי בְשָׁלֵם סֻכּוֹ
וּמְעוֹנָתוֹ בְצִיּוֹן׃

4 There
He broke the horrible fire off bows,
Shield, sword, and weapons, Selah.

ד שָׁמָּה
שִׁבַּר רִשְׁפֵי־קָשֶׁת
מָגֵן וְחֶרֶב וּמִלְחָמָה סֶלָה׃

5 O luminous,
You are august
Over devouring mountains.

ה נָאוֹר
אַתָּה אַדִּיר
מֵהַרְרֵי־טָרֶף׃

6 Ready to pillage,
The strong-hearted
Sleep their sleep;
None of the soldiers found their hands.

ו אֶשְׁתּוֹלְלוּ |
אַבִּירֵי לֵב
נָמוּ שְׁנָתָם
וְלֹא־מָצְאוּ כָל־אַנְשֵׁי־חַיִל יְדֵיהֶם׃

7 Before Your shouting rage
God of Jacob,
Both chariot and horse
Expire.

ז מִגַּעֲרָתְךָ
אֱלֹהֵי יַעֲקֹב
נִרְדָּם
וְרֶכֶב וָסוּס׃

8 You,
Awesome You are;
Who can stand before You,
When You are in rage?

ח אַתָּה |
נוֹרָא אַתָּה
וּמִי־יַעֲמֹד לְפָנֶיךָ
מֵאָז אַפֶּךָ׃

9 From Heaven
You proclaimed justice;
The earth was fearful but quiet,

ט מִשָּׁמַיִם
הִשְׁמַעְתָּ דִּין
אֶרֶץ יָרְאָה וְשָׁקָטָה׃

10 When God rose to judgment,
To save all the meek of the earth, Selah.

י בְּקוּם־לַמִּשְׁפָּט אֱלֹהִים
לְהוֹשִׁיעַ כָּל־עַנְוֵי־אֶרֶץ סֶלָה

11 Because human rage causes thanks to You
The leftover rages You will gird.

יא כִּי־חֲמַת אָדָם תּוֹדֶךָּ
שְׁאֵרִית חֵמֹת תַּחְגֹּר׃

12 Do make vows and redeem them
To the Eternal, your God,
All His surroundings;
Bring gifts to Him
Who is to be feared.

יב נִדְרוּ וְשַׁלְּמוּ
לַיהוָה אֱלֹהֵיכֶם
כָּל־סְבִיבָיו
יֹבִילוּ שַׁי
לַמּוֹרָא׃

13 He diminishes	יג יִ֭בְצֹר
The spirit of the leaders;	ר֣וּחַ נְגִידִ֑ים
He is awesome	נ֝וֹרָ֗א
To the kings of the earth!	לְמַלְכֵי־אָֽרֶץ׃

4. Comparing רשף to Accadic *risbu* "horrible fire".

13. The use of בצר here is an Aramaism, "He subtracts", not standard Hebrew "He fortifies".

Psalm 77

1 For the director, following Yedutun,
A psalm of Asaph.

א לַמְנַצֵּ֥חַ עַֽל־יְדִיתוּן [יְדוּת֗וּן]
לְאָסָ֥ף מִזְמֽוֹר׃

2 My voice is to God and I am lamenting,
My voice is to God,
May He lend His ear to me.

ב קוֹלִ֣י אֶל־אֱלֹהִ֣ים וְאֶצְעָ֑קָה
קוֹלִ֥י אֶל־אֱ֝לֹהִ֗ים
וְהַאֲזִ֥ין אֵלָֽי׃

3 The Almighty I sought
On the day of my distress;
My hand
Is stretched out in the night,
Is not being relaxed;
My soul refuses to be consoled.

ג בְּי֥וֹם צָרָתִי֮
אֲדֹנָ֪י דָּ֫רָ֥שְׁתִּי
יָדִ֤י ׀
לַ֣יְלָה נִ֭גְּרָה
וְלֹ֣א תָפ֑וּג
מֵאֲנָ֖ה הִנָּחֵ֣ם נַפְשִֽׁי׃

4 I am thinking of God and wailing;
I want to talk;
My spirit wraps itself up, Selah.

ד אֶזְכְּרָ֣ה אֱלֹהִ֣ים וְאֶהֱמָ֑יָה
אָשִׂ֓יחָה ׀
וְתִתְעַטֵּ֖ף רוּחִ֣י סֶֽלָה׃

5 You seized
The covers of my eyes,
I was palpitating,
I could not talk.

ה אָ֭חַזְתָּ
שְׁמֻר֣וֹת עֵינָ֑י
נִ֝פְעַ֗מְתִּי
וְלֹ֣א אֲדַבֵּֽר׃

6 I thought of days of old,
The years
From forever.

ו חִשַּׁ֣בְתִּי יָמִ֣ים מִקֶּ֑דֶם
שְׁ֝נ֗וֹת
עוֹלָמִֽים׃

7 I remember my song in the night,
I am talking to my heart,
My spirit is seeking.

ז אֶזְכְּרָ֥ה נְגִינָתִ֗י בַּ֫לָּ֥יְלָה
עִם־לְבָבִ֥י אָשִׂ֑יחָה
וַיְחַפֵּ֥שׂ רוּחִֽי׃

8 Does forever
The Almighty neglect,
Will He never again be pleased?

ח הַֽ֭לְעוֹלָמִים
יִזְנַ֥ח ׀ אֲדֹנָ֑י
וְלֹֽא־יֹסִ֖יף לִרְצ֣וֹת עֽוֹד׃

9 Is His kindness eternally nought?
Did He finalize the decree
For all generations?

ט הֶאָפֵ֣ס לָנֶ֣צַח חַסְדּ֑וֹ
גָּ֥מַר אֹ֝֗מֶר
לְדֹ֣ר וָדֹֽר׃

10 Did the Powerful forget to show favor?
Or did He in anger
Shut off His mercy? Selah.

י הֲשָׁכַ֣ח חַנּ֣וֹת אֵ֑ל
אִם־קָפַ֥ץ בְּ֝אַ֗ף
רַחֲמָ֥יו סֶֽלָה׃

11 But I will say:
It would be my emptiness,
A change
In the right hand of Most High?

יא וָ֭אֹמַר
חַלּ֣וֹתִי הִ֑יא
שְׁ֝נ֗וֹת
יְמִ֣ין עֶלְיֽוֹן׃

12 I (shall) remember the deeds of Yah,
When I proclaim Your previous wonders.

יב אֶזְכּ֥יר [אֶזְכּ֥וֹר] מַֽעַלְלֵי־יָ֑הּ
כִּֽי־אֶזְכְּרָ֖ה מִקֶּ֣דֶם פִּלְאֶֽךָ׃

13 I am studying all Your works,
I am talking about Your doings.

יג וְהָגִיתִי בְכָל־פָּעֳלֶךָ
וּבַעֲלִילוֹתֶיךָ אָשִׂיחָה׃

14 God,
Your way is in holiness;
Who is a power as great
As God?

יד אֱלֹהִים
בַּקֹּדֶשׁ דַּרְכֶּךָ
מִי־אֵל גָּדוֹל
כֵּאלֹהִים׃

15 You are the Power
Who performs wonders;
You publicized Your strength among nations.

טו אַתָּה הָאֵל
עֹשֵׂה פֶלֶא
הוֹדַעְתָּ בָעַמִּים עֻזֶּךָ׃

16 You saved Your people by force,
The sons of Jacob and Joseph, Selah.

טז גָּאַלְתָּ בִּזְרוֹעַ עַמֶּךָ
בְּנֵי־יַעֲקֹב וְיוֹסֵף סֶלָה׃

17 The waters saw You,
God,
The waters saw You, they trembled;
Also the depths shook.

יז רָאוּךָ מַּיִם ׀
אֱלֹהִים
רָאוּךָ מַּיִם יָחִילוּ
אַף יִרְגְּזוּ תְהֹמוֹת׃

18 Water streamed
From clouds,
Voice
The skies produced,
Also Your arrows
Went to and fro.

יח זֹרְמוּ מַּיִם ׀
עָבוֹת
קוֹל
נָתְנוּ שְׁחָקִים
אַף־חֲצָצֶיךָ
יִתְהַלָּכוּ׃

19 The voice of Your thunder in the spheres,
Lightning illuminates the terra firma,
Earth is shaking and quaking.

יט קוֹל רַעַמְךָ ׀ בַּגַּלְגַּל
הֵאִירוּ בְרָקִים תֵּבֵל
רָגְזָה וַתִּרְעַשׁ הָאָרֶץ׃

20 In the sea is Your way,
And Your path
In mighty waters,
But Your foot-steps
Cannot be known.

כ בַּיָּם דַּרְכֶּךָ
וּשְׁבִילְיךָ [וּשְׁבִילְךָ]
בְּמַיִם רַבִּים
וְעִקְּבוֹתֶיךָ
לֹא נֹדָעוּ׃

21 You led Your people like sheep
Through Moses and Aaron.

כא נָחִיתָ כַצֹּאן עַמֶּךָ
בְּיַד־מֹשֶׁה וְאַהֲרֹן׃

An introduction to Psalm 78.

11. חלל means "empty", as a derived form it is also a corpse, empty of life. חַלּוֹת is its noun of abstraction.

12. In the meanings is little difference between the *ketib* אזכיר "I will mention" (*piel*) and the *qere* אזכור "I will remember" (*qal*).

19. This is the first occurrence of גלגל for "heavenly sphere", the standard use of the word in the Middle Ages.

Psalm 78

1 A didactic poem by Asaph.
My people, listen
To my teaching,
Bend your ear
To my mouth's words.

א מַשְׂכִּיל לְאָסָף
הַאֲזִינָה עַמִּי
תּוֹרָתִי
הַטּוּ אָזְנְכֶם
לְאִמְרֵי־פִי׃

2 I shall open my mouth in a tale,
Express similes
Of old,

ב אֶפְתְּחָה בְמָשָׁל פִּי
אַבִּיעָה חִידוֹת
מִנִּי־קֶדֶם׃

3 Which we heard
And know them,
Which our fathers
Told us.

ג אֲשֶׁר שָׁמַעְנוּ
וַנֵּדָעֵם
וַאֲבוֹתֵינוּ
סִפְּרוּ־לָנוּ׃

4 We shall not withhold it
From their sons,
To a future generation,
Telling
The praises of the Eternal,
His power and His wonders
That He performed.

ד לֹא נְכַחֵד ׀
מִבְּנֵיהֶם
לְדוֹר אַחֲרוֹן
מְסַפְּרִים
תְּהִלּוֹת יהוה
וֶעֱזוּזוֹ וְנִפְלְאוֹתָיו
אֲשֶׁר עָשָׂה

5 He set up a testimonial
In Jacob,
A Torah
He gave in Israel
Which He commanded
To our forefathers,
To inform
Their children.

ה וַיָּקֶם עֵדוּת ׀
בְּיַעֲקֹב
וְתוֹרָה
שָׂם בְּיִשְׂרָאֵל
אֲשֶׁר־צִוָּה
אֶת־אֲבוֹתֵינוּ
לְהוֹדִיעָם
לִבְנֵיהֶם׃

6 So that they shall know,
The later generation,
The children who will be born to them.
They shall arise
And tell their children.

ו לְמַעַן יֵדְעוּ ׀
דּוֹר אַחֲרוֹן
בָּנִים יִוָּלֵדוּ
יָקֻמוּ
וִיסַפְּרוּ לִבְנֵיהֶם׃

7 They should put their trust in God,
Not forget
The deeds of the Powerful,
And keep His commandments.

ז וְיָשִׂימוּ בֵאלֹהִים כִּסְלָם
וְלֹא יִשְׁכְּחוּ
מַעַלְלֵי־אֵל
וּמִצְוֺתָיו יִנְצֹרוּ׃

8 They should not be like their fathers,
A generation
Unruly and rebellious,
A generation
With unprepared heart
Whose spirit was not faithful to the Power.

ח וְלֹא יִהְיוּ ׀ כַּאֲבוֹתָם
דּוֹר
סוֹרֵר וּמֹרֶה
דּוֹר
לֹא־הֵכִין לִבּוֹ
וְלֹא־נֶאֶמְנָה אֶת־אֵל רוּחוֹ׃

9 The sons of Ephraim,
Armed with lifted bows,
Turned around
In the day of battle.

ט בְּֽנֵי־אֶפְרַיִם
נוֹשְׁקֵי רוֹמֵי־קָשֶׁת
הָפְכוּ
בְּיוֹם קְרָב׃

10 They did not keep
God's covenant;
They refused to walk
In His Torah.

י לֹא שָׁמְרוּ
בְּרִית אֱלֹהִים
וּבְתוֹרָתוֹ
מֵאֲנוּ לָלֶכֶת׃

11 They forgot His deeds
And His wonders
That He had shown them.

יא וַיִּשְׁכְּחוּ עֲלִילוֹתָיו
וְנִפְלְאוֹתָיו
אֲשֶׁר הֶרְאָם׃

12 In front of their fathers
He performed miracles,
In the land of Egypt, the field of Ṣoan.

יב נֶגֶד אֲבוֹתָם
עָשָׂה פֶלֶא
בְּאֶרֶץ מִצְרַיִם שְׂדֵה־צֹעַן׃

13 He split the Sea
And led them through,
He erected the waters like a dike.

יג בָּקַע יָם
וַיַּעֲבִירֵם
וַיַּצֶּב־מַיִם כְּמוֹ־נֵד׃

14 He led them with a cloud by day
And the entire night
By the light of fire.

יד וַיַּנְחֵם בֶּעָנָן יוֹמָם
וְכָל־הַלַּיְלָה
בְּאוֹר אֵשׁ׃

15 He would split rocks
In the desert
And gave to drink
Like the deep underground.

טו יְבַקַּע צֻרִים
בַּמִּדְבָּר
וַיַּשְׁקְ
כִּתְהֹמוֹת רַבָּה׃

16 He produced fluids from rock
And brought water down like rivers.

טז וַיּוֹצִא נוֹזְלִים מִסָּלַע
וַיּוֹרֶד כַּנְּהָרוֹת מָיִם׃

17 But they continued
To sin against Him
To rebel against the Supreme One
In the desolation.

יז וַיּוֹסִיפוּ עוֹד
לַחֲטֹא־לוֹ
לַמְרוֹת עֶלְיוֹן
בַּצִּיָּה׃

18 They tempted the Powerful in their hearts
To ask for food for themselves.

יח וַיְנַסּוּ־אֵל בִּלְבָבָם
לִשְׁאָל־אֹכֶל לְנַפְשָׁם׃

19 They talked against God;
They said:
Can the Powerful
Set a table
In the wilderness?

יט וַיְדַבְּרוּ בֵּאלֹהִים
אָמְרוּ
הֲיוּכַל אֵל
לַעֲרֹךְ שֻׁלְחָן
בַּמִּדְבָּר׃

20 True, He hit the rock
And water flowed,
Streams flooded.
But can He give
Bread?:

כ הֵן הִכָּה־צוּר |
וַיָּזוּבוּ מַיִם
וּנְחָלִים יִשְׁטֹפוּ
הֲגַם־לֶחֶם
יוּכַל תֵּת

Or prepare meat for His people?

אִם־יָכִין שְׁאֵר לְעַמּוֹ׃

21 This
The Eternal heard,
And became angry, and fire
Was lit in Jacob,
Also rage
Rose against Israel.

כא לָכֵן ׀
שָׁמַע יהוה
וַיִּתְעַבָּר וְאֵשׁ
נִשְּׂקָה בְיַעֲקֹב
וְגַם־אַף
עָלָה בְיִשְׂרָאֵל׃

22 Because they did not trust
In God,
Did not have confidence
In His help.

כב כִּי לֹא הֶאֱמִינוּ
בֵּאלֹהִים
וְלֹא בָטְחוּ
בִּישׁוּעָתוֹ׃

23 He commanded the skies above
And opened the doors of heaven.

כג וַיְצַו שְׁחָקִים מִמָּעַל
וְדַלְתֵי שָׁמַיִם פָּתָח׃

24 He let Manna rain on them to eat,
Heavenly flour
He gave them.

כד וַיַּמְטֵר עֲלֵיהֶם מָן לֶאֱכֹל
וּדְגַן שָׁמַיִם
נָתַן לָמוֹ׃

25 The bread of superior beings
Man ate.
Provisions He sent them to fullness.

כה לֶחֶם אַבִּירִים
אָכַל אִישׁ
צֵידָה שָׁלַח לָהֶם לָשֹׂבַע׃

26 He made move the East wind
In the skies
And in His power led the South wind.

כו יַסַּע קָדִים
בַּשָּׁמָיִם
וַיְנַהֵג בְּעֻזּוֹ תֵימָן׃

27 He let meat rain on them like dust
And winged birds
Like Seas' sand.

כז וַיַּמְטֵר עֲלֵיהֶם כֶּעָפָר שְׁאֵר
וּכְחוֹל יַמִּים
עוֹף כָּנָף׃

28 He threw them down
In the middle of His camp,
All around
His dwelling place.

כח וַיַּפֵּל
בְּקֶרֶב מַחֲנֵהוּ
סָבִיב
לְמִשְׁכְּנֹתָיו׃

29 They ate and became very full;
Their desire
Was fulfilled.

כט וַיֹּאכְלוּ וַיִּשְׂבְּעוּ מְאֹד
וְתַאֲוָתָם
יָבִא לָהֶם׃

30 Their desire was not yet repugnant for them
Still
Their food was in their mouths,

ל לֹא־זָרוּ מִתַּאֲוָתָם
עוֹד
אָכְלָם בְּפִיהֶם׃

31 When God's rage
Caught up with them.
He killed
Of their fat ones
And tore down the select ones of Israel.

לא וְאַף אֱלֹהִים ׀
עָלָה בָהֶם
וַיַּהֲרֹג
בְּמִשְׁמַנֵּיהֶם
וּבַחוּרֵי יִשְׂרָאֵל הִכְרִיעַ׃

32 With all this
They continued to sin
And did not trust
In His wonders.

לב בְּכָל־זֹאת
חָטְאוּ־עוֹד
וְלֹא־הֶאֱמִינוּ
בְּנִפְלְאוֹתָיו׃

33 He finished their days in vapor
And their years
In confusion.

לג וַיְכַל־בַּהֶבֶל יְמֵיהֶם
וּשְׁנוֹתָם
בַּבֶּהָלָה׃

34 When He killed them, they sought Him,
Repented,
And implored The Mighty One

לד אִם־הֲרָגָם וּדְרָשׁוּהוּ
וְשָׁבוּ
וְשִׁחֲרוּ־אֵל׃

35 They remembered
That God is their rock
And The Supreme Power
Their redeemer.

לה וַיִּזְכְּרוּ
כִּי־אֱלֹהִים צוּרָם
וְאֵל עֶלְיוֹן
גֹּאֲלָם׃

36 They seduced Him with their mouths,
And with their tongues
They lied to Him.

לו וַיְפַתּוּהוּ בְּפִיהֶם
וּבִלְשׁוֹנָם
יְכַזְּבוּ־לוֹ׃

37 But their heart
Was not steadfast with Him;
They were not faithful
To His covenant.

לז וְלִבָּם
לֹא־נָכוֹן עִמּוֹ
וְלֹא נֶאֶמְנוּ
בִּבְרִיתוֹ׃

38 But He is merciful,
He covers up sin
And will not destroy;
Many times He
Withholds His anger
And does not kindle
All His rage.

לח וְהוּא רַחוּם |
יְכַפֵּר עָוֺן
וְלֹא־יַשְׁחִית
וְהִרְבָּה
לְהָשִׁיב אַפּוֹ
וְלֹא־יָעִיר
כָּל־חֲמָתוֹ׃

39 He remembers
That they are flesh,
A passing spirit
Who will not return.

לט וַיִּזְכֹּר
כִּי־בָשָׂר הֵמָּה
רוּחַ הוֹלֵךְ
וְלֹא יָשׁוּב׃

40 How many times they
Rebelled against Him in the wilderness,
Aggrieved Him
In the desert?

מ כַּמָּה
יַמְרוּהוּ בַמִּדְבָּר
עֲצִיבוּהוּ
בִּישִׁימוֹן׃

41 Repeatedly they tested the Powerful,
To the Holy of Israel they gave marks!

מא וַיָּשׁוּבוּ וַיְנַסּוּ אֵל
וּקְדוֹשׁ יִשְׂרָאֵל הִתְווּ׃

42 They did not remember His left hand,
The day
He redeemed them from the oppressor.

מב לֹא־זָכְרוּ אֶת־יָדוֹ
יוֹם
אֲשֶׁר־פָּדָם מִנִּי־צָר׃

43 When He put His signs
Into Egypt
And His wonders
In the fields of Ṣoan.

מג אֲשֶׁר־שָׂם בְּמִצְרַיִם
אֹתוֹתָיו
וּמוֹפְתָיו
בִּשְׂדֵה־צֹעַן׃

44 He turned into blood
Their streams;
Their fluids
Were undrinkable.

מד וַיַּהֲפֹךְ לְדָם
יְאֹרֵיהֶם
וְנֹזְלֵיהֶם
בַּל־יִשְׁתָּיוּן׃

45 He sent into them wild animals
Which ate them,
Also frogs
Which destroyed them.

מה יְשַׁלַּח בָּהֶם עָרֹב
וַיֹּאכְלֵם
וּצְפַרְדֵּעַ
וַתַּשְׁחִיתֵם׃

46 He gave their produce to the locust
And their exertion
To the grasshopper.

מו וַיִּתֵּן לֶחָסִיל יְבוּלָם
וִיגִיעָם
לָאַרְבֶּה׃

47 He killed their vines by hail
And their sycamores
By frost.

מז יַהֲרֹג בַּבָּרָד גַּפְנָם
וְשִׁקְמוֹתָם
בַּחֲנָמַל׃

48 He delivered their animals to hail,
And their herds
To pestilences.

מח וַיַּסְגֵּר לַבָּרָד בְּעִירָם
וּמִקְנֵיהֶם
לָרְשָׁפִים׃

49 He sent into them
The heat of His anger:
Rage, fury, and woe,
A pack
Of messengers of evils.

מט יְשַׁלַּח־בָּם ׀
חֲרוֹן אַפּוֹ
עֶבְרָה וָזַעַם וְצָרָה
מִשְׁלַחַת
מַלְאֲכֵי רָעִים׃

50 He cleared the way for His anger,
Did not spare their souls from death,
And their lives
He delivered to the plague.

נ יְפַלֵּס נָתִיב לְאַפּוֹ
לֹא־חָשַׂךְ מִמָּוֶת נַפְשָׁם
וְחַיָּתָם
לַדֶּבֶר הִסְגִּיר׃

51 He smote every firstborn in Egypt,
The primes of power
In the tents of Ham.:

נא וַיַּךְ כָּל־בְּכוֹר בְּמִצְרָיִם
רֵאשִׁית אוֹנִים
בְּאָהֳלֵי־חָם

52 He moved His people like sheep,
He lead them like a flock
In the wilderness.

נב וַיַּסַּע כַּצֹּאן עַמּוֹ
וַיְנַהֲגֵם כַּעֵדֶר
בַּמִּדְבָּר׃

53 He let them rest in safety
They were not afraid,
While the Sea
Covered their enemies.

נג וַיַּנְחֵם לָבֶטַח
וְלֹא פָחָדוּ
וְאֶת־אוֹיְבֵיהֶם
כִּסָּה הַיָּם׃

54 He brought them
To His holy precinct,
This mountain
Created by His right hand.

נד וַיְבִיאֵם
אֶל־גְּבוּל קָדְשׁוֹ
הַר־זֶה
קָנְתָה יְמִינוֹ׃

55 He drove peoples out before them,
He distributed
Their inheritance by rope,
And let the tribes of Israel
. Dwell in their tents

נה וַיְגָרֶשׁ מִפְּנֵיהֶם | גּוֹיִם
וַיַּפִּילֵם
בְּחֶבֶל נַחֲלָה
וַיַּשְׁכֵּן בְּאָהֳלֵיהֶם
שִׁבְטֵי יִשְׂרָאֵל׃

56 They tempted and rebelled
Against Supreme God,
Also His testimonials
They did not observe.

נו וַיְנַסּוּ וַיַּמְרוּ
אֶת־אֱלֹהִים עֶלְיוֹן
וְעֵדוֹתָיו
לֹא שָׁמָרוּ׃

57 They retreated and betrayed
Like their fathers;
They inverted
Like a treacherous bow.

נז וַיִּסֹּגוּ וַיִּבְגְּדוּ
כַּאֲבוֹתָם
נֶהְפְּכוּ
כְּקֶשֶׁת רְמִיָּה׃

58 They vexed Him with their high places,
And with their idols
They roiled Him.

נח וַיַּכְעִיסוּהוּ בְּבָמוֹתָם
וּבִפְסִילֵיהֶם
יַקְנִיאוּהוּ׃

59 God heard
And got angry,
He thoroughly despised
Israel.

נט שָׁמַע אֱלֹהִים
וַיִּתְעַבָּר
וַיִּמְאַס מְאֹד
בְּיִשְׂרָאֵל׃

60 He abandoned
The dwelling of Shilo,
The Tent
He made dwell among man.

ס וַיִּטֹּשׁ
מִשְׁכַּן שִׁלוֹ
אֹהֶל
שִׁכֵּן בָּאָדָם.

61 He gave His might into captivity,
And His splendor in the hand of the enemy.

סא וַיִּתֵּן לַשְּׁבִי עֻזּוֹ
וְתִפְאַרְתּוֹ בְיַד־צָר׃

62 He delivered His people to the sword
And against His inheritance
He was enraged.

סב וַיַּסְגֵּר לַחֶרֶב עַמּוֹ
וּבְנַחֲלָתוֹ
הִתְעַבָּר׃

63 The fire ate His young men,
His virgins
Were not fêted.

סג בַּחוּרָיו אָכְלָה־אֵשׁ
וּבְתוּלֹתָיו
לֹא הוּלָּלוּ׃

64 His priests
Fell by the sword;
His widows
Could not cry.

סד כֹּהֲנָיו
בַּחֶרֶב נָפָלוּ
וְאַלְמְנֹתָיו
לֹא תִבְכֶּינָה׃

65 The Almighty awoke like a sleeper,
Like a hero
Exhilarated by wine.

סה וַיִּקַץ כְּיָשֵׁן | אֲדֹנָי
כְּגִבּוֹר
מִתְרוֹנֵן מִיָּיִן׃

66 He slew his enemies backwards,
Permanent shame
He gave to them.

סו וַיַּךְ־צָרָיו אָחוֹר
חֶרְפַּת עוֹלָם
נָתַן לָמוֹ׃

67 He despised
The tent of Joseph,
The tribe of Ephraim
He did not choose.

סז וַיִּמְאַס
בְּאֹהֶל יוֹסֵף
וּבְשֵׁבֶט אֶפְרַיִם
לֹא בָחָר׃

68 He chose
The tribe of Judah,
Mount Zion
Beloved by Him.

סח וַיִּבְחַר
אֶת־שֵׁבֶט יְהוּדָה
אֶת־הַר צִיּוֹן
אֲשֶׁר אָהֵב׃

69 He built like on High
His holy place;
Like the earth
He gave it permanent foundations.

סט וַיִּבֶן כְּמוֹ־רָמִים
מִקְדָּשׁוֹ
כְּאֶרֶץ
יְסָדָהּ לְעוֹלָם׃

70 He chose
His servant David
And took him
From the sheep corrals.

ע וַיִּבְחַר
בְּדָוִד עַבְדּוֹ
וַיִּקָּחֵהוּ
מִמִּכְלְאֹת צֹאן׃

71 From after ewes He brought him
To shepherd
His people Jacob
And Israel
His inheritance.

עא מֵאַחַר עָלוֹת הֱבִיאוֹ
לִרְעוֹת
בְּיַעֲקֹב עַמּוֹ
וּבְיִשְׂרָאֵל
נַחֲלָתוֹ׃

72 He tended them
With his simple heart
And led them with his understanding hands.

עב וַיִּרְעֵם
כְּתֹם לְבָבוֹ
וּבִתְבוּנוֹת כַּפָּיו יַנְחֵם׃

7. Here כסל has the meaning "trust" as in *Prov.* 3:26, a property of which the loins are the repository; this contrasts with *Ps.* 49:14.

9. See *1Chr.* 7:21.

45. This is the traditional translation. It could as well mean "swarms of flies."

47. Nobody really knows the meaning of the hapax חנמל. The translation here follows R. Saadya Gaon (LXX "hoar frost"); the Targum and Rashi identify the word as name of a kind of locust.

Psalm 79

1 A Psalm of Asaph.
God,
Gentiles came
Into Your inheritance,
They defiled
Your holy hall,
They turned Jerusalem into ruins.

א מִזְמ֗וֹר לְאָ֫סָ֥ף
אֱלֹהִ֡ים
בָּ֤אוּ גוֹיִ֨ם ׀
בְּֽנַחֲלָתֶ֗ךָ
טִ֭מְּאוּ
אֶת־הֵיכַ֣ל קָדְשֶׁ֑ךָ
שָׂ֖מוּ אֶת־יְרוּשָׁלִַ֣ם לְעִיִּֽים׃

2 They gave
The corpses of Your servants
As food
To the birds of the sky,
The flesh of Your pious
To the beasts of the earth.

ב נָֽתְנ֡וּ
אֶת־נִבְלַ֬ת עֲבָדֶ֗יךָ
מַ֭אֲכָל
לְע֣וֹף הַשָּׁמָ֑יִם
בְּשַׂ֥ר חֲ֝סִידֶ֗יךָ
לְחַיְתוֹ־אָֽרֶץ׃

3 They spilled their blood like water
Around Jerusalem,
And nobody is burying.

ג שָׁפְכ֬וּ דָמָ֨ם ׀ כַּמַּ֗יִם
סְֽבִיב֥וֹת יְרוּשָׁלִָ֗ם
וְאֵ֣ין קוֹבֵֽר׃

4 We were a shame
To our neighbors,
Insult and spittle
To our surroundings.

ד הָיִ֣ינוּ חֶ֭רְפָּה
לִשְׁכֵנֵ֑ינוּ
לַ֥עַג וָ֝קֶ֗לֶס
לִסְבִיבוֹתֵֽינוּ׃

5 Until when, Eternal,
Will You be perpetually angry?
Will burn like fire
Your wrath?

ה עַד־מָ֣ה יְ֭הוה
תֶּאֱנַ֣ף לָנֶ֑צַח
תִּבְעַ֥ר כְּמוֹ־אֵ֝֗שׁ
קִנְאָתֶֽךָ׃

6 Pour out Your fury over the Gentiles
Who do not know You,
And over kingdoms
That Your Name
Do not invoke.

ו שְׁפֹ֤ךְ חֲמָתְךָ֨ אֶֽל־הַגּוֹיִ֗ם
אֲשֶׁ֣ר לֹֽא־יְדָ֫ע֥וּךָ
וְעַ֥ל מַמְלָכ֑וֹת
אֲשֶׁ֥ר בְּ֝שִׁמְךָ֗
לֹ֣א קָרָֽאוּ׃

7 Certainly,
Devoured is Jacob
And its champaign they laid waste.

ז כִּ֭י
אָכַ֣ל אֶֽת־יַעֲקֹ֑ב
וְֽאֶת־נָוֵ֥הוּ הֵשַֽׁמּוּ׃

8 Do not remember against us
The sins of earlier generations;
Soon
Your mercies may envelop us
Because we became very poor.

ח אַֽל־תִּזְכָּר־לָנוּ֮
עֲוֺנֹ֪ת רִאשֹׁ֫נִ֥ים
מַ֭הֵר
יְקַדְּמ֣וּנוּ רַחֲמֶ֑יךָ
כִּ֖י דַלּ֣וֹנוּ מְאֹֽד׃

9 Help us,
God of our salvation,
For the sake of Your name's honor,
Save us, and cover up our transgressions
Because of Your name.

ט עָזְרֵ֤נוּ ׀
אֱלֹהֵ֬י יִשְׁעֵ֗נוּ
עַל־דְּבַ֥ר כְּבֽוֹד־שְׁמֶ֑ךָ
וְהַצִּילֵ֥נוּ וְכַפֵּ֥ר עַל־חַ֝טֹּאתֵ֗ינוּ
לְמַ֣עַן שְׁמֶֽךָ׃

10 Why
    Should the Gentiles say:
    "Where is their God?"
Let be known to the haughty [Gentiles] before
    our eyes,
The revenge
    Of Your servants' spilled blood.

י לָ֤מָּה ׀
יֹאמְר֣וּ הַגּוֹיִם֮
אַיֵּ֪ה אֱלֹהֵ֫יהֶ֥ם
יִוָּדַ֣ע בַּגֹּיִים [בַּגּוֹיִ֣ם] לְעֵינֵ֑ינוּ
נִ֝קְמַ֗ת
דַּם־עֲבָדֶ֥יךָ הַשָּׁפֽוּךְ׃

11 May the groan of the prisoner
    Come before You.
Commensurate to the greatness of Your arm
Free
    Those about to die.

יא תָּב֤וֹא לְפָנֶ֗יךָ
אֶנְקַ֫ת אָ֥סִ֑יר
כְּגֹ֥דֶל זְרוֹעֲךָ֑
ה֝וֹתֵ֗ר
בְּנֵ֣י תְמוּתָֽה׃

12 And return to our neighbors sevenfold
    Into their bosom
The insult by which they insulted You,
    Almighty.

יב וְהָשֵׁ֬ב לִשְׁכֵנֵ֣ינוּ שִׁ֭בְעָתַיִם
אֶל־חֵיקָ֑ם
חֶרְפָּתָ֬ם אֲשֶׁ֖ר חֵרְפ֣וּךָ אֲדֹנָֽי׃

13 But we are Your people,
    The sheep of Your herd,
    We are forever thanking You;
In all generations
We shall tell
    Your praise.

יג וַאֲנַ֤חְנוּ עַמְּךָ֨ ׀
וְצֹ֬אן מַרְעִיתֶ֗ךָ
נ֤וֹדֶה לְּךָ֗ לְע֫וֹלָ֥ם
לְדֹ֥ר וָדֹ֑ר
נְ֝סַפֵּ֗ר
תְּהִלָּתֶֽךָ׃

3. This verse is quoted in *1Maccabees* 7:17.

4. About קלס see Ps. 44:14.

11. בני designates people having a designated property, not simply "children"; compare בן מות "condemned to death" (*1S.* 20:31).

Psalm 80

1 For the director, on Shoshannim
A testimonial, a Psalm of Asaph.

א לַמְנַצֵּחַ אֶל־שֹׁשַׁנִּים
עֵדוּת לְאָסָף מִזְמוֹר׃

2 Shepherd of Israel,
Please listen;
He who leads Joseph like sheep,
He who thrones above the Cherubim, please do appear.

ב רֹעֵה יִשְׂרָאֵל |
הַאֲזִינָה
נֹהֵג כַּצֹּאן יוֹסֵף
יֹשֵׁב הַכְּרוּבִים הוֹפִיעָה׃

3 In front of Ephraim,
Benjamin, and Manasse,
Awake Your strength
And come to save us.

ג לִפְנֵי אֶפְרַיִם |
וּבִנְיָמִן וּמְנַשֶּׁה
עוֹרְרָה אֶת־גְּבוּרָתֶךָ
וּלְכָה לִישֻׁעָתָה לָּנוּ׃

4 God, restore us,
Let Your face shine upon us
Then we will be saved.

ד אֱלֹהִים הֲשִׁיבֵנוּ
וְהָאֵר פָּנֶיךָ
וְנִוָּשֵׁעָה׃

5 Eternal, God of hosts,
Until when do You put smoke
Against the prayers of Your people?

ה יְהוָה אֱלֹהִים צְבָאוֹת
עַד־מָתַי עָשַׁנְתָּ
בִּתְפִלַּת עַמֶּךָ׃

6 You fed them
Bread of tears,
And made them drink
Tears from the measuring-bowl.

ו הֶאֱכַלְתָּם
לֶחֶם דִּמְעָה
וַתַּשְׁקֵמוֹ
בִּדְמָעוֹת שָׁלִישׁ׃

7 You made them a quarrel
For our neighbors;
Our enemies
Scoff at us.

ז תְּשִׂימֵנוּ מָדוֹן
לִשְׁכֵנֵינוּ
וְאֹיְבֵינוּ
יִלְעֲגוּ־לָמוֹ׃

8 God of Hosts, restore us,
Light up Your face
Then we shall be saved.

ח אֱלֹהִים צְבָאוֹת הֲשִׁיבֵנוּ
וְהָאֵר פָּנֶיךָ
וְנִוָּשֵׁעָה׃

9 A vine
You transported out of Egypt,
You drove out peoples
And planted it.

ט גֶּפֶן
מִמִּצְרַיִם תַּסִּיעַ
תְּגָרֵשׁ גּוֹיִם
וַתִּטָּעֶהָ׃

10 You cleared before it;
It spread it roots
And filled the land.

י פִּנִּיתָ לְפָנֶיהָ
וַתַּשְׁרֵשׁ שָׁרָשֶׁיהָ
וַתְּמַלֵּא־אָרֶץ׃

11 The mountains were covered by its shadow
And its branches
Were strong cedars.

יא כָּסּוּ הָרִים צִלָּהּ
וַעֲנָפֶיהָ
אַרְזֵי־אֵל׃

12 You send out its sprigs to the Sea
And to the River
Its suction roots.

יב תְּשַׁלַּח קְצִירֶהָ עַד־יָם
וְאֶל־נָהָר
יוֹנְקוֹתֶיהָ׃

13 Why
Did You breach its fences
That it can be plucked
By all who come along on the road?

יג לָמָּה
פָּרַצְתָּ גְדֵרֶיהָ
וְאָרוּהָ
כָּל־עֹבְרֵי דָרֶךְ׃

14 It is gnawed on by wild boar
And the crawling things from the field graze on it.

יד יְכַרְסְמֶנָּה חֲזִיר מִיָּעַר
וְזִיז שָׂדַי יִרְעֶנָּה׃

15 God of Host
Please return,
Look from Heaven and see,
And look up
This vine,

טו אֱלֹהִים צְבָאוֹת
שׁוּב־נָא
הַבֵּט מִשָּׁמַיִם וּרְאֵה
וּפְקֹד
גֶּפֶן זֹאת׃

16 The sapling
That Your right hand planted
And the son
You adopted,

טז וְכַנָּה
אֲשֶׁר־נָטְעָה יְמִינֶךָ
וְעַל־בֵּן
אִמַּצְתָּה לָּךְ׃

17 The one that is burned in fire, clipped.
They will be ruined by Your menacing face.

יז שְׂרֻפָה בָאֵשׁ כְּסוּחָה
מִגַּעֲרַת פָּנֶיךָ יֹאבֵדוּ׃

18 May Your hand be
On the man of Your right side,
On the human
You chose to give strength.

יח תְּהִי־יָדְךָ
עַל־אִישׁ יְמִינֶךָ
עַל־בֶּן־אָדָם
אִמַּצְתָּ לָּךְ׃

19 We shall not retreat from You;
Let us live,
Then we shall invoke Your name.

יט וְלֹא־נָסוֹג מִמֶּךָּ
תְּחַיֵּנוּ
בְשִׁמְךָ נִקְרָא׃

20 Eternal, God of Hosts, restore us,
Light up Your face
Then we shall be saved.

כ יְהוָה אֱלֹהִים צְבָאוֹת הֲשִׁיבֵנוּ
הָאֵר פָּנֶיךָ
וְנִוָּשֵׁעָה׃

12 The River is the Euphrates.

14 For זיז cf. *Ps.* 50.

Psalm 81

1 For the director,
On the Gittit, by Asaph.

א לַמְנַצֵּחַ ׀
עַל־הַגִּתִּית לְאָסָף׃

2 Jubilate
To our mighty God,
Modulate the trumpet
To the God of Jacob.

ב הַרְנִינוּ
לֵאלֹהִים עוּזֵּנוּ
הָרִיעוּ
לֵאלֹהֵי יַעֲקֹב׃

3 Prepare melody
And take the drum,
Pleasant guitar with harp.

ג שְׂאוּ־זִמְרָה
וּתְנוּ־תֹף
כִּנּוֹר נָעִים עִם־נָבֶל׃

4 Blow the horn for the New Moon,
When it is covered
For the day of our festival.

ד תִּקְעוּ בַחֹדֶשׁ שׁוֹפָר
בַּכֵּסֶה
לְיוֹם חַגֵּנוּ׃

5 Certainly, it is a rule for Israel,
A law
Of the God of Jacob.

ה כִּי חֹק לְיִשְׂרָאֵל הוּא
מִשְׁפָּט
לֵאלֹהֵי יַעֲקֹב

6 A testimonial
He put it in Jehoseph
When He went out
Over the land of Egypt.
An unknown language did I hear.

ו עֵדוּת ׀
בִּיהוֹסֵף שָׂמוֹ
בְּצֵאתוֹ
עַל־אֶרֶץ מִצְרָיִם
שְׂפַת לֹא־יָדַעְתִּי אֶשְׁמָע׃

7 "I removed the load from his shoulder,
His hands
Were taken from the hamper.

ז הֲסִירוֹתִי מִסֵּבֶל שִׁכְמוֹ
כַּפָּיו
מִדּוּד תַּעֲבֹרְנָה׃

8 You called in strait and I rescued you,
I answered you
From my hidden place with thunder,
I tried you at the waters of quarrel," Selah.

ח בַּצָּרָה קָרָאתָ וָאֲחַלְּצֶךָּ
אֶעֶנְךָ
בְּסֵתֶר רַעַם
אֶבְחָנְךָ עַל־מֵי מְרִיבָה סֶלָה׃

9 Listen, my people,
I shall call you as witness;
Israel,
If you would listen to me.

ט שְׁמַע עַמִּי
וְאָעִידָה בָּךְ
יִשְׂרָאֵל
אִם־תִּשְׁמַע־לִי׃

10 No strange power
Shall be among you;
Do not prostrate yourself
Before a foreign power.

י לֹא־יִהְיֶה בְךָ
אֵל זָר
וְלֹא תִשְׁתַּחֲוֶה
לְאֵל נֵכָר׃

11 I am
The Eternal, your God,
Who led you up
From the land of Egypt,
Open wide your mouth
And I shall fill it!

יא אָנֹכִי ׀
יְיָ אֱלֹהֶיךָ
הַמַּעַלְךָ
מֵאֶרֶץ מִצְרָיִם
הַרְחֶב־פִּיךָ
וַאֲמַלְאֵהוּ׃

12 But My people did not listen to My voice	יב וְלֹא־שָׁמַע עַמִּי לְקוֹלִי
And Israel	וְיִשְׂרָאֵל
Did not consent to Me.	לֹא־אָבָה לִי׃
13 Then I sent them away	יג וָאֲשַׁלְּחֵהוּ
After their heart's arbitrariness,	בִּשְׁרִירוּת לִבָּם
May they go	יֵלְכוּ
After their councils.	בְּמוֹעֲצוֹתֵיהֶם׃
14 If only My people	יד לוּ עַמִּי
Would listen to Me,	שֹׁמֵעַ לִי
Israel	יִשְׂרָאֵל
Would go in My ways,	בִּדְרָכַי יְהַלֵּכוּ׃
15 Shortly	טו כִּמְעַט
I would subdue their enemies,	אוֹיְבֵיהֶם אַכְנִיעַ
And against their oppressors	וְעַל־צָרֵיהֶם
I would turn My hand.	אָשִׁיב יָדִי׃
16 The haters of the Eternal	טז מְשַׂנְאֵי יהוה
Will be devoted to Him;	יְכַחֲשׁוּ־לוֹ
Their time will be forever.	וִיהִי עִתָּם לְעוֹלָם׃
17 He will feed him	יז וַיַּאֲכִילֵהוּ
From the fat of wheat	מֵחֵלֶב חִטָּה
And from the heart	וּמִצּוּר
Of honey will satiate you!	דְּבַשׁ אַשְׂבִּיעֶךָ׃

7

7 דוד usually in Semitic languages is "pot", but in Egyptian *didi* is a pan; here obviously taken as the builder's hamper.

17 Accadic *ṣurru* "heart, innermost, most important part"; accepted here following Dahood.

Psalm 82

1 A Psalm of Asaph.
God
Appears in Power's community.
God will judge from the inside.

א מִזְמ֗וֹר לְאָ֫סָ֥ף
אֱלֹהִ֗ים
נִצָּ֥ב בַּעֲדַת־אֵ֑ל
בְּקֶ֖רֶב אֱלֹהִ֣ים יִשְׁפֹּֽט׃

2 Until when will you judge wrongly
And will favor
The case of evildoers, Selah?

ב עַד־מָתַ֥י תִּשְׁפְּטוּ־עָ֑וֶל
וּפְנֵ֥י רְ֝שָׁעִ֗ים
תִּשְׂאוּ־סֶֽלָה׃

3 Do judge for the oppressed and the orphan,
Find innocent the downtrodden and destitute.

ג שִׁפְטוּ־דַ֥ל וְיָת֑וֹם
עָנִ֖י וָרָ֣שׁ הַצְדִּֽיקוּ׃

4 Let the oppressed and poor escape,
Save from the hand of criminals.

ד פַּלְּטוּ־דַ֥ל וְאֶבְי֑וֹן
מִיַּ֖ד רְשָׁעִ֣ים הַצִּֽילוּ׃

5 They know nothing,
Nor do they understand,
They amble in darkness.
They cause the collapse
Of all bases of earth.

ה לֹ֤א יָדְע֨וּ ׀
וְלֹ֥א יָבִ֗ינוּ
בַּחֲשֵׁכָ֥ה יִתְהַלָּ֑כוּ
יִ֝מּ֗וֹטוּ
כָּל־מ֥וֹסְדֵי אָֽרֶץ

6 I said,
You are godlike,
All of you are the sons of the Most High,

ו אֲֽנִי־אָ֭מַרְתִּי
אֱלֹהִ֣ים אַתֶּ֑ם
וּבְנֵ֖י עֶלְי֣וֹן כֻּלְּכֶֽם׃

7 However
You will die like a lowly man,
Or fall like one of the rulers.

ז אָ֭כֵן
כְּאָדָ֣ם תְּמוּת֑וּן
וּכְאַחַ֖ד הַשָּׂרִ֣ים תִּפֹּֽלוּ׃

8 Please rise, God,
Judge the earth,
For You will purify
All peoples.

ח קוּמָ֣ה אֱ֭לֹהִים
שָׁפְטָ֣ה הָאָ֑רֶץ
כִּֽי־אַתָּ֥ה֝ תִנְחַ֗ל
בְּכָל־הַגּוֹיִֽם׃

8 תנחל: Arabic نخل "to purify, to select the best".

Psalm 83

1 A song, a Psalm of Asaph.

א שִׁ֖יר מִזְמ֣וֹר לְאָסָֽף׃

2 God, do not be silent,
Powerful, do not be mute and quiet!

ב אֱלֹהִ֥ים אַל־דֳּמִי־לָ֑ךְ
אַל־תֶּחֱרַ֖שׁ וְאַל־תִּשְׁקֹ֣ט אֵֽל׃

3 Lo, behold Your enemies
Are seditious,
And those who hate You
Are aggressive.

ג כִּֽי־הִנֵּ֣ה א֭וֹיְבֶיךָ
יֶהֱמָי֑וּן
וּ֝מְשַׂנְאֶ֗יךָ
נָ֣שְׂאוּ רֹֽאשׁ׃

4 Against Your people
They conspire in malice,
They take counsel
Against Your hidden ones.

ד עַל־֭עַמְּךָ
יַעֲרִ֣ימוּ ס֑וֹד
וְ֝יִתְיָעֲצ֗וּ
עַל־צְפוּנֶֽיךָ׃

5 They say: Come,
Let us eliminate them as a people,
That the name of Israel should no more be mentioned!

ה אָֽמְר֗וּ לְ֭כוּ
וְנַכְחִידֵ֣ם מִגּ֑וֹי
וְלֹֽא־יִזָּכֵ֖ר שֵֽׁם־יִשְׂרָאֵ֣ל עֽוֹד׃

6 Truly, they consulted in unanimity.
Against You
They swear to a covenant.

ו כִּ֤י נוֹעֲצ֣וּ לֵ֣ב יַחְדָּ֑ו
עָ֝לֶ֗יךָ
בְּרִ֣ית יִכְרֹֽתוּ׃

7 The tents of Edom
And Ismaelites,
Moab and Hagarites.

ז אָהֳלֵ֣י אֱ֭דוֹם
וְיִשְׁמְעֵאלִ֗ים
מוֹאָ֥ב וְהַגְרִֽים׃

8 Jibal, Ammon,
And Amaleq,
Philistaea
With the inhabitants of Tyre.

ח גְּבָ֣ל וְ֭עַמּוֹן
וַעֲמָלֵ֑ק
פְּ֝לֶ֗שֶׁת
עִם־יֹ֥שְׁבֵי צֽוֹר׃

9 Assyria also
Accompanies them,
They lend their arms to the sons of Lot, Selah.

ט גַּם־אַ֭שּׁוּר
נִלְוָ֣ה עִמָּ֑ם
הָ֥יוּ זְר֖וֹעַ לִבְנֵי־ל֣וֹט סֶֽלָה׃

10 Treat them like Midian,
Like Sisera and Yavin
On Kishon brook.

י עֲשֵׂה־לָהֶ֥ם כְּמִדְיָ֑ן
כְּֽסִֽיסְרָ֥א כְ֝יָבִ֗ין
בְּנַ֣חַל קִישֽׁוֹן׃

11 They were destroyed at En Dor
They were dung
For the earth.

יא נִשְׁמְד֥וּ בְֽעֵין־דֹּ֑אר
הָ֥יוּ דֹּ֝֗מֶן
לָֽאֲדָמָֽה׃

12 Make them, their leaders,
Like Orev and Zeev
Like Zevah and Ṣalmunah
All their princes,

יב שִׁיתֵ֣מוֹ נְ֭דִיבֵמוֹ
כְּעֹרֵ֣ב וְכִזְאֵ֑ב
וּֽכְזֶ֥בַח וּ֝כְצַלְמֻנָּ֗ע
כָּל־נְסִיכֵֽמוֹ׃

13 Those who said	יג אֲשֶׁר אָמְרוּ
We shall grab for us	נִירֲשָׁה לָּנוּ
The champaigns of God.	אֵת נְאוֹת אֱלֹהִים׃
14 My God,	יד אֱלֹהַי
Treat them like tumbleweed,	שִׁיתֵמוֹ כַגַּלְגַּל
Like straw	כְּקַשׁ
Before the wind.	לִפְנֵי־רוּחַ׃
15 Like fire that consumes a forest,	טו כְּאֵשׁ תִּבְעַר־יָעַר
And a flame	וּכְלֶהָבָה
That burns mountains.	תְּלַהֵט הָרִים׃
16 So	טז כֵּן
Pursue them with Your storm	תִּרְדְּפֵם בְּסַעֲרֶךָ
And confound them with Your tornado.	וּבְסוּפָתְךָ תְבַהֲלֵם׃
17 Fill their faces with shame	יז מַלֵּא פְנֵיהֶם קָלוֹן
So they may seek Your name, Eternal.	וִיבַקְשׁוּ שִׁמְךָ יהוה׃
18 They should be ashamed and permanently confounded,	יח יֵבֹשׁוּ וְיִבָּהֲלוּ עֲדֵי־עַד
Be infamous and lost,	וְיַחְפְּרוּ וְיֹאבֵדוּ׃
19 And should know	יט וְיֵדְעוּ
That You, Whose name is Eternal, alone	כִּי־אַתָּה שִׁמְךָ יהוה לְבַדֶּךָ
Are supreme	עֶלְיוֹן
Over all the earth!	עַל־כָּל־הָאָרֶץ

8 Jibal is Biblos.

9 In *2S.* the helpers of Amon are Aramaic tribes from the Middle Euphrates.

10 While Sisera and Yavin belong to the story of Deborah, the others refer to the actions of Gideon against Midyan..

13 The root of נירשה is taken as Arabic נרש "to take avidly."

Psalm 84

1 For the director, on the *gittit,*
A psalm of the Qoraḥides.

א לַמְנַצֵּחַ עַל־הַגִּתִּית
לִבְנֵי־קֹרַח מִזְמוֹר׃

2 How lovely is Your dwelling place,
O Eternal of hosts.

ב מַה־יְּדִידוֹת מִשְׁכְּנוֹתֶיךָ
יְהוָה צְבָאוֹת׃

3 My soul
Is longing, even despairing,
For the courtyards of the Eternal.
My heart and my flesh
Pray in singing
To the the Living Power.

ג נִכְסְפָה וְגַם־כָּלְתָה |
נַפְשִׁי
לְחַצְרוֹת יְיָ
לִבִּי וּבְשָׂרִי
יְרַנְּנוּ
אֶל־אֵל חָי׃

4 Even the song-bird
Found a house
And the swallow
A nest for itself
To put there its nestlings.
Your altars,
Eternal of hosts,
My king
And my God.

ד גַּם־צִפּוֹר |
מָצְאָה בַיִת
וּדְרוֹר |
קֵן לָהּ
אֲשֶׁר־שָׁתָה אֶפְרֹחֶיהָ
אֶת־מִזְבְּחוֹתֶיךָ
יְיָ צְבָאוֹת
מַלְכִּי
וֵאלֹהָי׃

5 The dwellers in Your house
Are Blessed;
Eternally
They will praise You, Selah.

ה אַשְׁרֵי
יוֹשְׁבֵי בֵיתֶךָ
עוֹד
יְהַלְלוּךָ סֶּלָה׃

6 Blessed is the lowly man
Whose strength is in You,
Pillars
In their hearts.

ו אַשְׁרֵי אָדָם
עוֹז לוֹ־בָךְ
מְסִלּוֹת
בִּלְבָבָם׃

7 Those who pass
Through the valley of the baka tree
Settle down by the well,
With blessings
Would the winter rain envelop it.

ז עֹבְרֵי |
בְּעֵמֶק הַבָּכָא
מַעְיָן יְשִׁיתוּהוּ
גַּם־בְּרָכוֹת
יַעְטֶה מוֹרֶה׃

8 They walk
From stronghold to stronghold,
To appear before Mighty God in Zion.

ח יֵלְכוּ
מֵחַיִל אֶל־חָיִל
יֵרָאֶה אֶל־אֱלֹהִים בְּצִיּוֹן

9 Eternal, God of hosts,
Please listen to my prayer,
Please hear, God of Jacob, Selah.

ט יְהוָה אֱלֹהִים צְבָאוֹת
שִׁמְעָה תְפִלָּתִי
הַאֲזִינָה אֱלֹהֵי יַעֲקֹב סֶלָה׃

10 Our shield,
    See, o God,
And look
    At Your anointed.

י מָגִנֵּנוּ
רְאֵה אֱלֹהִים
וְהַבֵּט
פְּנֵי מְשִׁיחֶךָ׃

11 Because one day in Your Courts is better than thousand
,I chose to squat
    Before my God's House
Rather than dwell
    In the tents of evil.

יא כִּי טוֹב־יוֹם בַּחֲצֵרֶיךָ מֵאָלֶף
בָּחַרְתִּי הִסְתּוֹפֵף
בְּבֵית אֱלֹהַי
מִדּוּר
בְּאָהֳלֵי־רֶשַׁע׃

12 Because sun and shield
    Is the Eternal, God.
The Eternal will give
    Goodwill and honor.
He will not withhold the good
    From those who walk with integrity.

יב כִּי שֶׁמֶשׁ | וּמָגֵן
יְיָ אֱלֹהִים
חֵן וְכָבוֹד
יִתֵּן יְיָ
לֹא־יִמְנַע טוֹב
לַהֹלְכִים בְּתָמִים׃

13 Eternal of hosts,
Blessed is the lowly man
    Who is trusting You.

יג יְהוָה צְבָאוֹת
אַשְׁרֵי אָדָם
בֹּטֵחַ בָּךְ׃

4. On basis of the Arabic (צפר "to chirp"), it seems that צפור is a song bird, but עוף is any bird that flies.

6. Taking מסלה in the sense of Arabic מסלה "obelisc, coarse pin", rather than the inappropriate "roadway" which is the traditional (and Accadic) meaning of the word.

7. The baka trees play a role in *2Sam.* 5:23; the Baka valley is an area near Jerusalem.

11. הסתפף seems to mean "place myself close to the doorstep".

Psalm 85

1 For the director,
A psalm of the Qorahides.

א לַמְנַצֵּ֬חַ ׀
לִבְנֵי־קֹ֬רַח מִזְמֽוֹר׃

2 Eternal, please like Your land
Turn for the better
The changing fortunes of Jacob.

ב רָצִ֣יתָ יהוָ֣ה אַרְצֶ֑ךָ
שַׁ֝֗בְתָּ
שְׁבוּת [שְׁבִ֥ית] יַעֲקֹֽב׃

3 Forgive
The offence of Your people,
Cover up all their sins, Selah.

ג נָ֭שָׂאתָ
עֲוֺ֣ן עַמֶּ֑ךָ
כִּסִּ֖יתָ כָל־חַטָּאתָ֣ם סֶֽלָה׃

4 Collect all Your rage,
Turn back
From Your fiery anger.

ד אָסַ֥פְתָּ כָל־עֶבְרָתֶ֑ךָ
הֱ֝שִׁיב֗וֹתָ
מֵחֲר֥וֹן אַפֶּֽךָ׃

5 Return to us
God who helps us,
Annul Your ire against us.

ה שׁ֭וּבֵנוּ
אֱלֹהֵ֣י יִשְׁעֵ֑נוּ
וְהָפֵ֖ר כַּעַסְךָ֣ עִמָּֽנוּ׃

6 Will You be eternally enraged against us?
Will You draw out Your anger
For all generations?

ו הַלְעוֹלָ֥ם תֶּאֱנַף־בָּ֑נוּ
תִּמְשֹׁ֥ךְ אַ֝פְּךָ֗
לְדֹ֣ר וָדֹֽר׃

7 Only You
Can again revive us,
So Your people
Can rejoice in You.

ז הֲלֹא־אַ֭תָּה
תָּשׁ֣וּב תְּחַיֵּ֑נוּ
וְ֝עַמְּךָ֗
יִשְׂמְחוּ־בָֽךְ׃

8 Eternal, show us Your kindness,
Your help
Do give us.

ח הַרְאֵ֣נוּ יהוָ֣ה חַסְדֶּ֑ךָ
וְ֝יֶשְׁעֲךָ֗
תִּתֶּן־לָֽנוּ׃

9 May I hear what the Mighty Eternal
Will say,
Does He proclaim peace
For His people and His faithful,
For those that always are confident?

ט אֶשְׁמְעָ֗ה מַה־יְדַבֵּר֮
הָאֵ֪ל ׀ יְה֫וָ֥ה
כִּ֤י יְדַבֵּ֬ר שָׁל֗וֹם
אֶל־עַמּ֥וֹ וְאֶל־חֲסִידָ֑יו
וְאַל־יָשׁ֥וּבוּ לְכִסְלָֽה׃

10 But
His help is close for those who fear Him;
To let honor dwell in our land.

י אַ֤ךְ ׀
קָר֣וֹב לִירֵאָ֣יו יִשְׁע֑וֹ
לִשְׁכֹּ֖ן כָּב֣וֹד בְּאַרְצֵֽנוּ׃

11 Kindness and truth met,
Justice and peace kissed.

יא חֶֽסֶד־וֶאֱמֶ֥ת נִפְגָּ֑שׁוּ
צֶ֖דֶק וְשָׁל֣וֹם נָשָֽׁקוּ׃

12 Truth
Sprouts from the earth
And justice
Observes from Heaven.

יב אֱ֭מֶת
מֵאֶ֣רֶץ תִּצְמָ֑ח
וְ֝צֶ֗דֶק
מִשָּׁמַ֥יִם נִשְׁקָֽף׃

13 Certainly, the Eternal	יג גַּם־יְהוָה
Will provide the good;	יִתֵּן הַטּוֹב
Then our land	וְאַרְצֵנוּ
Will yield its produce.	תִּתֵּן יְבוּלָהּ׃
14 Just measure	יד צֶדֶק
Will walk before Him	לְפָנָיו יְהַלֵּךְ
Beauty is on the way of His steps.	וְיָשֵׂם לְדֶרֶךְ פְּעָמָיו׃

2. The translation follows the Ketib שבות "turning the fortune for the better"; the Qere might mean "captivity".

9. The last clause means literally: "Those who have no need to return to confidence" (since they never lost it.)

13. "The good" in this context has been justifiably identified by Dahood as the rain (to be added: when it falls in the right measure).

14. Following Dahood, identifying Hebrew ישם with Arabic ושם, Ugaritic *ysmt* , "fair, beautiful". Then צדק means neither "justice" nor "justification" but "just measure", most needed for rain.

Psalm 86

1 A prayer by David.
Eternal, bend Your ear, answer me.
Truly I am deprived and wretched.

א תְּפִלָּה לְדָוִד
הַטֵּה יהוה אָזְנְךָ עֲנֵנִי
כִּי־עָנִי וְאֶבְיוֹן אָנִי׃

2 Watch over my soul,
For I am pious,
You, my God,
Help your servant,
Who trusts in You.

ב שָׁמְרָה נַפְשִׁי
כִּי־חָסִיד אָנִי
הוֹשַׁע עַבְדְּךָ
אַתָּה אֱלֹהַי
הַבּוֹטֵחַ אֵלֶיךָ׃

3 Be graceful to me,
For to You I am calling
All day long.

ג חָנֵּנִי אֲדֹנָי
כִּי־אֵלֶיךָ אֶקְרָא
כָּל־הַיּוֹם׃

4 Give joy
To Your servant's soul,
Truly to You, Almighty,
I am offering my soul.

ד שַׂמֵּחַ
נֶפֶשׁ עַבְדֶּךָ
כִּי אֵלֶיךָ אֲדֹנָי
נַפְשִׁי אֶשָּׂא׃

5 Certainly You, Almighty,
Are good and forgiving,
And full of grace
For all who call on You.

ה כִּי־אַתָּה אֲדֹנָי
טוֹב וְסַלָּח
וְרַב־חֶסֶד
לְכָל־קֹרְאֶיךָ׃

6 Please listen, Eternal,
To my payer,
Please take notice
Of the sound of my supplications.

ו הַאֲזִינָה יהוה
תְּפִלָּתִי
וְהַקְשִׁיבָה
בְּקוֹל תַּחֲנוּנוֹתָי׃

7 On my day of distress
I an calling on You;
Certainly, You will answer me.

ז בְּיוֹם צָרָתִי
אֶקְרָאֶךָּ
כִּי תַעֲנֵנִי׃

8 Nothing among the powers is like You,
Almighty,
And nothing is like Your deeds.

ח אֵין־כָּמוֹךָ בָאֱלֹהִים ׀
אֲדֹנָי
וְאֵין כְּמַעֲשֶׂיךָ׃

9 All Nations
Which You made
Should come
And prostrate themselves before You,
Almighty
And give honor to Your Name.

ט כָּל־גּוֹיִם ׀
אֲשֶׁר עָשִׂיתָ
יָבוֹאוּ ׀
וְיִשְׁתַּחֲווּ לְפָנֶיךָ אֲדֹנָי
וִיכַבְּדוּ לִשְׁמֶךָ׃

10 For You are great,
And working wonders.
You alone are Supreme Power.

י כִּי־גָדוֹל אַתָּה
וְעֹשֵׂה נִפְלָאוֹת
אַתָּה אֱלֹהִים לְבַדֶּךָ׃

11 Eternal, teach me	יא הוֹרֵנִי יהוה |
Your way,	דַּרְכֶּךָ
I shall walk in Your truth.	אֲהַלֵּךְ בַּאֲמִתֶּךָ
Single out my heart	יַחֵד לְבָבִי
To fear Your Name.	לְיִרְאָה שְׁמֶךָ׃
12 I shall thank You	יב אוֹדְךָ |
Almighty, my God,	אֲדֹנָי אֱלֹהַי
With all my heart,	בְּכָל־לְבָבִי
And I shall always honor Your Name.	וַאֲכַבְּדָה שִׁמְךָ לְעוֹלָם׃
13 Truly Your grace	יג כִּי־חַסְדְּךָ
Is great over me;	גָּדוֹל עָלָי
You saved my soul	וְהִצַּלְתָּ נַפְשִׁי
From the Netherworld deep down.	מִשְּׁאוֹל תַּחְתִּיָּה׃
14 God,	יד אֱלֹהִים |
Evildoers stood up against me;	זֵדִים קָמוּ עָלַי
A group of cruel ones	וַעֲדַת עָרִיצִים
Desired my life,	בִּקְשׁוּ נַפְשִׁי
And did not put You before them.	וְלֹא שָׂמוּךָ לְנֶגְדָּם׃
15 But You, Almighty,	טו וְאַתָּה אֲדֹנָי
You are a Power merciful and compassionate,	אֵל־רַחוּם וְחַנּוּן
Long forgiving,	אֶרֶךְ אַפַּיִם
Of Infinite grace and truth.	וְרַב־חֶסֶד וֶאֱמֶת׃
16 Turn to me and show favor to me,	טז פְּנֵה אֵלַי וְחָנֵּנִי
Put Your might over Your servant	תְּנָה־עֻזְּךָ לְעַבְדֶּךָ
And save	וְהוֹשִׁיעָה
Your handmaiden's son.	לְבֶן־אֲמָתֶךָ
17 Give me a sign for betterment,	יז עֲשֵׂה־עִמִּי אוֹת לְטוֹבָה
So my haters shall see and be ashamed,	וְיִרְאוּ שֹׂנְאַי וְיֵבֹשׁוּ
For You, Eternal,	כִּי־אַתָּה יהוה
Helped me and consoled me.	עֲזַרְתַּנִי וְנִחַמְתָּנִי׃

15 As prayer quoted from *Num.* 14:18 which is inspired by the text *Ex.* 34:6.

Psalm 87

1 By the Qoraḥides.
A Psalm, a song.
He founded it
On the holy mountain.

א לִבְנֵי־קֹרַח
מִזְמוֹר שִׁיר
יְסוּדָתוֹ
בְּהַרְרֵי־קֹדֶשׁ׃

2 The Eternal loves
The gates of Zion
More than all
Dwellings of Jacob.

ב אֹהֵב יהוה
שַׁעֲרֵי צִיּוֹן
מִכֹּל
מִשְׁכְּנוֹת יַעֲקֹב׃

3 Important statements
Are made about you,
City of God, Selah!

ג נִכְבָּדוֹת
מְדֻבָּר בָּךְ
עִיר הָאֱלֹהִים סֶלָה׃

4 I am counting
Rahab and Babylon among my acquaintances,
Also Philistaea, Tyre, and Kush,
This one
Would be born there.

ד אַזְכִּיר | רַהַב וּבָבֶל לְיֹדְעָי
הִנֵּה פְלֶשֶׁת וְצוֹר עִם־כּוּשׁ
זֶה
יֻלַּד־שָׁם׃

5 But of Zion can be said
Everybody
Was born in it;
That is what the Almighty established it for.

ה וּלְצִיּוֹן | יֵאָמַר
אִישׁ וְאִישׁ
יֻלַּד־בָּהּ
וְהוּא יְכוֹנְנֶהָ עֶלְיוֹן׃

6 The Eternal will count
When He lists nations,
This one would be born there, Selah.

ו יהוה יִסְפֹּר
בִּכְתוֹב עַמִּים
זֶה יֻלַּד־שָׁם סֶלָה׃

7 And singers, as well as flute players,
All my thoughts are about you!

ז וְשָׁרִים כְּחֹלְלִים
כָּל־מַעְיָנַי בָּךְ׃

4 Rahab ("sea monster") is a symbolic name for Egypt; cf. *Is.* 30:7.
Kush in Genesis refers to *Kaššu* in central Iraq. In *Ez.* and *Esther* it refers to the Sudan. In Targum Jonathan to Prophets usually it is taken as referring to the Hindu-Kush. Here it seems to refer to a Phoenician territory.

Psalm 88

1 A song, a Psalm, by the Qoraḥides;
For the director, on fifes in antiphony,
A didactic poem
By Heyman the Zeraḥide.

א שִׁ֥יר מִזְמ֗וֹר לִבְנֵ֫י קֹ֥רַח
לַמְנַצֵּ֣חַ עַֽל־מָחֲלַ֣ת לְעַנּ֑וֹת
מַ֝שְׂכִּ֗יל
לְהֵימָ֥ן הָאֶזְרָחִֽי׃

2 Eternal,
God of my salvation,
Daily I am crying before You during the night.

ב יהוה
אֱלֹהֵ֥י יְשׁוּעָתִ֑י
יוֹם־צָעַ֖קְתִּי בַלַּ֣יְלָה נֶגְדֶּֽךָ׃

3 Before You shall come
My prayer,
Bend Your ear
To my supplication.

ג תָּב֣וֹא לְ֭פָנֶיךָ
תְּפִלָּתִ֑י
הַטֵּֽה־אָ֝זְנְךָ֗
לְרִנָּתִֽי׃

4 Truly, my soul is satiated with suffering,
My life
Touched the Netherworld.

ד כִּֽי־שָׂבְעָ֣ה בְרָע֣וֹת נַפְשִׁ֑י
וְ֝חַיַּ֗י
לִשְׁא֥וֹל הִגִּֽיעוּ׃

5 I am counted
With those who descend to the Pit,
I was
Like a powerless person.

ה נֶ֭חְשַׁבְתִּי
עִם־י֣וֹרְדֵי ב֑וֹר
הָ֝יִ֗יתִי
כְּגֶ֣בֶר אֵֽין־אֱיָֽל׃

6 Among the Dead is my sickbed,
Like corpses,
Lying in the grave,
Whom You do not consider any more,
And they
Were cut off by Your hand.

ו בַּמֵּתִ֗ים חָ֫פְשִׁ֥י
כְּמ֤וֹ חֲלָלִ֨ים ׀
שֹׁ֥כְבֵי קֶ֗בֶר
אֲשֶׁ֤ר לֹ֣א זְכַרְתָּ֣ם ע֑וֹד
וְ֝הֵ֗מָּה
מִיָּדְךָ֥ נִגְזָֽרוּ׃

7 You put me
In the lowest Pit,
In a dark place,
In ocean depths.

ז שַׁ֭תַּנִי
בְּב֣וֹר תַּחְתִּיּ֑וֹת
בְּ֝מַחֲשַׁכִּ֗ים
בִּמְצֹלֽוֹת׃

8 Upon me
Your rage presses down,
With all Your breaking waves
Did You cause pain, Selah.

ח עָ֭לַי
סָמְכָ֣ה חֲמָתֶ֑ךָ
וְכָל־מִ֝שְׁבָּרֶ֗יךָ
עִנִּ֥יתָ סֶּֽלָה׃

9 You removed my acquaintances from me,
You made me an abomination for them,
Jailed,
I cannot escape.

ט הִרְחַ֥קְתָּ מְיֻדָּעַ֗י מִ֫מֶּ֥נִּי
שַׁתַּ֣נִי תוֹעֵב֣וֹת לָ֑מוֹ
כָּ֝לֻ֗א
וְלֹ֣א אֵצֵֽא׃

10 My eye hurts from deprivation,
I am calling upon You, Eternal, all day long,
I am spreading my palms out to You.

י עֵינִ֥י דָאֲבָ֗ה מִנִּ֫י עֹ֥נִי
קְרָאתִ֣יךָ יהוה בְּכָל־י֑וֹם
שִׁטַּ֖חְתִּי אֵלֶ֣יךָ כַפָּֽי׃

11 Do You perform wonders for the dead?
Or would deceased rise,
Praise You, Selah?

יא הֲלַמֵּתִים תַּעֲשֶׂה־פֶּלֶא
אִם־רְפָאִים יָקוּמוּ |
יוֹדוּךָ סֶּלָה׃

12 Can Your kindness be recounted in the grave,
Your faithfulness
In perdition?

יב הַיְסֻפַּר בַּקֶּבֶר חַסְדֶּךָ
אֱמוּנָתְךָ
בָּאֲבַדּוֹן׃

13 Can Your miracle be known in the darkness,
And Your justice
In the Land of oblivion?

יג הֲיִוָּדַע בַּחֹשֶׁךְ פִּלְאֶךָ
וְצִדְקָתְךָ
בְּאֶרֶץ נְשִׁיָּה׃

14 But I,
Implored You, Eternal.
In the morning
My prayer to You is before all else.

יד וַאֲנִי |
אֵלֶיךָ יהוה שִׁוַּעְתִּי
וּבַבֹּקֶר
תְּפִלָּתִי תְקַדְּמֶךָּ׃

15 Why, Eternal,
Do you neglect my soul,
Do You hide Yourself before me?

טו לָמָה יהוה
תִּזְנַח נַפְשִׁי
תַּסְתִּיר פָּנֶיךָ מִמֶּנִּי׃

16 Deprived am I, and dying from youth
I am carrying Your fear, I am out of my wits.

טז עָנִי אֲנִי וְגֹוֵעַ מִנֹּעַר
נָשָׂאתִי אֵמֶיךָ אָפוּנָה׃

17 Upon me
Your rages passed,
Your horrors
Closed in on me.

יז עָלַי
עָבְרוּ חֲרוֹנֶיךָ
בִּעוּתֶיךָ
צִמְּתוּתֻנִי׃

18 They surround me like water
All day long,
They enclose me together.

יח סַבּוּנִי כַמַּיִם
כָּל־הַיּוֹם
הִקִּיפוּ עָלַי יָחַד׃

19 You removed from me
Lover and friend,
My acquaintance is darkness.

יט הִרְחַקְתָּ מִמֶּנִּי
אֹהֵב וָרֵעַ
מְיֻדָּעַי מַחְשָׁךְ׃

1. Heyman is mentioned, together with Eytan, the author of the next Psalm, as son on Zerah *1Chr* 6:2.

6. Cf. *2Kings* 15:5, בית החפשית, "the hospital"; found also in Ugaritic as חפּתת.

16. Following Ibn Ezra and most moderns, deriving אפונה from Arabic אפנ "to be out of one's wits", connected with Hebrew פנ "turned away".

17. צמתותני is obviously a poetic lengthening of צמתני when the poet needed two additional syllables for his melody.

Psalm 89

1 A didactic poem
By Ethan the Zeraḥide.

א מַשְׂכִּיל
לְאֵיתָן הָאֶזְרָחִי׃

2 I always shall sing
Of the Eternal's kindness,
For all generations
By my mouth I shall proclaim His faithfulness.

ב חַסְדֵי יהוה
עוֹלָם אָשִׁירָה
לְדֹר וָדֹר ׀
אוֹדִיעַ אֱמוּנָתְךָ בְּפִי׃

3 I insist to say:
The world
Was built by kindness;
The heavens,
Your faithfulness is more steadfast than they are.

ג כִּי־אָמַרְתִּי
עוֹלָם
חֶסֶד יִבָּנֶה
שָׁמַיִם ׀
תָּכִן אֱמוּנָתְךָ בָהֶם׃

4 "I concluded a covenant
With my chosen,
I swore
To my servant, David.

ד כָּרַתִּי בְרִית
לִבְחִירִי
נִשְׁבַּעְתִּי
לְדָוִד עַבְדִּי׃

5 Forever
I shall establish Your line,
I built your throne for all generations," Selah.

ה עַד־עוֹלָם
אָכִין זַרְעֶךָ
וּבָנִיתִי לְדֹר־וָדוֹר כִּסְאֲךָ סֶלָה׃

6 In the Heavens they praise Your promise,
Eternal,
Also Your faithfulness
In the assembly of the holy ones.

ו וְיוֹדוּ שָׁמַיִם פִּלְאֲךָ יהוה
אַף־אֱמוּנָתְךָ
בִּקְהַל קְדֹשִׁים׃

7 Because who in the sky
Can be valued like the Eternal,
Can be compared to the Eternal
Among the powerful?

ז כִּי מִי בַשַּׁחַק
יַעֲרֹךְ לַיהוה
יִדְמֶה לַיהוה
בִּבְנֵי אֵלִים׃

8 A dreadful power
In the great assembly of the holy ones,
And awesome
Over all His surroundings.

ח אֵל נַעֲרָץ
בְּסוֹד־קְדֹשִׁים רַבָּה
וְנוֹרָא
עַל־כָּל־סְבִיבָיו׃

9 Eternal,
God of Hosts,
Who is superior like You, Eternal,
And Your faithfulness
Is Your surroundings.

ט יהוה ׀
אֱלֹהֵי צְבָאוֹת
מִי־כָמוֹךָ חֲסִין ׀ יָהּ
וֶאֱמוּנָתְךָ
סְבִיבוֹתֶיךָ׃

10 You rule
Over the power of the Sea,
When its waves are ruinous
You smooth them.

י אַתָּה מוֹשֵׁל
בְּגֵאוּת הַיָּם
בְּשׂוֹא גַלָּיו
אַתָּה תְשַׁבְּחֵם׃

11 You subdued Rahab like a corpse,	יא אַתָּה דִכִּאתָ כֶחָלָל רָהַב
With Your powerful arm	בִּזְרוֹעַ עֻזְּךָ
You dispersed Your enemies.	פִּזַּרְתָּ אוֹיְבֶיךָ׃
12 Yours is heaven,	יב לְךָ שָׁמַיִם
Also Yours is the earth,	אַף־לְךָ אָרֶץ
The world and its contents	תֵּבֵל וּמְלֹאָהּ
You founded.	אַתָּה יְסַדְתָּם׃
13 North and South,	יג צָפוֹן וְיָמִין
You created them,	אַתָּה בְרָאתָם
Tabor and Hermon	תָּבוֹר וְחֶרְמוֹן
Sing to Your Name.	בְּשִׁמְךָ יְרַנֵּנוּ׃
14 You have the arm	יד לְךָ זְרוֹעַ
With strength,	עִם־גְּבוּרָה
Your left hand shall be strong,	תָּעֹז יָדְךָ
Your right hand uplifted.	תָּרוּם יְמִינֶךָ׃
15 Justice and law	טו צֶדֶק וּמִשְׁפָּט
Are the foundations of Your throne,	מְכוֹן כִּסְאֶךָ
Kindness and truth	חֶסֶד וֶאֱמֶת
Go before Your presence.	יְקַדְּמוּ פָנֶיךָ׃
16 Hail to the people	טז אַשְׁרֵי הָעָם
Who know friendship,	יוֹדְעֵי תְרוּעָה
Eternal,	יהוה
They walk in the light of Your presence.	בְּאוֹר־פָּנֶיךָ יְהַלֵּכוּן׃
17 In Your Name	יז בְּשִׁמְךָ
They rejoice every day,	יְגִילוּן כָּל־הַיּוֹם
And in Your justice they are elevated.	וּבְצִדְקָתְךָ יָרוּמוּ׃
18 Because You are the splendor of their power,	יח כִּי־תִפְאֶרֶת עֻזָּמוֹ אָתָּה
And in Your goodwill	וּבִרְצֹנְךָ
You lift our horn.	תָּרִים [תָּרוּם] קַרְנֵנוּ׃
19 Certainly from the Eternal	יט כִּי לַיהוה
Is our shield,	מָגִנֵּנוּ
Our king from the Holy One of Israel.	וְלִקְדוֹשׁ יִשְׂרָאֵל מַלְכֵּנוּ
20 Once You talked in a vision	כ אָז דִּבַּרְתָּ־בְחָזוֹן
To Your pious and said:	לַחֲסִידֶיךָ וַתֹּאמֶר
"I put help	שִׁוִּיתִי עֵזֶר
On the hero,	עַל־גִּבּוֹר
I elevated the chosen one from the people.	הֲרִימוֹתִי בָחוּר מֵעָם׃
21 I found	כא מָצָאתִי
My servant David.	דָּוִד עַבְדִּי
I anointed him with my holy oil.	בְּשֶׁמֶן קָדְשִׁי מְשַׁחְתִּיו׃
22 That my left hand	כב אֲשֶׁר יָדִי
Will be firm with him,	תִּכּוֹן עִמּוֹ
My arm will give him power.	אַף־זְרוֹעִי תְאַמְּצֶנּוּ

23 The enemy shall not destroy him
Nor the criminal
Hurt him.

כג לֹא־יַשִּׁא אוֹיֵב בּוֹ
וּבֶן־עַוְלָה
לֹא יְעַנֶּנּוּ׃

24 I shall smash his adversaries
And smite his haters.

כד וְכַתּוֹתִי מִפָּנָיו צָרָיו
וּמְשַׂנְאָיו אֶגּוֹף׃

25 My faithfulness and kindness are with him,
And in my Name
His horn will rise.

כה וֶאֱמוּנָתִי וְחַסְדִּי עִמּוֹ
וּבִשְׁמִי
תָּרוּם קַרְנוֹ׃

26 I shall put his left hand over the Sea
And his right hand over the rivers.

כו וְשַׂמְתִּי בַיָּם יָדוֹ
וּבַנְּהָרוֹת יְמִינוֹ׃

27 He shall call to Me
'You are my father,
You are my Powerful
And the rock of my help.'

כז הוּא יִקְרָאֵנִי
אָבִי אָתָּה
אֵלִי
וְצוּר יְשׁוּעָתִי׃

28 Also I
Will treat him like a first-born,
Superior
To the kings of the earth.

כח אַף־אָנִי
בְּכוֹר אֶתְּנֵהוּ
עֶלְיוֹן
לְמַלְכֵי־אָרֶץ׃

29 Forever
I shall keep my kindness for him
And my covenant
Will remain true for him.

כט לְעוֹלָם
אֶשְׁמוֹר [אֶשְׁמָר] ־לוֹ חַסְדִּי
וּבְרִיתִי
נֶאֱמֶנֶת לוֹ׃

30 I shall crown his descendants
And his throne
Like the days of heavens.

ל וְשַׂמְתִּי לָעַד זַרְעוֹ
וְכִסְאוֹ
כִּימֵי שָׁמָיִם׃

31 If his sons would abandon
My teachings
And not walk
In My statutes;

לא אִם־יַעַזְבוּ בָנָיו
תּוֹרָתִי
וּבְמִשְׁפָּטַי
לֹא יֵלֵכוּן׃

32 If they would desecrate My laws
And not keep
My commandments;

לב אִם־חֻקֹּתַי יְחַלֵּלוּ
וּמִצְוֹתַי
לֹא יִשְׁמֹרוּ׃

33 I shall punish their crime with a rod
And their sins with plagues;

לג וּפָקַדְתִּי בְשֵׁבֶט פִּשְׁעָם
וּבִנְגָעִים עֲוֺנָם׃

34 But my kindness
I shall not break from him,
I shall not be untrue
To my faithfulness.

לד וְחַסְדִּי
לֹא־אָפִיר מֵעִמּוֹ
וְלֹא־אֲשַׁקֵּר
בֶּאֱמוּנָתִי׃

35 I shall not desecrate my covenant,
And what came from my lips
I shall not change.

לה לֹא־אֲחַלֵּל בְּרִיתִי
וּמוֹצָא שְׂפָתַי
לֹא אֲשַׁנֶּה׃

36 One thing
I swore by My holiness
That I would not belie David.

לו אַחַת
נִשְׁבַּעְתִּי בְקָדְשִׁי
אִם־לְדָוִד אֲכַזֵּב׃

37 His line
Will be forever,
Before me his throne is like the sun.

לז זַרְעוֹ
לְעוֹלָם יִהְיֶה
וְכִסְאוֹ כַשֶּׁמֶשׁ נֶגְדִּי׃

38 Like the moon
It is set forever,
A witness in the sky,
Faithful, Selah."

לח כְּיָרֵחַ
יִכּוֹן עוֹלָם
וְעֵד בַּשַּׁחַק
נֶאֱמָן סֶלָה׃

39 But You have abandoned
And despised;
You were angry
Against Your anointed.

לט וְאַתָּה זָנַחְתָּ
וַתִּמְאָס
הִתְעַבַּרְתָּ
עִם־מְשִׁיחֶךָ׃

40 You annulled
The covenant with Your servant,
Desecrated down to the ground his crown.

מ נֵאַרְתָּה
בְּרִית עַבְדֶּךָ
חִלַּלְתָּ לָאָרֶץ נִזְרוֹ׃

41 You broke open all his fences,
Made his fortresses into rubble.

מא פָּרַצְתָּ כָל־גְּדֵרֹתָיו
שַׂמְתָּ מִבְצָרָיו מְחִתָּה׃

42 All passersby
Plundered him,
He became a shame
To his neighbors.

מב שַׁסֻּהוּ
כָּל־עֹבְרֵי דָרֶךְ
הָיָה חֶרְפָּה
לִשְׁכֵנָיו׃

4;3 You elevated
The right hand of his oppressors,
All his enemies
You made happy.

מג הֲרִימוֹתָ
יְמִין צָרָיו
הִשְׂמַחְתָּ
כָּל־אוֹיְבָיו׃

44 You blunted
The sharpness of his sword,
And did not support him
In war.

מד אַף־תָּשִׁיב
צוּר חַרְבּוֹ
וְלֹא הֲקֵימֹתוֹ
בַּמִּלְחָמָה׃

45 His splendor You made inactive;
Also his throne
You dragged to the ground.

מה הִשְׁבַּתָּ מִטְּהָרוֹ
וְכִסְאוֹ
לָאָרֶץ מִגַּרְתָּה׃

46 You shortened
The days of his youth,
You clothed him in shame, Selah.

מו הִקְצַרְתָּ
יְמֵי עֲלוּמָיו
הֶעֱטִיתָ עָלָיו בּוּשָׁה סֶלָה׃

47 Until when, Eternal,
Will You be permanently hidden,
Will Your rage burn like fire?

מז עַד־מָה יהוה
תִּסָּתֵר לָנֶצַח
תִּבְעַר כְּמוֹ־אֵשׁ חֲמָתֶךָ׃

48 I have to remember, how rusty,	מח זְכָר־אֲנִי מֶה־חָלֶד
How for nothingness	עַל־מַה־שָּׁוְא
You created all mankind.	בָּרָאתָ כָל־בְּנֵי־אָדָם׃
49 Who is the man who will live	מט מִי גֶבֶר יִחְיֶה
And not encounter death,	וְלֹא יִרְאֶה־מָּוֶת
Save himself from the grave, Selah?	יְמַלֵּט נַפְשׁוֹ מִיַּד־שְׁאוֹל סֶלָה׃
50 Where	נ אַיֵּה |
Is Your previous kindness, Almighty,	חֲסָדֶיךָ הָרִאשֹׁנִים | אֲדֹנָי
Which You swore to David	נִשְׁבַּעְתָּ לְדָוִד
In Your faithfulness?	בֶּאֱמוּנָתֶךָ׃
51 Remember, Almighty,	נא זְכֹר אֲדֹנָי
Your servants' shame,	חֶרְפַּת עֲבָדֶיךָ
My carrying on my breast	שְׂאֵתִי בְחֵיקִי
All the nobles of the peoples,	כָּל־רַבִּים עַמִּים׃
52 When Your enemies insulted,	נב אֲשֶׁר חֵרְפוּ אוֹיְבֶיךָ |
Eternal,	יְהוָה
Who insulted	אֲשֶׁר חֵרְפוּ
The heels of Your anointed.	עִקְּבוֹת מְשִׁיחֶךָ׃
53 Praised be the Eternal forever,	נג בָּרוּךְ יְהוָה לְעוֹלָם
Amen, Amen.	אָמֵן | וְאָמֵן׃

This Psalm is the peg on which to attach the belief in the Davidide Messiah.

1. For Ethan the Zerahide, cf. *Ps*. 88.

6. פלא is derived from the root "to make a clear vow" (*Lev*. 27:2).

16. For the meaning of תרועה cf. Rashi, *Num*. 23:21.

19. The shield and king is David, cf. Ibn Ezra.

23. ישיא is derived here from a root שוא "being catastrophic" (the root of *shoah*). There is also a meaning "to trick" which also might be acceptable.

30. Deriving לעד from the root עדי "jewel, diadem".

53. This last verse is the conclusion of the Third Book of Psalms, it is not part of the Psalm.

Book Four

Psalm 90

1 A prayer	א תְּפִלָּה
Of Moses, the godly man.	לְמֹשֶׁה אִישׁ־הָאֱלֹהִים
Almighty,	אֲדֹנָי
You were for us	מָעוֹן אַתָּה
A refuge	הָיִיתָ לָּנוּ
In every generation.	בְּדֹר וָדֹר׃
2 Before	ב בְּטֶרֶם |
Mountains were born,	הָרִים יֻלָּדוּ
You worked over Earth and inhabited land;	וַתְּחוֹלֵל אֶרֶץ וְתֵבֵל
From eternity to eternity	וּמֵעוֹלָם עַד־עוֹלָם
You are the Power.	אַתָּה אֵל׃
3 You turn a human back	ג תָּשֵׁב אֱנוֹשׁ
To pound him,	עַד־דַּכָּא
And You say:	וַתֹּאמֶר
Repent, simple people!	שׁוּבוּ בְנֵי־אָדָם׃
4 Certainly, a thousand years	ד כִּי אֶלֶף שָׁנִים
Are in Your eyes	בְּעֵינֶיךָ
Like yesterday	כְּיוֹם אֶתְמוֹל
After it is gone,	כִּי יַעֲבֹר
Or a watch in the night.	וְאַשְׁמוּרָה בַלָּיְלָה׃
5 You let them flow,	ה זְרַמְתָּם
To be a sleep;	שֵׁנָה יִהְיוּ
In the morning	בַּבֹּקֶר
It will pass by like grass.	כֶּחָצִיר יַחֲלֹף׃
6 In the morning	ו בַּבֹּקֶר
He will sprout and change,	יָצִיץ וְחָלָף
In the evening	לָעֶרֶב
He will wilt and dry up.	יְמוֹלֵל וְיָבֵשׁ׃
7 Truly, we are finished in Your anger,	ז כִּי־כָלִינוּ בְאַפֶּךָ
And we become frightened in Your rage.	וּבַחֲמָתְךָ נִבְהָלְנוּ׃
8 You put our sins before You,	ח שַׁתָּ [שַׁתָּה] עֲוֺנֹתֵינוּ לְנֶגְדֶּךָ
Our youth	עֲלֻמֵנוּ
To the light of Your face.	לִמְאוֹר פָּנֶיךָ׃
9 Truly, all our days	ט כִּי כָל־יָמֵינוּ
Are turned in Your rage;	פָּנוּ בְעֶבְרָתֶךָ
We finished our days as in one thought.	כִּלִּינוּ שָׁנֵינוּ כְמוֹ־הֶגֶה׃

10 The days of our years are up to seventy years,
And if there is strength
Eighty years,
Most of it
Exertion and misfortune,
Certainly quickly shorn
We are flown away.

י יְמֵי שְׁנוֹתֵינוּ בָהֶם שִׁבְעִים שָׁנָה
וְאִם בִּגְבוּרֹת |
שְׁמוֹנִים שָׁנָה
וְרָהְבָּם
עָמָל וָאָוֶן
כִּי־גָז חִישׁ
וַנָּעֻפָה׃

11 Who knows
The power of Your rage?
What is feared
Is Your wrath.

יא מִי־יוֹדֵעַ
עֹז אַפֶּךָ
וּכְיִרְאָתְךָ
עֶבְרָתֶךָ׃

12 To count our days
Please let us know,
We would have brought
The essence of wisdom.

יב לִמְנוֹת יָמֵינוּ
כֵּן הוֹדַע
וְנָבִא
לְבַב חָכְמָה׃

13 Turn back, Eternal,
Until when?
Have mercy
With Your servants.

יג שׁוּבָה יהוה
עַד־מָתָי
וְהִנָּחֵם
עַל־עֲבָדֶיךָ׃

14 Mornings satiate us in Your kindness,
Then we shall sing and rejoice
All our days long.

יד שַׂבְּעֵנוּ בַבֹּקֶר חַסְדֶּךָ
וּנְרַנְּנָה וְנִשְׂמְחָה
בְּכָל־יָמֵינוּ׃

15 Make us happy
Like the days You have deprived us,
The years
We saw bad luck.

טו שַׂמְּחֵנוּ
כִּימוֹת עִנִּיתָנוּ
שְׁנוֹת
רָאִינוּ רָעָה׃

16 May Your work appear to Your servants
And Your splendor
Over their children.

טז יֵרָאֶה אֶל־עֲבָדֶיךָ פָעֳלֶךָ
וַהֲדָרְךָ
עַל־בְּנֵיהֶם׃

17 Let
The Eternal's, our God, bounty be upon us.
Also our handiwork
Make enduring for us,
Our handiwork
Make it endure!

יז וִיהִי |
נֹעַם אֲדֹנָי אֱלֹהֵינוּ עָלֵינוּ
וּמַעֲשֵׂה יָדֵינוּ
כּוֹנְנָה עָלֵינוּ
וּמַעֲשֵׂה יָדֵינוּ
כּוֹנְנֵהוּ׃

Psalm 91

1 Sitting
In the shelter of the Most High,
In the shadow of the Powerful
Staying over night,

א יֹשֵׁב
בְּסֵתֶר עֶלְיוֹן
בְּצֵל שַׁדַּי
יִתְלוֹנָן׃

2 I say to the Eternal:
"My refuge and my fortress,
My God,
In Whom I trust".

ב אֹמַר לַיהוה
מַחְסִי וּמְצוּדָתִי
אֱלֹהַי
אֶבְטַח־בּוֹ׃

3 Truly He will save you
From the trapping snare,
From catastrophic plague.

ג כִּי הוּא יַצִּילְךָ
מִפַּח יָקוּשׁ
מִדֶּבֶר הַוּוֹת׃

4 With His pinions
He will cover you,
Under His wings you will find refuge,
His ell is long shield and round shield.

ד בְּאֶבְרָתוֹ ׀
יָסֶךְ לָךְ
וְתַחַת כְּנָפָיו תֶּחְסֶה
צִנָּה וְסֹחֵרָה אֲמִתּוֹ׃

5 You do not have to fear
The terror of night,
The arrow
Flying by day,

ה לֹא־תִירָא
מִפַּחַד לָיְלָה
מֵחֵץ
יָעוּף יוֹמָם׃

6 The plague
Stalking in the dark,
The burning fever
Robbing at noontime.

ו מִדֶּבֶר
בָּאֹפֶל יַהֲלֹךְ
מִקֶּטֶב
יָשׁוּד צָהֳרָיִם׃

7 At your left hand side may
Thousands fall,
And myriads at your right hand side,
To you
They will not come close.

ז יִפֹּל מִצִּדְּךָ ׀
אֶלֶף
וּרְבָבָה מִימִינֶךָ
אֵלֶיךָ
לֹא יִגָּשׁ׃

8 Just
Look with your eyes,
You can see the retribution for the wicked.

ח רַק
בְּעֵינֶיךָ תַבִּיט
וְשִׁלֻּמַת רְשָׁעִים תִּרְאֶה׃

9 "Truly, You, Eternal, are my refuge,"
The Most High
You put as your help.

ט כִּי־אַתָּה יהוה מַחְסִי
עֶלְיוֹן
שַׂמְתָּ מְעוֹנֶךָ׃

10 No evil will happen to you,
Harm
Will not come close to your tent.
:

י לֹא־תְאֻנֶּה אֵלֶיךָ רָעָה
וְנֶגַע
לֹא־יִקְרַב בְּאָהֳלֶךָ׃

11 Certainly, His angels
He will command to you
To watch you
On all your ways.

יא כִּי מַלְאָכָיו
יְצַוֶּה־לָּךְ
לִשְׁמָרְךָ
בְּכָל־דְּרָכֶיךָ׃

12 They will carry you on hands
Lest your foot should be hurt on a stone.

יב עַל־כַּפַּ֥יִם יִשָּׂא֑וּנְךָ
פֶּן־תִּגֹּ֖ף בָּאֶ֣בֶן רַגְלֶֽךָ׃

13 You may step on lion and python,
Crush lion's whelp and snake.

יג עַל־שַׁ֣חַל וָפֶ֣תֶן תִּדְרֹ֑ךְ
תִּרְמֹ֖ס כְּפִ֣יר וְתַנִּֽין׃

14 Because he desired Me,
I shall let him escape,
I shall lift him up
Because he knows My name.

יד כִּ֣י בִ֭י חָשַׁק
וַאֲפַלְּטֵ֑הוּ
אֲ֝שַׂגְּבֵ֗הוּ
כִּֽי־יָדַ֥ע שְׁמִֽי׃

15 He will call Me,
Then I shall answer him,
With him I shall be in straits,
I shall rescue him
And make him honored.

טו יִקְרָאֵ֨נִי ׀
וְֽאֶעֱנֵ֗הוּ
עִמּ֥וֹ אָנֹכִ֥י בְצָרָ֑ה
אֲ֝חַלְּצֵ֗הוּ
וַאֲכַבְּדֵֽהוּ׃

16 I shall make him full of
Length of days ,
I shall show him
My salvation.

טז אֹ֣רֶךְ יָ֭מִים
אַשְׂבִּיעֵ֑הוּ
וְ֝אַרְאֵ֗הוּ
בִּישׁוּעָתִֽי׃

9. Identifying מעון with Arabic מעאנה "help, aid".

Psalm 92

1 A Psalm, a song,
For the Sabbath Day.

א מִזְמ֥וֹר שִׁ֗יר
לְי֣וֹם הַשַּׁבָּֽת׃

2 It is good
To praise the Eternal,
And to sing to Your Name, Most High,

ב ט֗וֹב
לְהֹד֥וֹת לַיהוָ֑ה
וּלְזַמֵּ֖ר לְשִׁמְךָ֣ עֶלְיֽוֹן׃

3 To tell of Your kindness in the morning
And of Your faithfulness
During nights.

ג לְהַגִּ֣יד בַּבֹּ֣קֶר חַסְדֶּ֑ךָ
וֶ֝אֱמ֥וּנָתְךָ֗
בַּלֵּילֽוֹת׃

4 On a ten stringed instrument
And on a harp,
With thought-out melodies on the lute.

ד עֲלֵי־עָ֭שׂוֹר
וַעֲלֵי־נָ֑בֶל
עֲלֵ֖י הִגָּי֣וֹן בְּכִנּֽוֹר׃

5 Because You, Eternal, gladdened me with Your deed,
I shall chant about Your handiwork.

ה כִּ֤י שִׂמַּחְתַּ֣נִי יְהוָ֣ה בְּפָעֳלֶ֑ךָ
בְּֽמַעֲשֵׂ֖י יָדֶ֣יךָ אֲרַנֵּֽן׃

6 How great are Your works, Eternal,
Exceedingly
Deep are Your plans.

ו מַה־גָּדְל֣וּ מַעֲשֶׂ֣יךָ יְהוָ֑ה
מְ֝אֹ֗ד
עָמְק֥וּ מַחְשְׁבֹתֶֽיךָ׃

7 An uninstructed man
Cannot know,
And the silly
Cannot understand this.

ז אִֽישׁ־בַּ֭עַר
לֹ֣א יֵדָ֑ע
וּ֝כְסִ֗יל
לֹא־יָבִ֥ין אֶת־זֹֽאת׃

8 When the wicked are flowering
Like grass,
And there sprout
All evil doers,
To their everlasting destruction.

ח בִּפְרֹ֤חַ רְשָׁעִ֨ים ׀
כְּמ֥וֹ עֵ֗שֶׂב
וַ֭יָּצִיצוּ
כָּל־פֹּ֣עֲלֵי אָ֑וֶן
לְהִשָּֽׁמְדָ֥ם עֲדֵי־עַֽד׃

9 But You are sublime
Forever, Eternal.

ט וְאַתָּ֥ה מָר֗וֹם
לְעֹלָ֥ם יְהוָֽה׃

10 Truly, behold Your enemies,
Eternal,
Behold Your enemies go to ruin;
They will break up,
All who do evil.

י כִּ֤י הִנֵּ֪ה אֹיְבֶ֡יךָ ׀
יְהוָ֗ה
כִּֽי־הִנֵּ֣ה אֹיְבֶ֣יךָ יֹאבֵ֑דוּ
יִ֝תְפָּרְד֗וּ
כָּל־פֹּ֥עֲלֵי אָֽוֶן׃

11 But You lift my horn like the white antelope,
I am refreshed
With green oil.

יא וַתָּ֣רֶם כִּרְאֵ֣ים קַרְנִ֑י
בַּ֝לֹּתִ֗י
בְּשֶׁ֣מֶן רַעֲנָֽן׃

12 My eye gazes upon those who stare at me;
Of the criminals who rise against me
My ears can hear.

יב וַתַּבֵּ֥ט עֵינִ֗י בְּשׁ֫וּרָ֥י
בַּקָּמִ֣ים עָלַ֣י מְ֭רֵעִים
תִּשְׁמַ֥עְנָה אָזְנָֽי׃

13 The just
Will bloom like the date palm,
He will grow like a cedar on the Lebanon,

יג צַדִּיק
כַּתָּמָר יִפְרָח
כְּאֶרֶז בַּלְּבָנוֹן יִשְׂגֶּה

14 Planted
In the Eternal’s House,
In our God's courtyards they will flower.

יד שְׁתוּלִים
בְּבֵית יהוָה
בְּחַצְרוֹת אֱלֹהֵינוּ יַפְרִיחוּ׃

15 Still
Their sap will flow in old age,
They will be fat and green,

טו עוֹד
יְנוּבוּן בְּשֵׂיבָה
דְּשֵׁנִים וְרַעֲנַנִּים יִהְיוּ׃

16 To tell
That the Eternal is straight;
My rock,
No evil is in Him.

טז לְהַגִּיד
כִּי־יָשָׁר יהוָה
צוּרִי
וְלֹא־עַלָתָה [עַוְלָתָה] בּוֹ׃

Psalm 93

1 The Eternal reigns	א יְהוָ֣ה מָלָךְ֮
In majesty draped,	גֵּא֪וּת לָ֫בֵ֥שׁ
The Eternal is draped,	לָבֵ֣שׁ יְ֭הוה
Girded in strength;	עֹ֣ז הִתְאַזָּ֑ר
Surely You based the world,	אַף־תִּכּ֥וֹן תֵּ֝בֵ֗ל
It should not shake.	בַּל־תִּמּֽוֹט׃
2 Your throne is based from old;	ב נָכ֣וֹן כִּסְאֲךָ֣ מֵאָ֑ז
From eternity You are.	מֵעוֹלָ֣ם אָֽתָּה׃
3 The currents raised,	ג נָשְׂא֤וּ נְהָר֨וֹת ׀
Eternal,	יְהוָ֗ה
The currents raised their voices,	נָשְׂא֣וּ נְהָר֣וֹת קוֹלָ֑ם
The currents will raise their pounding.	יִשְׂא֖וּ נְהָר֣וֹת דָּכְיָֽם׃
4 More than the sounds	ד מִקֹּל֨וֹת ׀
Of mighty waters	מַ֤יִם רַבִּ֗ים
Mightier than the breakers of the Sea,	אַדִּירִ֣ים מִשְׁבְּרֵי־יָ֑ם
The Eternal is mighty on high.	אַדִּ֖יר בַּמָּר֣וֹם יְהוָֽה׃
5 Your assemblies	ה עֵֽדֹתֶ֨יךָ ׀
Are very true;	נֶאֶמְנ֬וּ מְאֹ֗ד
Holiness is appropriate for Your House,	לְבֵיתְךָ֥ נַאֲוָה־קֹ֑דֶשׁ
Eternal,	יְ֝הוָ֗ה
Forever.	לְאֹ֣רֶךְ יָמִֽים׃

As a song of the Creation and Temple, Ps. 93 is an appendix to Ps. 92. עֵֽדֹתֶ֨יךָ is derived from עדה "assembly".

Psalm 94

1 The avenging Power is the Eternal, The avenging Power appeared.	א אֵל־נְקָמוֹת יהוה אֵל נְקָמוֹת הוֹפִיעַ׃
2 Be elevated, Judge of the earth, Bring retribution Over the haughty!	ב הִנָּשֵׂא שֹׁפֵט הָאָרֶץ הָשֵׁב גְּמוּל עַל־גֵּאִים׃
3 Eternal, Until when will the wicked, Until when Will the wicked exult?	ג עַד־מָתַי רְשָׁעִים | יְהוָה עַד־מָתַי רְשָׁעִים יַעֲלֹזוּ׃
4 They pour forth, they speak as libertines, They make themselves leaders, All evil doers.	ד יַבִּיעוּ יְדַבְּרוּ עָתָק יִתְאַמְּרוּ כָּל־פֹּעֲלֵי אָוֶן׃
5 Eternal, they pound your people, And they torment Your inheritance.	ה עַמְּךָ יהוה יְדַכְּאוּ וְנַחֲלָתְךָ יְעַנּוּ׃
6 Widow And stranger they will kill, And routinely murder orphans,	ו אַלְמָנָה וְגֵר יַהֲרֹגוּ וִיתוֹמִים יְרַצֵּחוּ׃
7 While saying, The Eternal will not see, The God of Jacob Will not be minding.	ז וַיֹּאמְרוּ לֹא יִרְאֶה־יָּהּ וְלֹא־יָבִין אֱלֹהֵי יַעֲקֹב׃
8 Understand that, Uninstructed among the people; And fools, When will you comprehend?	ח בִּינוּ בֹּעֲרִים בָּעָם וּכְסִילִים מָתַי תַּשְׂכִּילוּ׃
9 He Who plants the ear, Will He not hear? If He creates the eye, Will He not gaze?	ט הֲנֹטַע אֹזֶן הֲלֹא יִשְׁמָע אִם־ יֹצֵר עַיִן הֲלֹא יַבִּיט׃
10 If He instructs peoples, Will He not chastise, He Who teaches knowledge to humans?	י הֲיֹסֵר גּוֹיִם הֲלֹא יוֹכִיחַ הַמְלַמֵּד אָדָם דָּעַת׃
11 The Eternal knows The thoughts of humans; Certainly they are vapor.	יא יהוה יֹדֵעַ מַחְשְׁבוֹת אָדָם כִּי הֵמָּה הָבֶל׃
12 Hail to the man Who is instructed by the Eternal, Whom You teach of Your Torah,	יב אַשְׁרֵי | הַגֶּבֶר אֲשֶׁר־תְּיַסְּרֶנּוּ יָּהּ וּמִתּוֹרָתְךָ תְלַמְּדֶנּוּ׃

13 To give him peace
After days of evil,
Until the pit is dug for the wicked.

יג לְהַשְׁקִיט לוֹ
מִימֵי רָע
עַד יִכָּרֶה לָרָשָׁע שָׁחַת׃

14 Certainly
The Eternal will not reject His people,
His inheritance
He will not abandon.

יד כִּי ׀
לֹא־יִטֹּשׁ יהוה עַמּוֹ
וְנַחֲלָתוֹ
לֹא יַעֲזֹב׃

15 Certainly for complete justice
He will return to judgment,
Followed by
All who are straight of heart.

טו כִּי־עַד־צֶדֶק
יָשׁוּב מִשְׁפָּט
וְאַחֲרָיו
כָּל־יִשְׁרֵי־לֵב׃

16 Who can stand up for me
Against criminals,
Who can put himself up for me
Against evil doers?

טז מִי־יָקוּם לִי
עִם־מְרֵעִים
מִי־יִתְיַצֵּב לִי
עִם־פֹּעֲלֵי אָוֶן׃

17 If the Eternal were not
A help for me,
Almost
I would already lie silent.

יז לוּלֵי יהוה
עֶזְרָתָה לִּי
כִּמְעַט ׀
שָׁכְנָה דוּמָה נַפְשִׁי׃

18 When I said:
"My foot was slipping",
Your kindness, Eternal,
Supported me.

יח אִם־אָמַרְתִּי
מָטָה רַגְלִי
חַסְדְּךָ יהוה
יִסְעָדֵנִי׃

19 With all my worries inside me,
Your consolations
Rejoiced my soul.

יט בְּרֹב שַׂרְעַפַּי בְּקִרְבִּי
תַּנְחוּמֶיךָ
יְשַׁעַשְׁעוּ נַפְשִׁי׃

20 Did they join against You
A seat of destruction,
Creating evil beyond the law?

כ הַיְחָבְרְךָ
כִּסֵּא הַוּוֹת
יֹצֵר עָמָל עֲלֵי־חֹק׃

21 They assemble
Against the person of the just,
They condemn innocent blood.

כא יָגוֹדּוּ
עַל־נֶפֶשׁ צַדִּיק
וְדָם נָקִי יַרְשִׁיעוּ׃

22 But the Eternal
Was my refuge,
And my God
A shelter rock.

כב וַיְהִי יהוה לִי לְמִשְׂגָּב
וֵאלֹהַי
לְצוּר מַחְסִי׃

23 He turned back over them
Their sins,
And in their wickedness silenced them,
He silenced them,
The Eternal, our God.

כג וַיָּשֶׁב עֲלֵיהֶם ׀
אֶת־אוֹנָם
וּבְרָעָתָם יַצְמִיתֵם
יַצְמִיתֵם
יהוה אֱלֹהֵינוּ׃

6. רוצֵחַ is the murderer but מְרַצֵּחַ is the professional killer.

23. We may derive צמת from Arabic "to be silent" instead from Rabbinic "to squeeze".

Psalm 95

1 Go,
Let us chant to the Eternal,
Let us trumpet
To the rock, our help!

א לְכוּ
נְרַנְּנָה לַיהוָה
נָרִיעָה
לְצוּר יִשְׁעֵנוּ׃

2 Let us appear before Him with thanks,
With melodies
We blow for Him.

ב נְקַדְּמָה פָנָיו בְּתוֹדָה
בִּזְמִרוֹת
נָרִיעַ לוֹ׃

3 Truly a great power is the Eternal,
A great king
Over all powers,

ג כִּי אֵל גָּדוֹל יְהוָה
וּמֶלֶךְ גָּדוֹל
עַל־כָּל־אֱלֹהִים׃

4 In Whose hands are
The recesses of the earth;
The lofty heights of mountains are His.

ד אֲשֶׁר בְּיָדוֹ
מֶחְקְרֵי־אָרֶץ
וְתוֹעֲפוֹת הָרִים לוֹ׃

5 His is the Sea,
He made it,
And the dry land,
His hands created.

ה אֲשֶׁר־לוֹ הַיָּם
וְהוּא עָשָׂהוּ
וְיַבֶּשֶׁת
יָדָיו יָצָרוּ׃

6 Come,
Let us prostrate ourselves and bow down,
Let us kneel
Before the Eternal, our Maker.

ו בֹּאוּ
נִשְׁתַּחֲוֶה וְנִכְרָעָה
נִבְרְכָה
לִפְנֵי־ יְהוָה עֹשֵׂנוּ׃

7 Because He is our God,
We are the people of His pasture,
The sheep of His hand,
Today,
If only you would listen to His voice.

ז כִּי הוּא אֱלֹהֵינוּ
וַאֲנַחְנוּ עַם מַרְעִיתוֹ
וְצֹאן יָדוֹ
הַיּוֹם
אִם־בְּקֹלוֹ תִשְׁמָעוּ׃

8 "Do not harden your hearts
Like at Meribah,
Like the day of Massah
In the desert,

ח אַל־תַּקְשׁוּ לְבַבְכֶם
כִּמְרִיבָה
כְּיוֹם מַסָּה
בַּמִּדְבָּר׃

9 Where your fathers
Tried Me,
Tested Me
Although they had seen My deeds.

ט אֲשֶׁר נִסּוּנִי
אֲבוֹתֵיכֶם
בְּחָנוּנִי
גַּם־רָאוּ פָעֳלִי׃

10 Forty years
I squabbled with the generation,
I said,
"They are a people of erring heart,
They
Did not know My ways,

י אַרְבָּעִים שָׁנָה ׀
אָקוּט בְּדוֹר
וָאֹמַר
עַם תֹּעֵי לֵבָב הֵם
וְהֵם
לֹא־יָדְעוּ דְרָכָי׃

11 About whom I had sworn in My rage
They shall never come
To My resting place."

יא אֲשֶׁר־נִשְׁבַּעְתִּי בְאַפִּי
אִם־יְבֹאוּן
אֶל־מְנוּחָתִי׃

8. See Ex. 17:7.

Psalm 96

1 Sing to the Eternal
A new song,
Sing to the Eternal
All earth.

א שִׁירוּ לַיהוה
שִׁיר חָדָשׁ
שִׁירוּ לַיהוה
כָּל־הָאָרֶץ׃

2 Sing to the Eternal,
Praise His name,
Announce daily
His salvation!

ב שִׁירוּ לַיהוה
בָּרְכוּ שְׁמוֹ
בַּשְּׂרוּ מִיּוֹם־לְיוֹם
יְשׁוּעָתוֹ׃

3 Tell His glory among the peoples,
Among all nations
His wonders.

ג סַפְּרוּ בַגּוֹיִם כְּבוֹדוֹ
בְּכָל־הָעַמִּים
נִפְלְאוֹתָיו׃

4 Truly the Eternal is great and much venerated,
Awesome is He
Above all powers.

ד כִּי גָדוֹל יהוה וּמְהֻלָּל מְאֹד
נוֹרָא הוּא
עַל־כָּל־אֱלֹהִים׃

5 Certainly
All gods of the nations are inanities
But the Eternal
Made the heavens.

ה כִּי |
כָּל־אֱלֹהֵי הָעַמִּים אֱלִילִים
וַיהוה
שָׁמַיִם עָשָׂה׃

6 Splendor and majesty are before Him,
Might and glory
In His sanctuary.

ו הוֹד־וְהָדָר לְפָנָיו
עֹז וְתִפְאֶרֶת
בְּמִקְדָּשׁוֹ׃

7 Give to the Eternal,
Families of nations,
Give to the Eternal
Honor and might,

ז הָבוּ לַיהוה
מִשְׁפְּחוֹת עַמִּים
הָבוּ לַיהוה
כָּבוֹד וָעֹז׃

8 Give to the Eternal
By the honor of His Name,
Carry a gift
And come to His courtyards.

ח הָבוּ לַיהוה
כְּבוֹד שְׁמוֹ
שְׂאוּ־מִנְחָה
וּבֹאוּ לְחַצְרוֹתָיו׃

9 Prostrate yourselves before the Eternal
In the glory of the Sanctuary.
Tremble before Him
All the earth.

ט הִשְׁתַּחֲווּ לַיהוה
בְּהַדְרַת־קֹדֶשׁ
חִילוּ מִפָּנָיו
כָּל־הָאָרֶץ׃

10 Say among the peoples:
The Eternal is king,
He has founded the world
So it should not totter,
He will judge nations
Straightforwardly.

י אִמְרוּ בַגּוֹיִם |
יהוה מָלָךְ
אַף־תִּכּוֹן תֵּבֵל
בַּל־תִּמּוֹט
יָדִין עַמִּים
בְּמֵישָׁרִים׃

11 May the heavens rejoice,	יא יִשְׂמְחוּ הַשָּׁמַיִם
And the earth be happy,	וְתָגֵל הָאָרֶץ
May the Sea thunder	יִרְעַם הַיָּם
All that is in it,	וּמְלֹאוֹ׃
12 May the field be glad	יב יַעֲלֹז שָׂדַי
And all that is in it,	וְכָל־אֲשֶׁר־בּוֹ
Then all trees of the forest	אָז יְרַנְּנוּ
Will chant.	כָּל־עֲצֵי־יָעַר׃
13 Before the Eternal,	יג לִפְנֵי יהוה |
When He comes,	כִּי בָא
He certainly comes	כִּי בָא
To judge the earth,	לִשְׁפֹּט הָאָרֶץ
He will judge the world in justice	יִשְׁפֹּט־תֵּבֵל בְּצֶדֶק
And nations	וְעַמִּים
In His faithfulness.	בֶּאֱמוּנָתוֹ׃

A very close copy of this Psalm appears in *1Chr*. 16:23-33 as the Levites' song at David's Tent of the Ark. For vv. *1Chr*. 16:8-22 cf. Psalm 106. As noted in the Introduction, the parallel can be used to determine the prose accents equivalent to the poetic accents used in Psalms, Proverbs, and Job.

Sing to the Eternal	כג שִׁירוּ לַיהוה
All earth.	כָּל־הָאָרֶץ
Announce daily	בַּשְּׂרוּ מִיּוֹם־אֶל־יוֹם
His salvation!	יְשׁוּעָתוֹ׃
Tell His glory	כד סַפְּרוּ בַגּוֹיִם
Among the peoples,	אֶת־כְּבוֹדוֹ
Among all nations	בְּכָל־הָעַמִּים
His wonders.	נִפְלְאֹתָיו׃
Truly	כה כִּי
The Eternal is great	גָדוֹל יהוה וּמְהֻלָּל
And much venerated,	מְאֹד
Awesome is He	וְנוֹרָא הוּא
Above all powers.	עַל־כָּל־אֱלֹהִים׃
Certainly	כו כִּי
All gods of the nations	כָּל־אֱלֹהֵי הָעַמִּים
Are inanities	אֱלִילִים
But the Eternal	וַיהוה
Made the heavens.	שָׁמַיִם עָשָׂה׃
Splendor and majesty	כז הוֹד וְהָדָר
Are before Him,	לְפָנָיו
Might and glory	עֹז וְחֶדְוָה
In His sanctuary.	בִּמְקֹמוֹ׃

Give to the Eternal,
Families of nations,
Give to the Eternal
Honor and might,

כח הָבוּ לַיהוה
מִשְׁפְּחוֹת עַמִּים
הָבוּ לַיְיָ
כָּבוֹד וָעֹז׃

Give to the Eternal
By the honor of His Name,
Carry a gift
And come before Him.
Prostrate yourselves before the Eternal
In the glory of the Sanctuary.

כט הָבוּ לַיהוָה
כְּבוֹד שְׁמוֹ
שְׂאוּ מִנְחָה
וּבֹאוּ לְפָנָיו
הִשְׁתַּחֲווּ לַיהוָה
בְּהַדְרַת־קֹדֶשׁ׃

Tremble before Him
All the earth.
Also He has founded the world
So it should not totter,

ל חִילוּ מִלְּפָנָיו
כָּל־הָאָרֶץ
אַף־תִּכּוֹן תֵּבֵל
בַּל־תִּמּוֹט׃

May the heavens rejoice,
And the earth be happy,
May the Gentiles say,
The Eternal is ruling.

לא יִשְׂמְחוּ הַשָּׁמַיִם
וְתָגֵל הָאָרֶץ
וְיֹאמְרוּ בַגּוֹיִם
יְיָ מָלָךְ׃

May the Sea thunder
All that is in it,
May the field be glad
And all that is in it.

לב יִרְעַם הַיָּם
וּמְלוֹאוֹ
יַעֲלֹץ הַשָּׂדֶה
וְכָל־אֲשֶׁר־בּוֹ׃

Then all trees of the forest,
Will chant.
Before the Eternal,
When He comes
To judge the earth.

לג אָז יְרַנְּנוּ
עֲצֵי הַיָּעַר
מִלִּפְנֵי יהוה
כִּי־בָא
לִשְׁפּוֹט אֶת־הָאָרֶץ׃

Psalm 97

1 The Eternal ruled!
The Land jubilated,
Many islands
Rejoiced.

א יְהוָה מָלָךְ
תָּגֵל הָאָרֶץ
יִשְׂמְחוּ
אִיִּים רַבִּים׃

2 Clouds and fog surround Him,
Equity and Justice
Are the foundation of His throne.

ב עָנָן וַעֲרָפֶל סְבִיבָיו
צֶדֶק וּמִשְׁפָּט
מְכוֹן כִּסְאוֹ׃

3 Fire
Goes before Him
And blazes all around Him.

ג אֵשׁ
לְפָנָיו תֵּלֵךְ
וּתְלַהֵט סָבִיב צָרָיו׃

4 His thunderbolts light up the world,
The Land saw it and trembled.

ד הֵאִירוּ בְרָקָיו תֵּבֵל
רָאֲתָה וַתָּחֵל הָאָרֶץ׃

5 The mountains
Melted like wax
Before the Eternal,
Before
The Master of all the earth.

ה הָרִים
כַּדּוֹנַג נָמַסּוּ
מִלִּפְנֵי יְהוָה
מִלִּפְנֵי
אֲדוֹן כָּל־הָאָרֶץ׃

6 The heavens tell His justice,
All nations saw His glory.

ו הִגִּידוּ הַשָּׁמַיִם צִדְקוֹ
וְרָאוּ כָל־הָעַמִּים כְּבוֹדוֹ׃

7 All worshippers of idols
Will come to naught, ,
Who pride themselves with their nothings.
All powers
Be prostrate before Him!

ז יֵבֹשׁוּ ׀
כָּל־עֹבְדֵי פֶסֶל
הַמִּתְהַלְלִים בָּאֱלִילִים
הִשְׁתַּחֲווּ־לוֹ
כָּל־אֱלֹהִים׃

8 Zion
Heard it and rejoiced,
The daughters of Judah
Jubilated,
For Your justice, Eternal.

ח שָׁמְעָה וַתִּשְׂמַח ׀
צִיּוֹן
וַתָּגֵלְנָה
בְּנוֹת יְהוּדָה
לְמַעַן מִשְׁפָּטֶיךָ יְהוָה׃

9 Truly, You are the Eternal,
Most high over all the Land,
Extremely elevated
Over all powers!

ט כִּי־אַתָּה יְהוָה
עֶלְיוֹן עַל־כָּל־הָאָרֶץ
מְאֹד נַעֲלֵיתָ
עַל־כָּל־אֱלֹהִים׃

10 Lovers of the Eternal, hate evil!
He preserves
The life of His pious;
From the hand of the wicked
He saves them.

י אֹהֲבֵי יְהוָה שִׂנְאוּ רָע
שֹׁמֵר
נַפְשׁוֹת חֲסִידָיו
מִיַּד רְשָׁעִים
יַצִּילֵם׃

11 Greenery is sown for the just,	יא אֹ֣ור זָרֻ֣עַ לַצַּדִּ֑יק
Joy for those straight of heart.	וּֽלְיִשְׁרֵי־לֵ֥ב שִׂמְחָֽה׃
12 Rejoice, o just ones,	יב שִׂמְח֣וּ צַ֭דִּיקִים
In the Eternal	בַּֽ֝יהֹוָ֗ה
And give thanks	וְ֝הוֹד֗וּ
To His holy Name!	לְזֵ֣כֶר קָדְשֽׁוֹ׃

1. Since the stanza starts with a perfect and continues with imperfect, one has to take this as the general narrative mode with *waw* conversive suppressed for poetic reasons. איים "islands" are far-away places; this usage is frequent in Isaiah.

3. For the meaning of צר "all around", parallel Rabbinic מיצר, cf. *Amos* 3:11.

12. With Rashi and Dahood, taking אור as masculine (Ugaritic, Canaanite) for otherwise documented אורה "(soup-)greens" (*2K.* 4:39); cf. Accadic *araru* "poppy".

Psalm 98

1 A psalm.	א מִזְמוֹר
Sing to the Eternal	שִׁירוּ לַיהוָה ׀
A new song	שִׁיר חָדָשׁ
For the wonders He did,	כִּי־נִפְלָאוֹת עָשָׂה
The help through His right hand	הוֹשִׁיעָה־לּוֹ יְמִינוֹ
And His holy arm.	וּזְרוֹעַ קָדְשׁוֹ׃
2 The Eternal made known	ב הוֹדִיעַ יהוה
His salvation,	יְשׁוּעָתוֹ
Before the eyes of the peoples	לְעֵינֵי הַגּוֹיִם
He uncovered His fairness.	גִּלָּה צִדְקָתוֹ׃
3 He remembered His kindness	ג זָכַר חַסְדּוֹ ׀
And faith	וֶאֱמוּנָתוֹ
For the house of Israel,	לְבֵית יִשְׂרָאֵל
All ends of the earth saw	רָאוּ כָל־אַפְסֵי־אָרֶץ
This,	אֵת
Our God's help.	יְשׁוּעַת אֱלֹהֵינוּ׃
4 Sound to the Eternal,	ד הָרִיעוּ לַיהוה
All the earth,	כָּל־הָאָרֶץ
Open your mouth, sing, and make music.	פִּצְחוּ וְרַנְּנוּ וְזַמֵּרוּ׃
5 Play to the Eternal on the lute,	ה זַמְּרוּ לַיהוָה בְּכִנּוֹר
On the lute	בְּכִנּוֹר
And the sound of instruments.	וְקוֹל זִמְרָה׃
6 With trumpets	ו בַּחֲצֹצְרוֹת
And the voice of the horn,	וְקוֹל שׁוֹפָר
Sound	הָרִיעוּ
Before	לִפְנֵי ׀
The King, Eternal.	הַמֶּלֶךְ יהוה׃
7 The ocean thunders	ז יִרְעַם הַיָּם
And all in it,	וּמְלֹאוֹ
The continents,	תֵּבֵל
And their inhabitants,	וְיֹשְׁבֵי בָהּ׃
8 Rivers clap their hands;	ח נְהָרוֹת יִמְחֲאוּ־כָף
Together,	יַחַד
Mountains jubilate.	הָרִים יְרַנֵּנוּ׃
9 Before the Eternal,	ט לִפְנֵי־יהוה
Who certainly comes	כִּי בָא
To judge the earth,	לִשְׁפֹּט הָאָרֶץ
He will judge the world in equity,	יִשְׁפֹּט־תֵּבֵל בְּצֶדֶק
And nations	וְעַמִּים
In straightness.	בְּמֵישָׁרִים׃

Psalm 99

1 The Eternal rules!	א יְהוָה מָלָךְ
Nations are in upheaval!	יִרְגְּזוּ עַמִּים
He Who thrones above Cherubim!	יֹשֵׁב כְּרוּבִים
The earth leaps!	תָּנוּט הָאָרֶץ׃
2 The Eternal	ב יהוה
Is great in Zion,	בְּצִיּוֹן גָּדוֹל
He is exalted	וְרָם הוּא
Over all nations.	עַל־כָּל־הָעַמִּים׃
3 They should praise Your Name	ג יוֹדוּ שִׁמְךָ
Which is great, awesome;	גָּדוֹל וְנוֹרָא
It is holy.	קָדוֹשׁ הוּא׃
4 The King's might	ד וְעֹז מֶלֶךְ
Loves justice.	מִשְׁפָּט אָהֵב
You	אַתָּה
Founded it straightforwardly,	כּוֹנַנְתָּ מֵישָׁרִים
You performed	מִשְׁפָּט וּצְדָקָה
Justice and equity	בְּיַעֲקֹב ׀
In Jacob.	אַתָּה עָשִׂיתָ׃
5 Exalt	ה רוֹמְמוּ
The Eternal, our God,	יְיָ אֱלֹהֵינוּ
Prostrate yourselves	וְהִשְׁתַּחֲווּ
Before the footstool of His feet;	לַהֲדֹם רַגְלָיו
He is holy.	קָדוֹשׁ הוּא׃
6 Moses and Aaron among	ו מֹשֶׁה וְאַהֲרֹן ׀
His priests,	בְּכֹהֲנָיו
And Samuel	וּשְׁמוּאֵל
Among those who call on His Name,	בְּקֹרְאֵי שְׁמוֹ
They call on the Eternal	קֹרְאִים אֶל־יהוה
And He answers them.	וְהוּא יַעֲנֵם׃
7 In a cloud pillar	ז בְּעַמּוּד עָנָן
He would talk to them;	יְדַבֵּר אֲלֵיהֶם
They kept His testimonials	שָׁמְרוּ עֵדֹתָיו
And the law He gave them.	וְחֹק נָתַן־לָמוֹ
8 Eternal, our God,	ח יְהוָה אֱלֹהֵינוּ
You answered them,	אַתָּה עֲנִיתָם
A forgiving Power	אֵל נֹשֵׂא
You were for them	הָיִיתָ לָהֶם
But avenging	וְנֹקֵם
Their transgressions.	עַל־עֲלִילוֹתָם׃
9 Exalt	ט רוֹמְמוּ
The Eternal, our God,	יְהוָה אֱלֹהֵינוּ

Prostrate yourselves	וְֽהִשְׁתַּחֲווּ
Before His holy mountain,	לְהַ֣ר קָדְשׁ֑וֹ
Truly holy	כִּֽי־קָ֝ד֗וֹשׁ
Is the Eternal, our God.	יְהוָ֥ה אֱלֹהֵֽינוּ׃

1. The root תנט of תניט is found in Ugaritic as נטט, in Arabic as נט "to leap".

Psalm 100

1 A Psalm for thanksgiving.	א מִזְמוֹר לְתוֹדָה
Sound for the Eternal	הָרִיעוּ לַיהוה
All the earth.	כָּל־הָאָרֶץ׃
2 Serve the Eternal in joy,	ב עִבְדוּ אֶת־יהוה בְּשִׂמְחָה
Come before Him	בֹּאוּ לְפָנָיו
In song.	בִּרְנָנָה׃
3 Know that the Eternal	ג דְּעוּ כִּי־יהוה
Is the Supreme Power,	הוּא אֱלֹהִים
He made us,	הוּא עָשָׂנוּ
Not we ourselves [And we are His],	וְלֹא [וְלוֹ] אֲנַחְנוּ
His people,	עַמּוֹ
And the sheep of His pasture.	וְצֹאן מַרְעִיתוֹ׃
4 Come to His gates	ד בֹּאוּ שְׁעָרָיו ׀
In thanksgiving,	בְּתוֹדָה
To His courtyards with praise,	חֲצֵרֹתָיו בִּתְהִלָּה
Thank Him,	הוֹדוּ לוֹ
Praise His Name.	בָּרֲכוּ שְׁמוֹ׃
5 Truly, the Eternal is good,	ה כִּי־טוֹב יהוה
His kindness is forever,	לְעוֹלָם חַסְדּוֹ
For all generations	וְעַד־דֹּר וָדֹר
His steadfastness.	אֱמוּנָתוֹ׃

3. In the fifth line, the text is that of the *ketib*; the *qere* text is in parenthesis. It seems that there were two traditions since in later pronunciation there is no difference in sound between the two versions.

Psalm 101

1 A Psalm of David.
I want to sing of kindness and justice;
To You, Eternal, I want to chant.

א לְדָוִד מִזְמוֹר
חֶסֶד־וּמִשְׁפָּט אָשִׁירָה
לְךָ יְהוָה אֲזַמֵּרָה

2 I try to understand
The simple way;
When
Will You come to me?
I lead my life in the simplicity of my heart
Within my house.

ב אַשְׂכִּילָה ׀
בְּדֶרֶךְ תָּמִים
מָתַי
תָּבוֹא אֵלָי
אֶתְהַלֵּךְ בְּתָם־לְבָבִי
בְּקֶרֶב בֵּיתִי׃

3 I will not tolerate
Evil things before my eyes;
I hate the making of perversion,
Never shall it cling to me.

ג לֹא־אָשִׁית ׀
לְנֶגֶד עֵינַי דְּבַר־בְּלִיָּעַל
עֲשֹׂה־סֵטִים שָׂנֵאתִי
לֹא יִדְבַּק בִּי׃

4 A crooked heart
Shall be removed from before me,
A wicked person
I shall ignore.

ד לֵבָב עִקֵּשׁ
יָסוּר מִמֶּנִּי
רָע
לֹא אֵדָע׃

5 He who slanders
His neighbor in secret,
Him I shall silence.
The haughty of eyes
And wide of heart,
Him
I cannot stand.

ה מְלָושְׁנִי [מְלָשְׁנִי] בַסֵּתֶר ׀
רֵעֵהוּ
אוֹתוֹ אַצְמִית
גְּבַהּ־עֵינַיִם
וּרְחַב לֵבָב
אֹתוֹ
לֹא אוּכָל׃

6 My eyes
Are upon the land's trustworthy
To have them sit with me.
He who walks
The simple way,
He
Shall serve me.

ו עֵינַי ׀
בְּנֶאֶמְנֵי־אֶרֶץ
לָשֶׁבֶת עִמָּדִי
הֹלֵךְ
בְּדֶרֶךְ תָּמִים
הוּא
יְשָׁרְתֵנִי׃

7 In my house
A trickster.
Shall not sit.
A teller of lies
Cannot endure
Before my eyes.

ז לֹא־יֵשֵׁב ׀
בְּקֶרֶב בֵּיתִי
עֹשֵׂה רְמִיָּה
דֹּבֵר שְׁקָרִים
לֹא־יִכּוֹן
לְנֶגֶד עֵינָי׃

8 Like cattle
I will silence all the wicked of the land,
To exterminate from the Eternal's city
All evil doers.

ח לַבְּקָרִים
אַצְמִית כָּל־רִשְׁעֵי־אָרֶץ
לְהַכְרִית מֵעִיר־יְיָ
כָּל־פֹּעֲלֵי אָוֶן׃

Psalm 102

1 A prayer
Of a fainting poor,
He pours out his despair.
Before the Eternal.

א תְּפִלָּה
לְעָנִי כִי־יַעֲטֹף
וְלִפְנֵי יהוה
יִשְׁפֹּךְ שִׂיחוֹ׃

2 Eternal,
Please listen to my prayer;
My supplication
May come before You.

ב יהוה
שִׁמְעָה תְפִלָּתִי
וְשַׁוְעָתִי
אֵלֶיךָ תָבוֹא׃

3 Do not hide Your presence
From me
On the day of my distress,
Bend Your ear to me;
On the day I shall call;
Answer me quickly.

ג אַל־תַּסְתֵּר פָּנֶיךָ ׀
מִמֶּנִּי
בְּיוֹם צַר לִי
הַטֵּה־אֵלַי אָזְנֶךָ
בְּיוֹם אֶקְרָא
מַהֵר עֲנֵנִי׃

4 Truly my days disappear like smoke;
My bones
Are scorched like a fireplace.

ד כִּי־כָלוּ בְעָשָׁן יָמָי
וְעַצְמוֹתַי
כְּמוֹ־קֵד נִחָרוּ׃

5 Smitten like grass,
My heart is dried out,
Truly I am withered,
Unable to eat my bread.

ה הוּכָּה־כָעֵשֶׂב
וַיִּבַשׁ לִבִּי
כִּי־שָׁכַחְתִּי
מֵאֲכֹל לַחְמִי׃

6 From the sound of my worry
My bone clings
To my flesh.

ו מִקּוֹל אַנְחָתִי
דָּבְקָה עַצְמִי
לִבְשָׂרִי׃

7 I compare to
A night bird in the desert
I am like
An owl in ruins.

ז דָּמִיתִי
לִקְאַת מִדְבָּר
הָיִיתִי
כְּכוֹס חֳרָבוֹת׃

8 I permanently am
Like a chirping bird,
A chatterer on the roof.

ח שָׁקַדְתִּי וָאֶהְיֶה
כְּצִפּוֹר
בּוֹדֵד עַל־גָּג׃

9 All day long
My enemies insult me,
Those who mock me
Use me as a swear-word.

ט כָּל־הַיּוֹם
חֵרְפוּנִי אוֹיְבָי
מְהוֹלָלַי
בִּי נִשְׁבָּעוּ׃

10 Truly I ate
Dust like bread
And my drinks
I offered with tears.

י כִּי־אֵפֶר
כַּלֶּחֶם אָכָלְתִּי
וְשִׁקֻּוַי
בִּבְכִי מָסָכְתִּי׃

11 Because of Your rage and anger
Since You lifted me up
And then threw me down.

יא מִפְּנֵי־זַעַמְךָ וְקִצְפֶּךָ
כִּי נְשָׂאתַנִי
וַתַּשְׁלִיכֵנִי׃

12 My days
Vanish like a shadow
And I
Will dry up like grass.

יב יָמַי
כְּצֵל נָטוּי
וַאֲנִי
כָּעֵשֶׂב אִיבָשׁ׃

13 But You, the Eternal,
Will throne forever;
You will be invoked
In all generations.

יג וְאַתָּה יהוה
לְעוֹלָם תֵּשֵׁב
וְזִכְרְךָ
לְדֹר וָדֹר׃

14 You will rise,
You will have mercy on Zion,
When it is time to be graceful to her,
When her term comes.

יד אַתָּה תָקוּם
תְּרַחֵם צִיּוֹן
כִּי־עֵת לְחֶנְנָהּ
כִּי־בָא מוֹעֵד׃

15 Your servants truly love
Her stones,
And they adore her dust.

טו כִּי־רָצוּ עֲבָדֶיךָ
אֶת־אֲבָנֶיהָ
וְאֶת־עֲפָרָהּ יְחֹנֵנוּ׃

16 Gentiles will fear
The Name of the Eternal,
And all kingdoms of the earth
Its glory,

טז וְיִירְאוּ גוֹיִם
אֶת־שֵׁם יהוה
וְכָל־מַלְכֵי הָאָרֶץ
אֶת־כְּבוֹדֶךָ׃

17 When the Eternal will have built Zion,
Will have appeared
In His glory.

יז כִּי־בָנָה יהוה צִיּוֹן
נִרְאָה
בִּכְבוֹדוֹ׃

18 He will have turned
To the prayer of the devastated,
He will not have rejected
Their prayer.

יח פָּנָה
אֶל־תְּפִלַּת הָעַרְעָר
וְלֹא־בָזָה
אֶת־תְּפִלָּתָם׃

19 May this be written down
For a future generation;
A people still to be created
Will praise the Eternal.

יט תִּכָּתֶב זֹאת
לְדוֹר אַחֲרוֹן
וְעַם נִבְרָא
יְהַלֶּל־יָהּ׃

20 When He will look down
From His holy heights,
The Eternal
Will gaze to the earth
From Heaven.

כ כִּי־הִשְׁקִיף
מִמְּרוֹם קָדְשׁוֹ
יהוה
מִשָּׁמַיִם |
אֶל־אֶרֶץ הִבִּיט׃

21 To listen
To the outcry of the bound,
To free
Those condemned to death.

כא לִשְׁמֹעַ
אֶנְקַת אָסִיר
לְפַתֵּחַ
בְּנֵי תְמוּתָה׃

22 To narrate in Zion
The Name of the Eternal
And His praise
In Jerusalem.

כב לְסַפֵּר בְּצִיּוֹן
שֵׁם יְהוָה
וּתְהִלָּתוֹ
בִּירוּשָׁלִָם׃

23 When nations will be assembled together,
And kingdoms,
To serve the Eternal.

כג בְּהִקָּבֵץ עַמִּים יַחְדָּו
וּמַמְלָכוֹת
לַעֲבֹד אֶת־יְהוָה׃

24 On the way He weakened me,
He shortened my days.

כד עִנָּה בַדֶּרֶךְ כֹּחו [כֹּחִי]
קִצַּר יָמָי׃

25 I am saying:
My God, do not take me away
With only half of my days,
Your years are for all generations.

כה אֹמַר
אֵלִי אַל־תַּעֲלֵנִי
בַּחֲצִי יָמָי
בְּדוֹר דּוֹרִים שְׁנוֹתֶיךָ׃

26 Earlier
You founded the earth;
The heavens are Your handiwork.

כו לְפָנִים
הָאָרֶץ יָסַדְתָּ
וּמַעֲשֵׂה יָדֶיךָ שָׁמָיִם׃

27 They will disappear
But You will persist;
They all
Will wear out like a dress;
You will change them like a garment and they will be replaced.

כז הֵמָּה | יֹאבֵדוּ
וְאַתָּה תַעֲמֹד
וְכֻלָּם
כַּבֶּגֶד יִבְלוּ
כַּלְּבוּשׁ תַּחֲלִיפֵם וְיַחֲלֹפוּ׃

28 You are the One,
Your years
Will never end.

כח וְאַתָּה־הוּא
וּשְׁנוֹתֶיךָ
לֹא יִתָּמּוּ׃

29 Your servants' sons will stay on,
Their descendants
Will be firmly before You.

כט בְּנֵי־עֲבָדֶיךָ יִשְׁכּוֹנוּ
וְזַרְעָם
לְפָנֶיךָ יִכּוֹן׃

1. For this meaning of שיח , see Rashi to *Job* 7:13.

8. For בדד, cf. Ugaritic בד, "sang, talked".

Psalm 103

1 By David.
My soul, praise
The Eternal,
All my inmost parts
His holy Name.

א לְדָוִד ׀
בָּרְכִי נַפְשִׁי
אֶת־יְהוָה
וְכָל־קְרָבַי
אֶת־שֵׁם קָדְשׁוֹ׃

2 My soul, praise
The Eternal,
Do not forget
All His benefits.

ב בָּרְכִי נַפְשִׁי
אֶת־יְהוָה
וְאַל־תִּשְׁכְּחִי
כָּל־גְּמוּלָיו׃

3 He Who forgives all your transgressions,
He Who heals
All your diseases.

ג הַסֹּלֵחַ לְכָל־עֲוֹנֵכִי
הָרֹפֵא
לְכָל־תַּחֲלֻאָיְכִי׃

4 He Who saves your life from destruction,
He Who crowns you
With kindness and mercy.

ד הַגּוֹאֵל מִשַּׁחַת חַיָּיְכִי
הַמְעַטְּרֵכִי
חֶסֶד וְרַחֲמִים׃

5 He Who satiates your old age with good,
Renews Your youth like the eagle's.

ה הַמַּשְׂבִּיעַ בַּטּוֹב עֶדְיֵךְ
תִּתְחַדֵּשׁ כַּנֶּשֶׁר נְעוּרָיְכִי׃

6 The Eternal acts in equity,
For the rights
Of all who are suppressed.

ו עֹשֵׂה צְדָקוֹת יְהוָה
וּמִשְׁפָּטִים
לְכָל־עֲשׁוּקִים׃

7 He made known His ways to Moses,
To the children of Israel
His clear instructions.

ז יוֹדִיעַ דְּרָכָיו לְמֹשֶׁה
לִבְנֵי יִשְׂרָאֵל
עֲלִילוֹתָיו׃

8 The Eternal is merciful and graceful,
Long forgiving and of mighty kindness.

ח רַחוּם וְחַנּוּן יְהוָה
אֶרֶךְ אַפַּיִם וְרַב־חָסֶד׃

9 He will not quarrel forever
Nor eternally bear a grudge.

ט לֹא־לָנֶצַח יָרִיב
וְלֹא לְעוֹלָם יִטּוֹר׃

10 Not according to our sins
Will He deal with us,
Not proportional to our transgressions
Did he mete out to us.

י לֹא כַחֲטָאֵינוּ
עָשָׂה לָנוּ
וְלֹא כַעֲוֹנֹתֵינוּ
גָּמַל עָלֵינוּ׃

11 But as high as heaven
Is over the earth,
So mighty is His kindness
Over those who fear Him.

יא כִּי כִגְבֹהַּ שָׁמַיִם
עַל־הָאָרֶץ
גָּבַר חַסְדּוֹ
עַל־יְרֵאָיו׃

12 As far as East
Is from the West,
He removed from us
Our sins.

יב כִּרְחֹק מִזְרָח
מִמַּעֲרָב
הִרְחִיק מִמֶּנּוּ
אֶת־פְּשָׁעֵינוּ׃

13 Like a father has mercy
On his children,
The Eternal had mercy
On those who fear Him.

יג כְּרַחֵ֣ם אָ֭ב
עַל־בָּנִ֑ים
רִחַ֥ם יְ֝הוָ֗ה
עַל־יְרֵאָֽיו׃

14 Truly He
Knows our instincts,
Being mindful
That we are dust.

יד כִּי־ה֭וּא
יָדַ֣ע יִצְרֵ֑נוּ
זָ֝כ֗וּר
כִּי־עָפָ֥ר אֲנָֽחְנוּ׃

15 A human:
His days are like greenery,
He sprouts
Like a wild flower.

טו אֱ֭נוֹשׁ
כֶּחָצִ֣יר יָמָ֑יו
כְּצִ֥יץ הַ֝שָּׂדֶ֗ה
כֵּ֣ן יָצִֽיץ׃

16 In case a wind blew over him, and he is no
more,
Nobody will recognize his place.

טז כִּ֤י ר֣וּחַ עָֽבְרָה־בּ֣וֹ וְאֵינֶ֑נּוּ
וְלֹא־יַכִּירֶ֖נּוּ ע֣וֹד מְקוֹמֽוֹ׃

17 But the kindness of the Eternal
From eternity to eternity
Is on those who fear Him,
And His equity
Is for mankind,

יז וְחֶ֤סֶד יהוה ׀
מֵעוֹלָ֣ם וְעַד־ע֭וֹלָם
עַל־יְרֵאָ֑יו
וְ֝צִדְקָת֗וֹ
לִבְנֵ֥י בָנִֽים׃

18 For those who keep His covenant
And remember His commandments
To execute them.

יח לְשֹׁמְרֵ֥י בְרִית֑וֹ
וּלְזֹכְרֵ֥י פִ֝קֻּדָ֗יו
לַעֲשׂוֹתָֽם׃

19 The Eternal based His throne
In Heaven,
Though His kingdom
Rules over everything.

יט יְֽהוָ֗ה בַּ֭שָּׁמַיִם
הֵכִ֣ין כִּסְא֑וֹ
וּ֝מַלְכוּת֗וֹ
בַּכֹּ֥ל מָשָֽׁלָה׃

20 His angels, praise the Eternal,
Powerful beings,
Executors of His word,
Who listen
To the sound of His word.

כ בָּרֲכ֥וּ יהוה מַלְאָכָ֗יו
גִּבֹּ֣רֵי כֹ֭חַ
עֹשֵׂ֣י דְבָר֑וֹ
לִ֝שְׁמֹ֗עַ
בְּק֣וֹל דְּבָרֽוֹ׃

21 Praise the Eternal
All His hosts,
His servants
Who execute His will.

כא בָּרֲכ֣וּ יְ֭הוָה
כָּל־צְבָאָ֑יו
מְ֝שָׁרְתָ֗יו
עֹשֵׂ֥י רְצוֹנֽוֹ׃

21 Praise the Eternal,
All His works
At all places of His rule;
Praise, my soul,
The Eternal

כב בָּרֲכ֤וּ יהוה
כָּֽל־מַעֲשָׂ֗יו
בְּכָל־מְקֹמ֥וֹת מֶמְשַׁלְתּ֑וֹ
בָּרֲכִ֥י נַ֝פְשִׁ֗י
אֶת־יְהוָֽה׃

.

5. Following the Targum, עדי is translated "old age", from a noun עוד "time", cf. Arabic עיד "old", but עִ֫יד "soft, young".

Psalm 104

1 My soul, praise the Eternal!
Eternal, my God,
You are very great,
Clothed in majesty and splendor.

א בָּרְכִי נַפְשִׁי אֶת־יהוָה
יהוָה אֱלֹהַי
גָּדַלְתָּ מְאֹד
הוֹד וְהָדָר לָבָשְׁתָּ׃

2 He is draped in light
As in a garment,
He spreads the skies
Like a carpet.

ב עֹטֶה אוֹר
כַּשַּׂלְמָה
נוֹטֶה שָׁמַיִם
כַּיְרִיעָה׃

3 With water He roofs His upper floors,
He takes clouds as His conveyance,
He proceeds
On the wings of wind.

ג הַמְקָרֶה בַמַּיִם עֲלִיּוֹתָיו
הַשָּׂם־עָבִים רְכוּבוֹ
הַמְהַלֵּךְ
עַל־כַּנְפֵי־רוּחַ׃

4 He takes winds as His messengers,
His servants
Are swirling fire.

ד עֹשֶׂה מַלְאָכָיו רוּחוֹת
מְשָׁרְתָיו
אֵשׁ לֹהֵט׃

5 He based the earth
On its foundations;
It should not totter
Forever.

ה יָסַד אֶרֶץ
עַל־מְכוֹנֶיהָ
בַּל־תִּמּוֹט
עוֹלָם וָעֶד׃

6 The depths
You covered as with cloth,
Waters would stand
On mountains.

ו תְּהוֹם
כַּלְּבוּשׁ כִּסִּיתוֹ
עַל־הָרִים
יַעַמְדוּ־מָיִם׃

7 They flee from Your rebuke;
From Your thunder's sound
They tremble.

ז מִן־גַּעֲרָתְךָ יְנוּסוּן
מִן־קוֹל רַעַמְךָ
יֵחָפֵזוּן׃

8 They rise up on mountains,
Go down into ravines,
To the place
That definitely
You set for them.

ח יַעֲלוּ הָרִים
יֵרְדוּ בְקָעוֹת
אֶל־מְקוֹם
זֶה ׀
יָסַדְתָּ לָהֶם׃

9 You put up a border
They cannot cross,
They cannot return
To cover the land.

ט גְּבוּל־שַׂמְתָּ
בַּל־יַעֲבֹרוּן
בַּל־יְשׁוּבוּן
לְכַסּוֹת הָאָרֶץ׃

10 He Who sends springs
Into rivers,
They are running
Between mountains .

י הַמְשַׁלֵּחַ מַעְיָנִים
בַּנְּחָלִים
בֵּין הָרִים
יְהַלֵּכוּן׃

11 They let drink
All beasts of the field;
Wild animals break their thirst.

יא יַשְׁקוּ
כָּל־חַיְתוֹ שָׂדָי
יִשְׁבְּרוּ פְרָאִים צְמָאָם׃

12 On them
Dwell the birds of the sky,
From amongst foliage
They raise their voices.

יב עֲלֵיהֶם
עוֹף־הַשָּׁמַיִם יִשְׁכּוֹן
מִבֵּין עֳפָאיִם
יִתְּנוּ־קוֹל׃

13 He Who soaks mountains
From His upper floors;
From the fruit of Your works
The earth is satiated.

יג מַשְׁקֶה הָרִים
מֵעֲלִיּוֹתָיו
מִפְּרִי מַעֲשֶׂיךָ
תִּשְׂבַּע הָאָרֶץ׃

14 He Who lets sprout greenery
For animals,
And grass
For man's exertion,
To produce bread
From the earth.

יד מַצְמִיחַ חָצִיר ׀
לַבְּהֵמָה
וְעֵשֶׂב
לַעֲבֹדַת הָאָדָם
לְהוֹצִיא לֶחֶם
מִן־הָאָרֶץ׃

15 But wine
Cheers up the spirit of men,
Makes their faces shine more than oil,
However bread
Nourishes the spirit of men.

טו וְיַיִן ׀
יְשַׂמַּח לְבַב־אֱנוֹשׁ
לְהַצְהִיל פָּנִים מִשָּׁמֶן
וְלֶחֶם
לְבַב־אֱנוֹשׁ יִסְעָד׃

16 The Eternal's trees
Are satiated,
The cedars of Lebanon
Which He planted,

טז יִשְׂבְּעוּ
עֲצֵי יְהוָה
אַרְזֵי לְבָנוֹן
אֲשֶׁר נָטָע׃

17 Where
Warblers build their nests.
The stork's
House is in the cypresses.

יז אֲשֶׁר־שָׁם
צִפֳּרִים יְקַנֵּנוּ
חֲסִידָה
בְּרוֹשִׁים בֵּיתָהּ׃

18 The high mountains
Are for the chamois,
Rocks
Are a refuge for hyrax.

יח הָרִים הַגְּבֹהִים
לַיְּעֵלִים
סְלָעִים
מַחְסֶה לַשְׁפַנִּים׃

19 He created the moon
For periods;
The sun
Knows when to disappear.

יט עָשָׂה יָרֵחַ
לְמוֹעֲדִים
שֶׁמֶשׁ
יָדַע מְבוֹאוֹ׃

20 You make darkness.
Then night falls
In which crawl
All animals of the forest.

כ תָּשֶׁת חֹשֶׁךְ
וִיהִי לָיְלָה
בּוֹ־תִרְמֹשׂ
כָּל־חַיְתוֹ־יָעַר׃

21 The lion cubs
Roar for their prey
And beg God for their food.

כא הַכְּפִירִים
שֹׁאֲגִים לַטָּרֶף
וּלְבַקֵּשׁ מֵאֵל אׇכְלָם

22 When the sun starts to shine
They return
And make themselves comfortable
In their lairs.

כב תִּזְרַח הַשֶּׁמֶשׁ
יֵאָסֵפוּן
וְאֶל־מְעוֹנֹתָם
יִרְבָּצוּן׃

23 Then man goes out to his toil,
His labor until evening.

כג יֵצֵא אָדָם לְפׇעֳלוֹ
וְלַעֲבֹדָתוֹ עֲדֵי־עָרֶב׃

24 How great are Your works,
Eternal,
All of them
You made in wisdom.
The earth is full
Of Your creations.

כד מָה־רַבּוּ מַעֲשֶׂיךָ ׀
יהוה
כֻּלָּם
בְּחׇכְמָה עָשִׂיתָ
מָלְאָה הָאָרֶץ
קִנְיָנֶךָ׃

25 In particular
The ocean is large,
Widely spread out,
There are crawling things
Without number,
Small animals
Together with large ones.

כה זֶה ׀
הַיָּם גָּדוֹל
וּרְחַב יָדָיִם
שָׁם רֶמֶשׂ
וְאֵין מִסְפָּר
חַיּוֹת קְטַנּוֹת
עִם־גְּדֹלוֹת׃

26 There
Ships traverse;
The Leviathan
You specially created to play with it.

כו שָׁם
אֳנִיּוֹת יְהַלֵּכוּן
לִוְיָתָן
זֶה יָצַרְתָּ לְשַׂחֶק־בּוֹ׃

27 All of them
Depend on You
To provide their food in time.

כז כֻּלָּם
אֵלֶיךָ יְשַׂבֵּרוּן
לָתֵת אׇכְלָם בְּעִתּוֹ׃

28 If You give it to them
They collect it;
If You open Your hand
They are filled with good things.

כח תִּתֵּן לָהֶם
יִלְקֹטוּן
תִּפְתַּח יָדְךָ
יִשְׂבְּעוּן טוֹב׃

29 If You hide Your presence,
They are perplexed,
If You remove their spirit
They die
And return to their dust.

כט תַּסְתִּיר פָּנֶיךָ
יִבָּהֵלוּן
תֹּסֵף רוּחָם
יִגְוָעוּן
וְאֶל־עֲפָרָם יְשׁוּבוּן׃

30 When You send Your spirit
They will be created,
You renew
The face of the earth.

ל תְּשַׁלַּח רוּחֲךָ
יִבָּרֵאוּן
וּתְחַדֵּשׁ
פְּנֵי אֲדָמָה׃

31 The glory of the Eternal persists forever,
The Eternal rejoices in His creation.

לא יְהִי כְבוֹד יְהוָה לְעוֹלָם
יִשְׂמַח יְהוָה בְּמַעֲשָׂיו׃

32 He gazes down to the earth
Then it trembles,
He touches mountains, then they emit smoke.

לב הַמַּבִּיט לָאָרֶץ
וַתִּרְעָד
יִגַּע בֶּהָרִים וְיֶעֱשָׁנוּ׃

33 I will sing to the Eternal all my life,
I shall chant to my God while I exist.

לג אָשִׁירָה לַיהוָה בְּחַיָּי
אֲזַמְּרָה לֵאלֹהַי בְּעוֹדִי׃

34 May my talk be sweet before Him.
I myself
Will rejoice in the Eternal.

לד יֶעֱרַב עָלָיו שִׂיחִי
אָנֹכִי
אֶשְׂמַח בַּ יהוָה׃

35 May sins vanish
From the earth,
And the wicked
Permanently disappear.
My soul, praise
The Eternal, Hallelujah.

לה יִתַּמּוּ חַטָּאִים ׀
מִן־הָאָרֶץ
וּרְשָׁעִים ׀
עוֹד אֵינָם
בָּרְכִי נַפְשִׁי
אֶת־ יהוָה הַלְלוּ־יָהּ׃

Psalm 105

1 Thank the Eternal,
Invoke His name,
Spread among nations the knowledge
Of His deeds!

א הוֹדוּ לַיהוה
קִרְאוּ בִּשְׁמוֹ
הוֹדִיעוּ בָעַמִּים
עֲלִילוֹתָיו׃

2 Sing to Him,
Chant to Him,
Talk
About all His wonders.

ב שִׁירוּ לוֹ
זַמְּרוּ־לוֹ
שִׂיחוּ
בְּכָל־נִפְלְאוֹתָיו׃

3 Praise yourselves
In His holy Name,
Let rejoice
The heart of
The seekers of the Eternal.

ג הִתְהַלְלוּ
בְּשֵׁם קָדְשׁוֹ
יִשְׂמַח
לֵב |
מְבַקְשֵׁי יהוָה׃

4 Inquire about the Eternal and His might,
Always desire His presence.

ד דִּרְשׁוּ יהוָה וְעֻזּוֹ
בַּקְּשׁוּ פָנָיו תָּמִיד׃

5 Remember
His wonders
Which He performed,
His signs
And the laws which He pronounced.

ה זִכְרוּ
נִפְלְאוֹתָיו
אֲשֶׁר עָשָׂה
מֹפְתָיו
וּמִשְׁפְּטֵי־פִיו׃

6 O seed
Of His servant Abraham,
The sons of Jacob, His elected.

ו זֶרַע
אַבְרָהָם עַבְדּוֹ
בְּנֵי יַעֲקֹב בְּחִירָיו׃

7 He is
The Eternal, our God,
Over all of earth
Are His laws.

ז הוּא
יהוָה אֱלֹהֵינוּ
בְּכָל־הָאָרֶץ
מִשְׁפָּטָיו׃

8 Forever He remembers His covenant,
The word He commanded
For a thousand generations,

ח זָכַר לְעוֹלָם בְּרִיתוֹ
דָּבָר צִוָּה
לְאֶלֶף דּוֹר׃

9 Which He concluded
With Abraham,
As well as His oath to Isaac.

ט אֲשֶׁר כָּרַת
אֶת־אַבְרָהָם
וּשְׁבוּעָתוֹ לְיִשְׂחָק׃

10 He erected it as standard for Jacob,
For Israel
As eternal covenant.

י וַיַּעֲמִידֶהָ לְיַעֲקֹב לְחֹק
לְיִשְׂרָאֵל
בְּרִית עוֹלָם׃

11 Meaning: to you
I shall give the land of Canaan,
The region
Of your inheritance.

יא לֵאמֹר לְךָ
אֶתֵּן אֶת־אֶרֶץ כְּנָעַן
חֶבֶל
נַחֲלַתְכֶם׃

12 When they were
Counted men,
Few,
And sojourning there.

יב בִּהְיוֹתָם
מְתֵי מִסְפָּר
כִּמְעַט
וְגָרִים בָּהּ׃

13 They wandered
From people to people,
From one state
To another nation.

יג וַיִּתְהַלְּכוּ
מִגּוֹי אֶל־גּוֹי
מִמַּמְלָכָה
אֶל־עַם אַחֵר׃

14 He let no man oppress them
And chastised kings about them.

יד לֹא־הִנִּיחַ אָדָם לְעָשְׁקָם
וַיּוֹכַח עֲלֵיהֶם מְלָכִים׃

15 “Do not touch my anointed,
And to my prophets
Do not do evil.”

טו אַל־תִּגְּעוּ בִמְשִׁיחָי
וְלִנְבִיאַי
אַל־תָּרֵעוּ׃

16 He called a famine
Over the land,
He broke every staff of bread.

ז וַיִּקְרָא רָעָב
עַל־הָאָרֶץ
כָּל־מַטֵּה־לֶחֶם שָׁבָר׃

17 He sent before them a personality;
As a slave
Joseph was sold.

יז שָׁלַח לִפְנֵיהֶם אִישׁ
לְעֶבֶד
נִמְכַּר יוֹסֵף׃

18 They hurt his feet [foot] with a rope,
Into irons
His person came.

יח עִנּוּ בַכֶּבֶל רַגְלָיו [רַגְלוֹ]
בַּרְזֶל
בָּאָה נַפְשׁוֹ׃

19 Until the time His word came,
The mandate of the Eternal refined him.

יט עַד־עֵת בֹּא־דְבָרוֹ
אִמְרַת יהוה צְרָפָתְהוּ׃

20 The king sent
And unbound him;
The ruler of nations
Set him free.

כ שָׁלַח־מֶלֶךְ
וַיַּתִּירֵהוּ
מֹשֵׁל עַמִּים
וַיְפַתְּחֵהוּ׃

21 He made him master of his house,
Ruler
Of all his possessions.

כא שָׂמוֹ אָדוֹן לְבֵיתוֹ
וּמֹשֵׁל
בְּכָל־קִנְיָנוֹ׃

22 He might arrest his princes at will;
His elders he should instruct.

כב לֶאְסֹר שָׂרָיו בְּנַפְשׁוֹ
וּזְקֵנָיו יְחַכֵּם׃

23 So Israel came to Egypt,
Jacob
Stayed in the land of Ham.

כג וַיָּבֹא יִשְׂרָאֵל מִצְרָיִם
וְיַעֲקֹב
גָּר בְּאֶרֶץ־חָם׃

24 He made His people grow very much,
Made it more powerful
Despite its enemies.

כד וַיֶּפֶר אֶת־עַמּוֹ מְאֹד
וַיַּעֲצִמֵהוּ
מִצָּרָיו׃

25 He turned their hearts
To hate His people,
To behave cruelly
To His servants.

כה הָפַךְ לִבָּם
לִשְׂנֹא עַמּוֹ
לְהִתְנַכֵּל
בַּעֲבָדָיו׃

26 He sent
His servant Moses,
Aaron
Whom He had selected.

כו שָׁלַח
מֹשֶׁה עַבְדּוֹ
אַהֲרֹן
אֲשֶׁר בָּחַר־בּוֹ׃

27 There they performed
The facts of His signs,
Wonders
In the land of Ham.

כז שָׂמוּ־בָם
דִּבְרֵי אֹתוֹתָיו
וּמֹפְתִים
בְּאֶרֶץ חָם׃

28 He sent darkness
And it became dark;
They did no longer oppose
His words [word].

כח שָׁלַח חֹשֶׁךְ
וַיַּחְשִׁךְ
וְלֹא־מָרוּ
אֶת־דְּבָרָיו [דְּבָרוֹ]׃

29 He turned their waters to blood
And killed
Their fishes.

כט הָפַךְ אֶת־מֵימֵיהֶם לְדָם
וַיָּמֶת
אֶת־דְּגָתָם׃

30 He made their land swarm with frogs
In the chambers
Of their kings.

ל שָׁרַץ אַרְצָם צְפַרְדְּעִים
בְּחַדְרֵי
מַלְכֵיהֶם׃

31 He commanded
And swarms came,
Lice
In all their districts.

לא אָמַר
וַיָּבֹא עָרֹב
כִּנִּים
בְּכָל־גְּבוּלָם׃

32 He turned their rains to hailstorms,
Swirling fire in their land.

לב נָתַן גִּשְׁמֵיהֶם בָּרָד
אֵשׁ לֶהָבוֹת בְּאַרְצָם׃

33 He hit their vines
And their fig trees,
Broke
The trees in their districts.

לג וַיַּךְ גַּפְנָם
וּתְאֵנָתָם
וַיְשַׁבֵּר
עֵץ גְּבוּלָם׃

34 He commanded
And brought locusts,
Grasshoppers
Without numbers.

לד אָמַר
וַיָּבֹא אַרְבֶּה
וְיֶלֶק
וְאֵין מִסְפָּר׃

35 They ate all the green in their land
They ate
The fruits of their earth.

לה וַיֹּאכַל כָּל־עֵשֶׂב בְּאַרְצָם
וַיֹּאכַל
פְּרִי אַדְמָתָם׃

36 He smote every firstborn in their land,
The first fruits
Of all their virility.

לו וַיַּךְ כָּל־בְּכוֹר בְּאַרְצָם
רֵאשִׁית
לְכָל־אוֹנָם

37 He lead them out
With silver and gold,
No one was stumbling among their tribes.

לז וַיּוֹצִיאֵם
בְּכֶסֶף וְזָהָב
וְאֵין בִּשְׁבָטָיו כּוֹשֵׁל׃

38 Egypt rejoiced in their leaving
Because their fear had fallen on them.

לח שָׂמַח מִצְרַיִם בְּצֵאתָם
כִּי־נָפַל פַּחְדָּם עֲלֵיהֶם

39 He spread a cloud as curtain,
And fire
To illuminate the night.

לט פָּרַשׂ עָנָן לְמָסָךְ
וְאֵשׁ
לְהָאִיר לָיְלָה׃

40 They asked and He brought quail;
With heavenly bread
He filled them.

מ שָׁאַל וַיָּבֵא שְׂלָו [שְׂלָיו]
וְלֶחֶם שָׁמַיִם
יַשְׂבִּיעֵם׃

41 He opened the rock
And let water flow;
They walked
In the desert with a river.

מא פָּתַח צוּר
וַיָּזוּבוּ מָיִם
הָלְכוּ
בַּצִּיּוֹת נָהָר׃

42 Truly, He remembered
His holy word,
His servant Abraham.

מב כִּי־זָכַר
אֶת־דְּבַר קָדְשׁוֹ
אֶת־אַבְרָהָם עַבְדּוֹ׃

43 He led out His people in joy,
In song
His elected.

מג וַיּוֹצִא עַמּוֹ בְשָׂשׂוֹן
בְּרִנָּה
אֶת־בְּחִירָיו׃

44 He gave them
The lands of the gentiles,
The toil of nations they inherited.

מד וַיִּתֵּן לָהֶם
אַרְצוֹת גּוֹיִם
וַעֲמַל לְאֻמִּים יִירָשׁוּ׃

45 In return
They must keep His laws
And preserve His teachings,
Halleluja.

מה בַּעֲבוּר ׀
יִשְׁמְרוּ חֻקָּיו
וְתוֹרֹתָיו יִנְצֹרוּ
הַלְלוּ־יָהּ׃

As noted for Psalm 96, the first part of this Psalm has a second version in *1Chr.* 16:8-22 in prose accents, mostly with regular four-line strophes:

Thank the Eternal,
Invoke His name,
Spread under the nations the knowledge
Of His deeds!

ח הוֹדוּ לַיהוָה
קִרְאוּ בִשְׁמוֹ
הוֹדִיעוּ בָעַמִּים
עֲלִילֹתָיו׃

Sing to Him,
Chant to Him,
Talk
About all His wonders.

ט שִׁירוּ לוֹ
זַמְּרוּ־לוֹ
שִׂיחוּ
בְּכָל־נִפְלְאֹתָיו׃

Praise yourselves
In His holy Name,
Let rejoice
The heart of
The seekers of the Eternal.

י הִתְהַלְלוּ֙
בְּשֵׁ֣ם קָדְשׁ֔וֹ
יִשְׂמַ֕ח
לֵ֖ב
מְבַקְשֵׁ֥י יְיָ׃

Inquire about the Eternal
And His might,
Always desire
His presence.

יא דִּרְשׁ֤וּ יהוה֙
וְעֻזּ֔וֹ
בַּקְּשׁ֥וּ פָנָ֖יו
תָּמִֽיד׃

Remember
His wonders
Which He performed,
His signs
And the laws which He pronounced.

יב זִכְר֗וּ
נִפְלְאֹתָיו֙
אֲשֶׁ֣ר עָשָׂ֔ה
מֹפְתָ֖יו
וּמִשְׁפְּטֵי־פִֽיהוּ׃

O seed
Of His servant Abraham,
The sons of Jacob,
His elected.

יג זֶ֚רַע
יִשְׂרָאֵ֣ל עַבְדּ֔וֹ
בְּנֵ֥י יַעֲקֹ֖ב
בְּחִירָֽיו׃

He is
The Eternal, our God,
Over all of earth
Are His laws.

יד ה֚וּא
יְהוָ֣ה אֱלֹהֵ֔ינוּ
בְּכָל־הָאָ֖רֶץ
מִשְׁפָּטָֽיו׃

Forever remember
His covenant,
The word He commanded
For a thousand generations,

טו זִכְר֤וּ לְעוֹלָם֙
בְּרִית֔וֹ
דָּבָ֥ר צִוָּ֖ה
לְאֶ֥לֶף דּֽוֹר׃

Which He concluded
With Abraham,
As well as His oath
To Isaac.

טז אֲשֶׁ֤ר כָּרַת֙
אֶת־אַבְרָהָ֔ם
וּשְׁבוּעָת֖וֹ
לְיִצְחָֽק׃

He erected it for Jacob
As standard,
For Israel
As eternal covenant

יז וַיַּעֲמִידֶ֤הָ לְיַעֲקֹב֙
לְחֹ֔ק
לְיִשְׂרָאֵ֖ל
בְּרִ֥ית עוֹלָֽם׃

Meaning:
To you
I shall give the land of Canaan,
The region
Of your inheritance.

יח לֵאמֹ֗ר
לְךָ֙
אֶתֵּ֣ן אֶֽרֶץ־כְּנָ֔עַן
חֶ֖בֶל
נַחֲלַתְכֶֽם׃

When they were
Counted men,
Few,
And sojourning there.

יט בִּֽהְיֽוֹתְכֶם֙
מְתֵ֣י מִסְפָּ֔ר
כִּמְעַ֖ט
וְגָרִ֥ים בָּֽהּ׃

They wandered
From people to people,
From one state
To another nation.

כ וַיִּתְהַלְּכוּ֙
מִגּ֣וֹי אֶל־גּ֔וֹי
וּמִמַּמְלָכָ֖ה
אֶל־עַ֥ם אַחֵֽר׃

He let no man
Oppress them
And chastised kings
About them.

כא לֹא־הִנִּ֤יחַ לְאִישׁ֙
לְעָשְׁקָ֔ם
וַיּ֥וֹכַח עֲלֵיהֶ֖ם
מְלָכִֽים׃

“Do not touch
My anointed,
And to my prophets
Do not do evil.”

כב אַל־תִּגְּעוּ֙
בִּמְשִׁיחָ֔י
וּבִנְבִיאַ֖י
אַל־תָּרֵֽעוּ׃

Psalm 106

1 Hallelujah!
Praise the Eternal, the most good,
Certainly His kindness is forever.

א הַלְלוּ יָהּ ׀
הוֹדוּ לַיהוָה כִּי־טוֹב
כִּי לְעוֹלָם חַסְדּוֹ׃

2 Who is it who can express
The mightiness of the Eternal,
Can tell
All His praise?

ב מִי יְמַלֵּל
גְּבוּרוֹת יהוָה
יַשְׁמִיעַ
כָּל־תְּהִלָּתוֹ׃

3 Hail to
Those who keep the law
Of Him Who acts equitably at all times.

ג אַשְׁרֵי
שֹׁמְרֵי מִשְׁפָּט
עֹשֵׂה צְדָקָה בְכָל־עֵת׃

4 Acknowledge me, Eternal,
With the goodwill of Your nation,
Remember me
With Your salvation.

ד זָכְרֵנִי יהוה
בִּרְצוֹן עַמֶּךָ
פָּקְדֵנִי
בִּישׁוּעָתֶךָ׃

5 That I may see
The benefit of Your select ones,
Rejoice
In the happiness of Your people,
To praise myself
With Your inheritance.

ה לִרְאוֹת ׀
בְּטוֹבַת בְּחִירֶיךָ
לִשְׂמֹחַ
בְּשִׂמְחַת גּוֹיֶךָ
לְהִתְהַלֵּל
עִם־נַחֲלָתֶךָ׃

6 We have sinned together with our fathers,
We have transgressed and produced evil.

ו חָטָאנוּ עִם־אֲבוֹתֵינוּ
הֶעֱוִינוּ הִרְשָׁעְנוּ׃

7 Our forefathers in Egypt
Did not understand Your wonders,
Did not recognize
Your many kind acts,
They rebelled on the Sea at the Sea of Reeds.

ז אֲבוֹתֵינוּ בְמִצְרַיִם ׀
לֹא־הִשְׂכִּילוּ נִפְלְאוֹתֶיךָ
לֹא זָכְרוּ
אֶת־רֹב חֲסָדֶיךָ
וַיַּמְרוּ עַל־יָם בְּיַם־סוּף׃

8 But He saved them
For the sake of His Name,
To proclaim
His might.

ח וַיּוֹשִׁיעֵם
לְמַעַן שְׁמוֹ
לְהוֹדִיעַ
אֶת־גְּבוּרָתוֹ

9 He screamed at the Sea of Reeds
And it became dry,
He lead them through the depths
As through a desert.

ט וַיִּגְעַר בְּיַם־סוּף
וַיֶּחֱרָב
וַיּוֹלִיכֵם בַּתְּהֹמוֹת
כַּמִּדְבָּר׃

10 He saved them
From the hand of the foe,
And delivered them
From the hand of the enemy.

י וַיּוֹשִׁיעֵם
מִיַּד שׂוֹנֵא
וַיִּגְאָלֵם
מִיַּד אוֹיֵב׃

11 The waters covered their oppressors,
Not one of them
Remained.

יא וַיְכַסּוּ־מַיִם צָרֵיהֶם
אֶחָד מֵהֶם
לֹא נוֹתָר׃

12 They believed in His words,
They sang
His praise.

יב וַיַּאֲמִינוּ בִדְבָרָיו
יָשִׁירוּ
תְּהִלָּתוֹ׃

13 Quickly
They forgot His deeds,
Did not wait for
His counsels.

יג מִהֲרוּ
שָׁכְחוּ מַעֲשָׂיו
\לֹא־חִכּוּ
לַעֲצָתוֹ׃

14 They craved a lust
In the desert,
They tried the Powerful
In the desolation.

יד וַיִּתְאַוּוּ תַאֲוָה
בַּמִּדְבָּר
וַיְנַסּוּ־אֵל
בִּישִׁימוֹן׃

15 He gave them
What they asked for
But sent consumption into them.

טו וַיִּתֵּן לָהֶם
שֶׁאֱלָתָם
וַיְשַׁלַּח רָזוֹן בְּנַפְשָׁם׃

16 They became jealous of Moses
In the camp,
Of Aaron,
The Eternal's holy one.

טז וַיְקַנְאוּ לְמֹשֶׁה
בַּמַּחֲנֶה
לְאַהֲרֹן
קְדוֹשׁ יהוה׃

17 Earth opened
And swallowed up Dathan,
And covered
The gang of Abiram.

יז תִּפְתַּח־אֶרֶץ
וַתִּבְלַע דָּתָן
וַתְּכַס
עַל־עֲדַת אֲבִירָם׃

18 Fire burned in their gang,
Blazes
Seared the sinners.

יח וַתִּבְעַר־אֵשׁ בַּעֲדָתָם
לֶהָבָה
תְּלַהֵט רְשָׁעִים׃

19 They made a calf at Horeb
And prostrated themselves
Before a molten image.

יט יַעֲשׂוּ־עֵגֶל בְּחֹרֵב
וַיִּשְׁתַּחֲווּ
לְמַסֵּכָה׃

20 They exchanged their glory
For the figure of an ox,
A grass eater.

כ וַיָּמִירוּ אֶת־כְּבוֹדָם
בְּתַבְנִית שׁוֹר
אֹכֵל עֵשֶׂב׃

21 They forgot
The Power Who saved them,
Who did great deeds in Egypt,

כא שָׁכְחוּ
אֵל מוֹשִׁיעָם
עֹשֶׂה גְדֹלוֹת בְּמִצְרָיִם׃

22 Wonders
In the land of Ham,
Awesome feats
On the Sea of Reeds.

כב נִפְלָאוֹת
בְּאֶרֶץ חָם
נוֹרָאוֹת
עַל־יַם־סוּף׃

23 He said to exterminate them;	כג וַיֹּאמֶר לְהַשְׁמִידָם
If not that	לוּלֵי
Moses, His selected,	מֹשֶׁה בְחִירוֹ
Had stood in the breach before Him	עָמַד בַּפֶּרֶץ לְפָנָיו
To turn back His rage	לְהָשִׁיב חֲמָתוֹ
From destroying.	מֵהַשְׁחִית׃
24 They despised	כד וַיִּמְאֲסוּ
The desirable land,	בְּאֶרֶץ חֶמְדָּה
Did not believe	לֹא־הֶאֱמִינוּ
In His word.	לִדְבָרוֹ׃
25 They griped in their tents,	כה וַיֵּרָגְנוּ בְאָהֳלֵיהֶם
Did not listen	לֹא שָׁמְעוּ
To the Eternal's word.	בְּקוֹל יהוה׃
26 He lifted His hand over them,	כו וַיִּשָּׂא יָדוֹ לָהֶם
To fell them	לְהַפִּיל אוֹתָם
In the desert,	בַּמִּדְבָּר׃
27 To fell their seed	כז וּלְהַפִּיל זַרְעָם
Among the Gentiles,	בַּגּוֹיִם
To winnow them	וּלְזָרוֹתָם
Among countries.	בָּאֲרָצוֹת׃
28 They yoked up	כח וַיִּצָּמְדוּ
With Baal Peor	לְבַעַל פְּעוֹר
And ate	וַיֹּאכְלוּ
Sacrifices for the dead.	זִבְחֵי מֵתִים׃
29 They caused anger	כט וַיַּכְעִיסוּ
By their crimes,	בְּמַעַלְלֵיהֶם
Among them spread	וַתִּפְרָץ־בָּם
Pestilence.	מַגֵּפָה׃
30 Phineas stood up	ל וַיַּעֲמֹד פִּינְחָס
And judged;	וַיְפַלֵּל
The pestilence	וַתֵּעָצַר
Was arrested.	הַמַּגֵּפָה׃
31 This was counted for him	לא וַתֵּחָשֶׁב לוֹ
As merit,	לִצְדָקָה
For all generations,	לְדֹר וָדֹר
Forever.	עַד־עוֹלָם׃
32 They caused anger	לב וַיַּקְצִיפוּ
At the Waters of Quarrel	עַל־מֵי מְרִיבָה
With bad consequences for Moses	וַיֵּרַע לְמֹשֶׁה
Because of them.	בַּעֲבוּרָם׃
33 Certainly they opposed his spirit	לג כִּי־הִמְרוּ אֶת־רוּחוֹ
And he expressed it	וַיְבַטֵּא
With his lips.	בִּשְׂפָתָיו׃

34 They did not destroy
The nations
That the Eternal had told them.

לד לֹא־הִשְׁמִידוּ
אֶת־הָעַמִּים
אֲשֶׁר אָמַר יהוה לָהֶם׃

35 They mingled with the Gentiles
And learned
From their practices.

לה וַיִּתְעָרְבוּ בַגּוֹיִם
וַיִּלְמְדוּ
מַעֲשֵׂיהֶם׃

36 They worshipped their abominations
Which were for them a trap.

לו וַיַּעַבְדוּ אֶת־עֲצַבֵּיהֶם
וַיִּהְיוּ לָהֶם לְמוֹקֵשׁ

37 They sacrificed their sons
And their daughters
To the spirits.

לז וַיִּזְבְּחוּ אֶת־בְּנֵיהֶם
וְאֶת־בְּנוֹתֵיהֶם
לַשֵּׁדִים׃

38 They spilled innocent blood,
Their sons' and daughters' blood,
Whom they sacrificed
To the abominations of Canaan,
So the land became desecrated
By blood.

לח וַיִּשְׁפְּכוּ דָם נָקִי
דַּם־בְּנֵיהֶם וּבְנוֹתֵיהֶם
אֲשֶׁר זִבְּחוּ
לַעֲצַבֵּי כְנָעַן
וַתֶּחֱנַף הָאָרֶץ
בַּדָּמִים׃

39 They became polluted by their deeds,
They prostituted themselves
By their deeds.

לט וַיִּטְמְאוּ בְמַעֲשֵׂיהֶם
וַיִּזְנוּ
בְּמַעַלְלֵיהֶם׃

40 The Eternal's anger burned against His people,
He despised
His inheritance.

מ וַיִּחַר־אַף יהוה בְּעַמּוֹ
וַיְתָעֵב
אֶת־נַחֲלָתוֹ

41 He gave them into the hands of Gentiles;
Their haters
Ruled over them.

מא וַיִּתְּנֵם בְּיַד־גּוֹיִם
וַיִּמְשְׁלוּ בָהֶם
שֹׂנְאֵיהֶם׃

42 Their enemies oppressed them,
They submitted
Under their hands.

מב וַיִּלְחָצוּם אוֹיְבֵיהֶם
וַיִּכָּנְעוּ
תַּחַת יָדָם׃

43 Many times
He saved them,
But they
Rebelled against their counsels
And sank low
By their sins.

מג פְּעָמִים רַבּוֹת יַצִּילֵם
וְהֵמָּה
יַמְרוּ בַעֲצָתָם
וַיָּמֹכּוּ
עֲוֹנָם׃

44 He saw
How they were in trouble
When He heard
Their supplications.

מד וַיַּרְא
צַּר לָהֶם
בְּשָׁמְעוֹ
אֶת־רִנָּתָם׃

45 He remembered His covenant with them
And had compassion
In His overwhelming kindness.

מה וַיִּזְכֹּר לָהֶם בְּרִיתוֹ
וַיִּנָּחֵם
כְּרֹב חֲסָדָו [חֲסָדָיו]׃

46 He had mercy with them
In spite of
All those that had captured them.

מו וַיִּתֵּן אוֹתָם לְרַחֲמִים
לִפְנֵי
כָּל־שׁוֹבֵיהֶם׃

47 Save us,
Eternal, our God,
Gather us in
From among the Gentiles,
That we may thank Your holy Name
And reassure ourselves
In Your praise.

מז הוֹשִׁיעֵנוּ ׀
יְהוָה אֱלֹהֵינוּ
וְקַבְּצֵנוּ
מִן־הַגּוֹיִם
לְהֹדוֹת
לְשֵׁם קָדְשֶׁךָ
לְהִשְׁתַּבֵּחַ
בִּתְהִלָּתֶךָ׃

48 Praise to the Eternal, the God of Israel,
From eternity
To eternity.
And all the people said Amen,
Halleluja.

מח בָּרוּךְ־יהוה אֱלֹהֵי יִשְׂרָאֵל
מִן־הָעוֹלָם ׀
וְעַד הָעוֹלָם
וְאָמַר כָּל־הָעָם אָמֵן
הַלְלוּיָהּ׃

43 וימכו seems to be a pun on ימקו, *Lev.*26:39.

48 “All the people” attending the Services at the Tent, *Ps.* 105 and *1Chr.* 15. This defines *Ps.* 106 as an appendix of the song of the Tent, *Ps.* 105.

Book Five

Psalm 107

1 Thank the Eternal for He truly is good, Certainly, His kindness is eternal,	א הֹדוּ לַיהוָה כִּי־טוֹב כִּי לְעוֹלָם חַסְדּוֹ׃
2 This shall say Those redeemed by the Eternal, Whom He did redeem From the hand of the oppressor,	ב יֹאמְרוּ גְּאוּלֵי יהוָה אֲשֶׁר גְּאָלָם מִיַּד־צָר׃
3 And from countries did collect, From East and West, From North and Seaside.	ג וּמֵאֲרָצוֹת קִבְּצָם מִמִּזְרָח וּמִמַּעֲרָב מִצָּפוֹן וּמִיָּם׃
4 Those that went astray in the wilderness, From the way in the desert; An inhabited town They did not find.	ד תָּעוּ בַמִּדְבָּר בִּישִׁימוֹן דָּרֶךְ עִיר מוֹשָׁב לֹא מָצָאוּ׃
5 Hungry, also thirsty, Their souls Started to become insane.	ה רְעֵבִים גַּם־צְמֵאִים נַפְשָׁם בָּהֶם תִּתְעַטָּף׃
6 They cried to the Eternal When they were in straits. From their distress He saved them,	ו וַיִּצְעֲקוּ אֶל־יהוה בַּצַּר לָהֶם מִמְּצוּקוֹתֵיהֶם יַצִּילֵם׃
7 And directed them To the straight way On which to go To an inhabited town.	ז וַיַּדְרִיכֵם בְּדֶרֶךְ יְשָׁרָה לָלֶכֶת אֶל־עִיר מוֹשָׁב׃
8 They thank the Eternal for His kindness And His wonders, For mankind,	ח יוֹדוּ לַיהוָה חַסְדּוֹ וְנִפְלְאוֹתָיו לִבְנֵי אָדָם׃
9 Because He satisfied Their insisting souls; A hungry person He filled with good things.	ט כִּי־הִשְׂבִּיעַ נֶפֶשׁ שֹׁקֵקָה וְנֶפֶשׁ רְעֵבָה מִלֵּא־טוֹב׃
10 Dwellers in darkness and deep shadow, Bound in torturing irons,	י יֹשְׁבֵי חֹשֶׁךְ וְצַלְמָוֶת אֲסִירֵי עֳנִי וּבַרְזֶל׃
11 Having rebelled against God's words And sneered at the advice of the Most High,	יא כִּי־הִמְרוּ אִמְרֵי־אֵל וַעֲצַת עֶלְיוֹן נָאָצוּ׃
12 He subdued their hearts in anguish, They stumbled And nobody helped.	יב וַיַּכְנַע בֶּעָמָל לִבָּם כָּשְׁלוּ וְאֵין עֹזֵר׃

13 They cried to the Eternal
When they were in straits,
From their distress
He saved them,

יג וַיִּזְעֲקוּ אֶל־יהוה
בַּצַּר לָהֶם
מִמְּצֻקוֹתֵיהֶם
יוֹשִׁיעֵם׃

14 He brought them out
From darkness and deep shadow
And broke their fetters.

יד יוֹצִיאֵם
מֵחֹשֶׁךְ וְצַלְמָוֶת
וּמוֹסְרוֹתֵיהֶם יְנַתֵּק׃

15 They thank the Eternal for His kindness
And His wonders,
In front of mankind,

טו יוֹדוּ לַיהוָה חַסְדּוֹ
וְנִפְלְאוֹתָיו
לִבְנֵי אָדָם׃

16 Because He broke
Brass gates
And lopped off pieces iron bolts.

טז כִּי־שִׁבַּר
דַּלְתוֹת נְחֹשֶׁת
וּבְרִיחֵי בַרְזֶל גִּדֵּעַ׃

17 The evil minded,
On the path of their misdeeds,
From their sins
They become tortured.

יז אֱוִלִים
מִדֶּרֶךְ פִּשְׁעָם
וּמֵעֲוֺנֹתֵיהֶם
יִתְעַנּוּ׃

18 Any food
They find unbearable
And so they come
To the gates of Death.

יח כָּל־אֹכֶל
תְּתַעֵב נַפְשָׁם
וַיַּגִּיעוּ
עַד־שַׁעֲרֵי מָוֶת׃

19 They cried to the Eternal
When they were in straits,
From their distress
He saved them,

יט וַיִּזְעֲקוּ אֶל־יהוה
בַּצַּר לָהֶם
מִמְּצֻקוֹתֵיהֶם
יוֹשִׁיעֵם׃

20 He sent His word
And healed them;
Let them escape
From their rut.

כ יִשְׁלַח דְּבָרוֹ
וְיִרְפָּאֵם
וִימַלֵּט
מִשְּׁחִיתוֹתָם׃

21 They thank the Eternal for His kindness,
And His wonders,
In front of mankind;

כא יוֹדוּ לַיהוה חַסְדּוֹ
וְנִפְלְאוֹתָיו
לִבְנֵי אָדָם׃

22 They bring
Thanksgiving sacrifices
And tell in song of His works.

כב וְיִזְבְּחוּ
זִבְחֵי תוֹדָה
וִיסַפְּרוּ מַעֲשָׂיו בְּרִנָּה׃

23 Those that go to Sea
In ships,
Do their work
On mighty waters,

כג יוֹרְדֵי הַיָּם
בָּאֳנִיּוֹת
עֹשֵׂי מְלָאכָה
בְּמַיִם רַבִּים׃

24 They could see
The deeds of the Eternal
And His wonders
In the deep.

כד הֵמָּה רָאוּ
מַעֲשֵׂי יהוה
וְנִפְלְאוֹתָיו
בִּמְצוּלָה׃

25 He would command and raise
A windstorm
That would turn high its waves.

כה וַיֹּאמֶר וַיַּעֲמֵד
רוּחַ סְעָרָה
וַתְּרוֹמֵם גַּלָּיו׃

26 They would rise to the sky,
Go down to the underworld,
Their souls
Would melt in disaster.

כו יַעֲלוּ שָׁמַיִם
יֵרְדוּ תְהוֹמוֹת
נַפְשָׁם
בְּרָעָה תִתְמוֹגָג׃

27 They would go in circles and move
Like a drunkard;
All their knowledge
Would swallow itself up.

כז יָחוֹגּוּ וְיָנוּעוּ
כַּשִּׁכּוֹר
וְכָל־חָכְמָתָם
תִּתְבַּלָּע׃

28 They cried to the Eternal
When they were in straits,
From their distress
He saved them.

כח וַיִּצְעֲקוּ אֶל־יהוה
בַּצַּר לָהֶם
וּמִמְּצוּקֹתֵיהֶם
יוֹצִיאֵם׃

29 He would erect the storm
Into silence
And quickly send away
Their waves.

כט יָקֵם סְעָרָה
לִדְמָמָה
וַיֶּחֱשׁוּ
גַּלֵּיהֶם׃

30 They rejoiced at the quieting down;
He led them
To the place they desired.

ל וַיִּשְׂמְחוּ כִי־יִשְׁתֹּקוּ
וַיַּנְחֵם
אֶל־מְחוֹז חֶפְצָם׃

31 They thank the Eternal for His kindness
And His wonders,
In front of mankind.

לא יוֹדוּ לַיהוָה חַסְדּוֹ
וְנִפְלְאוֹתָיו
לִבְנֵי אָדָם׃

32 They shall exalt Him
In a large assembly,
Praise Him in the council of the elders.

לב וִירוֹמְמוּהוּ
בִּקְהַל־עָם
וּבְמוֹשַׁב זְקֵנִים יְהַלְלוּהוּ׃

33 He may turn rivers into wilderness
And water sources
Into thirsty spots,

לג יָשֵׂם נְהָרוֹת לְמִדְבָּר
וּמֹצָאֵי מַיִם
לְצִמָּאוֹן׃

34 Fruit bearing land
Into salt flats,
Because of the badness
Of its inhabitants.

לד אֶרֶץ פְּרִי
לִמְלֵחָה
מֵרָעַת
יֹשְׁבֵי בָהּ׃

35 He will turn the wilderness
Into a water pond,
And desert land
Into water sources,

לה יָשֵׂם מִדְבָּר
לַאֲגַם־מַיִם
וְאֶרֶץ צִיָּה
לְמֹצָאֵי מָיִם׃

36 And put hungry people there to dwell,
For them to found
An inhabited town.

לו וַיּוֹשֶׁב שָׁם רְעֵבִים
וַיְכוֹנְנוּ
עִיר מוֹשָׁב׃

37 They sowed fields
And planted vineyards;
These yielded
Fruits and produce.

לז וַיִּזְרְעוּ שָׂדוֹת
וַיִּטְּעוּ כְרָמִים
וַיַּעֲשׂוּ
פְּרִי תְבוּאָה׃

38 He blessed them, they increased very much;
Their animals
Did not diminish.

לח וַיְבָרְכֵם וַיִּרְבּוּ מְאֹד
וּבְהֶמְתָּם
לֹא יַמְעִיט׃

39 So they diminished and flattened
Away barrenness, harm, and sorrow.

לט וַיִּמְעֲטוּ וַיָּשֹׁחוּ
מֵעֹצֶר רָעָה וְיָגוֹן׃

40 He pours scorn
On the nobles,
He leads them astray
In chaos without way.

מ שֹׁפֵךְ בּוּז
עַל־נְדִיבִים
וַיַּתְעֵם
בְּתֹהוּ לֹא־דָרֶךְ׃

41 But He lifts the needy out of deprivation,
Like sheep produces
Families.

מא וַיְשַׂגֵּב אֶבְיוֹן מֵעוֹנִי
וַיָּשֶׂם כַּצֹּאן
מִשְׁפָּחוֹת׃

42 May the straight ones see and rejoice,
And all crime
Close tight its mouth.

מב יִרְאוּ יְשָׁרִים וְיִשְׂמָח
וְכָל־עַוְלָה
קָפְצָה פִּיהָ׃

43 Who is wise enough to watch all this,
And ponder
The Eternal's kindness?

מג מִי־חָכָם וְיִשְׁמָר־אֵלֶּה
וְיִתְבּוֹנְנוּ
חַסְדֵי יהוה׃

Psalm 108

1 A song, a psalm of David.

א שִׁ֥יר מִזְמ֗וֹר לְדָוִֽד׃

2 My heart is steadfast in God;
I will sing and make music,
That is my honor.

ב נָכ֣וֹן לִבִּ֣י אֱלֹהִ֑ים
אָשִׁ֥ירָה וַ֝אֲזַמְּרָ֗ה
אַף־כְּבוֹדִֽי׃

3 Rise,
My harp and lute;
I will rise early in the morning.

ג ע֭וּרָה
הַנֵּ֣בֶל וְ֝כִנּ֗וֹר
אָעִ֥ירָה שָּֽׁחַר׃

4 I shall thank You amongst nations,
Eternal,
And I will compose songs about You
Among races.

ד אוֹדְךָ֖ בָעַמִּ֥ים ׀
יְהוָ֑ה
וַ֝אֲזַמֶּרְךָ֗
בַּל־אֻמִּֽים׃

5 For Your kindness is greater than Heaven
And Your steadfastness over skies.

ה כִּֽי־גָד֣וֹל מֵֽעַל־שָׁמַ֣יִם חַסְדֶּ֑ךָ
וְֽעַד־שְׁחָקִ֥ים אֲמִתֶּֽךָ׃

6 Be exalted over Heaven, God,
Over all of earth is Your splendor.

ו ר֣וּמָה עַל־שָׁמַ֣יִם אֱלֹהִ֑ים
וְעַ֖ל כָּל־הָאָ֣רֶץ כְּבוֹדֶֽךָ׃

7 So that
Your beloved may be extricated;
Please help by Your right hand and answer me.

ז לְ֭מַעַן
יֵחָלְצ֣וּן יְדִידֶ֑יךָ
הוֹשִׁ֖יעָה יְמִֽינְךָ֣ וַעֲנֵֽנִי׃

8 God
Spoke in His holy place, I shall rejoice.
I shall take Sichem as my part
And shall measure up the valley of Sukkot.

ח אֱלֹהִ֤ים ׀
דִּבֶּ֥ר בְּקָדְשׁ֗וֹ אֶ֫עְלֹ֥זָה
אֲחַלְּקָ֥ה שְׁכֶ֑ם
וְעֵ֖מֶק סֻכּ֣וֹת אֲמַדֵּֽד׃

9 Mine is Gilead
And mine is Manasseh,
Also Ephraim
Is my main stronghold,
Judah
My lawgiver's staff.

ט לִ֤י גִלְעָ֨ד ׀
לִ֤י מְנַשֶּׁ֗ה
וְ֭אֶפְרַיִם
מָע֣וֹז רֹאשִׁ֑י
יְ֝הוּדָ֗ה
מְחֹקְקִֽי׃

10 Moab
Is my washing bowl,
Over Edom
I shall throw my shoe,
To Philistia
I will get friendly.

י מוֹאָ֤ב ׀
סִ֬יר רַחְצִ֗י
עַל־אֱ֭דוֹם
אַשְׁלִ֣יךְ נַעֲלִ֑י
עֲלֵי־פְ֝לֶ֗שֶׁת
אֶתְרוֹעָֽע׃

11 Who will bring me
To the fortified city,
Who will guide me into Edom

יא מִ֣י יֹ֭בִלֵנִי
עִ֣יר מִבְצָ֑ר
מִ֖י נָחַ֣נִי עַד־אֱדֽוֹם׃

12 Will You, God, not abandon us?
Should God not march
With our armies?:

יב הֲלֹֽא־אֱלֹהִ֥ים זְנַחְתָּ֑נוּ
וְֽלֹא־תֵצֵ֥א אֱ֝לֹהִ֗ים
בְּצִבְאֹתֵֽינוּ׃

13 Give us help from the oppressor,	יג הָֽבָה־לָּ֣נוּ עֶזְרָ֣ת מִצָּ֑ר
Empty	וְ֝שָׁ֗וְא
Is the help of man.	תְּשׁוּעַ֥ת אָדָֽם׃
14 We shall do valiant things in God,	יד בֵּאלֹהִ֥ים נַעֲשֶׂה־חָ֑יִל
For He	וְ֝ה֗וּא
Will trample down our oppressors.	יָב֥וּס צָרֵֽינוּ׃

This Psalm recycles parts of *Psalms* 57 (8-12) and 60 (7-14).

Psalm 109

1 For the director,
A psalm of David.
God, Whom I praise,
Be not silent.

א לַמְנַצֵּחַ
לְדָוִד מִזְמוֹר
אֱלֹהֵי תְהִלָּתִי
אַל־תֶּחֱרַשׁ׃

2 For a criminal mouth
And a deceiving mouth
They opened against me,
They talked against me
With a lying tongue.

ב כִּי פִי רָשָׁע
וּפִי־מִרְמָה
עָלַי פָּתָחוּ
דִּבְּרוּ אִתִּי
לְשׁוֹן שָׁקֶר׃

3 Words of hate surround me,
They fight against me without cause.

ג וְדִבְרֵי שִׂנְאָה סְבָבוּנִי
וַיִּלָּחֲמוּנִי חִנָּם׃

4 For my love they accuse me
But I am prayer.

ד תַּחַת־אַהֲבָתִי יִשְׂטְנוּנִי
וַאֲנִי תְפִלָּה׃

5 They heap upon me evil
As swap for good,
And hatred
As swap for my love.

ה וַיָּשִׂימוּ עָלַי רָעָה
תַּחַת טוֹבָה
וְשִׂנְאָה
תַּחַת אַהֲבָתִי׃

6 Put a criminal in charge of him,
An accuser
May stand at his right side.

ו הַפְקֵד עָלָיו רָשָׁע
וְשָׂטָן
יַעֲמֹד עַל־יְמִינוֹ׃

7 When he will be judged,
May he be found guilty.
His prayer
May be counted as sinful.

ז בְּהִשָּׁפְטוֹ
יֵצֵא רָשָׁע
תְּפִלָּתוֹ
תִּהְיֶה לַחֲטָאָה׃

8 May his days be few,
Another may take
His office.

ח יִהְיוּ־יָמָיו מְעַטִּים
פְּקֻדָּתוֹ
יִקַּח אַחֵר׃

9 May his children be orphans,
His wife
A widow.

ט יִהְיוּ־בָנָיו יְתוֹמִים
וְאִשְׁתּוֹ
אַלְמָנָה׃

10 May his children wander about begging,
Asking
Out of their ruins.

י וְנוֹעַ יָנוּעוּ בָנָיו וְשִׁאֵלוּ
דָּרְשׁוּ
מֵחָרְבוֹתֵיהֶם׃

11 May the creditor dig out
All his property
And may others plunder what he worked for.

יא יְנַקֵּשׁ נוֹשֶׁה
לְכָל־אֲשֶׁר־לוֹ
וְיָבֹזּוּ זָרִים יְגִיעוֹ׃

12 Nobody should for him
Show sympathy;
Nobody should have mercy
For his orphans.

יב אַל־יְהִי־לוֹ
מֹשֵׁךְ חָסֶד
וְאַל־יְהִי חוֹנֵן
לִיתוֹמָיו׃

13 His future should be extermination,
In a future generation
Their name should be wiped out.

יג יְהִי־אַחֲרִיתוֹ לְהַכְרִית
בְּדוֹר אַחֵר
יִמַּח שְׁמָם׃

14 The crime of his ancestors
May be remembered
By the Eternal,
His mother's sin
Should not be wiped off.

יד יִזָּכֵר ׀
עֲוֺן אֲבֹתָיו
אֶל־יְהוָה
וְחַטַּאת אִמּוֹ
אַל־תִּמָּח׃

15 May they be always before the Eternal,
May He cut off their mention from the Land.

טו יִהְיוּ נֶגֶד־יְהוָה תָּמִיד
וְיַכְרֵת מֵאֶרֶץ זִכְרָם׃

16 Because
He did not remember
To show kindness, and persecuted
The deprived one and downtrodden,
The one mortally wounded in the heart.

טז יַעַן אֲשֶׁר ׀
לֹא זָכַר
עֲשׂוֹת חָסֶד וַיִּרְדֹּף
אִישׁ־עָנִי וְאֶבְיוֹן
וְנִכְאֵה לֵבָב לְמוֹתֵת׃

17 He loved curse;
May it come upon him.
He disliked blessing;
May it be far from him.

יז וַיֶּאֱהַב קְלָלָה
וַתְּבוֹאֵהוּ
וְלֹא־חָפֵץ בִּבְרָכָה
וַתִּרְחַק מִמֶּנּוּ׃

18 He wore cursing like a cloak,
It came like water into him
And like oil
Into his bones.

יח וַיִּלְבַּשׁ קְלָלָה כְּמַדּוֹ
וַתָּבֹא כַמַּיִם בְּקִרְבּוֹ
וְכַשֶּׁמֶן
בְּעַצְמוֹתָיו׃

19 May it be for him
Like a wrap-around suit,
Like a sash
That always will gird him.

יט תְּהִי־לוֹ
כְּבֶגֶד יַעְטֶה
לְמֵזַח
תָּמִיד יַחְגְּרֶהָ׃

20 That be the action against my accusers
From the Eternal,
Those who talk evil
Against me.

כ זֹאת פְּעֻלַּת שֹׂטְנַי
מֵאֵת יְהוָה
וְהַדֹּבְרִים רָע
עַל־נַפְשִׁי׃

21 But You, Eternal Almighty,
Act for me
For Your Name's sake,
For Your kindness is truly good,
Save me!

כא וְאַתָּה ׀ יְהוִה אֲדֹנָי
עֲשֵׂה־אִתִּי
לְמַעַן שְׁמֶךָ
כִּי־טוֹב חַסְדְּךָ
הַצִּילֵנִי׃

22 For I am deprived and downtrodden
And my heart
Is pierced inside me.

כב כִּי־עָנִי וְאֶבְיוֹן אָנֹכִי
וְלִבִּי
חָלַל בְּקִרְבִּי׃

23 I dragged myself like an evening shadow,
Buzzing
Like a locust.

כג כְּצֵל כִּנְטוֹתוֹ נֶהֱלָכְתִּי
נִנְעַרְתִּי
כָּאַרְבֶּה

24 My knees Stumble from fasting, My flesh Is lean, without fat.	כד בִּרְכַּי כָּשְׁלוּ מִצּוֹם וּבְשָׂרִי כָּחַשׁ מִשָּׁמֶן׃
25 Also I Was a curse word for them, When they would see me They would shake their heads.	כה וַאֲנִי | הָיִיתִי חֶרְפָּה לָהֶם יִרְאוּנִי יְנִיעוּן רֹאשָׁם׃
26 Help me, Eternal, my God, Save me by Your kindness.	כו עָזְרֵנִי יהוה אֱלֹהָי הוֹשִׁיעֵנִי כְחַסְדֶּךָ׃
27 They shall know That it is Your hand, That You, the Eternal, did it!	כז וְיֵדְעוּ כִּי־יָדְךָ זֹּאת אַתָּה יהוה עֲשִׂיתָהּ׃
28 Let them curse When You are blessing, Let them get up And be put to shame While Your servant will rejoice.	כח יְקַלְלוּ הֵמָּה וְאַתָּה תְבָרֵךְ קָמוּ | וַיֵּבֹשׁוּ וְעַבְדְּךָ יִשְׂמָח׃
29 May my accusers wear shame Be wrapped in dishonor as in a coat.	כט יִלְבְּשׁוּ שׂוֹטְנַי כְּלִמָּה יַעֲטוּ כַמְעִיל בָּשְׁתָּם
30 I shall thank the Eternal much by my mouth;, I shall praise him in the midst of grandees.	ל אוֹדֶה יהוה מְאֹד בְּפִי וּבְתוֹךְ רַבִּים אֲהַלְלֶנּוּ׃
31 Certainly, He will stand To the right hand of the downtrodden To save him From the judges of his person.	לא כִּי־יַעֲמֹד לִימִין אֶבְיוֹן לְהוֹשִׁיעַ מִשֹּׁפְטֵי נַפְשׁוֹ׃

10. The reading of דָּרְשׁוּ with *qamaṣ qaṭan* is confirmed by Rashi.

23. In Arabic, נער is the sound made by a mosquito (in standard Hebrew, the root as animal sound describes the sound of donkeys or horses.)

Psalm 110

1 For David, a Psalm.
The Eternal said
To my lord:
“Sit to My right hand side,
While I shall turn your enemies
Into your footstool.”

א לְדָוִד מִזְמוֹר
נְאֻם יהוֹה ׀
לַאדֹנִי
שֵׁב לִימִינִי
עַד־אָשִׁית אֹיְבֶיךָ
הֲדֹם לְרַגְלֶיךָ׃

2 Your mighty mace
The Eternal will send
From Zion,
Rule forcefully
Among your enemies.

ב מַטֵּה עֻזְּךָ
יִשְׁלַח יהוה
מִצִּיּוֹן
רְדֵה
בְּקֶרֶב אֹיְבֶיךָ׃

3 Your people volunteer
At the day of your army
In holy splendor
From birth, earliest childhood
Yours is
The dew of youth.

ג עַמְּךָ נְדָבֹת
בְּיוֹם חֵילֶךָ
בְּהַדְרֵי־קֹדֶשׁ
מֵרֶחֶם מִשְׁחָר
לְךָ
טַל יַלְדֻתֶיךָ׃

4 The Eternal has sworn
And will not back out:
“You are office holder forever,
By my command
King of Jerusalem.”

ד נִשְׁבַּע יהוֹה ׀
לֹא יִנָּחֵם
אַתָּה־כֹהֵן לְעוֹלָם
עַל־דִּבְרָתִי
מַלְכִּי־צֶדֶק׃

5 The Almighty, at your right hand,
Will smite kings on the day of His wrath.

ה אֲדֹנָי עַל־יְמִינְךָ
מָחַץ בְּיוֹם־אַפּוֹ מְלָכִים׃

6 He will judge among the Gentiles
Full of corpses,
Smashing heads
On a wide terrain.

ו יָדִין בַּגּוֹיִם
מָלֵא גְוִיּוֹת
מָחַץ רֹאשׁ
עַל־אֶרֶץ רַבָּה׃

7 From the brook
On the road he will drink,
Hence
He holds high his head.

ז מִנַּחַל
בַּדֶּרֶךְ יִשְׁתֶּה
עַל־כֵּן
יָרִים רֹאשׁ׃

4. Taking מלכי צדק (*Gen.* 14:18), and its parallel form אדני צדק (*Jos.* 10.1 ff.) as hereditary title of the king of Jerusalem.

Psalm 111

1 Praise the Eternal!
I will thank the Eternal
With all the heart,
In councils of the forthright and in public.

א הַֽלְלוּ יָהּ ׀
אוֹדֶה יהוה
בְּכׇל־לֵבָב
בְּסוֹד יְשָׁרִים וְעֵדָה׃

2 Great
Are the Eternal's works,
They can be investigated
By all who so desire.

ב גְּדֹלִים
מַעֲשֵׂי יהוה
דְּרוּשִׁים
לְכׇל־חֶפְצֵיהֶם׃

3 Splendor and majesty is His doing
And His justice
Stands forever.

ג הוֹד־וְהָדָר פׇּעֳלוֹ
וְצִדְקָתוֹ
עֹמֶדֶת לָעַד׃

4 A record He made
Of His wonders.
Gracious and merciful is the Eternal.

ד זֵכֶר עָשָׂה
לְנִפְלְאֹתָיו
חַנּוּן וְרַחוּם יהוה׃

5 Edibles
He gave to those who fear Him,
Forever He will remember His covenant.

ה טֶרֶף
נָתַן לִירֵאָיו
יִזְכֹּר לְעוֹלָם בְּרִיתוֹ׃

6 He told to His nation
The force of His deeds,
To give to them
The inheritance of peoples.

ו כֹּחַ מַעֲשָׂיו
הִגִּיד לְעַמּוֹ
לָתֵת לָהֶם
נַחֲלַת גּוֹיִם׃

7 The works of His hands
Are truth and law;
Trustworthy are
All His ordinances,

ז מַעֲשֵׂי יָדָיו
אֱמֶת וּמִשְׁפָּט
נֶאֱמָנִים
כׇּל־פִּקּוּדָיו׃

8 Supported forever,
Executed
In truth and equity.

ח סְמוּכִים לָעַד לְעוֹלָם
עֲשׂוּיִם
בֶּאֱמֶת וְיָשָׁר׃

9 Deliverance
He sent to His nation;
His covenant He ordained forever;
His name is holy and awesome.

ט פְּדוּת ׀
שָׁלַח לְעַמּוֹ
צִוָּה לְעוֹלָם בְּרִיתוֹ
קָדוֹשׁ וְנוֹרָא שְׁמוֹ׃

10 The start of wisdom
Is fear of the Eternal,
Good intelligence
For all who act on it,
His praise
Stands forever!

י רֵאשִׁית חָכְמָה ׀
יִרְאַת יהוה
שֵׂכֶל טוֹב
לְכׇל־עֹשֵׂיהֶם
תְּהִלָּתוֹ
עֹמֶדֶת לָעַד׃

Psalm 112

1 Praise the Eternal!
Hail to a man
Fearing the Eternal;
In His commandments
He takes great pleasure.

א הַלְלוּ יָהּ |
אַשְׁרֵי־אִישׁ
יָרֵא אֶת־יְהוָה
בְּמִצְוֺתָיו
חָפֵץ מְאֹד׃

2 His offspring will be
Strong in the land;
A generation
Virtuous, blessed.

ב גִּבּוֹר בָּאָרֶץ
יִהְיֶה זַרְעוֹ
דּוֹר
יְשָׁרִים יְבֹרָךְ׃

3 Wealth and riches are in his house.
Also his sincerity
Stands forever.

ג הוֹן־וָעֹשֶׁר בְּבֵיתוֹ
וְצִדְקָתוֹ
עֹמֶדֶת לָעַד׃

4 In the darkness shines light
For the virtuous.
He is Compassionate, Merciful, and Just..

ד זָרַח בַּחֹשֶׁךְ אוֹר
לַיְשָׁרִים
חַנּוּן וְרַחוּם וְצַדִּיק׃

5 A man acts sweetly
By being compassionate as creditor,
By supporting his actions in generosity.

ה טוֹב אִישׁ
חוֹנֵן וּמַלְוֶה
יְכַלְכֵּל דְּבָרָיו בְּמִשְׁפָּט׃

6 For eternally he will not stagger.
In eternal remembrance
He will be virtuous.

ו כִּי־לְעוֹלָם לֹא יִמּוֹט
לְזֵכֶר עוֹלָם
יִהְיֶה צַדִּיק׃

7 He will not fear
Bad news.
His intent is proper,
Trusting in the Eternal.

ז מִשְּׁמוּעָה רָעָה
לֹא יִירָא
נָכוֹן לִבּוֹ
בָּטֻחַ בַּיהוָה׃

8 His intent is supported,
He will not fear
Finally he will look down on his enemies.

ח סָמוּךְ לִבּוֹ
לֹא יִירָא
עַד אֲשֶׁר־יִרְאֶה בְצָרָיו׃

9 Alms
He gave to the needy;
His friendship
Stands for ever,
His horn
Will be lifted in honor.

ט פִּזַּר |
נָתַן לָאֶבְיוֹנִים
צִדְקָתוֹ
עֹמֶדֶת לָעַד
קַרְנוֹ
תָּרוּם בְּכָבוֹד׃

10 The criminal will see
And be angry
He will grind his teeth and despair;
The criminal's desire will disappear.

י רָשָׁע יִרְאֶה |
וְכָעָס
שִׁנָּיו יַחֲרֹק וְנָמָס
תַּאֲוַת רְשָׁעִים תֹּאבֵד׃

;

A private poem by David, not part of his official diwan, reflecting his partly Arabic language private life.

3,9. Reading צדק in the Arabic sense of "sincerity"

5. Reading טוב in the Arabic sense of “acting sweetly”, and שפט as Arabic שׂפט “generosity”.

10. נמס, cf. *Job* 9:23.

Psalm 113

1 Praise the Eternal!
Sing praise,
Servants of the Eternal,
Sing praise
Of the Eternal's Name.

א הַלְלוּ יָהּ |
הַלְלוּ
עַבְדֵי יְהוָה
הַלְלוּ
אֶת־שֵׁם יְהוָה׃

2 The Eternal's name shall be praised
From now on
To eternity.

ב יְהִי שֵׁם יְהוָה מְבֹרָךְ
מֵעַתָּה
וְעַד־עוֹלָם

3 From sunrise to its setting
Praised is
The Eternal's Name.

ג מִמִּזְרַח־שֶׁמֶשׁ עַד־מְבוֹאוֹ
מְהֻלָּל
שֵׁם יְהוָה׃

4 High over all peoples
Is the Eternal,
Higher than the Heavens is His glory.

ד רָם עַל־כָּל־גּוֹיִם |
יְהוָה
עַל הַשָּׁמַיִם כְּבוֹדוֹ׃

5 Who is
Like the Eternal our God,
He Who resides very high,

ה מִי
כַּיהוָה אֱלֹהֵינוּ
הַמַּגְבִּיהִי לָשָׁבֶת׃

6 He Who looks down very low
In heaven and on earth

ו הַמַּשְׁפִּילִי לִרְאוֹת
בַּשָּׁמַיִם וּבָאָרֶץ׃

7 He lifts up the poor from the dust,
From dunghills
He elevates the destitute,

ז מְקִימִי מֵעָפָר דָּל
מֵאַשְׁפֹּת
יָרִים אֶבְיוֹן׃

8 To seat him with the nobles,
With
His nation's nobles.

ח לְהוֹשִׁיבִי עִם־נְדִיבִים
עִם
נְדִיבֵי עַמּוֹ

9 He installs
The sterile of the house
As happy mother of children.
Praise the Eternal!

ט מוֹשִׁיבִי |
עֲקֶרֶת הַבַּיִת
אֵם־הַבָּנִים שְׂמֵחָה
הַלְלוּ־יָהּ׃

Psalm 114

1 When Israel moved out	א בְּצֵ֣את יִ֭שְׂרָאֵל
Of Egypt,	מִמִּצְרָ֑יִם
The house of Jacob	בֵּ֥ית יַ֝עֲקֹ֗ב
From a barbarous people,	מֵעַ֥ם לֹעֵֽז׃
2 Then Jehudah became His sanctuary,	ב הָיְתָ֣ה יְהוּדָ֣ה לְקָדְשׁ֑וֹ
Israel	יִ֝שְׂרָאֵ֗ל
His dominions.	מַמְשְׁלוֹתָֽיו׃
3 The Sea saw,	ג הַיָּ֣ם רָ֭אָה
And fled,	וַיָּנֹ֑ס
The Jordan	הַ֝יַּרְדֵּ֗ן
Turned backward,	יִסֹּ֥ב לְאָחֽוֹר׃
4 The mountains	ד הֶ֭הָרִים
Danced like rams,	רָקְד֣וּ כְאֵילִ֑ים
The hills	גְּ֝בָע֗וֹת
Like young sheep.	כִּבְנֵי־צֹֽאן׃
5 What ails you, o Sea,	ה מַה־לְּךָ֣ הַ֭יָּם
That you are fleeing,	כִּ֣י תָנ֑וּס
O Jordan,	הַ֝יַּרְדֵּ֗ן
That you are turning backward,	תִּסֹּ֥ב לְאָחֽוֹר׃
6 O mountains,	ו הֶ֭הָרִים
That you are dancing like rams,	תִּרְקְד֣וּ כְאֵילִ֑ים
Hills	גְּ֝בָע֗וֹת
Like young sheep?	כִּבְנֵי־צֹֽאן׃
7 Before the Master,	ז מִלִּפְנֵ֣י אָ֭דוֹן
Creator of the earth,	ח֣וּלִי אָ֑רֶץ
Before	מִ֝לִּפְנֵ֗י
Jacob's God,	אֱל֥וֹהַּ יַעֲקֹֽב׃
8 He Who turns the rock into a water pool,	ח הַהֹפְכִ֣י הַצּ֣וּר אֲגַם־מָ֑יִם
The pebble,	חַ֝לָּמִ֗ישׁ
Into a water source.	לְמַעְיְנוֹ־מָֽיִם׃

In the Yerushalmi (LXX) tradition, as well the Leningrad Codex, Psalm 115 is part of Psalm 114.

Psalm 115

1 Not to us, Eternal,
Not to us,
But to Your Name
Give honor,
For Your kindness,
For Your truth.

א לֹ֤א לָ֥נוּ יהוה
לֹ֥א לָ֑נוּ
כִּֽי־לְ֭שִׁמְךָ
תֵּ֣ן כָּב֑וֹד
עַל־חַ֝סְדְּךָ֗
עַל־אֲמִתֶּֽךָ׃

2 Why
Should the Gentiles say:
Where now
Is their God?

ב לָ֭מָּה
יֹאמְר֣וּ הַגּוֹיִ֑ם
אַיֵּה־נָ֝֗א
אֱלֹהֵיהֶֽם׃

3 But our God is in Heaven
Whatever He desires, He does.

ג וֵֽאלֹהֵ֥ינוּ בַשָּׁמָ֑יִם
כֹּ֖ל אֲשֶׁר־חָפֵ֣ץ עָשָֽׂה׃

4 Their idols
Are silver and gold,
Crafted by
The hands of men.

ד עֲ֭צַבֵּיהֶם
כֶּ֣סֶף וְזָהָ֑ב
מַ֝עֲשֵׂ֗ה
יְדֵ֣י אָדָֽם׃

5 They have a mouth
But cannot talk,
They have eyes
But cannot see.

ה פֶּֽה־לָ֭הֶם
וְלֹ֣א יְדַבֵּ֑רוּ
עֵינַ֥יִם לָ֝הֶ֗ם
וְלֹ֣א יִרְאֽוּ׃

6 They have ears
But cannot hear,
They have a nose
But cannot smell.

ו אָזְנַ֣יִם לָ֭הֶם
וְלֹ֣א יִשְׁמָ֑עוּ
אַ֥ף לָ֝הֶ֗ם
וְלֹ֣א יְרִיחֽוּן׃

7 With their hands
They cannot feel,
With their feet
They cannot walk,
No voice is
In their throats.

ז יְדֵיהֶ֤ם ׀
וְלֹ֬א יְמִישׁוּ
רַ֭גְלֵיהֶם
וְלֹ֣א יְהַלֵּ֑כוּ
לֹא־יֶ֝הְגּ֗וּ
בִּגְרוֹנָֽם׃

8 Like them
May be their makers,
All who trust in them.

ח כְּ֭מוֹהֶם
יִהְי֣וּ עֹשֵׂיהֶ֑ם
כֹּ֖ל אֲשֶׁר־בֹּטֵ֣חַ בָּהֶֽם׃

9 Israel,
Be trusting in the Eternal,
He is their help and shield.

ט יִ֭שְׂרָאֵל
בְּטַ֣ח בַּיהוָ֑ה
עֶזְרָ֖ם וּמָגִנָּ֣ם הֽוּא׃

10 House of Aaron,
Be trusting in the Eternal,
He is their help and shield.

י בֵּ֣ית אַ֭הֲרֹן
בִּטְח֣וּ בַיהוָ֑ה
עֶזְרָ֖ם וּמָגִנָּ֣ם הֽוּא׃

11 Those fearing the Eternal,
  Be trusting in the Eternal,;
He is their help and shield.

יא יִרְאֵי יהוה
בִּטְחוּ בַיהוָה
עֶזְרָם וּמָגִנָּם הוּא׃

12 The Eternal
  Will bless those who remember us,
Will bless
  The house of Israel,
Will bless
  The house of Aaron.

יב יהוה
זְכָרָנוּ יְבָרֵךְ
יְבָרֵךְ
אֶת־בֵּית יִשְׂרָאֵל
יְבָרֵךְ
אֶת־בֵּית אַהֲרֹן׃

13 He will bless
  Those who fear the Eternal,
The small ones
  With the great ones.

יג יְבָרֵךְ
יִרְאֵי יְהוָה
הַקְּטַנִּים
עִם־הַגְּדֹלִים׃

14 May the Eternal give increase to you,
To you
  And your sons.

יד יֹסֵף יְהוָה עֲלֵיכֶם
עֲלֵיכֶם
וְעַל־בְּנֵיכֶם׃

15 You are blessed
  Before the Eternal,
Maker
  Of Heaven and Earth.

טו בְּרוּכִים אַתֶּם
לַיהוָה
עֹשֵׂה
שָׁמַיִם וָאָרֶץ׃

16 The Heavens are Heavens
  For the Eternal,
But the earth
  He gave to mankind.

טז הַשָּׁמַיִם שָׁמַיִם
לַיהוָה
וְהָאָרֶץ
נָתַן לִבְנֵי־אָדָם׃

17 The dead
  Do not sing praise to the Eternal,
Nor do
  All those descending into Silence.

יז לֹא־הַמֵּתִים
יְהַלְלוּ־יָהּ
וְלֹא
כׇּל־יֹרְדֵי דוּמָה׃

18 But we
  Shall praise the Eternal,
From now to eternity.
  Hallelujah.

יח וַאֲנַחְנוּ ׀
נְבָרֵךְ יָהּ
מֵעַתָּה וְעַד־עוֹלָם
הַלְלוּ־יָהּ׃

Psalm 116

1 I am loving;
Certainly,
The Eternal listened,
To my voice,
My supplications.

א אָהַבְתִּי
כִּֽי־יִשְׁמַ֥ע ׀
יְהֹוָ֑ה
אֶת־ק֝וֹלִ֗י
תַּחֲנוּנָֽי׃

2 Truly He turned His ear to me
When I would call Him in my days.

ב כִּֽי־הִטָּ֣ה אָזְנ֣וֹ לִ֑י
וּבְיָמַ֥י אֶקְרָֽא׃

3 Fetters of Death
Surrounded me,
Netherworld's boundaries found me,
I would find sorrow and trouble.

ג אֲפָפ֤וּנִי ׀
חֶבְלֵי־מָ֗וֶת
וּמְצָרֵ֣י שְׁא֣וֹל מְצָא֑וּנִי
צָרָ֖ה וְיָג֣וֹן אֶמְצָֽא׃

4 But to the Eternal's Name I would appeal:
Please, Eternal,
Let my soul escape!

ד וּבְשֵׁם־יְהֹוָ֥ה אֶקְרָ֑א
אָנָּ֥ה יְ֝הֹוָ֗ה
מַלְּטָ֥ה נַפְשִֽׁי׃

5 The Eternal is kind and just,
And our God merciful.

ה חַנּ֣וּן יְהֹוָ֣ה וְצַדִּ֑יק
וֵ֖אלֹהֵ֣ינוּ מְרַחֵֽם׃

6 The Eternal watches over fools.
I became poor
But He will help me.

ו שֹׁמֵ֣ר פְּתָאיִ֣ם יְהֹוָ֑ה
דַּ֝לּוֹתִ֗י
וְלִ֣י יְהוֹשִֽׁיעַ׃

7 Return, my soul,
To your quiet,
Certainly the Eternal
Did favor you.

ז שׁוּבִ֣י נַ֭פְשִׁי
לִמְנוּחָ֑יְכִי
כִּֽי־יְ֝הֹוָ֗ה
גָּמַ֥ל עָלָֽיְכִי׃

8 Truly You rescued my soul from Death,
My eye from tears,
My foot from being pushed,

ח כִּ֤י חִלַּ֡צְתָּ נַפְשִׁ֬י מִמָּ֗וֶת
אֶת־עֵינִ֥י מִן־דִּמְעָ֑ה
אֶת־רַגְלִ֥י מִדֶּֽחִי׃

9 I shall wander
Before the Eternal,
In the Lands
Of the Living.

ט אֶ֭תְהַלֵּךְ
לִפְנֵ֣י יְהֹוָ֑ה
בְּ֝אַרְצ֗וֹת
הַֽחַיִּֽים׃

10 I did believe it
When I said,
"I am
Very deprived,"

י הֶ֭אֱמַנְתִּי
כִּ֣י אֲדַבֵּ֑ר
אֲ֝נִ֗י
עָנִ֥יתִי מְאֹֽד׃

11 I
Said rashly,
"All men are false."

יא אֲ֭נִי
אָמַ֣רְתִּי בְחָפְזִ֑י
כָּֽל־הָאָדָ֥ם כֹּזֵֽב׃

12 How shall I give back to the Eternal
All His bounties toward me?

יב מָה־אָשִׁיב לַ יהוָה
כָּל־תַּגְמוּלוֹהִי עָלָי׃

13 I shall lift up a cup of salvations,
And invoke the Eternal's Name.

יג כּוֹס־יְשׁוּעוֹת אֶשָּׂא
וּבְשֵׁם יהוָה אֶקְרָא׃

14 My vows
I shall pay to the Eternal,
In the presence
Of His entire people.

יד נְדָרַי
לַיהוָה אֲשַׁלֵּם
נֶגְדָה־נָּא
לְכָל־עַמּוֹ׃

15 Grave it is
In the Eternal's eyes
To hand His pious ones
Over to Death.

טו יָקָר
בְּעֵינֵי יהוָה
הַמָּוְתָה
לַחֲסִידָיו׃

16 O Eternal,
Because I am Your slave,
I am Your slave,
Son of Your bondmaid,
You unbound
My fetters.

טז אָנָּה יהוה
כִּי־אֲנִי עַבְדֶּךָ
אֲנִי עַבְדְּךָ
בֶּן־אֲמָתֶךָ
פִּתַּחְתָּ
לְמוֹסֵרָי׃

17 To You I shall bring
A sacrifice of thanksgiving,
I shall invoke the Eternal's Name.

יז לְךָ־אֶזְבַּח
זֶבַח תּוֹדָה
וּבְשֵׁם יהוָה אֶקְרָא׃

18 I shall pay my vows to the Eternal
In the presence
Of His entire people,

יח נְדָרַי לַיהוָה אֲשַׁלֵּם
נֶגְדָה־נָּא
לְכָל־עַמּוֹ׃

19 In the courtyards of
The Eternal's House,
In the center of Jerusalem,
Hallelujah!

יט בְּחַצְרוֹת |
בֵּית יהוה
בְּתוֹכֵכִי יְרוּשָׁלָם
הַלְלוּ־יָהּ׃

In this Psalm, as in the preceding one, Death is the eternal death of those who go down into Silence or the Pit; Life is eternal life in the Land of the Living souls.

15. Deriving יקר from Arabic וקר "grave".

Psalm 117

1 Sing the praise of the Eternal
All Gentiles,
Laud Him,
All nations,

א הַלְלוּ אֶת־יהוה
כָּל־גּוֹיִם
שַׁבְּחוּהוּ
כָּל־הָאֻמִּים׃

2 Truly, overpowering to us
Is His kindness
And the Eternal is true forever,
Hallelujah!

ב כִּי גָבַר עָלֵינוּ ׀
חַסְדּוֹ
וֶאֱמֶת־יהוָה לְעוֹלָם
הַלְלוּ־יָהּ

Psalm 118

1 Give thanks to the Eternal, the truly Good One,
Truly, His kindness is forever.

א הוֹדוּ לַיהוָה כִּי־טוֹב
כִּי לְעוֹלָם חַסְדּוֹ׃

2 Let Israel say:
Truly, His kindness is forever.

ב יֹאמַר־נָא יִשְׂרָאֵל
כִּי לְעוֹלָם חַסְדּוֹ׃

3 Let the house of Aaron say:
Truly, His kindness is forever.

ג יֹאמְרוּ נָא בֵית־אַהֲרֹן
כִּי לְעוֹלָם חַסְדּוֹ׃

4 Let those say
Who fear the Eternal:
Truly, His kindness is forever.

ד יֹאמְרוּ נָא
יִרְאֵי יהוָה
כִּי לְעוֹלָם חַסְדּוֹ׃

5 From distress
I called the Eternal;
He answered me in the Eternal's wideness.

ה מִן־הַמֵּצַר
קָרָאתִי יָּהּ
עָנָנִי בַמֶּרְחָב יָהּ׃

6 The Eternal is with me,
I shall not fear.
What can man do to me?

ו יהוָה לִי
לֹא אִירָא
מַה־יַּעֲשֶׂה לִי אָדָם׃

7 The Eternal is with me,
Among my helpers,
Then I
Shall look down on my enemies.

ז יהוָה לִי
בְּעֹזְרָי
וַאֲנִי
אֶרְאֶה בְשֹׂנְאָי׃

8 It is better
To seek shelter in the Eternal
Than to trust
In man;

ח טוֹב
לַחֲסוֹת בַּיהוָה
מִבְּטֹחַ
בָּאָדָם׃

9 It is better
To seek shelter in the Eternal
Than to trust
In princes.

ט טוֹב
לַחֲסוֹת בַּיהוָה
מִבְּטֹחַ
בִּנְדִיבִים׃

10 All Gentiles surround me,
But in the Name of the Eternal
I shall make them bend.

י כָּל־גּוֹיִם סְבָבוּנִי
בְּשֵׁם יְהוָה
כִּי אֲמִילַם׃

11 They encircle and surround me,
But in the Eternal's Name
I shall make them bend.

יא סַבּוּנִי גַם־סְבָבוּנִי
בְּשֵׁם יְהוָה
כִּי אֲמִילַם׃

12 They encircle me like bees,
They are destructive
Like fire of thorns,
But in the Eternal's Name
I shall make them bend.

יב סַבּוּנִי כִדְבוֹרִים
דֹּעֲכוּ
כְּאֵשׁ קוֹצִים
בְּשֵׁם יְהוָה
כִּי אֲמִילַם׃

13 You pushed me until I was falling,
But the Eternal helped me.

יג דָּחֹה דְחִיתַנִי לִנְפֹּל
וַיהוָה עֲזָרָנִי׃

14 The Eternal's power and cutting edge
Was my
Salvation.

יד עָזִּי וְזִמְרָת יָהּ
וַיְהִי־לִי
לִישׁוּעָה׃

15 A sound
Of song and salvation
Is in the tents of the just.
The Eternal's right hand
Does powerful deeds.

טו קוֹל ׀
רִנָּה וִישׁוּעָה
בְּאָהֳלֵי צַדִּיקִים
יְמִין יְהוָה
עֹשָׂה חָיִל׃

16 The Eternal's right hand
Is lifted up;
The Eternal's right hand
Does powerful deeds.

טז יְמִין יהוה
רוֹמֵמָה
יְמִין יְהוָה
עֹשָׂה חָיִל׃

17 I shall not die, certainly I shall live,
And I shall tell
The Eternal's works.

יז לֹא אָמוּת כִּי־אֶחְיֶה
וַאֲסַפֵּר
מַעֲשֵׂי יָהּ׃

18 The Eternal severely punished me,
But to Death
He did not hand me over.

יח יַסֹּר יִסְּרַנִּי יָּהּ
וְלַמָּוֶת
לֹא נְתָנָנִי׃

19 Open for me the gates of truth;
I shall enter them
And thank the Eternal.

יט פִּתְחוּ־לִי שַׁעֲרֵי־צֶדֶק
אָבֹא־בָם
אוֹדֶה יָהּ׃

20 This is the Eternal's Gate,	כ זֶה־הַשַּׁעַר לַיהוָה
The just	צַדִּיקִים
Will enter thereby.	יָבֹאוּ בוֹ׃
21 I am thanking You,	כא אוֹדְךָ
Since You answered me,	כִּי עֲנִיתָנִי
And You were	וַתְּהִי־לִי
My salvation.	לִישׁוּעָה׃
22 The stone	כב אֶבֶן
Rejected by the builders	מָאֲסוּ הַבּוֹנִים
Became	הָיְתָה
The cornerstone.	לְרֹאשׁ פִּנָּה׃
23 From the Eternal	כג מֵאֵת יהוה
This happened,	הָיְתָה זֹּאת
It is wonderful in our eyes.	הִיא נִפְלָאת בְּעֵינֵינוּ׃
24 This is the day	כד זֶה־הַיּוֹם
The Eternal made;	עָשָׂה יהוָה
Let us enjoy and be happy on it.	נָגִילָה וְנִשְׂמְחָה בוֹ׃
25 Please, Eternal,	כה אָנָּא יהוה
Please save!	הוֹשִׁיעָה נָּא
Please, Eternal,	אָנָּא יהוה
Please make succeed!	הַצְלִיחָה נָּא׃
26 Blessed is he who comes	כו בָּרוּךְ הַבָּא
In the Eternal's name,	בְּשֵׁם יהוָה
We bless you	בֵּרַכְנוּכֶם
From the Eternal's House.	מִבֵּית יהוָה׃
27 The Eternal	כז אֵל ׀
Is the Powerful,	יהוה
He enlightens us;	וַיָּאֶר לָנוּ
Bind the festival sacrifice with braided cord,	אִסְרוּ־חַג בַּעֲבֹתִים
To the corners	עַד קַרְנוֹת
Of the altar.	הַמִּזְבֵּחַ׃
28 You are my Powerful, I shall thank You,	כח אֵלִי אַתָּה וְאוֹדֶךָּ
My God,	אֱלֹהַי
I shall exalt You.	אֲרוֹמְמֶךָּ׃
29 Give thanks to the Eternal, the truly Good One;	כט הוֹדוּ לַיהוָה כִּי־טוֹב
Truly, His kindness is forever.	כִּי לְעוֹלָם חַסְדּוֹ

11 ff. Taking אמילם as regular causative of the Arabic root מיל "to bend".

14. This translation of עזי וזמרת follows Rashi to *Ex.* 15:2.

25. There is a suggestion to read אניהו "powerful one" instead of אנא ײ to eliminate the seemingly superfluous נא in the second line, but Oniyahu, known from a votive inscription in the Negev, could as well be a contraction of אנא ײ.

In contrast to Norzi and modern editions, all old sources treat the two parts of the verse as metrically equivalent (reading *hoshî`a nna, haṣlîḥa nna.*)

Psalm 119

1 Hail to those of perfect ways
Who walk
In the Eternal's teaching.

א אַשְׁרֵי תְמִימֵי־דָרֶךְ
הַהֹלְכִים
בְּתוֹרַת יהוָה׃

2 Hail to those
Who keep His testimonials
They seek Him with a full heart.

ב אַשְׁרֵי
נֹצְרֵי עֵדֹתָיו
בְּכָל־לֵב יִדְרְשׁוּהוּ׃

3 Clearly
They will do no evil
Going in His ways.

ג אַף
לֹא־פָעֲלוּ עַוְלָה
בִּדְרָכָיו הָלָכוּ׃

4 You
Commanded Your orders
To be scrupulously kept.

ד אַתָּה
צִוִּיתָה פִקֻּדֶיךָ
לִשְׁמֹר מְאֹד׃

5 I am praying
That my paths shall be firm
In keeping Your edicts.

ה אַחֲלַי
יִכֹּנוּ דְרָכָי
לִשְׁמֹר חֻקֶּיךָ׃

6 Then I shall not be put to shame
When I consider
All Your commandments.

ו אָז לֹא־אֵבוֹשׁ
בְּהַבִּיטִי
אֶל־כָּל־מִצְוֺתֶיךָ׃

7 I am thanking You
With a sincere heart
When I am studying
Your true laws.

ז אוֹדְךָ
בְּיֹשֶׁר לֵבָב
בְּלָמְדִי
מִשְׁפְּטֵי צִדְקֶךָ׃

8 Your edicts I shall keep,
Lest You abandon me, very strictly.

ח אֶת־חֻקֶּיךָ אֶשְׁמֹר
אַל־תַּעַזְבֵנִי עַד־מְאֹד׃

9 How can a youth choose
A winning way,
Other than by keeping
Your edicts?

ט בַּמֶּה יְזַכֶּה־נַּעַר
אֶת־אָרְחוֹ
לִשְׁמֹר
כִּדְבָרֶךָ׃

10 I sought You with all my hear;
Do not let me err
Away from Your commandments.

י בְּכָל־לִבִּי דְרַשְׁתִּיךָ
אַל־תַּשְׁגֵּנִי
מִמִּצְוֺתֶיךָ׃

11 In my heart
I hid Your instructions
So that
I should not sin against You.

יא בְּלִבִּי
צָפַנְתִּי אִמְרָתֶךָ
לְמַעַן
לֹא אֶחֱטָא־לָךְ׃

12 Praise to You, Eternal,
Who teaches His edicts to me.

יב בָּרוּךְ אַתָּה יהוָה
לַמְּדֵנִי חֻקֶּיךָ׃

13 With my lips I told
All
Laws of Your saying.

יג בִּשְׂפָתַי סִפַּרְתִּי
כֹּל
מִשְׁפְּטֵי־פִיךָ׃

14 Stating Your testimonials I rejoiced
More than about any wealth.

יד בְּדֶרֶךְ עֵדְוֺתֶיךָ שַׂשְׂתִּי
כְּעַל כָּל־הוֹן׃

15 I shall talk about Your orders
And gaze
Upon Your practices.

טו בְּפִקֻּדֶיךָ אָשִׂיחָה
וְאַבִּיטָה
אֹרְחֹתֶיךָ׃

16 I revel in Your edicts,
Never shall I forget Your word.

טז בְּחֻקֹּתֶיךָ אֶשְׁתַּעֲשָׁע
לֹא אֶשְׁכַּח דְּבָרֶךָ׃

17 Do a favor for Your servant, let me live,
So I can keep Your word.

יז גְּמֹל עַל־עַבְדְּךָ אֶחְיֶה
וְאֶשְׁמְרָה דְבָרֶךָ׃

18 Open my eyes so I can see
The wonders
Of Your teaching.

יח גַּל־עֵינַי וְאַבִּיטָה
נִפְלָאוֹת
מִתּוֹרָתֶךָ׃

19 A stranger I am in the Land,
Do not hide from me
Your commandments.

יט גֵּר אָנֹכִי בָאָרֶץ
אַל־תַּסְתֵּר מִמֶּנִּי
מִצְוֺתֶיךָ׃

20 My soul languishes with desire
For Your laws, at any time.

כ גָּרְסָה נַפְשִׁי לְתַאֲבָה
אֶל־מִשְׁפָּטֶיךָ בְכָל־עֵת׃

21 You roared
At cursed criminals
Who err away
From Your commandments.

כא גָּעַרְתָּ
זֵדִים אֲרוּרִים
הַשֹּׁגִים
מִמִּצְוֺתֶיךָ׃

22 Roll away from me
Shame and insult,
For I kept Your testimonials.

כב גַּל מָעָלַי
חֶרְפָּה וָבוּז
כִּי עֵדֹתֶיךָ נָצָרְתִּי׃

23 Even when the sinners
Talk together about me,
Your servant
Will continue talking about Your edicts.

כג גַּם יָשְׁבוּ שָׂרִים
בִּי נִדְבָּרוּ
עַבְדְּךָ
יָשִׂיחַ בְּחֻקֶּיךָ׃

24 Also Your testimonials
Are my enjoyment,
The men of my counsel.

כד גַּם־עֵדֹתֶיךָ
שַׁעֲשֻׁעָי
אַנְשֵׁי עֲצָתִי׃

24 I am glued to dust;
Revive me,
By Your word.

כה דָּבְקָה לֶעָפָר נַפְשִׁי
חַיֵּנִי
כִּדְבָרֶךָ׃

26 I noted my ways
And You answered me.
Teach me Your laws.

כו דְּרָכַי סִפַּרְתִּי
וַתַּעֲנֵנִי
לַמְּדֵנִי חֻקֶּיךָ׃

27 Let me understand the ways of Your ordinances;
Then I will talk
About your wonders.

כז דֶּֽרֶךְ־פִּקּוּדֶיךָ הֲבִינֵנִי
וְאָשִׂיחָה
בְּנִפְלְאוֹתֶֽיךָ׃

28 My heart is dripping
From sorrow.
Straighten me
By Your word.

כח דָּלְפָה נַפְשִׁי
מִתּוּגָה
קַיְּמֵנִי
כִּדְבָרֶֽךָ׃

29 Remove from me
Lying behavior
And favor me with Your teaching.

כט דֶּֽרֶךְ שֶׁקֶר
הָסֵר מִמֶּנִּי
וְתוֹרָתְךָ חָנֵּֽנִי׃

30 I chose the way of faith
And enforced Your judgments.

ל דֶּֽרֶךְ־אֱמוּנָה בָחָרְתִּי
מִשְׁפָּטֶיךָ שִׁוִּֽיתִי׃

31 I clang to Your testimonials;
Eternal,
Do not put me to shame.

לא דָּבַקְתִּי בְעֵדְוֺתֶיךָ
יהוה
אַל־תְּבִישֵֽׁנִי׃

32 I shall run in the way of Your commandments,
Because it widens my understanding.

לב דֶּֽרֶךְ־מִצְוֺתֶיךָ אָרוּץ
כִּי תַרְחִיב לִבִּֽי׃

33 Teach me, Eternal,
The understanding of Your edicts
And I shall preserve them consistently.

לג **ה**וֹרֵנִי יהוה
דֶּרֶךְ חֻקֶּיךָ
וְאֶצְּרֶנָּה עֵֽקֶב׃

34 Let me understand,
So I can preserve Your teaching
And keep it with a full heart.

לד הֲבִינֵנִי
וְאֶצְּרָה תֽוֹרָתֶךָ
וְאֶשְׁמְרֶנָּה בְכָל־לֵֽב׃

35 Instruct me
In the path of Your commandments
For that is my desire.

לה הַדְרִיכֵנִי
בִּנְתִיב מִצְוֺתֶיךָ
כִּי בוֹ חָפָֽצְתִּי׃

36 Bend my heart
To Your testimonials
And not to gain.

לו הַט־לִבִּי
אֶל־עֵדְוֺתֶיךָ
וְאַל אֶל־בָּֽצַע׃

37 Turn my eyes away
From seeing vain things,
Revive me by Your ways.

לז הַעֲבֵר עֵינַי
מֵרְאוֹת שָׁוְא
בִּדְרָכֶךָ חַיֵּֽנִי׃

38 Confirm to Your servant
Your directives,
Happiness
For those who fear You.

לח הָקֵם לְעַבְדְּךָ
אִמְרָתֶךָ
אֲשֶׁר
לְיִרְאָתֶֽךָ׃

39 Remove my shame
That I dreaded;
Truly, Your laws are good.

לט הַעֲבֵר חֶרְפָּתִי
אֲשֶׁר יָגֹרְתִּי
כִּי מִשְׁפָּטֶיךָ טוֹבִֽים׃

40 Lo,
I desire Your ordinances,
Revive me by Your justice.

מ הִנֵּה
תָּאַבְתִּי לְפִקֻּדֶיךָ
בְּצִדְקָתְךָ חַיֵּנִי׃

41 Eternal, may Your kindness bring me
Your salvation,
By Your directives.

מא וִיבֹאֻנִי חֲסָדֶךָ יהוה
תְּשׁוּעָתְךָ
כְּאִמְרָתֶךָ׃

42 Then I can answer my slanderers definitely
For I trusted
In Your word.

מב וְאֶעֱנֶה חֹרְפִי דָבָר
כִּי־בָטַחְתִּי
בִּדְבָרֶךָ׃

43 Do not snatch from my mouth the real truth
For I am yearning for Your laws.

מג וְאַל־תַּצֵּל מִפִּי דְבַר־אֱמֶת עַד־מְאֹד
כִּי לְמִשְׁפָּטֶךָ יִחָלְתִּי׃

44 May I keep Your teachings always,
Forever.

מד וְאֶשְׁמְרָה תוֹרָתְךָ תָמִיד
לְעוֹלָם וָעֶד׃

45 May I wander the wide road
For I seek Your commandments.

מה וְאֶתְהַלְּכָה בָרְחָבָה
כִּי פִקֻּדֶיךָ דָרָשְׁתִּי׃

46 I shall talk about Your testimonials
Before kings
And not be ashamed.

מו וַאֲדַבְּרָה בְעֵדֹתֶיךָ
נֶגֶד מְלָכִים
וְלֹא אֵבוֹשׁ׃

47 I shall relish Your commandments
Which I love.

מז וְאֶשְׁתַּעֲשַׁע בְּמִצְוֹתֶיךָ
אֲשֶׁר אָהָבְתִּי׃

48 I shall lift my hands to Your commandments
Which I love,
And talk about Your laws.

מח וְאֶשָּׂא כַפַּי אֶל־מִצְוֹתֶיךָ
אֲשֶׁר אָהָבְתִּי
וְאָשִׂיחָה בְחֻקֶּיךָ׃

49 Remember the word to Your servant
Which
You made me pray for.

מט זְכֹר־דָּבָר לְעַבְדֶּךָ
עַל
אֲשֶׁר יִחַלְתָּנִי׃

50 That is my consolation in my deprivation:
Truly, Your instruction keeps me alive.

נ זֹאת נֶחָמָתִי בְעָנְיִי
כִּי אִמְרָתְךָ חִיָּתְנִי׃

51 Criminals
Slandered me exceedingly,
From Your teaching
I did not swerve.

נא זֵדִים
הֱלִיצֻנִי עַד־מְאֹד
מִתּוֹרָתְךָ
לֹא נָטִיתִי׃

52 I remember Your laws from eternity,
Eternal,
And am consoled.

נב זָכַרְתִּי מִשְׁפָּטֶיךָ מֵעוֹלָם |
יהוה
וָאֶתְנֶחָם׃

53 Trembling gripped me,
Because of the wicked,
Those who abandon
Your teaching.

נג זַלְעָפָה אֲחָזַתְנִי
מֵרְשָׁעִים
עֹזְבֵי
תּוֹרָתֶךָ׃

54 Songs
Were Your laws to me
In the house where I dwell.

נד זְמִרוֹת
הָיוּ־לִי חֻקֶּיךָ
בְּבֵית מְגוּרָי׃

55 In the night I remember Your name, Eternal,
And I shall watch
Your teaching.

נה זָכַרְתִּי בַלַּיְלָה שִׁמְךָ יהוה
וָאֶשְׁמְרָה
תּוֹרָתֶךָ׃

56 That is my property:
That I kept Your orders.

נו זֹאת הָיְתָה־לִּי
כִּי פִקֻּדֶיךָ נָצָרְתִּי׃

57 My part, Eternal, I said,
Is to watch Your words.

נז **חֶ**לְקִי יהוה אָמַרְתִּי
לִשְׁמֹר דְּבָרֶיךָ׃

58 I am pleadimg before You with all my heart:
Be gracious to me,
As of Your instruction.

נח חִלִּיתִי פָנֶיךָ בְכָל־לֵב
חָנֵּנִי
כְּאִמְרָתֶךָ׃

59 I thought about my ways
And returned my feet
To Your testimonials.

נט חִשַּׁבְתִּי דְרָכָי
וָאָשִׁיבָה רַגְלַי
אֶל־עֵדֹתֶיךָ׃

60 I was quick
And did not tarry
To keep
Your commandments.

ס חַשְׁתִּי
וְלֹא הִתְמַהְמָהְתִּי
לִשְׁמֹר
מִצְוֹתֶיךָ׃

61 Bands of wicked ones walled me in,
Your teaching
I did not forget.

סא חֶבְלֵי רְשָׁעִים עִוְּדֻנִי
תּוֹרָתְךָ
לֹא שָׁכָחְתִּי׃

62 At midnight I get up
To thank You
For
Your just laws.

סב חֲצוֹת־לַיְלָה אָקוּם
לְהוֹדוֹת לָךְ
עַל
מִשְׁפְּטֵי צִדְקֶךָ׃

63 I am a comrade
Of all who fear You,
And of those who keep
Your ordinances.

סג חָבֵר אָנִי
לְכָל־אֲשֶׁר יְרֵאוּךָ
וּלְשֹׁמְרֵי
פִּקּוּדֶיךָ׃

64 Your kindness, Eternal,
Fills the Land;
Teach me Your laws
.

סד חַסְדְּךָ יְיָ
מָלְאָה הָאָרֶץ
חֻקֶּיךָ לַמְּדֵנִי׃

65 The best
You did with Your servant,
Eternal,
True to Your word.

סה **ט**וֹב
עָשִׂיתָ עִם־עַבְדְּךָ
יהוה
כִּדְבָרֶךָ׃

66 Teach me the best of reason and wisdom
For I believe in Your commandments.

סו טוּב טַעַם וָדַעַת לַמְּדֵנִי
כִּי בְמִצְוֹתֶיךָ הֶאֱמָנְתִּי׃

67 Before I reflected,
I was erring,
But now,
I kept Your instruction!

סז טֶרֶם אֶעֱנֶה
אֲנִי שֹׁגֵג
וְעַתָּה
אִמְרָתְךָ שָׁמָרְתִּי׃

68 You are good and doing good,
Teach me Your laws.

סח טוֹב־אַתָּה וּמֵטִיב
לַמְּדֵנִי חֻקֶּיךָ׃

69 Criminals heaped lies upon me.
As for me,
With all my heart
Shall I watch Your orders.

סט טָפְלוּ עָלַי שֶׁקֶר זֵדִים
אֲנִי
בְּכָל־לֵב ׀
אֱצֹּר פִּקּוּדֶיךָ׃

70 Fat as lard is their heart.
But for me,
Your teaching is my recreation.

ע טָפַשׁ כַּחֵלֶב לִבָּם
אֲנִי
תּוֹרָתְךָ שִׁעֲשָׁעְתִּי׃

71 It served me well that I was deprived
So that
I would study Your laws.

עא טוֹב־לִי כִי־עֻנֵּיתִי
לְמַעַן
אֶלְמַד חֻקֶּיךָ׃

72 The teaching of Your mouth is better for me
Than thousands
Of gold and silver.

עב טוֹב־לִי תוֹרַת פִּיךָ
מֵאַלְפֵי
זָהָב וָכָסֶף׃

73 Your hands made me
And planted me firmly;
Give me understanding,
So I may learn Your commandments.

עג יָדֶיךָ עָשׂוּנִי
וַיְכוֹנְנוּנִי
הֲבִינֵנִי
וְאֶלְמְדָה מִצְוֹתֶיךָ׃

74 Those who fear You,
Shall see me and enjoy,
For Your word I sought.

עד יְרֵאֶיךָ
יִרְאוּנִי וְיִשְׂמָחוּ
כִּי לִדְבָרְךָ יִחָלְתִּי׃

75 I know, Eternal
That Your judgment is just
And faithfulness
Deprived me.

עה יָדַעְתִּי יהוה
כִּי־צֶדֶק מִשְׁפָּטֶיךָ
וֶאֱמוּנָה
עִנִּיתָנִי׃

76 May now Your grace please console me,
By Your instruction to Your servant.

עו יְהִי־נָא חַסְדְּךָ לְנַחֲמֵנִי
כְּאִמְרָתְךָ לְעַבְדֶּךָ׃

77 May Your mercy come to me to enliven,
For Your teaching
Is my diversion.

עז יְבֹאוּנִי רַחֲמֶיךָ וְאֶחְיֶה
כִּי תוֹרָתְךָ
שַׁעֲשֻׁעָי׃

78 May the criminals come to shame,
For they indicted me by lies,
But I
Shall lecture about Your orders.

עח יֵבֹשׁוּ זֵדִים
כִּי־שֶׁקֶר עִוְּתוּנִי
אֲנִי
אָשִׂיחַ בְּפִקּוּדֶיךָ׃

79 Those who fear You may return to me,
And those who know
Your testimonials.

עט יָשׁוּבוּ־לִי יְרֵאֶיךָ
וְידְעו [וְיֹדְעֵי]
עֵדֹתֶיךָ׃

80 May my heart be perfect in Your laws
So that
I shall not come to shame.

פ יְהִי־לִבִּי תָמִים בְּחֻקֶּיךָ
לְמַעַן
לֹא אֵבוֹשׁ׃

81 My soul craves for Your salvation,
I am yearning for Your word.

פא כָּלְתָה לִתְשׁוּעָתְךָ נַפְשִׁי
לִדְבָרְךָ יִחָלְתִּי׃

82 My eyes crave
For Your instruction,
Expressing:
When will You console me?

פב כָּלוּ עֵינַי
לְאִמְרָתֶךָ
לֵאמֹר
מָתַי תְּנַחֲמֵנִי׃

83 For I was
Like a skin being smoked;
Your edicts
I did not forget.

פג כִּי־הָיִיתִי
כְּנֹאד בְּקִיטוֹר
חֻקֶּיךָ
לֹא שָׁכָחְתִּי׃

84 How many are the days of Your servant?
When will You pass judgment on my pursuers?

פד כַּמָּה יְמֵי עַבְדֶּךָ
מָתַי תַּעֲשֶׂה בְרֹדְפַי מִשְׁפָּט׃

85 Criminals dug trenches for me,
Not
According to Your teaching.

פה כָּרוּ־לִי זֵדִים שִׁיחוֹת
אֲשֶׁר
לֹא כְתוֹרָתֶךָ׃

86 All Your commandments are faithful.
With lies they pursued me; help me!

פו כָּל־מִצְוֹתֶיךָ אֱמוּנָה
שֶׁקֶר רְדָפוּנִי עָזְרֵנִי׃

87 Almost,
They destroyed me in the Land,
But I
Did not abandon Your ordinances.

פז כִּמְעַט
כִּלּוּנִי בָאָרֶץ
וַאֲנִי
לֹא־עָזַבְתִּי פִקֻּדֶיךָ׃

88 By Your kindness keep me alive
That I may keep
The testimonial of Your mouth.

פח כְּחַסְדְּךָ חַיֵּנִי
וְאֶשְׁמְרָה
עֵדוּת פִּיךָ׃

89 Forever, Eternal,
Your word
Is pitched in Heaven.

פט לְעוֹלָם יהוה
דְּבָרְךָ
נִצָּב בַּשָּׁמָיִם׃

90 For all generations
Is Your faithfulness.
You founded the earth
And it stood.

צ לְדֹר וָדֹר
אֱמוּנָתֶךָ
כּוֹנַנְתָּ אֶרֶץ
וַתַּעֲמֹד׃

91 In Your judgment
They are standing today,
Surely, all are Your servants.

צא לְמִשְׁפָּטֶיךָ
עָמְדוּ הַיּוֹם
כִּי הַכֹּל עֲבָדֶיךָ׃

92 If Your teachings
Were not my recreation
Then
I would have been lost in my suffering.

צב לוּלֵי תוֹרָתְךָ
שַׁעֲשֻׁעָי
אָז
אָבַדְתִּי בְעָנְיִי׃

93 Never
Shall I forget Your orders
For by them
You kept me alive.

צג לְעוֹלָם
לֹא־אֶשְׁכַּח פִּקּוּדֶיךָ
כִּי־בָם
חִיִּיתָנִי׃

94 I am Yours,
Save me,
For I am looking out for Your orders.

צד לְךָ־אֲנִי
הוֹשִׁיעֵנִי
כִּי פִקּוּדֶיךָ דָרָשְׁתִּי׃

95 Wicked men waited for me to destroy me,
Through Your testimonials
I got understanding.

צה לִי קִוּוּ רְשָׁעִים לְאַבְּדֵנִי
עֵדֹתֶיךָ
אֶתְבּוֹנָן׃

96 For all that can be measured,
I see a bound;
Your commandment is exceedingly wide.

צו לְכָל תִּכְלָה
רָאִיתִי קֵץ
רְחָבָה מִצְוָתְךָ מְאֹד׃

97 How did I love Your teaching;
All day long
It is my talk.

צז **מָ**ה־אָהַבְתִּי תוֹרָתֶךָ
כָּל־הַיּוֹם
הִיא שִׂיחָתִי׃

98 Over my enemies
Your commandment made me wise.
Truly it is mine forever.

צח מֵאֹיְבַי
תְּחַכְּמֵנִי מִצְוֹתֶךָ
כִּי לְעוֹלָם הִיא־לִי׃

99 From all my teachers did I learn
For Your testimonials
Are my talk.

צט מִכָּל־מְלַמְּדַי הִשְׂכַּלְתִּי
כִּי עֵדְוֺתֶיךָ
שִׂיחָה לִי׃

100 More than elders did I get understanding
For I kept Your orders.

ק מִזְּקֵנִים אֶתְבּוֹנָן
כִּי פִקּוּדֶיךָ נָצָרְתִּי׃

101 Away from any evil way
I locked up my feet
With the intent
Of keeping Your word.

קא מִכָּל־אֹרַח רָע
כָּלִאתִי רַגְלָי
לְמַעַן
אֶשְׁמֹר דְּבָרֶךָ׃

102 From Your law I did not deviate
Because You
Taught it to me.

קב מִמִּשְׁפָּטֶיךָ לֹא־סָרְתִּי
כִּי־אַתָּה
הוֹרֵתָנִי׃

103 How smooth for my palate
Is Your instruction,
Better than honey for my mouth.

קג מַה־נִּמְלְצוּ לְחִכִּי
אִמְרָתֶךָ
מִדְּבַשׁ לְפִי׃

104 From Your ordinances I become wise,
Therefore
I hate
Any lying practice.

קד מִפִּקּוּדֶיךָ אֶתְבּוֹנָן
עַל־כֵּן
שָׂנֵאתִי ׀
כָּל־אֹרַח שָׁקֶר׃

105 Your word is a candle for my foot,
And light
For my path.

קה **נֵ**ר־לְרַגְלִי דְבָרֶךָ
וְאוֹר
לִנְתִיבָתִי׃

106 I swear, and I shall persist in it:
To keep
Your just laws.

קו נִשְׁבַּעְתִּי וָאֲקַיֵּמָה
לִשְׁמֹר
מִשְׁפְּטֵי צִדְקֶךָ׃

107 I was very much tortured.
Eternal,
Revive me by Your word.

קז נַעֲנֵיתִי עַד־מְאֹד
יהוה
חַיֵּנִי כִדְבָרֶךָ׃

108 The offerings of my mouth
Please receive in pleasure, Eternal,
And teach me Your laws.

קח נִדְבוֹת פִּי
רְצֵה־נָא יהוה
וּמִשְׁפָּטֶיךָ לַמְּדֵנִי׃

109 My soul is always on my palms
And Your teaching
I did not forget.

קט נַפְשִׁי בְכַפִּי תָמִיד
וְתוֹרָתְךָ
לֹא שָׁכָחְתִּי׃

110 The wicked planted a trap for me
But from Your ordinances
I did not stray.

קי נָתְנוּ רְשָׁעִים פַּח לִי
וּמִפִּקּוּדֶיךָ
לֹא תָעִיתִי

111 I inherited Your testimonials forever
For they are the joy of my heart.

קיא נָחַלְתִּי עֵדְוֹתֶיךָ לְעוֹלָם
כִּי־שְׂשׂוֹן לִבִּי הֵמָּה׃

112 I bent my heart
To fulfill Your laws,
Forever, consistently.

קיב נָטִיתִי לִבִּי
לַעֲשׂוֹת חֻקֶּיךָ
לְעוֹלָם עֵקֶב׃

113 I hate scattered thoughts
But I love Your teaching.

קיג סֵעֲפִים שָׂנֵאתִי
וְתוֹרָתְךָ אָהָבְתִּי׃

114 Your are my refuge and shield,
I am yearning for Your word.

קיד סִתְרִי וּמָגִנִּי אָתָּה
לִדְבָרְךָ יִחָלְתִּי׃

115 Depart from me, evil doers,
So I may keep
My God's commandments.

קטו סוּרוּ מִמֶּנִּי מְרֵעִים
וְאֶצְּרָה
מִצְוֺת אֱלֹהָי׃

116 Support me by Your word, so I shall live, And
do not make me ashamed
Of my thoughts.

קטז סָמְכֵנִי כְאִמְרָתְךָ וְאֶחְיֶה
וְאַל־תְּבִישֵׁנִי
מִשִּׂבְרִי׃

117 Help me, then I will be saved
And always will enjoy Your edicts.

קיז סְעָדֵנִי וְאִוָּשֵׁעָה
וְאֶשְׁעָה בְחֻקֶּיךָ תָמִיד׃

118 You smashed
All who err from Your laws
For lie
Is their intent.

קיח סָלִיתָ
כָּל־שׁוֹגִים מֵחֻקֶּיךָ
כִּי־שֶׁקֶר
תַּרְמִיתָם׃

119 As slag
You locked out all the wicked of the land;
Therefore,
I love Your testimonials.

קיט סִגִים
הִשְׁבַּתָּ כָל־רִשְׁעֵי־אָרֶץ
לָכֵן
אָהַבְתִּי עֵדֹתֶיךָ׃

120 My flesh has goose pimples from terror of
I am afraid ofYour judgments.

קכ סָמַר מִפַּחְדְּךָ בְשָׂרִי
וּמִמִּשְׁפָּטֶיךָ יָרֵאתִי׃

121 I kept law and justice.
Do not lay me before
My oppressors.

קכא עָשִׂיתִי מִשְׁפָּט וָצֶדֶק
בַּל־תַּנִּיחֵנִי
לְעֹשְׁקָי׃

122 Guarantee Your servant the Good,
Not should the devilish oppress me.

קכב עֲרֹב עַבְדְּךָ לְטוֹב
אַל־יַעַשְׁקֻנִי זֵדִים׃

123 My eyes
Yearn for Your salvation,
And Your just instruction.

קכג עֵינַי
כָּלוּ לִישׁוּעָתֶךָ
וּלְאִמְרַת צִדְקֶךָ׃

124 Act towards Your servant in Your kindness,
And teach me Your edicts.

קכד עֲשֵׂה עִם־עַבְדְּךָ כְחַסְדֶּךָ
וְחֻקֶּיךָ לַמְּדֵנִי׃

125 I am Your servant, let me understand,
So I shall know
Your testimonials.

קכה עַבְדְּךָ אָנִי הֲבִינֵנִי
וְאֵדְעָה
עֵדֹתֶיךָ׃

126 It is a time
To act for the Eternal.
They transgress
Your teaching.

קכו עֵת
לַעֲשׂוֹת לַיהוָה
הֵפֵרוּ
תּוֹרָתֶךָ׃

127 Most High, Truthful,
I love Your commandments
Better than standard and refined gold.

קכז עַל־כֵּן
אָהַבְתִּי מִצְוֹתֶיךָ
מִזָּהָב וּמִפָּז׃

128 Most High, Truthful,
All Your orders, all is straight for me,
I hate all lying ways.

קכח עַל־כֵּן |
כָּל־פִּקּוּדֵי כֹל יִשָּׁרְתִּי
כָּל־אֹרַח שֶׁקֶר שָׂנֵאתִי׃

129 Your testimonials are wonderful,
Because of that
My soul preserves them.

קכט פְּלָאוֹת עֵדְוֹתֶיךָ
עַל־כֵּן
נְצָרָתַם נַפְשִׁי׃

130 Illuminate the beginning of Your words,
Who makes the silly understand.

קל פֵּתַח דְּבָרֶיךָ יָאִיר
מֵבִין פְּתָיִים׃

131 I open wide my mouth
And bray
In desire of Your commandments.

קלא פִּי־פָעַרְתִּי
וָאֶשְׁאָפָה
כִּי לְמִצְוֹתֶיךָ יָאָבְתִּי׃

132 Turn to me and be kind to me
As is the law
For the lovers of Your name.

קלב פְּנֵה־אֵלַי וְחָנֵּנִי
כְּמִשְׁפָּט
לְאֹהֲבֵי שְׁמֶךָ׃

133 My feet
Straightened by Your instruction,
Do not let any sin rule over me.

קלג פְּעָמַי
הָכֵן בְּאִמְרָתֶךָ
וְאַל־תַּשְׁלֶט־בִּי כָל־אָוֶן

134 Save me
From the oppression of man,
That I can keep
Your ordinances.

קלד פְּדֵנִי
מֵעֹשֶׁק אָדָם
וְאֶשְׁמְרָה
פִּקּוּדֶיךָ׃

135 Your presence
Let shine for Your servant
And teach me
Your edicts.

קלה פָּנֶיךָ
הָאֵר בְּעַבְדֶּךָ
וְלַמְּדֵנִי
אֶת־חֻקֶּיךָ׃

136 Water streams
Came down from my eyes
Over those
Who did not keep Your teaching.

קלו פַּלְגֵי־מַיִם
יָרְדוּ עֵינָי
עַל
לֹא־שָׁמְרוּ תוֹרָתֶךָ׃

137 You are just, Eternal,
And straightforward
Is Your law.

קלז צַדִּיק אַתָּה יהוה
וְיָשָׁר
מִשְׁפָּטֶיךָ׃

138 You commanded
Your just testimonials,
Very truthfully.

קלח צִוִּיתָ
צֶדֶק עֵדֹתֶיךָ
וֶאֱמוּנָה מְאֹד׃

139 My rage constricts me,
For my foes forgot Your words.

קלט צִמְּתַתְנִי קִנְאָתִי
כִּי־שָׁכְחוּ דְבָרֶיךָ צָרָי׃

140 Your instruction is very refined,
And Your servant loves it.

קמ צְרוּפָה אִמְרָתְךָ מְאֹד
וְעַבְדְּךָ אֲהֵבָהּ׃

141 I am young and despised,
Your orders
I did not forget.

קמא צָעִיר אָנֹכִי וְנִבְזֶה
פִּקֻּדֶיךָ
לֹא שָׁכָחְתִּי׃

142 Your justice
Is eternal justice
And Your teaching is truth.

קמב צִדְקָתְךָ
צֶדֶק לְעוֹלָם
וְתוֹרָתְךָ אֱמֶת׃

143 Straits and distress found me;
Your commandments
Are my recreation.

קמג צַר־וּמָצוֹק מְצָאוּנִי
מִצְוֹתֶיךָ
שַׁעֲשֻׁעָי׃

144 Your testimonials are eternally just,
Give me understanding, then I shall live.

קמד צֶדֶק עֵדְוֹתֶיךָ לְעוֹלָם
הֲבִינֵנִי וְאֶחְיֶה׃

145 I called with all my heart:
Answer me, Eternal.
I shall keep Your edicts.

קמה קָרָאתִי בְכָל־לֵב
עֲנֵנִי יהוה
חֻקֶּיךָ אֶצֹּרָה׃

146 I call upon You, save me,
Then I can keep
Your testimonials.

קמו קְרָאתִיךָ הוֹשִׁיעֵנִי
וְאֶשְׁמְרָה
עֵדֹתֶיךָ׃

147 I start early in the evening
And pray.
I am yearning for Your words [word].

קמז קִדַּמְתִּי בַנֶּשֶׁף
וָאֲשַׁוֵּעָה
לִדְבָרְיךָ [לִדְבָרְךָ] יִחָלְתִּי

148 My eyes search
During night watches
To talk
About Your instructions.

קמח קִדְּמוּ עֵינַי
אַשְׁמֻרוֹת
לָשִׂיחַ
בְּאִמְרָתֶךָ׃

149 My voice
Please do hear in Your kindness,
Eternal,
Let me live by Your laws.

קמט קוֹלִי
שִׁמְעָה כְחַסְדֶּךָ
יהוה
כְּמִשְׁפָּטֶךָ חַיֵּנִי׃

150 Those that run after lewdness
Come close.
They are far from Your teaching.

קנ קָרְבוּ
רֹדְפֵי זִמָּה
מִתּוֹרָתְךָ רָחָקוּ׃

151 You are close, Eternal,
And all Your commandments are truth.

קנא קָרוֹב אַתָּה יהוה
וְכָל־מִצְוֹתֶיךָ אֱמֶת׃

152 I had innate knowledge
Of Your testimonials
For You founded them eternally

קנב קֶדֶם יָדַעְתִּי
מֵעֵדֹתֶיךָ
כִּי לְעוֹלָם יְסַדְתָּם׃

153 See my deprivation and extricate me
Truly, Your teaching
I did not forget.

קנג רְאֵה־עָנְיִי וְחַלְּצֵנִי
כִּי־תוֹרָתְךָ
לֹא שָׁכָחְתִּי׃

154 Fight my fight
And free me;
By Your instruction make me Live.

קנד רִיבָה רִיבִי
וּגְאָלֵנִי
לְאִמְרָתְךָ חַיֵּנִי׃

155 Salvation is far from the wicked
Since They did not seek
Your laws.

קנה רָחוֹק מֵרְשָׁעִים יְשׁוּעָה
כִּי־חֻקֶּיךָ
לֹא דָרָשׁוּ׃

156 Your mercy is great, Eternal,
By Your law make me Live.

קנו רַחֲמֶיךָ רַבִּים | יהוה
כְּמִשְׁפָּטֶיךָ חַיֵּנִי׃

157 Many are
My pursuers and foes,
But from Your testimonials
I did not swerve.

קנז רַבִּים
רֹדְפַי וְצָרָי
מֵעֵדְוֺתֶיךָ
לֹא נָטִיתִי׃

158 I saw traitors
And started to quarrel
Since Your instruction
They did not keep

קנח רָאִיתִי בֹגְדִים
וָאֶתְקוֹטָטָה
אֲשֶׁר אִמְרָתְךָ
לֹא שָׁמָרוּ׃

159 Look,
Truly I loved Your ordinances.
Eternal,
By Your kindness make me Live.

קנט רְאֵה
כִּי־פִקּוּדֶיךָ אָהָבְתִּי
יהוה
כְּחַסְדְּךָ חַיֵּנִי׃

160 The essence of Your word is truth
And eternal
Is every just law of Yours.

קס רֹאשׁ־דְּבָרְךָ אֱמֶת
לְעוֹלָם
כָּל־מִשְׁפַּט צִדְקֶךָ׃

161 The corrupt
Persecute me without cause,
But my heart trembles
Before Your words {word].

קסא שָׂרִים
רְדָפוּנִי חִנָּם
וּמִדְּבָרֶיךָ [וּמִדְּבָרְךָ]
פָּחַד לִבִּי׃

162 I rejoice
In Your instructions
Like one who finds
Large booty.

קסב שָׂשׂ אָנֹכִי
עַל־אִמְרָתֶךָ
כְּמוֹצֵא
שָׁלָל רָב׃

163 I hate lies
And despise.
I love Your teaching.

קסג שֶׁקֶר שָׂנֵאתִי
וַאֲתַעֵבָה
תּוֹרָתְךָ אָהָבְתִּי׃

164 Seven times a day
I am praising You,
According to
Your just laws.

קסד שֶׁבַע בַּיּוֹם
הִלַּלְתִּיךָ
עַל
מִשְׁפְּטֵי צִדְקֶךָ

165 Boundless peace is
For the lovers of Your instruction;
For them there is no stumbling-block.

קסה שָׁלוֹם רָב
לְאֹהֲבֵי תוֹרָתֶךָ
וְאֵין לָמוֹ מִכְשׁוֹל׃

166 I am yearning for Your salvation, Eternal,
I executed Your commandments.

קסו שִׂבַּרְתִּי לִישׁוּעָתְךָ יהוה
וּמִצְוֺתֶיךָ עָשִׂיתִי

167 My soul kept
Your testimonials;
I love them very much.

קסז שָׁמְרָה נַפְשִׁי
עֵדֹתֶיךָ
וָאֹהֲבֵם מְאֹד׃

168 I kept Your ordinances
And testimonials;
Truly all my ways are with You in mind.

קסח שָׁמַרְתִּי פִקּוּדֶיךָ
וְעֵדֹתֶיךָ
כִּי כָל־דְּרָכַי נֶגְדֶּךָ׃

169 May my wailing come before You, Eternal,
By Your word, give me understanding.

קסט תִּקְרַב רִנָּתִי לְפָנֶיךָ יהוה
כִּדְבָרְךָ הֲבִינֵנִי׃

170 May my supplication come before You;
By Your instruction
Save me!

קע תָּבוֹא תְחִנָּתִי לְפָנֶיךָ
כְּאִמְרָתְךָ
הַצִּילֵנִי׃

171 May my lips express praise
As You teach me Your laws.

קעא תַּבַּעְנָה שְׂפָתַי תְּהִלָּה
כִּי תְלַמְּדֵנִי חֻקֶּיךָ׃

172 May my tongue repeat Your instructions. Certainly all Your commandments are just.	קעב תַּעַן לְשׁוֹנִי אִמְרָתֶךָ כִּי כָל־מִצְוֹתֶיךָ צֶּדֶק׃
173 May Your hand be my aid For I chose Your ordinances.	קעג תְּהִי־יָדְךָ לְעָזְרֵנִי כִּי פִקּוּדֶיךָ בָחָרְתִּי׃
174 I am thirsting for Your salvation, Eternal, And Your teaching Is my enjoyment.	קעד תָּאַבְתִּי לִישׁוּעָתְךָ יְהוָה וְתוֹרָתְךָ שַׁעֲשֻׁעָי׃
175 May my soul be Living And praise You And Your judgment help me.	קעה תְּחִי־נַפְשִׁי וּתְהַלְלֶךָּ וּמִשְׁפָּטֶךָ יַעֲזְרֻנִי׃
176 If I should err, Seek Your servant Like a stray sheep, For Your commandments I did not forget.	קעו תָּעִיתִי כְּשֶׂה אֹבֵד בַּקֵּשׁ עַבְדֶּךָ כִּי מִצְוֹתֶיךָ לֹא שָׁכָחְתִּי׃

23, 161. Arabic שאר "to act maliciously".

32. Arabic דרכ "understandng, achievement, accomplishment. Similarly in Accadic (Note to *Ps*. 1.).

38. Reading אשֶׁר for bland and unpoetic אֲשֶׁר .

42 Compare Arabic דבר "final statement".

61. For the root עוד cf. Arabic עוֹד, עיד "to take refuge" (Note of E. Ben Yehuda).

103. Arabic מלצ "to be smooth".

Psalm 120

1 A song of ascent.
When I am in straits,
To the Eternal
I am calling,
And He answers me.

א שִׁיר הַמַּעֲלוֹת
אֶל־יְהוָה
בַּצָּרָתָה לִּי
קָרָאתִי
וַיַּעֲנֵנִי׃

2 Eternal,
Save my soul
From lying lips,
From swindling tongues.

ב יְהוָה
הַצִּילָה נַפְשִׁי
מִשְּׂפַת־שֶׁקֶר
מִלָּשׁוֹן רְמִיָּה׃

3 What can you get
And what is in for you
From a swindling tongue?

ג מַה־יִּתֵּן לְךָ
וּמַה־יֹּסִיף לָךְ
לָשׁוֹן רְמִיָּה

4 Sharpened warrior's arrows
With
Broom's embers.

ד חִצֵּי גִבּוֹר שְׁנוּנִים
עִם
גַּחֲלֵי רְתָמִים׃

5 Woe to me
If I have to stay in Moesia,
If I have to dwell
By the tents of Qedar.

ה אוֹיָה לִי
כִּי־גַרְתִּי מֶשֶׁךְ
שָׁכַנְתִּי
עִם־אָהֳלֵי קֵדָר׃

6 Too much
Has my soul to lie down
With
The haters of peace.

ו רַבַּת
שָׁכְנָה־לָּהּ נַפְשִׁי
עִם
שׂוֹנֵא שָׁלוֹם׃

7 I am for peace,
And that I am expressing,
But they
Are for war.

ז אֲנִי־שָׁלוֹם
וְכִי אֲדַבֵּר
הֵמָּה
לַמִּלְחָמָה׃

Psalm 121

1 A song of ascent.
I lift my eyes
To the mountains:
From where
Will my help come?

א שִׁיר לַמַּעֲלוֹת
אֶשָּׂא עֵינַי
אֶל־הֶהָרִים
מֵאַיִן
יָבֹא עֶזְרִי׃

2 My help
Is from the Eternal,
The Creator
Of Heaven and Earth.

ב עֶזְרִי
מֵעִם יהוָה
עֹשֵׂה
שָׁמַיִם וָאָרֶץ׃

3 He will not let your foot slip;
Your guard
Will not slumber.

ג אַל־יִתֵּן לַמּוֹט רַגְלֶךָ
אַל־יָנוּם
שֹׁמְרֶךָ׃

4 Lo, He will not slumber
Nor sleep,
The guard
Of Israel.

ד הִנֵּה לֹא יָנוּם
וְלֹא יִישָׁן
שׁוֹמֵר
יִשְׂרָאֵל׃

5 The Eternal is your guard,
The Eternal is your shadow
At your right hand side.

ה יהוָה שֹׁמְרֶךָ
יהוָה צִלְּךָ
עַל־יַד יְמִינֶךָ׃

6 During daytime
The sun will not strike you,
Nor will the moon during nighttime.

ו יוֹמָם
הַשֶּׁמֶשׁ לֹא־יַכֶּכָּה
וְיָרֵחַ בַּלָּיְלָה׃

7 The Eternal
May guard you from all evil,
May guard
Your soul.

ז יהוה
יִשְׁמָרְךָ מִכָּל־רָע
יִשְׁמֹר
אֶת־נַפְשֶׁךָ׃

8 The Eternal
May guard your going and your coming
From now on
And forever.

ח יהוה
יִשְׁמָר־צֵאתְךָ וּבוֹאֶךָ
מֵעַתָּה
וְעַד־עוֹלָם׃

Psalm 122

1 A song of ascent, for David.
I am rejoicing
When people tell me
"We shall go to the Eternal's House.

א שִׁיר הַֽמַּעֲלוֹת לְדָ֫וִ֥ד
שָׂ֭מַחְתִּי
בְּאֹמְרִ֣ים לִ֑י
בֵּ֖ית יהוָ֣ה נֵלֵֽךְ׃

2 Standing
Were our feet
In your gates,
Jerusalem.

ב עֹ֭מְדוֹת
הָי֣וּ רַגְלֵ֑ינוּ
בִּ֝שְׁעָרַ֗יִךְ
יְרוּשָׁלָֽם׃

3 Built-up Jerusalem,
Truly a city
Tightly connected.

ג יְרוּשָׁלַ֥ם הַבְּנוּיָ֑ה
כְּ֝עִ֗יר
שֶׁחֻבְּרָה־לָּ֥הּ יַחְדָּֽו׃

4 Where the tribes ascended,
The Eternal's tribes
A testimonial for Israel,
To confess in
The Eternal's Name.

ד שֶׁשָּׁ֨ם עָל֪וּ שְׁבָטִ֡ים
שִׁבְטֵי־יָ֭הּ
עֵד֣וּת לְיִשְׂרָאֵ֑ל
לְ֝הֹד֗וֹת
לְשֵׁ֣ם יהוָֽה׃

5 Truly there
Are law courts sitting,
Courts
Of the dynasty of David.

ה כִּ֤י שָׁ֨מָּה ׀
יָשְׁב֣וּ כִסְא֣וֹת לְמִשְׁפָּ֑ט
כִּ֝סְא֗וֹת
לְבֵ֣ית דָּוִֽד׃

6 Ask for
The peace of Jerusalem;
May there be serenity
For those who love you.

ו שַׁ֭אֲלוּ
שְׁל֣וֹם יְרוּשָׁלָ֑ם
יִ֝שְׁלָ֗יוּ
אֹהֲבָֽיִךְ׃

7 May there be peace in your watchtowers,
Serenity
In your palaces.

ז יְהִי־שָׁל֥וֹם בְּחֵילֵ֑ךְ
שַׁ֝לְוָ֗ה
בְּאַרְמְנוֹתָֽיִךְ׃

8 For the sake of
My brothers and friends,
I shall proclaim peace in you.

ח לְמַ֣עַן
אַחַ֣י וְרֵעָ֑י
אֲדַבְּרָה־נָּ֖א שָׁל֣וֹם בָּֽךְ׃

9 For the sake of
The house of the Eternal, our God,
I am seeking your good.

ט לְ֭מַעַן
בֵּית־יהוָ֣ה אֱלֹהֵ֑ינוּ
אֲבַקְשָׁ֖ה ט֣וֹב לָֽךְ׃

Psalm 123

1 A song of ascent.
To You
I am raising my eyes,
You who thrones
In Heaven.

2 Lo, like slaves' eyes
To their masters' hand,
Like the eyes of a slave girl
To the hand of her mistress
So our eyes are
Upon the Eternal, our God,
Until
He may show us grace.

3 Show us grace, Eternal, show us grace,
Certainly more than enough
We had our fill of contempt.

4 Too much
Of it filled our soul,
The scorn of the nonchalant,
The contempt
Of the dangerous haughty.

א שִׁ֗יר הַֽמַּ֫עֲל֥וֹת
אֵ֭לֶיךָ
נָשָׂ֣אתִי אֶת־עֵינַ֑י
הַ֝יֹּשְׁבִ֗י
בַּשָּׁמָֽיִם׃

ב הִנֵּ֨ה כְעֵינֵ֪י עֲבָדִ֡ים
אֶל־יַ֬ד אֲדוֹנֵיהֶ֗ם
כְּעֵינֵ֣י שִׁפְחָה֮
אֶל־יַ֪ד גְּבִ֫רְתָּ֥הּ
כֵּ֣ן עֵ֭ינֵינוּ
אֶל־יהוָ֣ה אֱלֹהֵ֑ינוּ
עַ֝֗ד
שֶׁיְּחָנֵּֽנוּ׃

ג חָנֵּ֣נוּ יהוָ֣ה חָנֵּ֑נוּ
כִּי־רַ֝֗ב
שָׂבַ֥עְנוּ בֽוּז׃

ד רַבַּת֮
שָׂבְעָה־לָּ֪הּ נַ֫פְשֵׁ֥נוּ
הַלַּ֥עַג הַשַּׁאֲנַנִּ֑ים
הַ֝בּ֗וּז
לִגְאֵ֥יוֹנִֽים׃

Psalm 124

1 A song of ascents, for David.	א שִׁיר הַמַּעֲלוֹת לְדָוִד
If the Eternal	לוּלֵי יהוה
Were not with us,	שֶׁהָיָה לָנוּ
So shall say	יֹאמַר־נָא
Israel,	יִשְׂרָאֵל׃
2 If the Eternal	ב לוּלֵי יהוה
Were not with us	שֶׁהָיָה לָנוּ
When men arose against us,	בְּקוּם עָלֵינוּ אָדָם׃
3 Then	ג אֲזַי
They would have swallowed us alive	חַיִּים בְּלָעוּנוּ
When their rage was burning against us;	בַּחֲרוֹת אַפָּם בָּנוּ׃
4 Then	ד אֲזַי
The waters would have swept us away	הַמַּיִם שְׁטָפוּנוּ
A torrent	נַחְלָה
Would have passed over us.	עָבַר עַל־נַפְשֵׁנוּ׃
5 Then	ה אֲזַי
There would have passed over us	עָבַר עַל־נַפְשֵׁנוּ
The waters,	הַמַּיִם
The vicious ones.	הַזֵּידוֹנִים׃
6 Praised be the Eternal	ו בָּרוּךְ יְהוָה
Who did not let us be prey	שֶׁלֹּא נְתָנָנוּ טֶרֶף
To their teeth.	לְשִׁנֵּיהֶם׃
7 Our life	ז נַפְשֵׁנוּ
Escaped like a bird	כְּצִפּוֹר נִמְלְטָה
From the trapping snare.	מִפַּח יוֹקְשִׁים
The snare is broken,	הַפַּח נִשְׁבָּר
And we escaped!	אֲנַחְנוּ נִמְלָטְנוּ
8 Our help	ח עֶזְרֵנ
Is in the Eternal's name,	בְּשֵׁם יְהוָה
The creator	עֹשֵׂה
Of Heaven and Earth.	שָׁמַיִם וָאָרֶץ׃

Psalm 125

1 A song of ascents.
Those who trust in the Eternal
Are like unshakeable Mount Zion,
Forever inhabited.

א שִׁיר הַמַּעֲלוֹת
הַבֹּטְחִים בַּיהוָה
כְּהַר־צִיּוֹן לֹא־יִמּוֹט
לְעוֹלָם יֵשֵׁב׃

2 Jerusalem, Mountains
Around it, and the Eternal
Surrounds His people,
From now
To eternity.

ב יְרוּשָׁלַםהָרִים
סָבִיב לָהּ וַיהוה
סָבִיב לְעַמּוֹ
מֵעַתָּה
וְעַד־עוֹלָם׃

3 For the mace of the wicked
Shall not rest
On
The lot of the just,
Lest
The just would try to grasp ill gotten gains.

ג כִּי לֹא יָנוּחַ
שֵׁבֶט הָרֶשַׁע
עַל־
גּוֹרַל הַצַּדִּיקִים
לְמַעַן
לֹא־יִשְׁלְחוּ הַצַּדִּיקִים בְּעַוְלָתָה יְדֵיהֶם׃

4 Eternal, please benefit
The good ones
And those straightforward
In their hearts.

ד הֵיטִיבָה יהוה
לַטּוֹבִים
וְלִישָׁרִים
בְּלִבּוֹתָם׃

5 But the crooked ones in their distorted ways,
May the Eternal lead them away,
The evil doers.
Peace
Over Israel.

ה וְהַמַּטִּים עֲקַלְקַלּוֹתָם
יוֹלִיכֵם יהוה
אֶת־פֹּעֲלֵי הָאָוֶן
שָׁלוֹם
עַל־יִשְׂרָאֵל׃

Psalm 126

1 A song of ascents.
When the Eternal turned
The fortunes of Israel
We were
Like convalescents.

א שִׁיר הַמַּעֲלוֹת
בְּשׁוּב יְהוָה
אֶת־שִׁיבַת צִיּוֹן
הָיִינוּ
כְּחֹלְמִים׃

2 Then laughter would fill our mouth,
And song our tongue.
Then
Among the Gentiles one would say:
Great deeds the Eternal
Did perform with these.

ב אָז יִמָּלֵא שְׂחוֹק
פִּינוּ
וּלְשׁוֹנֵנוּ רִנָּה
אָז
יֹאמְרוּ בַגּוֹיִם
הִגְדִּיל יְהוָה
לַעֲשׂוֹת עִם־אֵלֶּה

3 Great Deeds the Eternal
Did perform with us;
We were happy.

ג הִגְדִּיל יְהוָה
לַעֲשׂוֹת עִמָּנוּ
הָיִינוּ שְׂמֵחִים

4 Turn, Eternal,
Our fortunes
Like wadis in the Negev.

ד שׁוּבָה יְהוָה
אֶת־שְׁבוּתֵנוּ [שְׁבִיתֵנוּ]
כַּאֲפִיקִים בַּנֶּגֶב׃

5 They who sow in tears
Shall harvest in song.

ה הַזֹּרְעִים בְּדִמְעָה
בְּרִנָּה יִקְצֹרוּ׃

6 Continuously moving,
And crying,
Is the carrier of the seed container,
Returning he shall come in song,
Carrying
His sheaves.

ו הָלוֹךְ יֵלֵךְ ׀
וּבָכֹה
נֹשֵׂא מֶשֶׁךְ־הַזָּרַע
בֹּא־יָבוֹא בְרִנָּה
נֹשֵׂא
אֲלֻמֹּתָיו׃

1. Taking חלם as Rabbinic Hebrew "mentally recuperating, sane".

Psalm 127

1 A song of ascents for Salomon.
If the Eternal
    Will not build the house
In vain
    Its builders labor on it;
If the Eternal will not guard a city,
    In vain
    The watchman is diligent.

א שִׁיר הַמַּעֲלוֹת לִשְׁלֹמֹה
אִם־ יְהוָה |
לֹא־יִבְנֶה בַיִת
שָׁוְא |
עָמְלוּ בוֹנָיו בּוֹ
אִם־ יְהוָה לֹא־יִשְׁמָר־עִיר
שָׁוְא |
שָׁקַד שׁוֹמֵר׃

2 In vain for you
    Who get up early,
    Who turn in late,
But eat
    The bread of idols,
The Truthful will provide a change for His dear.

ב שָׁוְא לָכֶם |
מַשְׁכִּימֵי קוּם
מְאַחֲרֵי־שֶׁבֶת
אֹכְלֵי
לֶחֶם הָעֲצָבִים
כֵּן יִתֵּן לִידִידוֹ שֵׁנָא׃

3 Lo, Sons are an inheritance from the Eternal,
A reward
    The fruit of the womb.

ג הִנֵּה נַחֲלַת יְיָ בָּנִים
שָׂכָר
פְּרִי הַבָּטֶן׃

4 Like arrows in the hand of the warrior,
So are
    Sons born in youth.

ד כְּחִצִּים בְּיַד־גִּבּוֹר
כֵּן
בְּנֵי הַנְּעוּרִים׃

5 Hail to the man
Who filled his quiver with them,
They will not be ashamed
But will subdue the enemies at the gate.

ה אַשְׁרֵי הַגֶּבֶר
אֲשֶׁר מִלֵּא אֶת־אַשְׁפָּתוֹ מֵהֶם
לֹא יֵבֹשׁוּ
כִּי־יְדַבְּרוּ אֶת־אוֹיְבִים בַּשָּׁעַר׃

2. Following Dahood, we read עֲצָבִים as identical with עֲצַבִּים "idols", and taking שנא as Rabbinic Hebrew "change, difference".

Psalm 128

1 A song of ascent.	א שִׁיר הַמַּעֲלוֹת
Fortunate is	אַשְׁרֵי
Everyone who fears the Eternal,	כָּל־יְרֵא יהוָה
Who walks	הַהֹלֵךְ
In His ways.	בִּדְרָכָיו׃
2 From the effort of your hand	ב יְגִיעַ כַּפֶּיךָ
You will eat well,	כִּי תֹאכֵל
You are fortunate	אַשְׁרֶיךָ
And the Good is yours.	וְטוֹב לָךְ׃
3 Your wife	ג אֶשְׁתְּךָ ׀
Is like a fruit bearing vine	כְּגֶפֶן פֹּרִיָּה
On the walls of your house;	בְּיַרְכְּתֵי בֵיתֶךָ
Your sons	בָּנֶיךָ
Are like olive tree saplings	כִּשְׁתִלֵי זֵיתִים
Surrounding	סָבִיב
Your table.	לְשֻׁלְחָנֶךָ׃
4 Behold, truly so	ד הִנֵּה כִי־כֵן
Will the man be blessed	יְבֹרַךְ גָּבֶר
Who fears the Eternal.	יְרֵא יהוִה׃
5 May the Eternal bless You from Zion;	ה יְבָרֶכְךָ יהוֹה מִצִּיּוֹן
May you see	וּרְאֵה
The fortune of Jerusalem	בְּטוּב יְרוּשָׁלָםִ
All	כֹּל
The days of your life.	יְמֵי חַיֶּיךָ׃
6 May you see your children's children.	ו וּרְאֵה־בָנִים לְבָנֶיךָ
Peace	שָׁלוֹם
Over Israel.	עַל־יִשְׂרָאֵל׃

Psalm 129

1 A song of ascent.
Enormously
They were hostile to me from my youth
So shall Israel say;

א שִׁ֗יר הַֽמַּ֫עֲל֥וֹת
רַ֭בַּת
צְרָר֣וּנִי מִנְּעוּרָ֑י
יֹֽאמַר־נָ֝א
יִשְׂרָאֵֽל׃

2 Enormously
They were hostile to me from my youth,
However
They could not overcome me.

ב רַ֭בַּת
צְרָר֣וּנִי מִנְּעוּרָ֑י
גַּ֝ם
לֹא־יָ֥כְלוּ לִֽי׃

3 On my back
The tillers tilled,
They made their furrows
Extra long
.

ג עַל־גַּ֭בִּי
חָרְשׁ֣וּ חֹרְשִׁ֑ים
הֶ֝אֱרִ֗יכוּ
לְמַֽעֲנוֹתָֽם [לְמַֽעֲנִיתָֽם]׃

4 The Eternal is just,
He cut
The ropes of the wicked.

ד יְהוָ֥ה צַדִּ֑יק
קִ֝צֵּ֗ץ
עֲב֣וֹת רְשָׁעִֽים׃

5 They shall be put to shame
And turned backwards,
All
The haters of Zion.

ה יֵ֭בֹשׁוּ
וְיִסֹּ֣גוּ אָח֑וֹר
כֹּ֝֗ל
שֹׂנְאֵ֥י צִיּֽוֹן׃

6 They shall be
Like greenery growing on roofs,
Which is dry before it can be bunched,

ו יִ֭הְיוּ
כַּחֲצִ֣יר גַּגּ֑וֹת
שֶׁקַּדְמַ֖ת שָׁלַ֣ף יָבֵֽשׁ׃

7 Of which the harvester cannot fill his hand,
Nor his vessel the binder of sheaves,

ז שֶׁלֹּ֤א מִלֵּ֖א כַפּ֥וֹ ק֝וֹצֵ֗ר
וְחִצְנ֥וֹ מְעַמֵּֽר׃

8 Neither did the passers-by say:
The Eternal's blessing on you;
We bless you
In the Eternal's Name.

ח וְלֹ֤א אָֽמְר֨וּ ׀ הָעֹבְרִ֗ים
בִּרְכַּ֣ת יְיָ֣ אֲלֵיכֶ֑ם
בֵּרַ֥כְנוּ אֶ֝תְכֶ֗ם
בְּשֵׁ֣ם יְיָ׃

Psalm 130

1 A song of ascent.
From the depth I am calling You, Eternal.

א שִׁ֥יר הַֽמַּֽעֲל֑וֹת
מִמַּעֲמַקִּ֖ים קְרָאתִ֣יךָ יְהוָֽה׃

2 Almighty,
Please listen to my voice,
May Your ears
Be attentive
To the sound
Of my supplication.

ב אֲדֹנָי֮
שִׁמְעָ֪ה בְק֫וֹלִ֥י
תִּהְיֶ֣ינָה אָ֭זְנֶיךָ
קַשֻּׁב֑וֹת
לְ֝ק֗וֹל
תַּחֲנוּנָֽי׃

3 Yah, If You would keep records of sins,
Almighty
Who could endure?

ג אִם־עֲוֺנ֥וֹת תִּשְׁמָר־יָ֑הּ
אֲ֝דֹנָ֗י
מִ֣י יַעֲמֹֽד׃

4 But with You is forgiveness,
So that
You shall be feared.

ד כִּֽי־עִמְּךָ֥ הַסְּלִיחָ֑ה
לְ֝מַ֗עַן
תִּוָּרֵֽא׃

5 I am hoping for the Eternal,
My soul is hoping,
I am yearning for His word

ה קִוִּ֣יתִי יְ֭הוָה
קִוְּתָ֣ה נַפְשִׁ֑י
וְֽלִדְבָר֥וֹ הוֹחָֽלְתִּי׃

6 In my soul, for the Almighty,
More than watchmen for dawn,
Watchmen for dawn!

ו נַפְשִׁ֥י לַאדֹנָ֑י
מִשֹּׁמְרִ֥ים לַ֝בֹּ֗קֶר
שֹׁמְרִ֥ים לַבֹּֽקֶר׃

7 Israel, yearn for the Eternal,
Because kindness is the Eternal's,
And much deliverance with Him,

ז יַחֵ֥ל יִשְׂרָאֵ֗ל אֶל־ יְה֫וָ֥ה
כִּֽי־עִם־יְהוָ֥ה הַחֶ֑סֶד
וְהַרְבֵּ֖ה עִמּ֣וֹ פְדֽוּת

8 So He
Will deliver Israel
From all
Its sins.

ח וְה֗וּא
יִפְדֶּ֥ה אֶת־יִשְׂרָאֵ֑ל
מִ֝כֹּ֗ל
עֲוֺנֹתָֽיו׃

Psalm 131

1 A song of ascent by David.
Eternal,
    My heart was not haughty,
    My eyes were not overbearing,
Nor did I decide
    On matters too great and wonderful for me.

2 But rather I prayed,
    And silenced my soul
Like a baby
    By its mother.
Like a baby my soul is for me.

4 Israel, yearn
    For the Eternal,
From now
    To eternity.

א שִׁ֥יר הַֽמַּעֲל֗וֹת לְדָ֫וִ֥ד
יְהוָ֤ה ׀
לֹא־גָבַ֣הּ לִ֭בִּי
וְלֹא־רָמ֣וּ עֵינַ֑י
וְלֹֽא־הִלַּ֓כְתִּי ׀
בִּגְדֹל֖וֹת וּבְנִפְלָא֣וֹת מִמֶּֽנִּי׃

ב אִם־לֹ֤א שִׁוִּ֨יתִי ׀
וְדוֹמַ֗מְתִּי נַ֫פְשִׁ֥י
כְּ֭גָמֻל
עֲלֵ֣י אִמּ֑וֹ
כַּגָּמֻ֖ל עָלַ֣י נַפְשִֽׁי׃

ג יַחֵ֣ל יִ֭שְׂרָאֵל
אֶל־יְהוָ֑ה
מֵ֝עַתָּ֗ה
וְעַד־עוֹלָֽם׃

Psalm 132

1 A song of ascent.
Remember, Eternal, for David
All
His deprivations.

א שִׁיר הַֽמַּעֲלוֹת
זְכוֹר־ יהוָה לְדָוִד
אֵת
כָּל־עֻנּוֹתוֹ׃

2 That he swore
To the Eternal,
Made a vow
To the Mighty of Jacob:

ב אֲשֶׁר נִשְׁבַּע
לַיהוָה
נָדַר
לַאֲבִיר יַעֲקֹב׃

3 That I should not come
To the shelter of my house,
Nor climb
On my laid-out couch,

ג אִם־אָבֹא
בְּאֹהֶל בֵּיתִי
אִם־אֶעֱלֶה
עַל־עֶרֶשׂ יְצוּעָי׃

4 Nor give sleep to my eyes
Nor slumber to my eyelashes,

ד אִם־אֶתֵּן שְׁנַת לְעֵינָי
לְעַפְעַפַּי תְּנוּמָה׃

5 Until I shall have found a place
For the Eternal,
A residence
For the Mighty of Jacob.

ה עַד־אֶמְצָא מָקוֹם
לַיהוָה
מִשְׁכָּנוֹת
לַאֲבִיר יַעֲקֹב׃

6 But now we heard it in Ephrat,
We found it
On a wooded field.

ו הִנֵּה־שְׁמַעֲנוּהָ בְאֶפְרָתָה
מְצָאנוּהָ
בִּשְׂדֵי־יָעַר׃

7 Let us come to His abode
Let us prostrate ourselves
Before His footstool.

ז נָבוֹאָה לְמִשְׁכְּנוֹתָיו
נִשְׁתַּחֲוֶה
לַהֲדֹם רַגְלָיו׃

8 Rise, Eternal,
To Your resting place,
You
And the ark of Your might.

ח קוּמָה יהוה
לִמְנוּחָתֶךָ
אַתָּה
וַאֲרוֹן עֻזֶּךָ׃

9 May Your priest be clothed in justice,
And Your pious rejoice.

ט כֹּהֲנֶיךָ יִלְבְּשׁוּ־צֶדֶק
וַחֲסִידֶיךָ יְרַנֵּנוּ׃

10 For the sake of
Your servant David,
Do not abandon
Your anointed.

י בַּעֲבוּר
דָּוִד עַבְדֶּךָ
אַל־תָּשֵׁב
פְּנֵי מְשִׁיחֶךָ׃

11 The Eternal swore
To David in truth,
He will not turn away from him,
From your body's fruit
I shall put
On your throne.

יא נִשְׁבַּע יהוה | לְדָוִד
אֱמֶת
לֹא־יָשׁוּב מִמֶּנָּה
מִפְּרִי בִטְנְךָ
אָשִׁית
לְכִסֵּא־לָךְ׃

12 If your sons will keep	יב אִם־יִשְׁמְרוּ בָנֶיךָ |
My covenant	בְּרִיתִי
And this testimonial I shall teach them,	וְעֵדֹתִי זוֹ אֲלַמְּדֵם
Then their descendants forever	גַּם־בְּנֵיהֶם עֲדֵי־עַד
Shall sit	יֵשְׁבוּ
On your throne.	לְכִסֵּא־לָךְ׃
13 For the Eternal did select Zion,	יג כִּי־בָחַר יהוה בְּצִיּוֹן
Desired it	אִוָּהּ
As His seat.	לְמוֹשָׁב לוֹ׃
14 This is my eternal resting place,	יד זֹאת־מְנוּחָתִי עֲדֵי־עַד
Here I shall reside	פֹּה אֵשֵׁב
For I desired it.	כִּי אִוִּתִיהָ׃
15 Her provisions	טו צֵידָהּ
I shall bless multiply,	בָּרֵךְ אֲבָרֵךְ
Its poor	אֶבְיוֹנֶיהָ
I shall make full with bread,	אַשְׂבִּיעַ לָחֶם׃
16 Its priests	טז וְכֹהֲנֶיהָ
I shall dress in salvation	אַלְבִּישׁ יֶשַׁע
And its pious	וַחֲסִידֶיהָ
Shall sing continuously.	רַנֵּן יְרַנֵּנוּ׃
17 There I shall let grow a horn for David,	יז שָׁם אַצְמִיחַ קֶרֶן לְדָוִד
I will have set a light	עָרַכְתִּי נֵר
For my anointed.	לִמְשִׁיחִי׃
18 His enemies	יח אוֹיְבָיו
I shall dress in shame,	אַלְבִּישׁ בֹּשֶׁת
But on him	וְעָלָיו
His crown shall sparkle.	יָצִיץ נִזְרוֹ׃

13., 14. R. Gordis points out that the root אוה contains a double entendre, as a Hebrew root "to desire" and an Arabic root (אוי) "to choose as a dwelling".

Psalm 133

1 A song of ascent, by David.
Behold, how good
And how pleasant
The sitting of brothers together!

א שִׁיר הַֽמַּעֲלוֹת לְדָוִד
הִנֵּה מַה־טּוֹב
וּמַה־נָּעִים
שֶׁבֶת אַחִים גַּם־יָחַד׃

2 Like the good oil
On the head,
Dripping down
To the beard, Aaron's beard,
Dripping down
To the rim of his garments;

ב כַּשֶּׁמֶן הַטּוֹב ׀
עַל־הָרֹאשׁ
יֹרֵד
עַל־הַזָּקָן זְקַן אַהֲרֹן
שֶׁיֹּרֵד
עַל־פִּי מִדּוֹתָיו׃

3 Like the dew of Hermon descending
On the mountains of Zion,
For there
The Eternal has commanded
Blessing:
Life
Forever!

ג כְּטַל־חֶרְמוֹן שֶׁיֹּרֵד
עַל־הַרְרֵי צִיּוֹן
כִּי שָׁם ׀
צִוָּה יהוה
אֶת־הַבְּרָכָה
חַיִּים
עַד־הָעוֹלָם׃

Psalm 134

1 A song of ascent.
Behold,
Praise the Eternal,
All the Eternal's servants,
Standing in the Eternal's House
During nights.

א שִׁיר הַֽמַּעֲלוֹת
הִנֵּה ׀
בָּרְכוּ אֶת־יהוה
כָּל־עַבְדֵי יהוה
הָעֹמְדִים בְּבֵית־יהוה
בַּלֵּילוֹת׃

2 Lift your hands to the Holy
And praise
The Eternal.

ב שְׂאוּ־יְדֵכֶם קֹדֶשׁ
וּבָרְכוּ
אֶת־יהוה׃

3 May the Eternal bless you
From Zion,
The creator
Of Heaven and Earth.

ג יְבָרֶכְךָ יהוה
מִצִּיּוֹן
עֹשֵׂה
שָׁמַיִם וָאָרֶץ׃

Psalm 135

1 Exalt the Eternal,
Exalt
The Eternal's Name
Exalt,
Servants of the Eternal,

א הַֽלְלוּ יָ֨הּ ׀
הַֽ֭לְלוּ
אֶת־שֵׁ֣ם יהוה
הַֽ֝לְלוּ
עַבְדֵ֥י יהוה׃

2 Who are standing
In the Eternal's House,
In the courtyards of
Our God's House.

ב שֶׁ֣עֹמְדִים
בְּבֵ֣ית יהוה
בְּ֝חַצְר֗וֹת
בֵּ֣ית אֱלֹהֵֽינוּ׃

3 Exalt the Eternal,
For the Eternal is good;
Sing to His Name
For He is pleasant.

ג הַֽלְלוּ־יָ֭הּ
כִּי־ט֣וֹב יהוה
זַמְּר֥וּ לִ֝שְׁמ֗וֹ
כִּ֣י נָעִֽים׃

4 Truly the Eternal selected Jacob
For Himself,
Israel
As His treasure.

ד כִּֽי־יַ֭עֲקֹב
בָּחַ֣ר ל֣וֹ יָ֑הּ
יִ֝שְׂרָאֵ֗ל
לִסְגֻלָּתֽוֹ׃

5 I know for certain
That the Eternal is great,
Our Master,
Over all powers.

ה כִּ֤י אֲנִ֣י יָ֭דַעְתִּי
כִּֽי־גָד֣וֹל יהוה
וַ֝אֲדֹנֵ֗ינוּ
מִכָּל־אֱלֹהִֽים׃

6 All that the Eternal desires He made,
In heaven and on earth,
In the oceans
And all depths.

ו כֹּ֤ל אֲשֶׁר־חָפֵ֥ץ יהוה עָ֫שָׂ֥ה
בַּשָּׁמַ֥יִם וּבָאָ֑רֶץ
בַּ֝יַּמִּ֗ים
וְכָל־תְּהוֹמֽוֹת׃

7 He raises clouds
From the ends of the earth,
He made lightning for rain,
Sending out wind
From His storehouses.

ז מַֽעֲלֶ֪ה נְשִׂאִ֡ים
מִקְצֵ֬ה הָאָ֗רֶץ
בְּרָקִ֣ים לַמָּטָ֣ר עָשָׂ֑ה
מֽוֹצֵא־ר֝֗וּחַ
מֵאֽוֹצְרוֹתָֽיו׃

8 When He smote
The firstborn of Egypt,
From man
To animal.

ח שֶׁ֭הִכָּה
בְּכוֹרֵ֣י מִצְרָ֑יִם
מֵ֝אָדָ֗ם
עַד־בְּהֵמָֽה׃

9 He sent
Signs and wonders
Into Egypt,
Over Pharao
And all his servants

ט שָׁלַ֤ח ׀
אֹת֣וֹת וּ֭מֹפְתִים
בְּתוֹכֵ֣כִי מִצְרָ֑יִם
בְּ֝פַרְעֹ֗ה
וּבְכָל־עֲבָדָֽיו׃

10 When He smote
Enormous peoples
And killed
Powerful kings,

י שֶׁהִכָּה
גּוֹיִם רַבִּים
וְהָרַג
מְלָכִים עֲצוּמִים׃

11 Sihon,
The king of the Emorite,
And Og
The king of Bashan,
And all
Kingdoms of Canaan.

יא לְסִיחוֹן ׀
מֶלֶךְ הָאֱמֹרִי
וּלְעוֹג
מֶלֶךְ הַבָּשָׁן
וּלְכֹל
מַמְלְכוֹת כְּנָעַן׃

12 And gave their land as inheritance,
Inheritance
To His people Israel.

יב וְנָתַן אַרְצָם נַחֲלָה
נַחֲלָה
לְיִשְׂרָאֵל עַמּוֹ׃

13 Eternal,
Your Name is forever,
Eternal,
You are eternally invoked.

יג יהוה
שִׁמְךָ לְעוֹלָם
יהוה
זִכְרְךָ לְדֹר־וָדֹר׃

14 Truly the Eternal will judge His people
And about His servants
He will sing.

יד כִּי־יָדִין יהוה עַמּוֹ
וְעַל־עֲבָדָיו
יִתְנֶחָם׃

15 The idols of the Gentiles are
Silver and gold,
The product
Of human hands.

טו עֲצַבֵּי הַגּוֹיִם
כֶּסֶף וְזָהָב
מַעֲשֵׂה
יְדֵי אָדָם׃

16 They have a mouth
But cannot talk,
They have eyes
But cannot see,

טז פֶּה־לָהֶם
וְלֹא יְדַבֵּרוּ
עֵינַיִם לָהֶם
וְלֹא יִרְאוּ׃

17 They have ears
But cannot listen,
A nose,
In their mouths is no existing spirit.

יז אָזְנַיִם לָהֶם
וְלֹא יַאֲזִינוּ
אַף
אֵין־יֶשׁ־רוּחַ בְּפִיהֶם׃

18 Like them
May be their makers,
Everybody
Trusting in them.

יח כְּמוֹהֶם
יִהְיוּ עֹשֵׂיהֶם
כֹּל
אֲשֶׁר־בֹּטֵחַ בָּהֶם׃

19 House of Israel,
Praise the Eternal,
House of Aaron,
Praise the Eternal,

יט בֵּית יִשְׂרָאֵל
בָּרְכוּ אֶת־ יהוה
בֵּית אַהֲרֹן
בָּרְכוּ אֶת־יהוה׃

20 House of Levi,
Praise the Eternal,
Those who fear the Eternal
Praise the Eternal.

כ בֵּית הַלֵּוִי
בָּרְכוּ אֶת־ יהוה
יִרְאֵי יהוה בָּרְכוּ
אֶת־ יהוה׃

21 The Eternal is praised
From Zion;
He Who dwells in Jerusalem.
Hallelujah!

כא בָּ֘ר֤וּךְ יְהֹוָ֨ה ׀
מִצִּיּ֗וֹן
שֹׁ֘כֵ֤ן יְֽרוּשָׁלָ֗ם
הַֽלְלוּ־יָֽהּ׃

14 In a victory song it does not make much sense to declare that the Eternal consoles himself about His servants. The verb here is not Arabic נחם "to sigh, groan", but נח̇ם "to chant, to sing".

Psalm 136

1 Thank the truly good Eternal,
Truly His kindness is forever.

א הוֹדוּ לַיהוָה כִּי־טוֹב
כִּי לְעוֹלָם חַסְדּוֹ׃

2 Thank
The Highest Power,
Truly His kindness is forever.

ב הוֹדוּ
לֵאלֹהֵי הָאֱלֹהִים
כִּי לְעוֹלָם חַסְדּוֹ׃

3 Thank
The Master of masters,
Truly His kindness is forever.

ג הוֹדוּ
לַאֲדֹנֵי הָאֲדֹנִים
כִּי לְעוֹלָם חַסְדּוֹ׃

4 Who alone works great wonders,
Truly His kindness is forever.

ד לְעֹשֵׂה נִפְלָאוֹת גְּדֹלוֹת לְבַדּוֹ
כִּי לְעוֹלָם חַסְדּוֹ׃

5 Who made the heavens
With understanding,
Truly His kindness is forever.

ה לְעֹשֵׂה הַשָּׁמַיִם
בִּתְבוּנָה
כִּי לְעוֹלָם חַסְדּוֹ׃

6 Who spreads out the land
Over the waters,
Truly His kindness is forever

ו לְרֹקַע הָאָרֶץ
עַל־הַמָּיִם
כִּי לְעוֹלָם חַסְדּוֹ׃

7 Who makes
Great lights,
Truly His kindness is forever.

ז לְעֹשֵׂה
אוֹרִים גְּדֹלִים
כִּי לְעוֹלָם חַסְדּוֹ׃

8 The sun
To reign by day,
.Truly His kindness is forever.

ח אֶת־הַשֶּׁמֶשׁ
לְמֶמְשֶׁלֶת בַּיּוֹם
כִּי לְעוֹלָם חַסְדּוֹ׃

9 The moon and stars
To reign by night,
Truly His kindness is forever.

ט אֶת־הַיָּרֵחַ וְכוֹכָבִים
לְמֶמְשְׁלוֹת בַּלָּיְלָה
כִּי לְעוֹלָם חַסְדּוֹ׃

10 Who smites Egypt
Through their firstborn,
Truly His kindness is forever.

י לְמַכֵּה מִצְרַיִם
בִּבְכוֹרֵיהֶם
כִּי לְעוֹלָם חַסְדּוֹ׃

11 And leads Israel out
From their midst,
Truly His kindness is forever.

יא וַיּוֹצֵא יִשְׂרָאֵל
מִתּוֹכָם
כִּי לְעוֹלָם חַסְדּוֹ׃

12 With strong hand
And outstretched arm,
Truly His kindness is forever.

יב בְּיָד חֲזָקָה
וּבִזְרוֹעַ נְטוּיָה
כִּי לְעוֹלָם חַסְדּוֹ׃

13 Who cuts the reed sea
Into strips,
Truly His kindness is forever.

יג לְגֹזֵר יַם־סוּף
לִגְזָרִים
כִּי לְעוֹלָם חַסְדּוֹ׃

14 And made Israel pass through it,
Truly His kindness is forever.

יד וְהֶעֱבִיר יִשְׂרָאֵל בְּתוֹכוֹ
כִּי לְעוֹלָם חַסְדּוֹ׃

15 And emptied Pharaoh and his army into the reed Sea,
Truly His kindness is forever.

טו וְנִעֵר פַּרְעֹה וְחֵילוֹ בְיַם־סוּף
כִּי לְעוֹלָם חַסְדּוֹ׃

16 Who leads His people
In the desert,
Truly His kindness is forever.

טז לְמוֹלִיךְ עַמּוֹ
בַּמִּדְבָּר
כִּי לְעוֹלָם חַסְדּוֹ׃

17 Who smites
Great kings,
Truly His kindness is forever.

יז לְמַכֵּה
מְלָכִים גְּדֹלִים
כִּי לְעוֹלָם חַסְדּוֹ׃

18 And kills
Mighty kings,
Truly His kindness is forever.

יח וַיַּהֲרֹג
מְלָכִים אַדִּירִים
כִּי לְעוֹלָם חַסְדּוֹ׃

19 Siḥon
King of the Emorite
Truly His kindness is forever.

יט לְסִיחוֹן
מֶלֶךְ הָאֱמֹרִי
כִּי לְעוֹלָם חַסְדּוֹ׃

20 And Og
King of the Bashan,
Truly His kindness is forever.

כ וּלְעוֹג
מֶלֶךְ הַבָּשָׁן
כִּי לְעוֹלָם חַסְדּוֹ׃

21 And gave their land as inheritance,
Truly His kindness is forever.

כא וְנָתַן אַרְצָם לְנַחֲלָה
כִּי לְעוֹלָם חַסְדּוֹ׃

22 Inheritance
Of His servant Israel,
Truly His kindness is forever.

כב נַחֲלָה
לְיִשְׂרָאֵל עַבְדּוֹ
כִּי לְעוֹלָם חַסְדּוֹ׃

23 Who in our low state
Remembered us,
Truly His kindness is forever.

כג שֶׁבְּשִׁפְלֵנוּ
זָכַר־לָנוּ
כִּי לְעוֹלָם חַסְדּוֹ׃

24 And delivered us from our attackers,
Truly His kindness is forever.

כד וַיִּפְרְקֵנוּ מִצָּרֵינוּ
כִּי לְעוֹלָם חַסְדּוֹ׃

25 He gives food
To all flesh,
Truly His kindness is forever.

כה נֹתֵן לֶחֶם
לְכָל־בָּשָׂר
כִּי לְעוֹלָם חַסְדּוֹ׃

26 Thank
Heaven's Power,
Truly His kindness is forever.

כו הוֹדוּ
לְאֵל הַשָּׁמָיִם
כִּי לְעוֹלָם חַסְדּוֹ׃

Psalm 137

1 By the rivers of Babylon,
There we sat.
How we cried
When we remembered
All of Zion.

2 On the willow trees in her midst
We hung up
Our lutes,

3 For there our captors asked from us
Lyrical compositions,
Joy, our mockers:
“Sing to us
Of the anthems of Zion!”

4 How
Can we sing the Eternal’s anthem
On
Foreign soil?

5 If I should forget you, o Jerusalem,
May my right hand wither,

6 May my tongue be glued to my palate
If I should not remember you,
If I should not lift
Jerusalem
On
The head on my wedding feast.

7 Remember, Eternal,
The sons of Edom
On
The Day of Jerusalem,
Who were saying:
"Strip! strip!
To
The bare rock under it!"

8 Daughter Babylon, the one to be plundered,
Hail to him who will pay you back,
The sum total
Of what you did to us!

9 Hail to him
Who will grab and smash your babies.
On the rock.

א עַל־נַהֲרוֹת | בָּבֶל
שָׁם יָשַׁבְנוּ
גַּם־בָּכִינוּ
בְּזָכְרֵנוּ
אֶת־צִיּוֹן׃

ב עַל־עֲרָבִים בְּתוֹכָהּ
תָּלִינוּ
כִּנֹּרוֹתֵינוּ׃

ג כִּי שָׁם שְׁאֵלוּנוּ שׁוֹבֵינוּ
דִּבְרֵי־שִׁיר
וְתוֹלָלֵינוּ שִׂמְחָה
שִׁירוּ לָנוּ
מִשִּׁיר צִיּוֹן׃

ד אֵיךְ
נָשִׁיר אֶת־שִׁיר־יְהוָה
עַל
אַדְמַת נֵכָר׃

ה אִם־אֶשְׁכָּחֵךְ יְרוּשָׁלִָם
תִּשְׁכַּח יְמִינִי׃

ו תִּדְבַּק־לְשׁוֹנִי | לְחִכִּי
אִם־לֹא אֶזְכְּרֵכִי
אִם־לֹא אַעֲלֶה
אֶת־יְרוּשָׁלִַם
עַל
רֹאשׁ שִׂמְחָתִי׃

ז זְכֹר יְהוָה |
לִבְנֵי אֱדוֹם
אֵת
יוֹם יְרוּשָׁלִָם
הָאֹמְרִים
עָרוּ | עָרוּ
עַד
הַיְסוֹד בָּהּ׃

ח בַּת־בָּבֶל הַשְּׁדוּדָה
אַשְׁרֵי שֶׁיְשַׁלֶּם־לָךְ
אֶת־גְּמוּלֵךְ
שֶׁגָּמַלְתְּ לָנוּ׃

ט אַשְׁרֵי |
שֶׁיֹּאחֵז וְנִפֵּץ אֶת־עֹלָלַיִךְ
אֶל־הַסָּלַע

3. דברי שיר are not “words of song” but “lyrical compositions”.

5. Following a hint in Ibn Ezra, expanded by Krochmal, we see in תשכח a poetic metathesis of תכחש "should dry up". Another possibility, hinted at by Ibn Janaḥ, is to see in תשכח an Aramaism, "should (not) be found".

8. Deriving גמלך not from the Hebrew root גמל used in the first and third occurrence, but an Arabic גמל "to sum".

Psalm 138

1 Of David.
I thank You with all my heart,
Before mighty ones I shall sing of You.

א לְדָוִד |
אוֹדְךָ בְכָל־לִבִּי
נֶגֶד אֱלֹהִים אֲזַמְּרֶךָּ׃

2 I prostrate myself before Your holy Hall
And thank Your name
For Your kindness and truth
For even greater than Your reputation
Is Your word.

ב אֶשְׁתַּחֲוֶה אֶל־הֵיכַל קָדְשְׁךָ
וְאוֹדֶה אֶת־שְׁמֶךָ
עַל־חַסְדְּךָ וְעַל־אֲמִתֶּךָ
כִּי־הִגְדַּלְתָּ עַל־כָּל־שִׁמְךָ
אִמְרָתֶךָ׃

3 On the day that I called
You answered me,
You stirred up might in my soul.

ג בְּיוֹם קָרָאתִי
וַתַּעֲנֵנִי
תַּרְהִבֵנִי בְנַפְשִׁי עֹז׃

4 All kings on earth
Shall thank You, Eternal,
When they hear
The command of Your mouth.

ד יוֹדוּךָ יהוה
כָּל־מַלְכֵי־אָרֶץ
כִּי שָׁמְעוּ
אִמְרֵי־פִיךָ׃

5 May they sing
Of the Eternal's rule:
Truly great
Is the Eternal's glory.

ה וְיָשִׁירוּ
בְּדַרְכֵי יהוה
כִּי גָדוֹל
כְּבוֹד יהוה׃

6 For the Eternal is exalted
But the lowly one He sees,
The haughty
He will punish from far.

ו כִּי־רָם יהוה
וְשָׁפָל יִרְאֶה
וְגָבֹהַּ
מִמֶּרְחָק יְיֵדָע׃

7 When I march
Into trouble, You will keep me alive,
Also on my enemies
You will bring down Your left hand,
You right hand will make me victorious.

ז אִם־אֵלֵךְ |
בְּקֶרֶב צָרָה תְּחַיֵּנִי
עַל אַף אֹיְבַי
תִּשְׁלַח יָדֶךָ
וְתוֹשִׁיעֵנִי יְמִינֶךָ׃

8 The Eternal
Will do good things for me!
Eternal,
Your kindness is forever!
Do not let go of the work of Your hands.

ח יהוה
יִגְמֹר בַּעֲדִי
יהוה
חַסְדְּךָ לְעוֹלָם
מַעֲשֵׂי יָדֶיךָ אַל־תֶּרֶף׃

6. Following Rashi and Ibn Ezra who recognize a *hif'il* meaning "to punish" of the root ידע in *Jud.* 8:16.

Psalm 139

1 For the director,
A Psalm of David.
Eternal, You investigated me
And You know.

א לַמְנַצֵּחַ
לְדָוִד מִזְמוֹר
יְהוָה חֲקַרְתַּנִי
וַתֵּדָע׃

2 You know
My sitting down and getting up.
You realized friendship for me
From early times.

ב אַתָּה יָדַעְתָּ
שִׁבְתִּי וְקוּמִי
בַּנְתָּה לְרֵעִי
מֵרָחוֹק׃

3 My paths and my lying down You measured by a
hand's span
And all my ways are well-known to You.

ג אָרְחִי וְרִבְעִי זֵרִיתָ
וְכָל־דְּרָכַי הִסְכַּנְתָּה׃

4 There is no word on my tongue
But that You, Eternal,
Know it completely.

ד כִּי אֵין מִלָּה בִּלְשׁוֹנִי
הֵן יְהֹוָה
יָדַעְתָּ כֻלָּהּ׃

5 Behind and before me You straitened me
And put Your hand upon me.

ה אָחוֹר וָקֶדֶם צַרְתָּנִי
וַתָּשֶׁת עָלַי כַּפֶּכָה׃

6 Too wonderful it is, for me to understand,
Too majestic
I fail in it.

ו פְּלָאִיה [פְּלִיאָה] דַעַת מִמֶּנִּי
נִשְׂגְּבָה
לֹא־אוּכַל לָהּ׃

7 Where
May I go from Your spirit,
And where
Can I flee from Your presence?

ז אָנָה
אֵלֵךְ מֵרוּחֶךָ
וְאָנָה
מִפָּנֶיךָ אֶבְרָח׃

8 If I climb to the sky
There You are,
And if would bed down in the Netherworld,
You are there.

ח אִם־אֶסַּק שָׁמַיִם
שָׁם אָתָּה
וְאַצִּיעָה שְּׁאוֹל הִנֶּךָּ׃

9 If I would take the wings of dawn,
I would dwell
At the farthest West,

ט אֶשָּׂא כַנְפֵי־שָׁחַר
אֶשְׁכְּנָה
בְּאַחֲרִית יָם׃

10 There also
Your left hand would direct me,
Your right hand would grab me.

י גַּם־שָׁם
יָדְךָ תַנְחֵנִי
וְתֹאחֲזֵנִי יְמִינֶךָ׃

11 If I would say:
"But darkness would encompass me
And night
Should be the light around me."

יא וָאֹמַר
אַךְ־חֹשֶׁךְ יְשׁוּפֵנִי
וְלַיְלָה
אוֹר בַּעֲדֵנִי׃

12 But darkness
Is not dark before You,
And night
Will radiate like day,
Like darkness,
Like light.

יב גַּם־חֹשֶׁךְ
לֹא־יַחְשִׁיךְ מִמֶּךָ
וְלַיְלָה
כַּיּוֹם יָאִיר
כַּחֲשֵׁיכָה
כָּאוֹרָה׃

13 For You
Did create my kidneys,
You sheltered me
In my mother's womb.

יג כִּי־אַתָּה
קָנִיתָ כִלְיֹתָי
תְּסֻכֵּנִי
בְּבֶטֶן אִמִּי׃

14 I thank You
For that in tremendous ways I was distinguished;
Your works are wonderful,
My soul
Knows it very well.

יד אוֹדְךָ
עַל כִּי נוֹרָאוֹת נִפְלֵיתִי
נִפְלָאִים מַעֲשֶׂיךָ
וְנַפְשִׁי
יֹדַעַת מְאֹד׃

15 My essence was not hidden from You
When I was made in secret,
Stitched together
In the depths of the earth.

טו לֹא־נִכְחַד עָצְמִי מִמֶּךָּ
אֲשֶׁר־עֻשֵּׂיתִי בַסֵּתֶר
רֻקַּמְתִּי
בְּתַחְתִּיּוֹת אָרֶץ׃

16 My unformed body
Was seen by Your eyes,
In Your ledger
They are all written down
The days bundled
Before one of them happened.

טז גָּלְמִי ׀
רָאוּ עֵינֶיךָ
וְעַל־סִפְרְךָ
כֻּלָּם יִכָּתֵבוּ
יָמִים יֻצָּרוּ
וְלֹא [וְלוֹ] אֶחָד בָּהֶם׃

17 Regarding me,
How precious is Your friendship, Powerful!
How powerful
Their heads.

יז וְלִי
מַה־יָּקְרוּ רֵעֶיךָ אֵל
מֶה עָצְמוּ
רָאשֵׁיהֶם׃

18 If I would count them,
They would be more numerous than sand;
I am waking up
And I am still with You.

יח אֶסְפְּרֵם
מֵחוֹל יִרְבּוּן
הֱקִיצֹתִי
וְעוֹדִי עִמָּךְ׃

19 If You, God, will kill the wicked,
Men of blood guilt
Depart from me.

יט אִם־תִּקְטֹל אֱלוֹהַּ ׀ רָשָׁע
וְאַנְשֵׁי דָמִים
סוּרוּ מֶנִּי׃

20 Those who talk about You
For their perjury,
Elevated for nothing in Your cities.

כ אֲשֶׁר יֹאמְרֻךָ
לִמְזִמָּה
נָשֻׂא לַשָּׁוְא עָרֶיךָ׃

21 So Your haters, Eternal,
I shall hate,
And those who rebel against You
I shall abhor. כב תַּכְלִית שִׂנְאָה שְׂנֵאתִים

כא הֲלוֹא־מְשַׂנְאֶיךָ יְיָ ׀
אֶשְׂנָא
וּבִתְקוֹמְמֶיךָ
אֶתְקוֹטָט׃

22 With absolute hate I hate them,
As enemies
They were for me.

לְאוֹיְבִים
הָיוּ לִי׃

23 Investigate me, Powerful,
And know my heart,
Test me,
And know my thoughts.

כג חָקְרֵנִי אֵל
וְדַע לְבָבִי
בְּחָנֵנִי
וְדַע שַׂרְעַפָּי׃

24 And see
If any idolatrous way is in me;
And direct me
On the way to eternity.

כד וּרְאֵה
אִם־דֶּרֶךְ־עֹצֶב בִּי
וּנְחֵנִי
בְּדֶרֶךְ עוֹלָם׃

Psalm 140

1 For the director,
A Psalm of David.

א לַמְנַצֵּחַ
מִזְמוֹר לְדָוִד׃

2 Rescue me, Eternal,
From evil people,
From violent men protect me.

ב חַלְּצֵנִי יהוה
מֵאָדָם רָע
מֵאִישׁ חֲמָסִים תִּנְצְרֵנִי׃

3 Who think evil in the heart,
All day long
They plan wars.

ג אֲשֶׁר חָשְׁבוּ רָעוֹת בְּלֵב
כָּל־יוֹם
יָגוּרוּ מִלְחָמוֹת׃

4 They sharpen their tongue
Like a snake,
The venom of spiders
Is under their lips, Selah.

ד שָׁנְנוּ לְשׁוֹנָם
כְּמוֹ־נָחָשׁ
חֲמַת עַכְשׁוּב
תַּחַת שְׂפָתֵימוֹ סֶלָה׃

5 Guard me, Eternal,
From the hands of the wicked,
From violent men protect me
Who are planning
To trip up my steps.

ה שָׁמְרֵנִי יהוה |
מִידֵי רָשָׁע
מֵאִישׁ חֲמָסִים תִּנְצְרֵנִי
אֲשֶׁר חָשְׁבוּ
לִדְחוֹת פְּעָמָי׃

6 The haughty buried a trap
For me, and ropes,
They spread as a net,
Close to the cart-way.
Snares they put down for me, Selah.

ו טָמְנוּ גֵאִים | פַּח
לִי וַחֲבָלִים
פָּרְשׂוּ רֶשֶׁת
לְיַד מַעְגָּל
מֹקְשִׁים שָׁתוּ־לִי סֶלָה׃

7 I said: Eternal,
You are my Powerful,
Listen, Eternal,
To the sound of my supplication.

ז אָמַרְתִּי לַיהוה
אֵלִי אָתָּה
הַאֲזִינָה יהוה
קוֹל תַּחֲנוּנָי׃

8 Eternal, Almighty,
Strength of my victory,
You sheltered my head
On the day of arms.

ח יהוה אֲדֹנָי
עֹז יְשׁוּעָתִי
סַכֹּתָה לְרֹאשִׁי
בְּיוֹם נָשֶׁק׃

9 Eternal, do not fulfill,
The desires of the wicked,
Do not execute his intent,
Which would elevate them, Selah.

ט אַל־תִּתֵּן יהוה
מַאֲוַיֵּי רָשָׁע
זְמָמוֹ אַל־תָּפֵק
יָרוּמוּ סֶלָה׃

10 The poison of those who surround me,
The perfidy of their lips may overwhelm them.

י רֹאשׁ מְסִבָּי
עֲמַל שְׂפָתֵימוֹ יְכַסֵּיוּמוֹ [יְכַסֵּמוֹ]׃

11 Embers may rain down on them,
May He throw them into fire,
In ditches
Not to resurrect.

יא יִמִּיטוּ [יִמּוֹטוּ] עֲלֵיהֶם גֶּחָלִים
בָּאֵשׁ יַפִּלֵם
בְּמַהֲמֹרוֹת
בַּל־יָקוּמוּ׃

12 The man of the tongue,
May he not be firm in the land.
The violent, evil man,
May be caught
To be pushed down.

יב אִישׁ לָשׁוֹן
בַּל־יִכּוֹן בָּאָרֶץ
אִישׁ־חָמָס רָע
יְצוּדֶנּוּ
לְמַדְחֵפֹת׃

13 I know
That the Eternal will wage
The lawsuit of the deprived,
Judgment
Of the meek.

יג יָדַעְתָּ [יָדַעְתִּי]
כִּי־יַעֲשֶׂה יהוה
דִּין עָנִי
מִשְׁפַּט
אֶבְיֹנִים׃

14 Only the just ones
Will thank Your Name;
The straightforward will sit
In Your presence.

יד אַךְ צַדִּיקִים
יוֹדוּ לִשְׁמֶךָ
יֵשְׁבוּ יְשָׁרִים
אֶת־פָּנֶיךָ׃

2. The grammatical form is collective, not singular.

10. Reading עמל as Arabic עמלה “perfidy”.

Psalm 141

1 A psalm of David.
Eternal, I called You,
Be quick for me,
Listen to my voice,
When I call upon You.

א מִזְמוֹר לְדָוִד
יְהוָה קְרָאתִיךָ
חוּשָׁה לִּי
הַאֲזִינָה קוֹלִי
בְּקָרְאִי־לָךְ׃

2 Prepare my prayer as incense before You,
The uplifting of my hands
As evening offering.

ב תִּכּוֹן תְּפִלָּתִי קְטֹרֶת לְפָנֶיךָ
מַשְׂאַת כַּפַּי
מִנְחַת־עָרֶב׃

3 Eternal, please put
A guard to my mouth,
A muzzle
On the door of my lips.

ג שִׁיתָה יהוה
שָׁמְרָה לְפִי
נִצְּרָה
עַל־דַּל שְׂפָתָי׃

4 Do not bend my heart to evil things,
To plan criminal plans
With men working in villainy,
And I shall not eat
Of their delicacies.

ד אַל־תַּט לִבִּי לְדָבָר | רָע
לְהִתְעוֹלֵל עֲלִלוֹת | בְּרֶשַׁע
אֶת־אִישִׁים פֹּעֲלֵי־אָוֶן
וּבַל־אֶלְחַם
בְּמַנְעַמֵּיהֶם׃

5 The Just One may smite me
In kindness
And admonish me.
Poison oil
May not hinder my head,
On and on my prayer is
Against their evil doings.

ה יֶהֶלְמֵנִי־צַדִּיק |
חֶסֶד
וְיוֹכִיחֵנִי
שֶׁמֶן רֹאשׁ
אַל־יָנִי רֹאשִׁי
כִּי־עוֹד וּתְפִלָּתִי
בְּרָעוֹתֵיהֶם׃

6 In the hands of the Rock their judges-rulers
Are let lose;
May they hear my sayings,
For they are pleasing.

ו נִשְׁמְטוּ בִידֵי־סֶלַע
שֹׁפְטֵיהֶם
וְשָׁמְעוּ אֲמָרַי
כִּי נָעֵמוּ׃

7 Like one who is cleaving and tearing up the earth
They would spread our bones
At the doors of the Netherworld.

ז כְּמוֹ פֹלֵחַ וּבֹקֵעַ בָּאָרֶץ
נִפְזְרוּ עֲצָמֵינוּ
לְפִי שְׁאוֹל׃

8 But on You,
Eternal Almighty, are my eyes,
In You I take refuge,
Do not pour out my soul!

ח כִּי אֵלֶיךָ |
יְהוִה אֲדֹנָי עֵינָי
בְּכָה חָסִיתִי
אַל־תְּעַר נַפְשִׁי׃

9 Keep me
From the trap
    They baited for me,
And the snares
    Of the evil doers!

ט שָׁמְרֵנִי
מִידֵי פַח
יָקְשׁוּ לִי
וּמֹקְשׁוֹת
פֹּעֲלֵי אָוֶן׃

10 May the criminals fall into their pits
Together, until I
    Will have passed by.

י יִפְּלוּ בְמַכְמֹרָיו רְשָׁעִים
יַחַד אָנֹכִי
עַד־אֶעֱבוֹר׃

2 For the meaning "to prepare" of the root כון cf. Amos 4:12.

6 The Suffete is a political office.

Psalm 142

1 A didactic poem of David,
A prayer when he was in the cave.

א מַשְׂכִּיל לְדָוִד
בְּהְיוֹתוֹ בַמְּעָרָה תְפִלָּה׃

2 With my voice
I am crying to the Eternal,
With my voice
I beseech the Eternal.

ב קוֹלִי
אֶל־יהוה אֶזְעָק
קוֹלִי
אֶל־יהוָה אֶתְחַנָּן׃

3 I shall pour out my talk before Him,
My problems
I shall tell before Him,

ג אֶשְׁפֹּךְ לְפָנָיו שִׂיחִי
צָרָתִי
לְפָנָיו אַגִּיד׃

4 While my spirit
Is fainting in me
You
Know my track,
On this path that I am following
They covered a trap for me.

ד בְּהִתְעַטֵּף עָלַי ׀
רוּחִי
וְאַתָּה
יָדַעְתָּ נְתִיבָתִי
בְּאֹרַח־זוּ אֲהַלֵּךְ
טָמְנוּ פַח לִי׃

5 Look, Giver of luck, and see:
No one wants to know me,
All refuge is lost for me,
No one cares for me.

ה הַבֵּיט יָמִין ׀ וּרְאֵה
וְאֵין־לִי מַכִּיר
אָבַד מָנוֹס מִמֶּנִּי
אֵין דּוֹרֵשׁ לְנַפְשִׁי׃

6 I cried to You, Eternal,
I said:
You are my shelter,
My part
In the Land of Life.

ו זָעַקְתִּי אֵלֶיךָ יהוָה
אָמַרְתִּי
אַתָּה מַחְסִי
חֶלְקִי
בְּאֶרֶץ הַחַיִּים׃

7 Take note of my entreaty
For I am very poor,
Save me from my pursuers
For they are more powerful than I am.

ז הַקְשִׁיבָה ׀ אֶל־רִנָּתִי
כִּי־דַלּוֹתִי מְאֹד
הַצִּילֵנִי מֵרֹדְפַי
כִּי אָמְצוּ מִמֶּנִּי׃

8 Take my soul out from confinement
To thank Your Name;
In me
The just may find a crown
When You do good to me.

ח הוֹצִיאָה מִמַּסְגֵּר ׀ נַפְשִׁי
לְהוֹדוֹת אֶת־שְׁמֶךָ
בִּי
יַכְתִּרוּ צַדִּיקִים
כִּי תִגְמֹל עָלָי׃

Psalm 143

1 A psalm of David.
Eternal,
Hear my prayer,
Give ear to my appeal,
In Your faithfulness answer me,
In Your righteousness.

א מִזְמוֹר לְדָוִד
יְהוָה |
שְׁמַע תְּפִלָּתִי
הַאֲזִינָה אֶל־תַּחֲנוּנַי
בֶּאֱמֻנָתְךָ עֲנֵנִי
בְּצִדְקָתֶךָ׃

2 Do not bring to court
Your servant
For before You no living being is virtuous.

ב וְאַל־תָּבוֹא בְמִשְׁפָּט
אֶת־עַבְדֶּךָ
כִּי לֹא־יִצְדַּק לְפָנֶיךָ כָל־חָי׃

3 But the Foe pursued
My soul,
Trampled to Earth
My living spirit,
Put me into darkness
Like the eternally dead.

ג כִּי רָדַף אוֹיֵב |
נַפְשִׁי
דִּכָּא לָאָרֶץ
חַיָּתִי
הוֹשִׁיבַנִי בְמַחֲשַׁכִּים
כְּמֵתֵי עוֹלָם׃

4 My spirit fainted in me,
Inside me
My heart grew silent.

ד וַתִּתְעַטֵּף עָלַי רוּחִי
בְּתוֹכִי
יִשְׁתּוֹמֵם לִבִּי׃

5 I remembered the days
Of old,
I was studying all Your works,
About Your handiwork I would talk.

ה זָכַרְתִּי יָמִים |
מִקֶּדֶם
הָגִיתִי בְכָל־פָּעֳלֶךָ
בְּמַעֲשֵׂה יָדֶיךָ אֲשׂוֹחֵחַ׃

6 I am spreading my hands out before You,
My soul
Is like parched land before You, Selah.

ו פֵּרַשְׂתִּי יָדַי אֵלֶיךָ
נַפְשִׁי |
כְּאֶרֶץ־עֲיֵפָה לְךָ סֶלָה׃

7 Quickly answer me,
Eternal,
My spirit is finished,
Do not hide Your presence from me
Or I could be compared
To those who descend to the Pit.

ז מַהֵר עֲנֵנִי |
יְהוָה
כָּלְתָה רוּחִי
אַל־תַּסְתֵּר פָּנֶיךָ מִמֶּנִּי
וְנִמְשַׁלְתִּי
עִם־יֹרְדֵי בוֹר׃

8 In the morning, make me hear
Your kindness.
Certainly in You I trust;
Make me know
The particular way I have to go;
Truly to You
I am lifting my soul.

ח הַשְׁמִיעֵנִי בַבֹּקֶר |
חַסְדֶּךָ
כִּי־בְךָ בָטָחְתִּי
הוֹדִיעֵנִי
דֶּרֶךְ־זוּ אֵלֵךְ
כִּי־אֵלֶיךָ
נָשָׂאתִי נַפְשִׁי׃

9 Save me from my Foe,
Eternal,
I am following You step by step.

ט הַצִּילֵנִי מֵאֹיְבַי |
יְהוָה
אֵלֶיךָ כִסִּתִי׃

10 Teach me	י לַמְּדֵנִי ׀
To do Your will	לַעֲשׂוֹת רְצוֹנֶךָ
Truly You are my God,	כִּי־אַתָּה אֱלוֹהָי
Your good spirit	רוּחֲךָ טוֹבָה
Will make me rest	תַּנְחֵנִי
In a flat Land.	בְּאֶרֶץ מִישׁוֹר׃
11 For Your Name's sake, Eternal, let me live,	יא לְמַעַן־שִׁמְךָ יהוה תְּחַיֵּנִי
In Your righteousness	בְּצִדְקָתְךָ ׀
Lead my soul out of trouble.	תּוֹצִיא מִצָּרָה נַפְשִׁי׃
12 And in Your kindness	יב וּבְחַסְדְּךָ
Squeeze my Foe,	תַּצְמִית אֹיְבָי
Make lost	וְהַאֲבַדְתָּ
All those who trouble my soul,	כָּל־צֹרְרֵי נַפְשִׁי
Certainly	כִּי
I am Your servant!	אֲנִי עַבְדֶּךָ׃

3.7. The Foe is the Satan, the representation of one's evil inclinations. The Pit is the storage place for the useless souls which have no part in the future World.

9. Deriving כסיתי from Arabic כסא "to follow someone step by step". Based on Accadic *kasu* "to be bound", one could also translate "To You I am bound"

Psalm 144

1 Of David.
Praised be the Eternal,
My rock,
Who trains my hands for combat,
My fingers
For war.

א לְדָוִד |
בָּרוּךְ יהוה |
צוּרִי
הַמְלַמֵּד יָדַי לַקְרָב
אֶצְבְּעוֹתַי
לַמִּלְחָמָה׃

2 My protector and fortress,
My refuge and shelter,
My shield
In Whom I rely,
Who flattens my people under me.

ב חַסְדִּי וּמְצוּדָתִי
מִשְׂגַּבִּי וּמְפַלְטִי לִי
מָגִנִּי
וּבוֹ חָסִיתִי
הָרוֹדֵד עַמִּי תַחְתָּי׃

3 Eternal, what is man
That You should know him,
A mortal
That You should consider him?

ג יהוה מָה־אָדָם
וַתֵּדָעֵהוּ
בֶּן־אֱנוֹשׁ
וַתְּחַשְּׁבֵהוּ׃

4 Man
Compares to vapor,
His days
Like a passing shadow.

ד אָדָם
לַהֶבֶל דָּמָה
יָמָיו
כְּצֵל עוֹבֵר׃

5 Eternal,
Bend Your heavens and descend,
Touch mountains and let them smoke.

ה יהוה
הַט־שָׁמֶיךָ וְתֵרֵד
גַּע בֶּהָרִים וְיֶעֱשָׁנוּ׃

6 Lighten lightning
And disperse them,
Equip Your arrows
And confuse them.

ו בְּרוֹק בָּרָק
וּתְפִיצֵם
שְׁלַח חִצֶּיךָ
וּתְהֻמֵּם׃

7 Send Your hands from up high,
Rescue me and save me
From enormous waters,
From the hand
Of alien people.

ז שְׁלַח יָדֶיךָ מִמָּרוֹם
פְּצֵנִי וְהַצִּילֵנִי
מִמַּיִם רַבִּים
מִיַּד
בְּנֵי נֵכָר׃

8 Whose mouth is
Vain speech
And their right arms
Right arms of perjury.

ח אֲשֶׁר פִּיהֶם
דִּבֶּר־שָׁוְא
וִימִינָם
יְמִין שָׁקֶר׃

9 God,
A new song
I shall sing to You,
With the ten stringed harp
I shall chant to You.

ט אֱלֹהִים
שִׁיר חָדָשׁ
אָשִׁירָה לָּךְ
בְּנֵבֶל עָשׂוֹר
אֲזַמְּרָה־לָּךְ׃

10 He Who gives victory to kings,
Who rescues
His servant David
From the evil sword

י הַנּוֹתֵן תְּשׁוּעָה לַמְּלָכִים
הַפּוֹצֶה
אֶת־דָּוִד עַבְדּוֹ
מֵחֶרֶב רָעָה׃

11 Rescue me and save me
From the hands of alien people
Whose mouth is
Vain speech
And their right arms
Right arms of perjury.

יא פְּצֵנִי וְהַצִּילֵנִי
מִיַּד בְּנֵי־נֵכָר
אֲשֶׁר־פִּיהֶם
דִּבֶּר־שָׁוְא
וִימִינָם
יְמִין שָׁקֶר׃

12 Happily, our sons
Are like planted trees
Cared for in their youth,
Our daughters like corners stones
Cut out
For the building of a palace.

יב אֲשֶׁר בָּנֵינוּ | כִּנְטִעִים
מְגֻדָּלִים בִּנְעוּרֵיהֶם
בְּנוֹתֵינוּ כְזָוִיֹּת
מְחֻטָּבוֹת
תַּבְנִית הֵיכָל׃

13 Our storage barns are full,
Yielding from kind to kind,
Our sheep multiply by thousands,
Go by myriads
In our streets.

יג מְזָוֵינוּ מְלֵאִים
מְפִיקִים מִזַּן אֶל־זַן
צֹאונֵנוּ מַאֲלִיפוֹת
מְרֻבָּבוֹת
בְּחוּצוֹתֵינוּ׃

14 Our oxen are well loaded;
There is neither breach
Nor loss,
Nor wailing
In our squares.

יד אַלּוּפֵינוּ מְסֻבָּלִים
אֵין פֶּרֶץ
וְאֵין יוֹצֵאת
וְאֵין צְוָחָה
בִּרְחֹבֹתֵינוּ׃

15 Hail to the people
Whose lot is this,
Hail to the people,
Whose God is the Eternal.

טו אַשְׁרֵי הָעָם
שֶׁכָּכָה לּוֹ
אַשְׁרֵי הָעָם
שֶׁיְהוָה אֱלֹהָיו׃

12. An alternate translation is: "Our daughters are very brilliant, Adorned, fitting for a Temple."

Psalm 145

1 A Psalm of David.
I shall elevate You my God, King,
And bless Your Name
Eternally.

א תְּהִלָּה לְדָוִד
אֲרוֹמִמְךָ אֱלוֹהַי הַמֶּלֶךְ
וַאֲבָרְכָה שִׁמְךָ
לְעוֹלָם וָעֶד׃

2 Every day I shall bless You
And praise Your Name
Eternally.

ב בְּכָל־יוֹם אֲבָרְכֶךָּ
וַאֲהַלְלָה שִׁמְךָ
לְעוֹלָם וָעֶד׃

3 Great is the Eternal and much praised,
His greatness
Cannot be investigated.

ג גָּדוֹל יהוה וּמְהֻלָּל מְאֹד
וְלִגְדֻלָּתוֹ
אֵין חֵקֶר׃

4 One generation to the next
Shall praise Your works,
And tell of Your mightiness.

ד דּוֹר לְדוֹר
יְשַׁבַּח מַעֲשֶׂיךָ
וּגְבוּרֹתֶיךָ יַגִּידוּ׃

5 The splendor
Of Your majesty's glory
And the data of Your wonders I shall utter.

ה הֲדַר
כְּבוֹד הוֹדֶךָ
וְדִבְרֵי נִפְלְאוֹתֶיךָ אָשִׂיחָה׃

6 And of Your awesome might they shall speak,
Of Your greatness they shall tell.

ו וֶעֱזוּז נוֹרְאֹתֶיךָ יֹאמֵרוּ
וּגְדוּלָּתְיךָ [וּגְדוּלָּתְךָ] אֲסַפְּרֶנָּה׃

7 They gush to mention Your enormous good
And sing of Your truth.

ז זֵכֶר רַב־טוּבְךָ יַבִּיעוּ
וְצִדְקָתְךָ יְרַנֵּנוּ׃

8 The Eternal is graceful and merciful
Long forgiving
And great in kindness.

ח חַנּוּן וְרַחוּם יהוה
אֶרֶךְ אַפַּיִם
וּגְדָל־חָסֶד׃

9 The Eternal is good to all,
His mercies are
For all His creatures.

ט טוֹב־יהוה לַכֹּל
וְרַחֲמָיו
עַל־כָּל־מַעֲשָׂיו׃

10 All Your creatures, Eternal,
Shall thank You,
And Your pious
Shall bless You.

י יוֹדוּךָ יהוה
כָּל־מַעֲשֶׂיךָ
וַחֲסִידֶיךָ
יְבָרְכוּכָה׃

11 They talk about the Your kingdom’s glory
And speak of Your might.

יא כְּבוֹד מַלְכוּתְךָ יֹאמֵרוּ
וּגְבוּרָתְךָ יְדַבֵּרוּ׃

12 To proclaim to mankind
His might
And the glory
Of His kingdom's majesty.

יב לְהוֹדִיעַ לִבְנֵי הָאָדָם
גְּבוּרֹתָיו
וּכְבוֹד
הֲדַר מַלְכוּתוֹ׃

13 Your kingdom
Is kingdom over all worlds
And Your rule
Over all generations.

יג מַלְכוּתְךָ
מַלְכוּת כָּל־עֹלָמִים
וּמֶמְשַׁלְתְּךָ
בְּכָל־דּוֹר וָדוֹר׃

14 The Eternal supports
All who are falling,
And straightens
All who are bent.

יד סוֹמֵךְ יהוה
לְכָל־הַנֹּפְלִים
וְזוֹקֵף
לְכָל־הַכְּפוּפִים׃

15 The eyes of all
Hope for You,
You give them their food in its time,

טו עֵינֵי כֹל
אֵלֶיךָ יְשַׂבֵּרוּ
וְאַתָּה נוֹתֵן־לָהֶם אֶת־אָכְלָם בְּעִתּוֹ׃

16 Opening Your hand
And satisfying all living with goodwill.

טז פּוֹתֵחַ אֶת־יָדֶךָ
וּמַשְׂבִּיעַ לְכָל־חַי רָצוֹן׃

17 The Eternal is just
In all His ways
And gracious
In all His works.

יז צַדִּיק יהוה
בְּכָל־דְּרָכָיו
וְחָסִיד
בְּכָל־מַעֲשָׂיו׃

18 The Eternal is close
To all who call on Him,
To all who call on Him in truth.

יח קָרוֹב יהוה
לְכָל־קֹרְאָיו
לְכֹל אֲשֶׁר יִקְרָאֻהוּ בֶאֱמֶת׃

19 The desire of those who fear Him he will do,
Their supplication He will hear
And save them.

יט רְצוֹן־יְרֵאָיו יַעֲשֶׂה
וְאֶת־שַׁוְעָתָם יִשְׁמַע
וְיוֹשִׁיעֵם׃

20 The Eternal watches
Over all who love Him
But all the wicked He will destroy.

כ שׁוֹמֵר יהוה
אֶת־כָּל־אֹהֲבָיו
וְאֵת כָּל־הָרְשָׁעִים יַשְׁמִיד׃

21 My mouth shall lead the Eternal's praise:
May all flesh bless
His holy Name
For all eternity.

כא תְּהִלַּת יהוה יְדַבֶּר־פִּי
וִיבָרֵךְ כָּל־בָּשָׂר
שֵׁם קָדְשׁוֹ
לְעוֹלָם וָעֶד׃

The Septuagint has a spurious verse 13a for the missing letter נ: "Faithful is the Lord in all His sayings, and according to the nature in all His works."

Psalm 146

1 Praise Yah!
Praise, my soul,
The Eternal.

א הַֽלְלוּ־יָהּ
הַלְלִי נַפְשִׁי
אֶת־יהוָה׃

2 I shall praise the Eternal while I live,
I shall sing to my God while I am still here.

ב אֲהַלְלָה יהוָה בְּחַיָּי
אֲזַמְּרָה לֵאלֹהַי בְּעוֹדִי׃

3 Do not trust nobles;
Man
Who cannot give victory.

ג אַל־תִּבְטְחוּ בִנְדִיבִים
בְּבֶן־אָדָם |
שֶׁאֵין לוֹ תְשׁוּעָה׃

4 His ghost will leave,
He will return to his earth,
On that day
His schemes are lost.

ד תֵּצֵא רוּחוֹ
יָשֻׁב לְאַדְמָתוֹ
בַּיּוֹם הַהוּא
אָבְדוּ עֶשְׁתֹּנֹתָיו׃

5 Hail to him,
For whom the Strong of Jacob is his help,
His hope is
On the Eternal, his God,

ה אַשְׁרֵי
שֶׁאֵל יַעֲקֹב בְּעֶזְרוֹ
שִׂבְרוֹ
עַל־יהוה אֱלֹהָיו׃

6 Who makes
Heaven and earth,
The sea and all that is in it,
Who keeps truth forever,

ו עֹשֶׂה |
שָׁמַיִם וָאָרֶץ
אֶת־הַיָּם וְאֶת־כָּל־אֲשֶׁר־בָּם
הַשֹּׁמֵר אֱמֶת לְעוֹלָם׃

7 Who provides justice
For the oppressed,
Gives bread
To the hungry.
The Eternal
Releases the bound;

ז עֹשֶׂה מִשְׁפָּט |
לָעֲשׁוּקִים
נֹתֵן לֶחֶם
לָרְעֵבִים
יהוה
מַתִּיר אֲסוּרִים׃

8 The Eternal
Opens the eyes of the blind;
The Eternal
Straightens the bent;
The Eternal.
Loves the just ones.

ח יהוָה |
פֹּקֵחַ עִוְרִים
יהוה
זֹקֵף כְּפוּפִים
יהוה
אֹהֵב צַדִּיקִים׃

9 The Eternal
Guards the strangers;
He encourages orphan and widow
But the way of the wicked He curbs.

ט יהוָה |
שֹׁמֵר אֶת־גֵּרִים
יָתוֹם וְאַלְמָנָה יְעוֹדֵד
וְדֶרֶךְ רְשָׁעִים יְעַוֵּת׃

10 The Eternal will rule forever,
Your God, Zion,
For all generations,
Praise the Eternal!

י יִמְלֹךְ יהוה | לְעוֹלָם
אֱלֹהַיִךְ צִיּוֹן
לְדֹר וָדֹר
הַלְלוּ יָהּ׃

The Septuagint attributes this and the next two Psalms to the prophets Haggai and Zacharia.

Psalm 147

1 Praise Yah!
Certainly it is good
To chant to our God
Certainly it is pleasant
Agreeable praise.

א הַֽלְלוּ־יָ֨הּ ׀
כִּי־ט֭וֹב
זַמְּרָ֣ה אֱלֹהֵ֑ינוּ
כִּֽי־נָ֝עִ֗ים
נָאוָ֥ה תְהִלָּֽה׃

2 The Eternal is builder of Jerusalem,
He gathers the dispersed one of Israel.

ב בּוֹנֵ֣ה יְרוּשָׁלַ֣͏ִם יהוָ֑ה
נִדְחֵ֖י יִשְׂרָאֵ֣ל יְכַנֵּֽס׃

3 He Who heals
The heart-boken
And dresses
Their hurts.

ג הָ֭רוֹפֵא
לִשְׁב֣וּרֵי לֵ֑ב
וּ֝מְחַבֵּ֗שׁ
לְעַצְבוֹתָֽם׃

4 He is counting the number
Of stars,
To all of them
He gives names.

ד מוֹנֶ֣ה מִ֭סְפָּר
לַכּוֹכָבִ֑ים
לְ֝כֻלָּ֗ם
שֵׁמ֥וֹת יִקְרָֽא׃

5 Our Lord is great and very powerful,
His insight
Cannot be recorded.

ה גָּד֣וֹל אֲדוֹנֵ֣ינוּ וְרַב־כֹּ֑חַ
לִ֝תְבוּנָת֗וֹ
אֵ֣ין מִסְפָּֽר׃

6 The Eternal encourages the meek,
He humiliates criminals to the ground.

ו מְעוֹדֵ֣ד עֲנָוִ֣ים יהוָ֑ה
מַשְׁפִּ֖יל רְשָׁעִ֣ים עֲדֵי־אָֽרֶץ׃

7 Form a chorus for the Eternal in thanks,
Chant to our God with the lute.

ז עֱנ֣וּ לַייָ֣ בְּתוֹדָ֑ה
זַמְּר֖וּ לֵאלֹהֵ֣ינוּ בְכִנּֽוֹר׃

8 He who covers the sky with clouds
Who prepares rain for the earth
Who makes hills growing greenery.

ח הַֽמְכַסֶּ֬ה שָׁמַ֨יִם ׀ בְּעָבִ֗ים
הַמֵּכִ֣ין לָאָ֣רֶץ מָטָ֑ר
הַמַּצְמִ֖יחַ הָרִ֣ים חָצִֽיר׃

9 He provides nourishment for livestock,
The raven's young
What they call for.

ט נוֹתֵ֣ן לִבְהֵמָ֣ה לַחְמָ֑הּ
לִבְנֵ֥י עֹ֝רֵ֗ב
אֲשֶׁ֣ר יִקְרָֽאוּ׃

10 He has no pleasure in the horse's strength
Nor desire for man's splint-bone.

י לֹ֤א בִגְבוּרַ֣ת הַסּ֣וּס יֶחְפָּ֑ץ
לֹֽא־בְשׁוֹקֵ֖י הָאִ֣ישׁ יִרְצֶֽה׃

11 The Eternal has desire
For those who fear Him,
Those who are expecting His grace.

יא רוֹצֶ֣ה יהוה
אֶת־יְרֵאָ֑יו
אֶת־הַֽמְיַחֲלִ֥ים לְחַסְדּֽוֹ׃

12 Jerusalem, praise
The Eternal,
Zion, glorify your God.

יב שַׁבְּחִ֣י יְ֭רוּשָׁלַ͏ִם
אֶת־יהוָ֑ה
הַֽלְלִ֖י אֱלֹהַ֣יִךְ צִיּֽוֹן׃

13 Truly He strengthened
Your gates' locking bolts,
He blessed you sons in your midst

יג כִּֽי־חִ֭זַּק
בְּרִיחֵ֣י שְׁעָרָ֑יִךְ
בֵּרַ֖ךְ בָּנַ֣יִךְ בְּקִרְבֵּֽךְ׃

14 He pacified your domain;
He satiated you
With the fat of wheat.

יד הַשָּׂם גְּבוּלֵךְ שָׁלוֹם
חֵלֶב חִטִּים
יַשְׂבִּיעֵךְ׃

15 He sends His commands to the earth,
Very quickly
Runs His word.

טו הַשֹּׁלֵחַ אִמְרָתוֹ אָרֶץ
עַד־מְהֵרָה
יָרוּץ דְּבָרוֹ׃

16 He provides snow like wool
Frost
He disperses like ashes.

טז הַנֹּתֵן שֶׁלֶג כַּצָּמֶר
כְּפוֹר
כָּאֵפֶר יְפַזֵּר׃

17 He strews his ice like small breads;
Who is able to withstand
His freeze?

יז מַשְׁלִיךְ קַרְחוֹ כְפִתִּים
לִפְנֵי קָרָתוֹ
מִי יַעֲמֹד׃

18 He sends His word and melts it.
His wind blows,
Water flows.

יח יִשְׁלַח דְּבָרוֹ וְיַמְסֵם
יַשֵּׁב רוּחוֹ
יִזְּלוּ־מָיִם׃

19 He tells His word [words] to Jacob,
His laws and regulations
To Israel,

יט מַגִּיד דְּבָרוֹ [דְּבָרָיו] לְיַעֲקֹב
חֻקָּיו וּמִשְׁפָּטָיו
לְיִשְׂרָאֵל׃

20 What He not did so
To any nation
Who are ignorant of regulations,
Hallelujah!

כ לֹא עָשָׂה כֵן |
לְכָל־גּוֹי
וּמִשְׁפָּטִים בַּל־יְדָעוּם
הַלְלוּ־יָהּ׃

4 Cf. Note to *Ps*. 40:8.

9 It seems that *yiqrā’u* is onomatopoetic for the raven’s call *kra, kra.*

19 The *qere* is singular “His word”, stipulating a single Sinaitic source of Divine law.

Psalm 148

1 Praise Yah!
Praise the Eternal
From Heaven.
Praise Him
In the Heights.

א הַלְלוּ־יָהּ ׀
הַלְלוּ אֶת־יהוה
מִן־הַשָּׁמַיִם
הַלְלוּהוּ
בַּמְּרוֹמִים׃

2 Praise Him, all His messengers
Praise Him,
All His hosts.

ב הַלְלוּהוּ כָל־מַלְאָכָיו
הַלְלוּהוּ
כָּל־צְבָאָו [צְבָאָיו]׃

3 Praise Him
Sun and Moon,
Praise Him
All light-stars.

ג הַלְלוּהוּ
שֶׁמֶשׁ וְיָרֵחַ
הַלְלוּהוּ
כָּל־כּוֹכְבֵי אוֹר׃

4 Praise Him
The highest Heavens
And the waters
Which are
Higher than the Heavens.

ד הַלְלוּהוּ
שְׁמֵי הַשָּׁמָיִם
וְהַמַּיִם
אֲשֶׁר ׀
מֵעַל הַשָּׁמָיִם׃

5 Praise
The Eternals' Name,
Truly He commanded and they were created.

ה יְהַלְלוּ
אֶת־שֵׁם יְהוָה
כִּי הוּא צִוָּה וְנִבְרָאוּ׃

6 He erected them forever;
A law He gave
Never to be violated.

ו וַיַּעֲמִידֵם לָעַד לְעוֹלָם
חָק־נָתַן
וְלֹא יַעֲבוֹר׃

7 Praise the Eternal
From the earth,
Reptiles
And all depths,

ז הַלְלוּ אֶת־יהוה
מִן־הָאָרֶץ
תַּנִּינִים
וְכָל־תְּהֹמוֹת׃

8 Fire and hail,
Snow and smoke,
Hurricane winds
His word makes.

ח אֵשׁ וּבָרָד
שֶׁלֶג וְקִיטוֹר
רוּחַ סְעָרָה
עֹשָׂה דְבָרוֹ׃

9 Mountains and all valleys,
Fruit trees
And all cedars.

ט הֶהָרִים וְכָל־גְּבָעוֹת
עֵץ פְּרִי
וְכָל־אֲרָזִים׃

10 Wild animals and all domesticated ones
Vermin
And winged birds.

י הַחַיָּה וְכָל־בְּהֵמָה
רֶמֶשׂ
וְצִפּוֹר כָּנָף׃

11 Kings on earth	יא מַלְכֵי־אֶרֶץ
And all nations	וְכָל־לְאֻמִּים
Rulers	שָׂרִים
And all judges on earth.	וְכָל־שֹׁפְטֵי אָרֶץ׃
12 Bachelors and also maids	יב בַּחוּרִים וְגַם־בְּתוּלוֹת
Old men	זְקֵנִים
With young men.	עִם־נְעָרִים׃
13 Praise	יג יְהַלְלוּ ׀
The Eternal's Name	אֶת־שֵׁם יהוה
For His Name alone is illustrious,	כִּי־נִשְׂגָּב שְׁמוֹ לְבַדּוֹ
His splendor	הוֹדוֹ
On earth and sky.	עַל־אֶרֶץ וְשָׁמָיִם׃
14 He raises the horn	יד וַיָּרֶם קֶרֶן ׀
Of His people,	לְעַמּוֹ
A praise for all His pious,	תְּהִלָּה לְכָל־חֲסִידָיו
The Children of Israel,	לִבְנֵי יִשְׂרָאֵל
The people close to Him,	עַם־קְרֹבוֹ
Hallelujah!	הַלְלוּ־יָהּ׃

2 The *qere* reads: "all His host" unless it is archaic deficient spelling.

4 Here the prose particle אשר is totally unnecessary in the composition. If it is used anyhow and given prominence in a separate line it is either that the existence of water higher than the highest Heaven is not implied in the story of Creation where the water is asserted to be "on top of the spread", a material sky, or because an allusion is made to the root אשר "riches".

11 The best translation here of שופט is "organizer".

Psalm 149

1 Praise Yah!
Sing to the Eternal
A new song,
His praise
In the assembly of the pious ones.

א הַלְלוּ יָהּ ׀
שִׁירוּ לַיהוה
שִׁיר חָדָשׁ
תְּהִלָּתוֹ
בִּקְהַל חֲסִידִים׃

2 Let Israel enjoy in its Maker,
Zion's sons
Jubilate in their King.

ב יִשְׂמַח יִשְׂרָאֵל בְּעֹשָׂיו
בְּנֵי־צִיּוֹן
יָגִילוּ בְמַלְכָּם׃

3 Praise His Name with flutes;
With drum and lute
Chant to Him.

ג יְהַלְלוּ שְׁמוֹ בְמָחוֹל
בְּתֹף וְכִנּוֹר
יְזַמְּרוּ־לוֹ׃

4 Truly the Eternal desires His people,
He will glorify the meek
By salvation.

ד כִּי־רוֹצֶה יהוה בְּעַמּוֹ
יְפָאֵר עֲנָוִים
בִּישׁוּעָה׃

5 The pious ones will exult in honor;
They will sing
On their couches.

ה יַעְלְזוּ חֲסִידִים בְּכָבוֹד
יְרַנְּנוּ
עַל־מִשְׁכְּבוֹתָם׃

6 God's supremacy
In their throats
And a double-edged sword in their hands.

ו רוֹמְמוֹת אֵל
בִּגְרוֹנָם
וְחֶרֶב פִּיפִיּוֹת בְּיָדָם׃

7 To execute vengeance
On the peoples,
Censure
on No-nations.

ז לַעֲשׂוֹת נְקָמָה
בַּגּוֹיִם
תּוֹכֵחֹת
בַּל־אֻמִּים׃

8 To tie their kings with fetters
And their notables
With iron ropes,

ח לֶאְסֹר מַלְכֵיהֶם בְּזִקִּים
וְנִכְבְּדֵיהֶם
בְּכַבְלֵי בַרְזֶל׃

9 To execute on them
The written judgment.
He is splendor
For all His pious ones,
Hallelujah!

ט לַעֲשׂוֹת בָּהֶם ׀
מִשְׁפָּט כָּתוּב
הָדָר הוּא
לְכָל־חֲסִידָיו
הַלְלוּ־יָהּ׃

3 Everywhere the Septuagint translates מחול with *choros*, which means "circular dance; choir (dancing), troup (performing)". The usual תוף ומחול cannot mean "drums and dances" but is the common "drums and fifes"; the root חול "turn around in circles" refers to the fact that fifes are circular wooden pipes with a circular hole in the middle.

7 The traditional texts read בַּלְאֻמִּים "on nations".

Psalm 150

1 Praise Yah!	א הַֽלְלוּ יָ֨הּ ׀
Praise God in His sanctuary,	הַֽלְלוּ־אֵ֥ל בְּקָדְשׁ֑וֹ
Praise Him	הַ֝לְל֗וּהוּ
In His strong sky.	בִּרְקִ֥יעַ עֻזּֽוֹ׃
2 Praise him in His strengths,	ב הַֽלְל֥וּהוּ בִגְבוּרֹתָ֑יו
Praise Him	הַ֝לְל֗וּהוּ
In His enormous greatness.	כְּרֹ֣ב גֻּדְלֽוֹ׃
3 Praise Him	ג הַֽ֭לְלוּהוּ
By blowing the horn,	בְּתֵ֣קַע שׁוֹפָ֑ר
Praise Him	הַ֝לְל֗וּהוּ
With harp and lute.	בְּנֵ֣בֶל וְכִנּֽוֹר׃
4 Praise Him	ד הַֽ֭לְלוּהוּ
With drum and fife,	בְתֹ֣ף וּמָח֑וֹל
Praise Him	הַ֝לְל֗וּהוּ
With strings and organ.	בְּמִנִּ֥ים וְעוּגָֽב׃
5 Praise Him with cymbals sounding,	ה הַֽלְל֥וּהוּ בְצִלְצְלֵי־שָׁ֑מַע
Praise Him,	הַ֝לְל֗וּהוּ
With cymbals trembling.	בְּֽצִלְצְלֵ֥י תְרוּעָֽה׃
6 Every soul	ו כֹּ֣ל הַ֭נְּשָׁמָה
Praise Yah,	תְּהַלֵּ֥ל יָ֗הּ
Hallelujah!	הַֽלְלוּ־יָֽהּ׃

Here the source of the difference between three- and four-liners is whether the following ב is soft or hard. An opinion regarding he antiquity of this change in style depends on whether one accepts an old Phoenician source for *begad-kefat* changes or not. In any case, the second הללו always carries a separating accent.

4 Clearly מָחֺול cannot mean "circular dance" but is round wooden instrument known as fife and always associated with drums. One may ask whether מֵן "hair, string" is the source of rabbinic נימה "hair, string" and not, as commonly noted, the Greek νῆμα..

Index of Hebrew words

Index of Names